112959350

ZK-2

LIFE AND LETTERS OF
MARY EMMA WOOLLEY

Life and Letters of Mary Emma Woolley

Jeannette Marks

Author of "Genius and Disaster," "Family
of the Barrett," and other books

PUBLIC AFFAIRS PRESS, WASHINGTON D. C.

PREFACE

Life and Letters of Mary Emma Woolley is not a formal biography but informal and personal. Its purpose is to reveal something of what Mary Woolley accomplished and of what she felt and thought—the mosaic of the life she lived. Wherever possible the story is set down in her own words, whether the "words" come from recorded or recalled conversations; lectures or letters; or from her "Notes on Autobiography" —her own title for the autobiography she had intended to write. With the exception of Chapters 1 and 2, each chapter opens with a saying by Mary Emma Woolley. In the coining of pithy sayings, her great-uncle, Isaac Sherwood Beers, was her progenitor. It was this great-uncle who said: "Everybody is rating against the climate: it's like the abolition cause, if they knew more about it, they would say less"; and his great-niece wrote: "Life is a succession of making choices and education will help you make wise ones." The integrating source of the biography is the companionship of some fifty-two years, during which in one place and another Mary Woolley and the author were together.

We shall hear Mary Woolley speak again, both as a child and as a mature woman, not imaginary sentences but the words she actually spoke. We shall be with her when her father is carrying her on the pommel of his saddle to school; see her on the way to her beloved grandmother and grandfather Ferris in South Norwalk; have glimpses of her in high school in Providence; go with her to Wheaton and to Brown University where she came under the lasting influence of Dr. E. Benjamin Andrews—all, together with her fortunate home life, the source influences of her leadership in education and in peace.

And, later, friends will talk with her when she was a young Professor at Wellesley College; and be with her on the day she was inaugurated as President of Mount Holyoke College. Or we shall try to keep up with that brisk step of Mary Woolley's as, with packed briefcase, she goes out to the office building at our home on Lake Champlain—sometimes with our collies—or crosses College Street to the President's Office at Mount Holyoke College where by ceaseless toil in "brickmaking" and with the cooperation of her faculty and students and the help of her trustees and alumnae she was building one of the great colleges for women.

In her letters friends known and unknown will travel with her to Korea, Japan and China. They will go with her to Geneva, too, where as the first woman delegate appointed by the United States to a Disarmament Conference, she is cooperating with an international group of men and women in work for peace. With her we shall see many "pictures" of contemporary value in history, among them that of John Foster Dulles earning his shoulder straps in international diplomacy. With her, readers will meet not only famous American men and women but also English men and women among the great of their day. Yet despite the surrounding complexities of her days, we shall find that, as one Mount Holyoke alumna said, "Her simplicity was restful; her quietness deep."

Year after year, in the making, we shall watch with her the immense power for peace of a united womanhood and hear her speak again and again about "women as human beings". Finally, we shall see her struggle to maintain in a woman's college the right of leadership *of* women *for* women, and watch her as she pays her utmost on *behalf* of women. Mary Woolley came to understand well what one Quaker has called "the cold of the heart and the pain of the spirit."

If someone asks—the biographer did—why the story of Mary Woolley's life could not complete itself without its intimate and heroic close, the following words can be quoted from a letter Elizabeth Barrett Browning wrote to Robert Browning: "We should all be ready to say that if the secrets of our daily lives and inner souls may instruct other surviving souls, let them be open to men hereafter, even as they are to God now . . ."

JEANNETTE MARKS

Westport, New York

ACKNOWLEDGMENTS

The author makes grateful acknowledgments for permissions to the following photographers: Bachrach, Emily Huttin, Katharine Mc-Clellan, John H. B. Mills and Eric Stahlberg, owner of the profile portrait of Mary Woolley. Gratefully, also, do I acknowledge the biography's debt to the Class of '99 at Wellesley College, to the Park Place Congregational Church of Pawtucket, Rhode Island, and to several libraries, among them the Institute of Jamaica Library, the Island Record Office of Jamaica, the Library of the Boston Athenaeum, the Wellesley College Library, the Williston Memorial Library at Mount Holyoke College and the Yale University Library. Among the newspapers and magazines I am grateful for permissions given by *Brown Magazine, Good Housekeeping Magazine, Harper's Bazaar, New York Herald-Tribune, Holyoke Daily Transcript, Ladies Home Journal, Providence Sunday Journal, Mount Holyoke Alumnae Quarterly, New York Sun, New York Times, Springfield Republican, Washington Post, Wheaton Alumnae Magazine.*

Among the consoling memories I have in writing this documentary are my indebtedness to the colleagues and friends of Mary Woolley, to those whose names appear within the biography as well as to the following: Katharine McC. Arnett, Edith Thornton Cabot, Dorothy Foster, Eleanor Green, Lena Blake Greene, Dorothea Knowles, Clemewell Lay, Flora Belle Ludington, Irene Moran Maloney, Maude Meagher, Marion Randall, Fannie Ratchford, Dr. Martha Hale Shackford, Harriet Slaney, Rebecca Smaltz, Marguerite Smith, Elenita Watson.

In conclusion I am grateful for material and for permission to Maxwell Armfield, R.A., Dorothy Burgess, Dame Kathleen Courtney, Dorothy Detzer, the Honorable Herbert Hoover, Frances Perkins, John D. Rockefeller, Jr., Countess Russell, and Thomas J. Watson.

CONTENTS

"I shall light a candle of understanding in thine heart which shall not be put out."—Esdras II

CHAPTER 1

LOVE

"I should rather be in exile, than have those I esteem unhappy hereafter on my account."—MARY ANN BEERS

The door opened. The wistful eyes of a young woman looked in, saw the green backlog smoldering and a cat asleep on the cushion in the curved rocking chair before the hearth. Then the door closed gently, and the room, except for the pendulum motion of a grandfather clock, was again silent. The place was Wilton, Connecticut; the year 1836 in February; the old mansion home was Bald Hill. The smoldering backlog in the dignified dining room gave off no firelight yet the interior of the room was luminous, holding the color of both sky and sea—its light brightening the highboy against the west wall and the china on the polished dining room table and upon the plate rail of the wainscoting.

The door opened again, and the young woman came in with an arm full of fire wood which she dropped into the heavy basket-like wood box. Taking the big iron poker from its corner and hooking it into the backlog, she turned over the log, sending showers of sparks up the chimney. After that she put on some of the wood she had brought in, and flames shot up.

Going to the east window, Mary Ann Beers looked off to the nearby snow of Bald Hill and the far-away Long Island Sound. Then she took a heavy old shawl which was folded over the back of the chair and, carrying it back to the hearth, she folded it into a soft pad and placed it on the floor, not too near the fire but near enough. Lifting the gray cat from the chair, she held Boss lovingly against her shoulder and cheek before she set her down on the shawl.

"There, Boss," she said, "you will be contented and Mary Ann can read her letters! Boss, one is from Isaac. Do you hear, Boss? I said 'Isaac'!"

Despite the meow of recognition and an outburst of purring at Isaac's name, the young woman seemed more lonely than ever as she settled down to read her letters. She picked up Isaac's letter first, then

1

put it aside: that was the best—she would save it till the last. As she took up the second letter, she murmured to herself: "I wonder where pa is!"

Folding up this letter, Mary Ann sat on in silence for some seconds. Speaking to Boss again, she said: "I wonder where pa is?"

To that Boss did not reply even by a meow. Opening the thick letter which was addressed to her at Bald Hill and had come from her brother Isaac—a brother but one year younger than she was—the young woman read:

New York Feby 20th, 1836

Dearest Sister:

. . . I cannot but think that Pa feels . . . unhappy at the loss of our Dear Mother; that is natural and to seek for someone to fill the void is natural. And I think if such is his intention he cannot be too careful in his selection. If he should be so unlucky as to . . .

Mary Ann paused in the reading of her brother's letter and listened: yes, there was the sound of foot steps—sharp, alert steps. The door opened and Captain Samuel Beers, slender, erect, black haired, entered the dining room.

"Well, pa," said Mary Ann, "I've been wondering where you were!" She gathered up her papers and arose.

Captain Sam came another step closer to Mary Ann and the fire, saying: "I've something to say to you, child, would better be said now. I've been over to South Norwalk. Next week I'm bringing home a step-ma for you—best for us all, for you, for little Henry whether he do or don't live on in Ridgefield with Grandma Keeler, and better for me."

"Yes, pa," agreed Mary Ann gently, "better for us all. She is not ma but she is a good woman."

"So you knew?" asked Captain Sam.

"Yes, pa, I knew, but does Grandma Keeler know in Ridgefield?"

Captain Sam replied: "Not that I know of, child. You are Esther's daughter. Make yourself a messenger to Ridgefield to tell her and Isaac Keeler—and your little brother."

After a second of silence Mary Ann inquired: "Pa, where is Big Kitty?"

"She came in when I did and made off for the kitchen."

"I'll stop my letter reading and writing and get your tea now."

Captain Beers took up the big poker, gave the backlog a thrust and a turn which set the fire again to showering sparks, replaced the fore-log, put on some fresh wood and sat down staring into the deep fire-place. Tick-tock, tick-tock swung the pendulum of the clock. The

light was going and with it dusk had come and gone. Captain Sam
got up to light the candles on the table.

"Here, pa," said Mary Ann, entering. "Here's our supper!"

She put down a big tray, setting out on the beautiful old table
plates of scrambled eggs and sausages, fresh-heated muffins, butter,
hot apple sauce, hot milk and a pot of coffee. She pulled the sugar
bowl over to Captain Sam's place.

Then she said: "Come, pa, there is snow on the road and if we're
planning to be on time at prayer meeting, we must eat our supper."

Her father rose, sat down at the table and swiftly asked a blessing.

Some hours later in her low-ceilinged warm bedroom above the
kitchen, she sat by a lighted candle, unfolded Isaac's letter and went
on reading:

> In regard to the subject which is to me as well as to yourself the burden
> of your letter I take the liberty to reply freely. . . . I am well aware of
> the state of your feelings in regard to Stephen Ferris and have been for
> these two years and can with safety assert that nothing would be wanting
> on your part to make such an alliance . . . entitled to as much happiness
> as one can reasonably expect. . . . Marriage has been often termed the
> lottery of life and every one that draws stands a chance to draw a blank.
> . . . Now I intend to take a venture at some future day, *but not among*
> strangers. . . . If the case were mine I would, like you, ask advice and
> then if I loved and was aware that affection was reciprocated—I would
> suffer no more time to intervene than was necessary to make arrange-
> ments. . . . One thing I will say which is no more complimentary than
> true—that if Providence will allot to me a companion possessed of as much
> affection and virtue as you can boast of, I shall be contented. . . . You
> must not worry about my going South at present for hot weather will be
> along soon and then the cooler the better. Give my love to Pa, Henry,
> Boss and Big Kitty as members of our household and Grandma Keeler as
> being the nearest Mother I have got. . . . If I could roll in the mine of
> Golconda it would be tasteless without a parent's or sister's affection. . . .
> Mary you must write as I do. I like to read long letters quite as well as
> I love to write them—don't take night just as you are going to bed and
> scratch down a few sleepy ideas—let's have them wide awake and a good
> many of them—just get a large sheet like this and begin it as soon as you
> get this and write some every day till you get it full, then send it directly
> —write about everything you can think of the chickens—pigs, hoss ETC
> ETC. Tell Henry I should like to see him & also Grandma. Tell Grandma
> I have put the tract she gave me in a . . . pocket Bible so that every time
> I open the bible I cannot help but see it. . . . Give Boss some supper to-
> night and feed the chickens for me.
>
> Your very affectionate but sleepy Brother
> I. S. Beers
>
> P.S. Mr. Stevenson inquires after you and says he thinks B[ald] Hill
> a beautiful place maybe its on your account. He appears to be a fine
> young man. . . . I hope to hear from home, about home, just wind a string

around your flights of fancy and embrace in the scope of your general intelligence something nearer home.

Mary Ann sat thinking about her brother's letter, one hand upon it.
She was to treasure his letters to the day of her death. In them Isaac
recounts his journeys by land to Augusta, Georgia, and his voyages by
sea to Charleston, he tells about his work as a wholesale grocer, his
failure and his successes—letters memorable for their vivid accounts
of travel, for pictures of Congress and of John Quincy Adams, of the
New York City of the early nineteenth century, and memorable too
for the warmth of feeling Isaac had for the whole business of living.
This young man who was making a great success as an apprentice in
the wholesale grocery business in New York City and, later, in Augusta,
had the culture of wide interests, not least among them the political
life of the country. Every once in a while Isaac used an unforgettable
phrase—a trenchant saying such as "a prostration of silence", or the
description of city acquaintances as "cool 'goodmorning' friends"; or a
description of his own face which, because of ill health, had become
thinner and "almost sharp enough," he wrote, "to split pumpkins"; or
"Everybody is rating against this climate: its like the abolition cause,
if they knew more about it they would say less." Notable—and it has
to be remembered that he was only twenty-one years old—are his
sound standards of education, the strength of his moral nature, his love
for his home, its brooks and its meadows, his family loyalty, and his
unfailing sense of justice and love for peace. Virtually all his letters,
fascinating from beginning to end, are in the best tradition of good
letter-writing. What he says about education and peace, justice, and
politics are especially interesting in the light of his kinship to Mary
Emma Woolley, his great-niece.

❖   ❖   ❖   ❖

That spring and early summer the months passed slowly for the
lonely and puzzled Mary Ann. Almost every week on Saturday afternoon Stephen Ferris called on the young lady and spent the evening
with her at Bald Hill.[1] After that he walked the twelve miles back
from Wilton to South Norwalk. As for Mary Ann, her brother's words
turned over and over in her thoughts: "If I loved and was aware that
affection was reciprocated—I would suffer no more time to intervene
than was necessary." Yes, she did love and yet she was allowing time
"to intervene". Finally, one Thursday evening in August 1837, Mary
Ann sat down while pa and step-ma were at a meeting in the Village of
Wilton, and wrote Stephen the most decisive letter of her life:

These photographs show Mary Emma Woolley when she was five years old (top left); her mother, Mary Augusta Woolley (top right); father, Joseph Judah Woolley (bottom left); and grandmother, Mary Ann Beers Ferris (bottom right).

At left is a photograph of Mary E. Woolley as President-elect of Mount Holyoke College. At right she is seen with Dr. Coffin in her last academic procession in 1937.

Williston Memorial Library

Friend S. . . . If we had time to converse verbally, perhaps we might
understand each other better. You ask for an expression of my feelings—
My friendship towards yourself has stood the test of years, without being
diminished by time or absence and is still all that you could wish, provided you was decided in favour of the union proposed. I cannot with
propriety specify anything further on this subject until you have fully
made up your mind. I hope your duty may be made plain, and satisfac-
tory to yourself—I should rather be in exile, than have those I esteem unhappy hereafter on my account. Indeed I could not consent to a proposal
of this kind if I thought your hesitancy proceeded from this cause. So
far as I know there is but one feeling but what is unison with yours— and
that is a sorrow all my own—I mean the want of that peace of mind origi-
nating from a consciousness of acceptance with our heavenly Father. . . .
I am sensible that this world cannot afford any permanent satisfaction.
All real enjoyment must be derived from God—and hoping we may be
guided by Him through all the changing scenes of this life, and eventually
be prepared to meet in a better world, I will conclude writing, with sub-
scribing myself

Yours respectfully,

Mary Ann Beers

In South Norwalk, Stephen worked harder and harder, blocking
hats faster and faster in a trade which since 1732 had not only the
incentive of love but also the incentive of international competition
with the London hatters beginning to complain of Connecticut competition. Stephen was successful in love, he was successful in learning how to block hats, yet he was never successful financially. On
the cold morning of April 5, 1838, the edges of the brook were still
laced with ice when Mary Ann and Stephen were married in Wilton.
Her brother Isaac wrote from Augusta, Georgia: "I suppose before
this reaches you, the yes and no of life will be said and you will be
placed on the summit of the throne of human affections—at least you
will be on the summit of your Brothers."

When Isaac's letter reached them, even the moving into a little house
with a leak in it had been completed. It was in this house that their
first child, Mary Augusta Ferris, was born on March 4, 1839. In those
days parents had no inhibitions about rocking chairs and lullabies.
And it was in the rocking chair which had moved to South Norwalk
with them and from which Mary Ann had removed Boss that she
rocked her first child, sang her first lullaby as she nursed the baby she
called "Sis" or "Sunshine". This little girl had other pet names such
as "Mamie" and "Manie" and "Mary Gus". A second name, "Augusta",
had been given the child. Almost as soon as she could walk Mary Gus
began dancing; and as soon as she began dancing, she began talking
gaily and flirting with her large dark eyes. Her first flirtations were,

of course, with her father. Two years later her brother Francis Arthur
—usually called Frank—was born in the same little house with the
leak in it. Quickly this boy came to love his sister better than anyone
else in the world. When she was first sent to school, a cousin wrote:
"Grandmother says Mary Augusta goes to school so I think you and
Frank must be rather lonely during the day. I can hardly see how he
busys himself without Sis he is so fond of her."

It must have been sometime in 1843 that Mary Ann, Stephen and
their two children had moved into their new house at 8 West Avenue,
South Norwalk, which had been built with Mary Ann's money. It
was there that the last of their children, Emma Jane, was born. It was
there that they continued for many, many years to be one of the
happiest of families. Today this sort of home life sounds like a fairy
tale. It was, however, a sober fact in which a handsome little boy
adored his sister and occupied himself by "digging little wells 'Faxi-
foxi hunting'", whatever that means; and the young uncle sent them
this message: "I conclude Mary Augusta goes to school. Tell her I
want her to learn so fast that she can by fall read like a lady." And
in an even more adult mood: "Kiss Mary Augusta and Frank on each
cheek twenty times and tell the dear creatures it came from Uncle
Henry."

These children went on many visits. Their mother always dressed
them in clean underclothes and fresh suits and sent them off with some
spare pantalettes packed in their luggage.

Mary Ann wrote her older daughter:

> Aunt Mary [Trowbridge] expects to go to Wilton tomorrow (if I hear
> from you today that you can do without me). She will go to Ridgefield
> and all about before she returns. Your father expects to spend next Sab-
> bath with Frank and wants Emma to go with him. I will have to be very
> busy this week to get her ready. I am going to fix a garibaldi and let her
> wear her old dresses. She wants me to tell you her hat will be pressed
> with the sides turned up like Georgie's.

And again she wrote of this much-loved youngest child, Emma: "You
will laugh when I tell you the braid is all off my dress. It was too
troublesome spending a half hour to clear out the dust every time I
went in the street. It will do to trim Emma's winter dress with."

Yes, certainly the travel habit—call it "going into the street" or
"stirring about"—was characteristic of the Beers, Ferris and Woolley
families. Even when these elders had nothing but coaches, riding
horses, shanks' mare, buggies and slow belching old trains, with an
occasional steamer or sleigh thrown in to take them somewhere, nothing
was more remarkable than the "speed" and the frequency with which

the members of the Beers, the Ferris, and eventually the Woolley families, got around the four sides of the quadrangle made by Bridge-port, where the Woolleys lived; Danbury, where Aunt Kate Trow-bridge had her home; Wilton with its beautiful Bald Hill home and Captain Beers and South Norwalk, where young Deacon Ferris and Mary Ann Beers had settled to bring up their family. Of this quad-rangle Grandpa Beers would write: "I got home safe that day that I went to Norwalk about dark and your ma and I went to Ridgefield yesterday to visit Mrs. Rockwell. We had a very pleasant sleigh ride. I have been stirring about pretty well this week." And no doubt this time he stopped in at Ridgefield at Grandma Keeler's whom Isaac loved so much and with whom Henry had lived for many years. Yes, it was all very different in these modern 1840's, for when Grandpa Beers was a boy, if any member of the family or community took a trip across the state line between Connecticut and New York in order to go to Buffalo, prayers were offered in the churches for the safety of the traveller. But that was all changed now, and like all up-to-date people they much preferred what they considered to be their "modern world" in which, without fear of Indians, their pastor, Gus Beard, rode all the way from Maine to Connecticut on horseback and Grandpa Beers dashed around the quadrangle at the reckless speed of eight miles an hour!

CHAPTER 2

SORROW

"One should never give up a plan because of bad weather."
—J. J. WOOLLEY

Josie, holding his hands behind him, stood looking down at his four-year-old sister, his thin sensitive face twitching as he asked: "Is Hattie no better?"

"No better," replied his mother, dipping her hand into the basin and wringing out the cloth. She sponged it tenderly over the child's forehead and temples and pushed back the child's damp hair from the sides of her face.

"Could the stars foretell anything about Hattie?" Josie asked suddenly.

"Precious lamb, that would be superstition!" exclaimed his mother. "Whatever put that thought into your head?"

"A book at school which tells about Indians, mother."

"Ask your father when he comes home."

The boy was still holding his hands behind him as he said: "Mother, here is somewhat for you!"

"What is 'somewhat', Josie?" asked Fanny Burroughs Woolley, looking up to smile as, knitting a gray wool sock, she sat on beside her sick child Harriet Augusta. Looking fondly at Josie she repeated her question: "You have 'somewhat' for me?"

"Mother, have you forgotten," he asked.

"Forgotten what, Josie?"

"What day it is: St. Valentine's Day, the fourteenth of February, anno domini eighteen hundred and forty-two, mother."

"I had—forgotten it altogether."

"It is the trouble we bear now, mother, makes you forget the days as they come and as they go," Joseph Woolley spoke gravely for a ten-year-old boy and with quaint precision.

"Give me the 'somewhat', dear," said his mother, holding out her hand.

Taking it from behind his back, Josie said as he gave her the valentine: "I made it!"

8

Fanny Burroughs Woolley, taking it eagerly, looked at the forget-me-nots which were a bright blue on the lacy valentine and at her son's clear, strong handwriting.

"Beautiful!" she exclaimed. "Let us read it aloud together."

Josie looking over her shoulder, shy and content, they read aloud:

To My Dear Mother
May God help you
May he bless you
And take care of you
In all your troubles

My Dearest Friend
J. J. Woolley

She drew him towards her, her arm about him. She had several sons but for her there had never been another boy like this son, Joseph, who in time was to become Mary Woolley's father. Fanny Burroughs smiled at herself for such worship of her own son. She was not a pretty woman but like her features, her motions were full of strength and definiteness. "Different" is the word which might have described her as well as this son.

"Mother, where did father go?"

"He rode to South Norwalk and then rides on by way of Wilton where he sees Captain Sam Beers and then on to Ridgefield to ask Isaac Keeler's advice about making some hardware needed this spring for one of his boats."

"Was father riding Aldwell or Sally?"

"Aldwell, dear. When he returns it may be he can give you some facts about the stars. As a boy he knew your grandfather Stephen Burroughs well and has treasured every word my father spoke about the stars and the sea."

"Was it before he became blind that Grandpa Burroughs studied the stars?"

"Yes, and afterwards, too!"

Of her eight children of whom she was to lose three—John, Harriet and Eveline—Josie was closest to her, for as troubles increased so did Joseph's devotion to her seem to grow.

A cry came from the sick child, and Fanny Woolley lifted Hattie in her arms, walking up and down, humming Isaac Watts' lullaby:

Soft and easy is thy cradle
Coarse and hard thy Savior lay
When his birthplace was a stable,
And his softest bed was hay.

*   *   *   *

It had been an open winter throughout Connecticut and this St. Valentine's Day was more like the coming of spring than the close of winter. With only thin patches of snow here and there down to the harbor's edge, the sun was setting in the west, casting clear, almost warm light eastward upon the Sound. In the open barn door Josie stood waiting for his father to come home and watching the sunlight prick out shining spots on distant Long Island. Hearing the approaching clip-clop of a horse he ran out. Shading his eyes with his hand he looked into the sunlight. Yes, they were coming down the sandy lane. As they reached the barn door, taking Aldwell's bridle Josie said: "Father, I have fed Sally." From within the barn came a whinny which was answered by Aldwell, and Josie added: "They all but speak."

Swinging himself off Aldwell, Joseph replied: "Thank you, son. We'll have to wait till after supper before we feed Aldwell. Give him now a sup of water—no more!"

With Josie's help, Joseph Woolley began lifting the saddle bags off the horse's rump, while Josie, expert as any groom, grabbed a cloth with which to rub down the sweat, talking as he darted hither and yon helping: "Father, today I could see that Hattie grows weaker. If Grandpa Burroughs were living would he not read the stars to help Hattie get well?"

"No, Josie, *no*," replied Joseph emphatically, slipping the bridle out of Aldwell's mouth and patting the gelding as the horse walked off to its stall, "never that! He would have done for Hattie exactly what your mother is doing. He had many children of his own and he knew well how little physicians know about the fevers and ailments of children. He did not believe in omens pointing to the future and he condemned all forms of ignorance which could lead to superstition. '*Science*', he would say, 'is *to know; ignorance* is *not* to know.' And somehow it seemed as if your grandfather thought there was somewhat of willfulness in ignorance—that a man did not *know* because he did not *wish* to know. He would have made a good and honest physician—but never an Indian medicine man!"

"But, father, we need to know more or Hattie will die."

"Yes, son," answered Joseph Woolley, "but even if loss must come again, we are better off here in this northern climate with its better health than the Woolleys were in the Island of Jamaica where putrid fever killed off many of my family and cramp in the stomach—cholera they are calling that nowadays—killed off the rest including mother's first child, whom they called 'Joseph'. When a year later I was born they named me 'Joseph' after that brother. But almost before I could walk my father was taken sick and died. Mother, lest I, too, be lost, sent me quickly by ship with some friends here to Bridgeport, while she made haste to settle your grandfather's estate in order that she might follow me. Sarah was her name, she was from New York, and a good business woman. But the cholera caught up with her, too, and she died. Except for the fact that mother, after my father's death, had shipped me off quickly I might not have survived. And, as I said, Josie, even here—though Hattie is the third of our children to fall ill —we are better off."

But Josie was not to be easily reassured, for he persisted: "Do mothers *have* to lose more children than they can keep?"

"It seems that way, does it not!" But noticing the expression in his son's eyes, he said: "Come now Josie, let us set our thoughts elsewhere lest we make the day's end harder for your mother. Look out there and beyond to Long Island! See those ships beating their way towards our harbor: that square-rigged brig, maybe with a cargo from some distant part of the world. And that sloop flying the British flag of England, where the Woolleys once lived until my father Joseph Woolley and uncle James went to Jamaica."

"And," said Josie in the sing-song voice of a tired boy repeating the last line of this well-known family story, "where Grandfather and Grandmother Woolley had gold watches and slaves and ships, horses and saddles and spurs, swords and guns, silver plate and land, much land." [1-5]

"A true story, son, not make-believe. Come now, let us go into the house to your mother who is waiting for me to tell her about Sam Beers's second wife. She is keeping our supper hot for us."

                    *   *   *   *

Some records in Connecticut and some documents in the Record Office at Spanish Town, Jamaica, some black and white broken china with scenes of English landscape, a Bible published 125 years ago (torn and scuffed by children's hands, scribbled upon yet still containing entries and some clipped poems), inscriptions on a few tombstones in Bridgeport, genealogical data in the Bridgeport Library concerning Josie's fabulous grandfather Captain Stephen Burroughs (a successful merchant, a ship builder and owner, a navigator, the inventor of the decimal system now in use in America, a philosopher given to deep speculations, an authority in astronomy)—these still survive from those colonial West Indian days and the early days of Connecticut.

Possessed of boundless vitality, physical as well as mental, young Joseph Judah Woolley, better known as "Josie" to all who loved him and they were many, stayed in school for only a few years and then, still a boy, went into "business". What that business was is not known. When he was about eighteen years old, in the language of the time, he "became converted" and decided to study for the ministry. This study he began about 1852 under the direction of Professor Northrop of Yale. From his pencilled notes, it is evident that, like everything else about him, young Woolley's conversion was direct and simple and could be summed up in five words: *to live a good life.*

Two years later his "dearest Friend", his mother, Fanny Burroughs Woolley, died on November 3, 1854. One month and three days later her son Joseph, twenty-two years old, married Mary Emma Brisco in Ridgefield, Connecticut. In those Ridgefield days, the young minister, an elder who had still to be ordained, and Mary Emma Brisco were "the talk of the village". On December 6, 1854, the pews of the Methodist Episcopal Church were filled to capacity when the Reverend Thomas G. Osborn married the couple. The only extant letter to this first wife is one which tells of his success as an elder in meeting the requirements of his ordination:

> Mrs. J. J. Woolley
> Ridgefield, Conn.
>
> My precious wife
> God bless you my darling. While away from you, I have an opportunity to think of the past and from my heart of hearts I bless God for my own Dear Wife. Your influence lives with me. It is around me, it wraps me like a mantel, the memory of yourself, your sweet, loving uncomplaining nature, and disposition. I owe to you much. I am not insensible to the fact that to you I owe more than to any other. I thank God for the refreshing times & seasons of memory. I long to be with you today. I know you will miss me, but God has ordered otherwise. I am to be ordained tomorrow, afternoon after service. I was the only one in the class of the 4th year and am the only Elder to be ordained. God bless thee darling. This is written during conference in haste.
>
> Joseph [6]

On the back of the letter at different angles and apparently written at different times in the microscopic handwriting of his wife were two poems. On the front page of their little Bible, next to the cover, a slip of white paper was pasted and in the same handwriting on the label was written:

> Joseph J. Woolley
> Emma Woolley

It had been their Bible from 1854 when they were married. Also in the front of the Bible, pasted opposite the title page, was the picture of a child, "Avery Sc."—a little girl with chubby arms and a chubby face. Was this the little one for whom Mary Emma and J. J. Woolley had hoped? Or a suggestion of the sister Joseph had lost? And in this Bible these two lovers seemed to "talk" to and fro on its pages, he with his pencilled notes and transcriptions: "All knowledge is not wisdom. . . . A man may have all knowledge and yet not have the wisdom of life"; she, already ill and in need of courage, in her unmistakable handwritten verses:

"Come to the land of peace!"
Come where the tempest hath no longer sway,
The shadow passes from the soul away,
The sounds of weeping cease.

There were, too, a clipping of John Greenleaf Whittier's poem *Angel of Patience*; and a bookmarker made by Mary Emma Brisco. On the flyleaf at the end of the Old Testament, in J. J. Woolley's handwriting, this entry was made:

Died
Mary Emma—wife of
Joseph J. Woolley
Died May 6—1860
Aged 28 years, 6 months—
lacking 4 days

In Bridgeport a tombstone marks the place of Mary Emma's burial.[7]

CHAPTER 3

DARLING FAMILY

"There was never a happier home, I am convinced, than ours."

In that West Avenue home in South Norwalk educational ambitions as well as love came early and stayed late. Charlotte Raymond was not only the school teacher for the children, but also their Sunday School instructor. By 1850 Mary Augusta, then eleven years old, and Frank, nine, were using the same school book, into which they copied for their mother some lines from the *Improvement of the Mind*, a textbook in use at Mount Holyoke Seminary in 1837 and for many years thereafter.

On July 30, 1853, when Charlotte Raymond, the children's teacher, wrote them from South Hadley, Massachusetts, where Mary Lyon had not much more than started her famous Mount Holyoke Seminary, Mary Augusta was fourteen years old and Frank Arthur twelve—still virtually children. Yet Charlotte Raymond expected to receive their interest and their understanding:

South Hadley July 30 1853

Dear Mary Augusta and Francis,

. . . This is, indeed, a lovely place; mountains, and hills, and valleys, all mingle here; while little streams and fairy glens add their gentler beauties. . . . But all this beautiful scenery is little compared with the advantages enjoyed by this happy household. I would give anything to have some of my dear girls with me a while. . . . The teachers are so good and kind and *love* seems to be the watchword, the keynote of all. . . . I have addressed this to both of you because I could not very well find time to write you separately. I do not suppose you will quarrel about it! I wish I might have a *line or two* from you if you receive this soon enough. I shall probably return Friday or Saturday of next week. I have concluded not to teach again this summer and shall probably go "West" in the Fall. Will you be kind enough to make it known as far as possible; perhaps it would be well if your Father would speak to Mr. W. H. B. about it also; . . . In some respects it will be a great trial to me, and from none will it be harder to part than from your family. . . . With much love to your parents and a kiss for the baby I remain

Your sincere friend

Charlotte E. Raymond

14

As these children approached the zenith of their fortunate youth, it might well have been a problem to find out just how earnest and happy or just how frivolous and silly Mary Augusta and Frank could be in their adolescence. Scraps of paper still tell the story in diaries, letters and verses. When he was fifteen, Frank wrote this gay song about his sister:

> Mary Gus for French has a passion
> Ribbons are all the fashion
> They say its all the go
> Now Mrs. Ferris you dont mean so
> "You little thing you want a spanking"
> For which you will get no thanking
> Mary Gus feels mighty fine
> I can find nothing to rhyme
> Oh how delightful blow the breezes
> And whisper among the treeses
> Shic shu shu le lu
> After rain the sky is blue

Having a fine voice, Frank went about the house singing to tease his sister and please himself. As for Mary Gus, more and more certain was she that the world was her friend while she talked on blithely and tied on fresh ribbons.

It was three years later that the climax of her frivolity was to be found in her diaries. Whether the name be Smith or Brown, no doubt Mary Gus thought she was playing the part of power in the life of love-sick swains. When she went to get some "bandoline" for her black abundant hair and met George, she entered in her diary: ". . . we walked down together and had a delightful walk he was between us and Neal says 'a thistle between two roses' . . . in a moment he had her between us." On October 31st comes this entry:

> Last night Ed W and Sylvester spent the evening here till nearly 12 o'clock had a splendid time, sat on the sofa by S most of the time. Ed has his ring, says he will get it for me this morning they went uptown to church last Sunday evening—I wonder if *he* cares much for me; hope they will come *again soon* S is going home tomorrow night Deacon Bouton fell while plastering the church and broke his neck—how sad it is—,

The following day was busy, she staying on at "church in the evening to practice some pieces for the funeral". Again about Sylvester she wrote: "Sylver here in the evening and staid till 11 o'clock. I have his ring and he said he wished it on for six months but I shall give it to him in a few days."

These words followed in a few days: "Oh! if I could only see him to give him his ring for I do not wish to wear it." The stories of the rings—and there were many—were seldom resolved satisfactorily.

Her diaries reveal that the boy-sequence was endless and Mary Gus's appetite for rings insatiable. However, feeling that not enough that was "new" happened, she sat herself down to knit a pair of slippers for her mother—who had never flirted even with Boss the Cat and had known one love and one only. Mary Gus carried her flirtations even into the very fastnesses of the school in which the eighteen-year-old girl was then teaching.

But something sobering was beginning to happen to her, for on a Friday in March of 1858 she entered in her diary: "I hope Mr. W(oolley) will *not* stay to our house all night." Seven lines further down the page Mary Augusta copied into her Journal: "True love is founded on esteem, and esteem is the result of intimate acquaintance and confidential intercourse", and followed that with another quotation:

> "At ten a child; at twenty, wild;
> At thirty, strong, if ever;
> At forty, wise; at fifty, rich;
> At sixty, good, or never."

And as she was reaching the most important event in her life, she wrote about her own diary: "I am *sure* I should be ashamed to show this journal to any one for it does seem so foolish to read it over."

❋   ❋   ❋   ❋

After the death of Mary Emma Brisco, J. J. Woolley was a somber figure. Some eight months later, at an evening skating party on the night of December 29, 1860, when the men rose from putting on the skates of the girls and for an instant stood in a group together, the young Pastor looked around vaguely and said: "Frank, do you think Mary Augusta will come back for New Year's?"

"She had a lot of paper work to correct before school opens. Sis promised she would come back, Mr. Woolley, and we hope she will."

"Danbury is not far away. Why do you call her 'Sis'?" asked J. J.

"Ma and all her friends call her 'Sunshine' or 'Mamie'," replied her brother. "I don't; I like 'Sis' better. Come, Mr. Woolley, they're waiting for us, let's get our girls now!"

After the skating party was over there followed three letters to Mary Augusta—one from her brother, a note from her mother and a letter from her friend Minnie. In the case of all three the court of appeal was "Mr. Woolley": "Mr. Woolley wants to be remembered"; "Mr. Woolley came in and staid till 10"; "I wonder if Mr. Woolley could intercede & persuade & make you know how much you are wanted."

On the return to South Norwalk from Danbury where she was living with some cousins the Trowbridges and teaching school, Mary Augusta was looking from the train window and back to her lap and a pad of paper on which she had been writing and rewriting a Valentine. When the New Year holiday was over there would be no time before St. Valentine's Day came and she must be ready. Ready for what? But what would others think if they knew all that she had said to this man she loved? Well, there was no turning back now. She had to go on and she did into this final stanza:

> Should you refuse her great will be her woes
> And much she begs that you will not expose
> To a censorious world the step she's took
> Lest she should be by all her friends forsook
> Act just to her who loves no one but you
> And she will be your Valentine most true.

The "quadrangle" was busier than ever when the summer came with its holidays—Danbury to Ridgefield, Ridgefield to Wilton, Wilton to South Norwalk, then off to Bridgeport and the "family" and friends there. By that time everybody knew that the young pastor of the Methodist Episcopal Church in Ridgefield was engaged to Mary Augusta Ferris—Deacon and Mrs. Ferris's daughter. But nobody knew when they would be married. Nor did they themselves know. In September Mary Augusta wrote to her brother Frank:

> Here I am at home again—I come down in the eleven o'clock train and expect to go back on Thursday afternoon. . . . Remember that we are all to be at home on Josie's birthday (D-V) the 17th of Sept. Thank you very much for my trunk—its *grand*. It is late so good-night—dear brother. All send love.
>
> Your loving sister,
Mamie.

In the air those days there were more suggestions of coming change and separation than a trunk, symbol of travel, for the Civil War had had its first battle on April 12, 1861. And now, eight months later, as they prepared for Josie's birthday on September 17th, there were many and inconclusive discussions about his enlisting.

After the celebration of his birthday, plans gained momentum. Yet uncertainty remained until Mary Ann Ferris wrote her father, Captain Sam Beers:

> South Norwalk Dec 11th [1861]
>
> Dear Father—I write this to tell you that Mr. Woolley and Mary were married this morning a half an hour previous to his leaving for Annapolis. It was not decided until after breakfast that they would be married this winter—You see there was no time to invite any one or make any wedding. I hope it may all be for the best. . . . Love to Ma—
>
> Your daughter Mary Ann

When Abraham Lincoln sent out his call for 75,000 volunteers, there was not even one militia company ready in Connecticut. Then immediately Governor Buckingham issued his call and, quickly, fifty-four companies of volunteers were made ready—five times the required quota from the state. No state in the Union was a more devoted supporter in the struggle to free the slaves.

Two weeks after her mother's note to Captain Sam, young Mary Augusta Woolley followed with this longer letter for her grandfather at Bald Hill:

South Norwalk Dec 30th

My dear Grand Pa,
. . . I should have liked very much to have had you and Grandma here when we were married but it was so unexpected that there was no time to invite our friends. We hear from Joseph (Mr. Woolley) every day and sometimes twice a day. He is well—they are at Annapolis yet but expect to leave there soon. . . . He is doing a great deal for the soldiers and I hope will do them good. There are some sick ones in the hospital and he visits them several times during the day and then at their dress parade at five o'clock he has prayers. Sunday evening he lectures and Thursday evening they have prayer meetings he enjoys very much. He preaches on the Sabbath at three o'clock and has Sabbath school at one o'clock and prayer meeting in the evening. His tent is the post-office and he is post-master and he receives for the soldiers from one to three hundred letters every day. You will love him as your Grand-son—wont you? . . . All send love to Grandma and you.

Your loving Grand-daughter
Mary A.

❊   ❊   ❊   ❊

Chaplain Woolley had been in the thick of the Civil War at Fredericksburg and elsewhere. One incident about him survives from this period. A soldier went with a message to the Chaplain's tent. When the shells began to fall "alarmingly near", the soldier mounted his horse to beat a retreat. But the only comment the Chaplain made was "Let 'em shoot. I'm going to finish my breakfast." However, and whatever his courage, busied by night and by day in the care of the wounded and dying, he himself fell ill finally and was sent home to recover.

Following a partial recovery, Chaplain Woolley was offered the post of minister to the "Congregational Church at the Center" in Meriden where on July 25, 1862, he preached his first sermon.[1] It was one year later—on July 13, 1863, to be exact—that Mary Augusta became the mother of their first child: Mary Emma Woolley. The baby was born in South Norwalk at her grandmother's home at 8 West Avenue at eleven in the morning.

It was about the middle of August when little Mary Woolley was only a few weeks old that the beloved and loving grandmother of this child wrote the following letter to the child's mother:

Sunday evening [1863]

My precious Mary—I promised you we would write. There is nothing new to say. We are all well as usual and anxious to hear from you. Your friends here . . . think you ought to have remained at home till your health was more established. I hope no harm will come to you from going. *Save yourself and let Ellen and Georgie take care of baby till you are stronger.* I went with Emma to Mrs. Halenbecks last night. . . . We came home very tired and before taking off my shawl I was fast asleep on the lounge. Emma began to think it was time to take our tea—and so we ate our supper after 8 o'clock. This morning we felt rested and all went to Church. Gus Beard preached a most excellent sermon from the text "Beware of the leaven of the Pharisees". Practical and sweeping. It does us good to have the evil lifted so as to see by what motives we are actuated. . . . We miss you and baby so much. I wish she was on my lap this very minute. Your father and Emma have gone to the concert and Aunt Mary is asleep. I hear nothing but the ticking of the clock and the catydids— its very monotonous—even little May's crying would be preferable. I think she would enjoy one of those pleasant excursions I have so often given her. Kiss her every day for me and let it comfort you to know how largely you all share in our affection. . . .

Love to all
Ever your loving
Mother

The Ferris and Woolley family life was that of young people—children coming, many visits, many plans and boundless hopes. Six months after the baby was born Grandma and her young daughter Emma decided to visit the Woolleys in Meriden. Their arrival was recorded in JJ's diary by four words: "Mother and Emma came." But Stephen Ferris was not given to "four word writing". The day they left home, he wrote:

Home 3/2 P.M. Sunday
Jan'y 10th/64

Darling family,

. . . I came home at nine found all safe, heated and read till ten, went to bed slept well—got up at eight—fir'd up in the kitchen which was very cold—had broil'd ham etc, etc, etc, etc, for breakfast, made as much as possible of Tinie's company—put things in order—at ½ past ten started for Church, heard Rev. Mr. Bardwell in behalf of the contrabands for cash on old clo etc. etc. etc. etc.—got home at 12/2 . . . gave Pet his bath, got my dinner in the oven—went at the Independent—(call Josie's attention to the S. S. article by the Editor—a good text for a talk). . . . I hope you will all read Beecher's sermon in the Independent or let Josie read it to you, especially the last half. You will be instructed I think. Monday 8 A.M. Well and ready. A little colder than yesterday.

Yours Affg, Father

Five weeks later, on Monday, February 22, 1864, there was a return visit, for J. J. Woolley made this entry in his diary: "Went to Norwalk with Mrs. W & Baby." The next day: "I returned to M—attended funeral of Mr. Lucas child—infant." On March 4 he was still alone in Meriden and set down the words: "Mrs. Woolley Birth Day." A week later came this entry: "Paid E. Wilcox for Baby chair $1.25." In June after selling his horse and carriage for $400, he paid a number of bills which were owing in Meriden, took Mrs. Woolley and Baby May again to Norwalk, and left them at Grandma's. The day following he went down to New York, bought a baby carriage for $20.00, a family Bible for $6.50 and paid the Treasurer of the A & B Society $30.00 to make Levi Yale a life member. Quite a day! The next day he returned to Meriden, stayed all night with his friend Deacon Wood and sent Mrs. Woolley $10. Shortly afterwards he set down on July 9th (his daughter's birthday was due on July 13th) that from Mr. Platt at the "B-Company" he had bought a silver spoon for seventy-five cents. And on July 12th—one day before little Mary Emma's birthday, he himself left for South Norwalk. Their infant daughter Mary Emma Woolley in the first year of her life had, therefore, been provided with a high chair, a baby carriage deluxe for those days, and a silver spoon. The eyes of young "Papa" Woolley twinkled and the tip of his nose twitched a little—it always did when he was happy or successful—as during their vacation at Grandma's he glanced back over that wonderful year.

Not less good was the fact that Mother and Father and Baby were all on vacation in South Norwalk at Grandma's. On July 18, five days after baby's birthday, he wrote this joyous letter.

> Dear Bro Yale
> . . . We are all very well and enjoying ourselves finely. Today Father and I had a fine sail down the harbor in a sail boat. You would have been amused to have seen me, sitting in the stern of a sail boat, with the brim of my hat turned down all around, my feet on the seat opposite, guiding the little craft as she was driven by the winds through dancing, sparkling water. . . . With ever so much love, I am
>
> Ever your Afft Pastor
> J. J. Woolley

Vacation was over, and they took up their usual home life together, its duties in pastoral calls, its Sunday services and sermons, its weekly services, its weddings and its baptisms and its funerals. Whether he had married Frederick Monkmeyer to Sophia Ulbrand for $3 or James Hays to Frances Palmeter for $5 or Charles N. Paddock to Nancy Hall for $10, whatever the amount of the wedding fee, the Chaplain always gave it to Mrs. Woolley. Whereupon she promptly took it upstairs to place the fee in her savings box in her top bureau drawer.

As his journals make clear, among the "pastoral" duties of young Joseph Woolley were those he carried on at home. These entries are many and revealing, among them "Kittie sick." Noted for his tenderness of heart for all fellow creatures: dogs and cats, birds and cows and horses, immediately we "see" him caring for a sick kitten. But a little later this mental picture is shattered by this entry: "Had Kitty shod"! It was said of J. J. Woolley that he had a heart as big as an ox. At the very commencement of his pastorate at the Center Congregational Church in Meriden, J. J. Woolley had endeared himself greatly to the entire church membership by risking his life in his selfless devotion to those to whom he ministered.

Now a few years later, erect young soldier that he was, we see him going peacefully about his chores in the barn, then swift of step going into the house to make this entry: "My little brood hatched." Among the records of that home life in Meriden are many "farm" bills: "Paid E. Miller for Pasture." "Paid B. Rice for hay", "bought hay $14.20 paid", and the triumphant entry: "Cow calved". More and more did a little girl with large dark eyes, tiny braids of dark hair, on week days wearing a bright dress of Scotch plaid covered by a short little black pinafore, white stockings and high buttoned shoes, follow him from hen to horse, and calf to cow as he fed the creatures they both loved, and milked the family cow. One of his daughter's first episodes was in that Meriden barn. Dressed this time in her "Sunday best", a white dress with a white sun bonnet tied under her chin, late on that Sunday afternoon she took one gay step too many backwards and sat down in a full pail of milk.

It was on another Sunday when, suddenly, after the exit of some guests, little May was missed. Her father ran from room to room calling "May! May!" and her mother followed, opening closet doors, looking everywhere. No May to be found!

"Mama," said J. J., "she's not here. I'll get Kittie!"

He rushed out of the house, bridled Kittie and flung himself onto the mare's back. Touching her flank he was off at a swift gallop southward. He thought he knew where that child was going. He did, for about a quarter of a mile out of town he saw a little figure in white under a white sun bonnet trudging southward down the middle of the road.

Overtaken, the child looked up at her father surprised, but said nothing.

"May, where are you going?" asked the chaplain.

"May is goin' to Grandma's," was the unruffled, succinct reply.

"We'll put that off to another day," said her father, dismounting. He picked up his little daughter, placing her almost on Kittie's mane, saying: "There, hold on!" Mounting, he put his left arm about the child who was holding on for dear life with both hands to Kittie's mane. With his right hand grasping the bridle reins the chaplain and his daughter cantered back home. Home again, they found Mary Augusta walking up and down the lawn in front of their house. As she saw them riding in she burst into tears of joy.

On November 17, 1866, another child, a son, Erving Yale Woolley, was born to the Woolleys. An active and brilliant boy, he was soon toddling after his sister. Now young Chaplain Woolley had two children and not just one to "do" his "barn chores" with him. Three years later Papa Woolley made this entry in South Norwalk at Grandma's": "May Birthday party. Six birthday candles and in the center of the cake a seventh candle for the coming year."

For these Connecticut New Englanders the climax for every year came in late November with "Thanksgiving at Grandma's", and to the end of her days Mary Woolley remembered as if it were yesterday the color, the fragrance, the taste of those Thanksgivings. On the journey there they had gone through miles of gray autumn. It was after dark of a sharp November day and the snow was falling when they reached the house in South Norwalk on Thanksgiving Eve. Stepping out of the falling snow they entered the house and flung themselves into Grandma's arms.

Later, Grandma said they could visit the pantry to look at, mind you just look at and sniff, the fragrance of the mince and pumpkin pies, while they ate their bedtime milk and crackers. As they went upstairs to bed the children went on asking questions: "Mama, ask Grandma can we go skating tomorrow?" or "Mama, will Grandpa let us coast on his sled?" Tucked into bed, they were still asking questions when suddenly they fell sound asleep. No children were ever any happier, for their sense of well being and love had brought them the first peace a child can know: peace of heart with its security and its love.

The next morning they went to Church with Grandpa and Uncle Henry, while Grandma and their mother stayed home to help get the dinner. At last Thanksgiving dinner was ready. May Woolley remembered it all, admitting in later years that on the whole her recollections were decidedly material: turkey and squash and turnip and onions and potatoes, cranberry sauce and mince and pumpkin pies; the old fashioned Indian pudding and mammoth chicken pie—both baked in her grandmother's brick oven at 8 West Avenue. And she never forgot another memory in her seventh year: their grandmother, Mary Ann, urging her brother Henry to take some turkey and his refusal as he said: "But I have turkey every day at my hotel in New York." Even this seven-year-old child knew that there was something wrong with that reply—that the feast they shared at Grandma's with its "world of strife shut out and world of love shut in" was somehow *not* just turkey!

CHAPTER 4

PINK GLOVES AND GENTLEMEN CALLERS

*"Often the most bitter enemy of a good man is one who envies
him because of his superior qualities, until envy, carefully nurtured, changes to hate*

They left Meriden in 1871, when the young chaplain was called to
take over the active ministry of the Congregational Church in Pawtucket, Rhode Island, of which the Reverend Constantine Blodgett,
D.D., still occupying the parsonage, had been pastor for thirty-five
years, and now had become "Retired Pastor". In Pawtucket the young
pastor and his wife and their two children, May and Erving, making
such adjustments as they could to hotel life, lived for three years in
the Pawtucket Hotel owned and run by Mr. and Mrs. Jilson. It was
located on lower Broadway just over the Main Street Bridge, near
the Congregational Church. During these transition years of hotel life,
the habit pattern of "going to Grandma's" became even more evident.
There at Grandma's on May 9, 1873, in South Norwalk, May's sister
Grace Ferris Woolley was born. In a letter written in August by Dr.
Blodgett there lingers still the echo of children's voices:

> We are as usual, & regret that your *last born* had been thus earlier
> put upon the discipline of life in the suffering of pain. . . . You will assure
> Mrs. W. & the dear children of our love. Tell the children to hurry home
> that they may enliven Walcott Street with their joyous voices. . . .

The Woolley family, with the ailing Gracie then about four months
old, were still "at Grandma's". From the reference in Dr. Blodgett's
letter it is evident that little Gracie was suffering. Because of their
temporary homelessness, Gracie's arrival, and their father's immersion
in new pastoral duties, the ten-year-old Mary Emma Woolley and
her seven-year-old brother Erving were probably somewhat adrift and
running up and down Walcott Street.

The church members soon found out that the young pastor's energy
was boundless and that among other facts he enjoyed springing upstairs three steps at a time. Not long after he transferred from
Meriden to Pawtucket one of his parishioners looked at him askance

24

and said for public consumption that she did not see how anyone could trust a minister who went upstairs three steps at a time! And there was another parishioner who after a certain sermon the Chaplain had preached, in which the young pastor had said "Some prayers go no higher than the ceiling," attacked J. J. Woolley, much to his amusement, for this statement. The only comment the pastor made was: "What made you think I was referring to you?" Another time a visiting minister preached on and on. One hour had already been ticked off the clock for a suffering congregation when the Chaplain finally leaned forward and pulled the minister's coattail.

About that time Mary Woolley's mother allowed her to spend the night in Amesbury with a little friend, the head of whose family was the Quaker poet John Greenleaf Whittier. The day before returning home together the two children called on the poet to say goodbye. It was then that John Greenleaf Whittier said to little May Woolley: "Thee canst tell thy mother thee hast been a good girl." Years later when she had become a woman and was telling this story, she added: "If we could always tell our mothers the same thing, we'd be doing quite all right!" Early did this child develop a sense of decorum. When she called on her childhood friend Edith Conant in 1872 in Pawtucket, young Mary Emma Woolley was aged nine and was wearing a pair of pink gloves! But however much the child may have brightened life with pink gloves, there was loneliness in this letter:

> Pawtucket
> Dec 10, 1873
>
> Dear Grandma:
> We were alone this evening and I thought I would write to you. We had a very nice time coming up. Your lunch proved very acceptable coming up. (We) had a nice supper at seven o'clock out of it. . . . I must stop now, so good bye. Love to all. from your little May.

Eight months later on August 1, 1874, the little sister—who was, according to her mother's Bible, "1 year 2 months 22 days old"—died. Four days afterward the child's mother spread out over the top of the black walnut bureau in her bedroom some of Gracie's little things: a baby ring, a locket, a pair of tiny baby shoes, the dress she had made for her. She was laying these things away in a hard wood box when May turned the door knob and came in. At the moment her mother had in her hands Gracie's baby shoes. May's warm dark eyes were anxious as she looked at her mother: "Mama, what are you doing?"

"Putting away Gracie's things."

Then she turned back to the bureau, tears rolling down her cheeks as she picked up the child's locket.

Standing stiff and helpless beside her mother, May asked: "Won't God be good to Gracie?"

There was no answer.

"So we can be with her again, won't God take us to Gracie?"

Still no answer. Frightened by this widening separation of silence and tears, the child quietly left the room.

It was to be three years before her mother would either speak or write about the loss of Gracie. Then in 1877, pregnant once more, she wrote a strange poem with the title "Little Gracie Went Home." Not without power, it begins:

> " 'Who plucked the Flower?' cried the gardener as he walked through
> the garden.
> "His fellow servant answered, 'The Master.'
> "And the gardener held his peace."

As she sought in the ensuing dialogue between her Soul and her Earthly Motherhood for comfort, she could at last say:

> "This little shining head we lay
> In the Redeemer's bosom.
> She *is not dead*, but only lieth sleeping. . . .
> Not dead, but sleeping, not even gone
> But present still. . . .
> Lord of the living and the dead,
> Our Savior dear,
> *We lay in silence at Thy feet*
> This sad, sad year."

The holiday season had come and had gone, bringing to the child May Woolley the largesse of Christmas and the New Year of 1875. Always independent and resourceful, she sat down to write a letter, this time to her Grandpa Ferris. The "rule" with her was writing to Grandma, so that the little New Year's Day letter to Grandpa is an exception which proves that rule, and perhaps an apology for her sauciness of which she wrote years later: "Grandfather was always sweet and self-controlled. I never knew him to flame up but once. Then I was saucy to Grandma. MY! How I felt his indignation and I never was saucy to her again." In her New Year's Night letter to Grandpa she said:

> Pawtucket
> Friday evening
> Jan 1, 1875
>
> I wish you a happy New Year Grandpa. I thought that you would like
> a little note from me. I have just got up from supper. Did you make

PINK GLOVES AND GENTLEMEN CALLERS

I did. here is a list of the gentlemen who called on me. Willie Cheney,
Arthur Clapp, Lyman Goff, Freddie Cheney. I received callers from
three to five o'clock. Is Aunt Emma going to the wedding? I should
go if I were her. Tell her to look real nice if she goes. Tell Grandma
that I shall write to her soon. I had a New Years present of a dollar
bill from Mrs. Jilson. Wasn't that nice. Give my love to all write soon.
Good night from your loving little May.[1]

This letter has a golden butterfly on the flap of its tiny envelope and
at the heading of the paper. But right in the midst of all its glories a
big ink blot mars the triumphant "I received callers". Having dispatched New Year's Day about which she showed an unusual knowledge of the difference between the calls "gentlemen" made, the calls
"ladies" received and the proper costuming for a wedding, three days
over three weeks later she followed with a vivacious report on her
successes on Christmas Day. Written a month after Christmas, the
child's memory and ability to list the gifts she had are worth noting, as
well as the depth of her delight in her own presents—always characteristic of her. Thus early did she enjoy success and no doubt thus
early did she play, as always, a whole-hearted part in that success.
She wrote to her "Cousin" Nancy Yale—an adopted "relative" of the
Meriden years.

Pawtucket
Sunday evening
January 24, 1875

Dear Cousin Nancy.
I haven't seen you for so long that I have a great deal to tell you. I
had a splendid Christmas. We had a Christmas tree here in the Hotel
for the children. There are six children in the Hotel. We had our tree
on Christmas eve, on Christmas night we went over to Mr. Goffs to another tree. Mama gave me a photograph album. Papa gave three hand-
kerchiefs. Grandma gave me a writing desk, Ervie gave me a handkerchief and a pair of cuffs. Mr Shippie (one of the boarders) gave me a
bottle of cologne. Mr. Crawford (another boarder) gave me a work box.
Mr. Ingraham gave me a bottle of cologne. Mrs. Leonard gave me a
roman necktie. The next night at Mrs. Goff's Christmas tree Aunt Saidie
Goff gave me a handkerchiefe. Uncle Jack gave me a book. Bessie Goff
gave me a box of paper, and Mrs. Goff gave me five dollars. Don't you
think Santa Claus treated me well? I had lots of candy and mottoes.
When we get in our new house you must come and see us. Goodby from
your loving little Cousin M.

Young May Woolley's faults were not those of ill will. Her home-
grown sins—if they can be called such—were those of the much-loved
child: the slammed door, clothes thrown angrily on the floor, a somewhat adult form of "name-calling", and crying when she could not

have something she wanted. But at heart she was never spoiled or complex or confused, and in her affections she was direct and whole-hearted. The torture many human beings endure in collisions with themselves was seldom hers. But as she grew up she did make the mistake of thinking human beings better than they are. For a while she paid little for this decent and generous blunder but later the "cost" was heavy.

For the Chaplain's and Mary Augusta's child in Meriden, Connecticut, there had been Mrs. Augur's school in the basement of the Church with pupils numbering between four and eight. It was there in Meriden the child had her first failure on one of her first school days at age five. These days "were spent," wrote Mary Woolley, "at a small private school in the basement of the Center Congregational Church, opened by Mrs. Fannie Augur at the suggestion of my Father for a group of little children. This somewhat reluctantly entered upon by Mrs. Augur, became a successful private school. . . . I recall my humiliation at the mature age of five or six when I misspelled 'bowl'!" The child recalled other incidents of her life in Meriden, ranking high among those memories her envy for a little playmate whose father owned a candy store.

In the manufacturing city of Pawtucket she was to be a pupil successively in three different and larger private schools: Miss Bliss's opposite St. Paul's Episcopal Church; Mrs. Lord's on the second floor of Deacon Bowen's store; and Mrs. Davis's *Private School for Young Ladies.* Set down by her in "Notes on Autobiography", Mary Woolley's own recollections of those school days are matchless: "I soon found myself enrolled in another small private school, known as 'Miss Bliss's.' It is a social rather than an academic recollection which persists from those far-away days. In the school group were the two little Sayles girls, cousins, Martha—then known as 'Mattie'—and Carrie, both of them my good friends for the remainder of their lives. . . . The one 'episode' at Miss Bliss's School which has stayed in my memory all these years is connected with a knitted muffler, an exceedingly useful article of apparel on a wintry day, but, from my point of view, an exceedingly ugly one. That opinion was shared by 'Carrie', who said without circumlocution one morning: 'I think that muffler is homely.' 'I don't,' immediately said another, more diplomatic but less honest little schoolmate, 'I think it's pretty.' That is the single and only incident that stands out in connection with Miss Bliss's School—a remark seventy years old and more. It is interesting—and somewhat startling —to realize how early children form their estimates of character, and how unerring they generally are. Many times in after years, when I had learned to rely upon straightforward Carrie Sayles Holls, I recalled: 'I don't think it is pretty—I think it's homely!' . . . These early scholastic adventures were all of them somewhat ecclesiastical in character: the first, Mrs. Augur's, in the basement of my Father's Congregational Church in Meriden; the second, Miss Bliss's, opposite St. Paul's, one of the two Episcopal churches in Pawtucket; the third, over the store kept by my Father's senior deacon, a white haired, patriarchal figure, whose kindly attitude toward the noisy boys and girls trooping up and down the wooden stairs just outside his 'general store', I love to remember. . . . Many recollections cluster about the several years in Mrs. Lord's School. . . . One day when lobster was being prepared at home, a generous supply of lobster claws travelled back to school, some of them being stored in my desk for another day. But an unexpected visit from favorite cousins meant absence from school . . . followed by a week-end, at the close of which a trail of discovery led directly to my desk. It is not difficult to understand my unpopularity for a season with the powers that were. Another incident of those days, indelibly imprinted on my memory is of the lanky, yellow-haired boy—name forgotten—who, finding it difficult to get the cork out of his ink bottle, tried his teeth as an opener, with speedy and unqualified success.

"A primitive little school, that could be tucked into a corner of one of the many palatial grade schools of today, that little school of Mrs. Lord's . . . I have a vivid memory of that little schoolmistress, slight, somewhat bent, not at all impressive, teaching an invaluable lesson, namely, that school is a place in which to work, that learning one's lesson is not just good luck—but the direct result of effort. I wish that the little widow with a little shawl over her shoulders, working hard to support two little girls, could know how grateful one of her scholars . . . is to her, even after the lapse of many years.

"My fourth educational venture was at 'Mrs. Davis's Private School for Young Ladies'. This meant a long step forward, not only socially, into 'young ladyhood'—but also educationally. I doubt whether my Father had ever heard of the 'preceptorial system', but that was the kind of education which he wished his children to have, small classes and personal attention. Mrs. Davis's schoolhouse would look very insignificant today,—'equipment' was practically non-existent, but good teaching was not. Annie Peck, winning world-wide fame at a later day as a mountain-climber, kept the members of her classes on their toes, mentally, if not physically. *The* teacher, however, was of quite a different type. Lois Green was a Friend, a graduate of Vassar in the early days, whose personality is as vivid to me today as it was fifty or sixty years ago. Of medium height, with crinkly—rather than wavy—black hair, a firm mouth, serious expression, and steady black eyes that could look right through one and detect 'instanter' whether you knew or were pretending. But the firm mouth had humorous corners, and the penetrating eyes a humorous twinkle, which more than once relieved the situation. To have one's beginning lessons in Latin with a teacher like Lois Green was a happy fortune for which I gave thanks many times in my later academic career.

"Mrs. Davis herself was a worthy fore-runner of the headmistress of today, and of the combined 'careerist and homemaker'. The three 'm's'—manners, morals and mentality—received as much emphasis as the 'three r's'. She made us feel that the reputation of the school rested on our shoulders; that 'Mrs. Davis's School' might succeed independently of us, but that the 'for young ladies' was preeminently *our* responsibility!"

Among his quaint but democratic customs the Chaplain spoke to all he met. His daughter was walking down town with him one day when, as she wrote, "I was 'young and foolish', and said: 'Why do you speak to every one? Do you know the name of that man we just passed?'" She had intended to trip him up with this inquiry, but her father answered cheerfully: "Well I cannot recall his name, but I am sure that I know him." Chaplain Woolley was loved by all who knew him. To men who worked in the streets he was known as "Father Woolley". Whether it was night or day, bad weather or good weather, rich man or thief, he went to those who needed him — the servant of every brother and every sister in the Pawtucket neighborhood and on beyond the boundaries of Rhode Island and, if need be, to the confines of Heaven or Hell. For both the common people and the unfortunate he claimed the rights and freedom of the church, including pews which did not have to be paid for and were free to all.

But by 1880 this democratic emphasis did not suit the ruling "aristocracy" of the church. Dr. Blodgett, conscious of an oncoming storm, had counselled the young minister he loved to be thinking of starting a new church on the west side of the river where the growth of the factory population was continuous and rapid. By March 3rd of 1881 letters from the Providence Press and elsewhere were being received by the Chaplain assuring him of their confidence in him and their loyalty to him. Some of these letters begin "Dear Pastor", some "Dear Friend". Some of the letters speak out and some do not.

The year preceding the division of the church Chaplain Woolley's father, Joseph Woolley, was with them, and had died in March at their Pawtucket house. Thus came to an end the life of the little boy who had been born in Jamaica eighty years ago. At that time Mary Augusta's son Frank was just three years and one month old. So great was Mrs. Woolley's suffering about church conditions that in the oncoming storm of dissension she prayed that her son Frank might not become a minister. In all this distress, one day, hearing a call from downstairs, hastily she picked up Frank, missed her footing and fell to the bottom of the stairs. The doctor came and reported no broken bones. But in the following years the lameness grew worse; it wasn't until years later that Mrs. Woolley discovered she had a broken hip and that it was too late then to help the lameness.

The yellowed pages of the data which have survived that ecclesiastical explosion reveal how deep the wound was. In this "Dagger at the Heart" letter, as Chaplain Woolley called it, he wrote in the course of his flaming protest:

> I am moved by deep love for this church of which I am a member, and by an earnest desire to preserve it from ruin and destruction at the hands of these men and those in league with them.
> I am moved by a sense of self-preservation, the preservation and welfare of my family, and my continuance in the work to which I have been called both by God and His Church, which these men are seeking to impair and to destroy. . . .
> I am moved by the Consciousness that God is with me and approves the steps I now take. I have suffered long and prayed much. I have taken all possible steps in the circumstances to escape from this trouble. . . . *I have borne insults and slights—the dagger has been put to the handle into my breast and for more than a year I have buttoned my coat over it.* I have passed sleepless nights—walking the floor of my chamber until morning.
> I, therefore, call upon the church to unite with me in putting down the creators and fomentors of this trouble.

In this last year young May Woolley was to have at the Providence High School before her father took her out, she wrote a remarkable paper entitled "Respect". This essay with its clear, perfect handwriting—something which the older Mary Woolley lost under pressure— is tied with a white ribbon and bears upon its last page a proud "A". It takes up not only respect for others but also the far more difficult subject of self-respect. In this essay there is similarity of experience, which, as is noted in the following paragraph, is almost prophetic of what was to happen in her father's career, and to herself in the last decade of her own life: often the most bitter enemy of a good man is one who envies him because of his superior qualities, until envy, carefully nurtured, changes to hate.

Of her Providence High School days Mary Woolley wrote years later: "From Mrs. Davis's School for Young Ladies to the Classical Department of the Providence High School was quite a leap. The contrast was a sharp one and probably just what was needed. Coeducational, a small group of girls in a room full of boys; no social life; and no informal 'give and take' in the classroom. One certainly had to be on one's toes mentally, in Greek and Latin and mathematics, the three subjects on which I spent my days and parts of my nights. It was good discipline for the girl who had always known the sympathetic atmosphere of the informal classroom. Of the three men whom we had as teachers, Mr. Peck, the principal—and the brother of my former teacher at Mrs. Davis's—did occasionally give a fraction of a second to collect one's thoughts—but Mr. Webster, who took classes in Latin and Greek on alternate days, allowed never an instant of grace. An immediate answer—or next! . . . Two distinguished citizens of a later day—George Pierce Baker of Harvard and Yale, and Theodore Francis Green, Governor of Rhode Island and United States Senator— I remember vividly as boys at the blackboard successfully solving the 'originals' which had laid low most of the class."

Comparatively young, healthy, athletic, incorruptible and devout, if Chaplain Woolley had made mistakes in gathering up the dragon's teeth which were sown in the Church, the mistakes were those of youthful courage. Worn by the conflict, it seemed best that he should travel in Europe for a few months before new plans were formulated. The journal he kept as he journeyed through England, Ireland, France, and Italy is full of thoughtful interpretations of what he heard and saw. Many years later Mary Woolley said that her father's "belief in the social mission of the church was far in advance of his day," and that "Anything short of this ideal was a failure, no matter how prosperous it might be as an organization."

On his return home, Chaplain Woolley found a letter dated at Pawtucket, August 23, 1882, asking him to preach and do pastoral work for one year for the constituency of a "new Congregational Church". Among those friends who heard their chaplain give his first talk in the temporary home of the new Park Place Congregational Church was the contralto choir singer of the former church, Seraphine Goodale, about whom the young chaplain had said many times jokingly that "Seraphine used to back me up," for in the old days the choir singers were located behind and a little above the pulpit. Also in the congregation of that church was Seraphine's little daughter, Nettie Serena Goodale, who was to become an intimate friend of Mary Woolley's at Brown University. It was a great homecoming for the new church society which had been organized during his absence—the old church home reborn in song, in service and in friends.

CHAPTER 5

LADDER AND THE ANGELS

*"Life is a succession of making choices and education will help
you make wise ones."*

Early that spring of 1882 before her father's travels began, May
Woolley had been taken out of the Providence High School where she
had as schoolmates, George Pierce Baker, and Theodore Francis
Green, and sent with her mother and the children to Grandma Ferris's
to stay till her father's return. The social life of South Norwalk had
its possibilities, and this fact had played, perhaps, into her meek acceptance of the paternal law-making, for there was plenty of opportunity at South Norwalk for May's social inclinations and her fondness
for clothes. She had graduated from pink gloves but had plunged into
Japanese parasols. Her cousin Belle Ferris, who for some time lived
with Grandma Ferris, used to sit on fence posts with Carrie Platt to
see May and her friends all dressed up, walk up and down the street
in Norwalk, the Japanese parasols held "just so" over their heads. Said
Belle: "It was quite a sight!"

But with her father's return from Europe in August of 1882, and in
line with these delightful school-free months of her father's absence,
daughter May presented him with her educational program for the
future: lessons in French and music and a winter of social events at
home and of travel abroad.

Her father's succinct reply was: "You are going to Wheaton." Two
weeks later she went to Wheaton, entering, because of advanced standing, the Class of '84.

Within a year at Wheaton, May felt thoroughly at home and was
engaged not only in study and in laughter at her own and the foibles
of her fellow students but also in jesting at the pedantry of the teachers
and of the teaching of her school days. In an article by her in the
Wheaton school paper called *Rushlight* for December 1863, she wrote:

> Mental science is the branch which enters most into our daily life.
> Every meta-physician seems to have a different opinion, so by believing
> all that each one says, we have something to suit every condition. When

34

we are next afflicted with a toothache we are going to remember that
Bishop Berkeley says there is no matter but only ideas, consequently we
have no teeth, and hence no toothache. The mercury is zero, the wind
blowing furiously, and we must take one hour and a half of exercise, but
do not stop to put on your idea of a cloak. Those snow-drifts which you
think you see exist only in your mind, and anyway, a dotted swiss *idea*
will keep you as warm as a fur one.

More important, showing the early development of her interest in
and loyalty to women, it was at Wheaton in 1884 in which she wrote
Portraits of Our Grandmothers. This sketch closes: "The curtain falls,
but we carry away with us the pictures of the women of past time, to
whom we owe no less, if not more, than to the forefathers of history."
These words suggest that she was for the first time looking into the
deep self of her racial inheritance as a woman. At Wheaton she was
to spend two years as student and five as teacher. In "Notes on Autobiography" she wrote:

> It is not strange, I think, that the simple events of so long ago have
> left such vivid memories. . . . Evening prayers were often followed by
> talks on manners, talks which had a way of "staying put". For instance,
> I shall never forget that the way we ate soup indicated the kind of home
> from which we came! . . . The second aspect which grows more vivid with
> the passing of the years was the intellectual. Wheaton was not a college
> in my day, but had a vitality of intellectual life any college might envy.
> . . . The two student years at Wheaton were followed—after a brief in-
> terim—by four and one half faculty years. . . .

Of these faculty years and the opportunity they brought for travel
in Europe, she wrote:

> The summer of 1890 was marked by my first trip to Europe, an event in
> my life, for "Going abroad" fifty years ago was something quite different
> from the casual crossings of our recent pre-war years and this first trip
> was a real tour, including more of Europe than I ever saw in the later
> "treks". It was a party under the leadership of Dr. Blodgett, for many
> years head of the Department of Music at Smith College, and was largely
> a Smith group, with the addition of four of us from Wheaton faculty,—
> Miss Pike, Elizabeth Palmer, Nellie Hopkins and I. Within the two
> months and a little more, we visited England including of course, London,
> the Lake Region, Oxford and Cambridge, several of the Cathedral towns,
> Stratford, Liverpool, Chester, et cetera. . . . Since that time I have never
> felt critical of the "grand tour". For one woman in her twenties, it opened
> a new world. Indirectly, it opened another new world.

❧   ❧   ❧   ❧

The great and formative element in Mary Woolley's life was the
happiness of her home life. There were birthdays always remembered
and celebrated by a birthday dinner. In that home there were, too,
what might be called the "Saturday Celebrations" when invariably,

winter or summer, the Chaplain brought home some flowers for Mrs. Woolley. And there were the daughter's own home-comings from Wheaton when she made the rounds with her father to hear his caged birds sing, see the new tricks of their dog, and go for a drive with her father and his high-stepping horse. There was the development of her little brother Frank, then about ten years old, to watch, and his witty comments to remember. Arriving home and setting down her vacation luggage, she would say, big-sister-wise: "Now, Frank, will you, please,—." But Frank, before she could finish the sentence, retorted: "Not if it's upstairs!" There were the games of parchesi about which they all had so much and such noisy argument they had to stop playing. There were the laughter and—well, it can be called nothing else: the unashamed giggling of the brothers and sister over some of the amusing events of their family life,—"stitches" of mirth as they bent double in their merriment. "Love and nothing else is soon nothing else," writes Walter Lippmann, and it was never that in the Woolley family.

One memory was that of an exceedingly hot summer Sunday when a famous English evangelist preached in their new Park Place Church, attired, as was usual, in a heavy Prince Albert coat. Upon reaching the Woolley home after service, he had asked Mrs. Woolley whether she would mind if he came to dinner in his "Honolulu suit". Mrs. Woolley had not the remotest idea as to what a Honolulu suit might be, but, of course, replied: "Certainly not." The family went out on the side lawn, which opened onto the street, to enjoy a bit of fresh air while waiting for their guest to come downstairs. After a few minutes the Rev. H. V. appeared, attired in what, to the eyes of the family as well as of the neighbors, was indistinguishable from a very tight-fitting pair of white silk pajamas. Seating himself in a comfortable chair, he leaned back and fanned himself, to the delight of passers-by on Summit Street who had never before seen such an apparition on Chaplain Woolley's lawn.

There was the first time the Congregational Club of Rhode Island, made up of men, on one of their semi-annual "ladies' nights", had invited a woman as speaker. "The woman," said Mary Woolley, "was Alice Freeman Palmer and the debatable question was whether her husband should be summoned to the feast. The president of the club, a near neighbor, came over to consult with my father" and found him playing games with his family. "It was finally decided to invite Professor Palmer, but this parting remark of the agitated president indicated that *courtesy*, not *conviction*, had turned the scale: 'Well, I sup-

ield Memorial Gateway of Mount Holyoke College.

A photograph of Tyke, Turvey, and their Missus.

Home at Fleur de Lys.

The Porte Cochere and beyond.

pose it is all right, but I must say that it seems queer to ask a man to come from Boston to Providence to hear his *wife* talk!"

*   *   *   *

When Mary Woolley followed her father's mandate "You are going to Wheaton!", a great New England Quaker and poet, a trustee of Brown University in Providence, John Greenleaf Whittier—little May Woolley's former friend—was at work for larger educational opportunities for women. "At this time Brown University had several Quaker trustees," wrote Anne Tillinghast Weeden. In age Whittier was in the seventies. About that time, too, another New Englander of a different type, a man noted for his courtly charm, light touch and devotion to learning, Colonel Thomas Wentworth Higginson, wrote an essay entitled "Ought Women to Learn the Alphabet?" During these years for the first time in Rhode Island there was brought before the public the possibility of admitting women on equal terms with men to the universities under private corporation. In fact several liberal men spoke to the Rhode Island Women's Club on the subject of higher education for women; and during these years of campaigning for equal rights for women in education the Club entertained Dr. and Mrs. Andrews of Brown, and the subject was discussed.

It was the visit Mary Woolley paid to Cambridge in 1890 under the leadership of Dr. Blodgett which, with its glimpse of Oxford and Cambridge, had quickened in her the desire for a college education. Her father at dinner in Providence with President Andrews spoke of his daughter's wish to study at Oxford. This was followed by Dr. Andrews' immediate inquiry: "Why doesn't she come to Brown?" Dr. Andrews and Chaplain Woolley were old acquaintances: the Chaplain's son Erving Yale Woolley had graduated from Brown in 1888, later marrying Mary Emily, the daughter of Governor John Davis of Rhode Island.

May Woolley went to Brown. Under what conditions? She did not know. At that time the first "female" applicants for learning were Clara Comstock, Maude Anne Donner, Nettie Serena Goodale, Maria Storrs Peck, Sally Peckham, Anne Tillinghast Weeden and Mary E. Woolley. In the second year of their course at Pembroke-Brown, Lida Shaw King, a Vassar graduate, joined the group of women students. She had been a teacher at Vassar, and a graduate student at Radcliffe. Already she had won wide reputation as a classical scholar; and she was to become one of the intimate friends of Mary Woolley, as well as of Eleanor Green, sister of Theodore Francis Green, Mary Woolley's schoolmate at Providence High School. The note which May received at home in Pawtucket on September 29th from Dr. Andrews is not among the treasured Mary E. Woolley papers. But Nettie Serena Goodale, the daughter of Chaplain Woolley's contralto choir singer, still treasures her note, no doubt identical with others which Dr. Andrews sent. It is given here:

> Providence, Sept. 29: Dear Miss Goodale. The classes begin as above, tomorrow, Oct. 1, in the University School room, up stairs, opposite my house, on College Street. Go in at the front door. You see that the first exercise is French. It is taught by Mr. Crowell. Dr. Manning has the Math, Prof Bennett the Greek, and Mr. Everett the Latin. Hoping to see you at the house.
>
> Yours,   E. Benj. Andrews.

On October 1 Nettie Serena came by train from Pawtucket. At the time stated by Dr. Andrews she was "climbing College Hill, a steep and rather strange hill to me then—noisy too, for a cable car with its clanging bell and rumbling cable was continuously going up and down." Although there has been a legend at Brown that Mary Woolley was the "first woman", it was Nettie Serena Goodale and Sally Brown Peckham who were the "first women" to enter the classroom of Brown University. Brilliant, both were valedictorians of their high schools in Bristol and Pawtucket.

An hour later on that "first" afternoon for "first" women students at Brown, Clara Comstock, Maude Anne Donner and Mary Woolley reached the University at half past three for a class in mathematics with Dr. Manning. On this unforgettable afternoon after the mathematics class was over they went into Professor Walter C. Everett's class in Latin, and there were joined by two other girls, Anne Tillinghast Weeden and Maria Storrs Peck.

The journal of young Dr. Manning has survived. From it the following excerpts give an interesting picture of the classes and the life of those first seven women students at Brown:

> Oct. 2 . . . We are fairly started. The College opened Sept. 16 . . . The class of young ladies that the President has been so much interested in is just started. Yesterday afternoon I met them for the first time and assigned them a lesson for next Monday. We are to meet four times a week. . . . I think it will be a bright class and very pleasant to teach and will add quite a little to my income.
>
> Nov. 1 . . . The young ladies' class has been getting along nicely and almost caught up with the boys . . . There was no special understanding with President Andrews as to the terms nor do I know how much I shall receive nor how often it will come, but last Monday I received a check for $30 as a beginning. It may be that there will be that amount paid me each month or each half term.

Jan. 31, 1892 . . . I received $10 from President Andrews for the young ladies' class, making $40 received in all for the fall term . . . Examinations began Dec. 14. The young ladies did excellently.

One of those "first" classes which was most memorable for May Woolley was Dr. Andrews' class in philosophy. The other classes of those days were two in history — American and English, with Dr. Jameson and one in Oriental history with Dr. James Richard Jewett, with whom also she took three terms in the Study of Hebrew. In the course of philosophy—ethics actually—May Woolley entered a little old-fashioned recitation room and quietly sat down next to a boy whose name was Gorham Noble Norton. The boy became nervous, not because May Woolley was the nice-looking girl she was, but because the boy somehow guessed she was what, fifty years later, in a letter he wrote her, he was to call a "smart kid". The next morning going into a huddle at breakfast with another Brown boy whose name was Marshal Brown, he discovered the worst was true: May Woolley was a "smart kid". Little did those Brown boys know then that the girl with the dark Madonna eyes, the rosy cheeks and the look of distinction was, as one of those "first women" said, "equal to any situation", and was coaching the other six of the immortal seven not to "seem to notice" the boys or to look either to right or to left when they had to walk across the campus, "for", she added, "it depends on us in a very large measure whether there is ever a woman's college in Brown."

❋   ❋   ❋   ❋

When later May Woolley was asked: "What was the attitude of Brown students towards the Woman's College?", "I do not know how they felt," was her reply, "I can tell you how they acted. During the four years I received nothing but the utmost courtesy from any student at Brown, an evidence of the calibre of Brown men which I have enjoyed recalling." One might add, too, that it was evidence of the calibre of these "first" Brown University women. In her senior year the editorial board of the *Brown Magazine* elected her as one of their members. Here was an authentic "first"—the first time a woman ever had served on the editorial board of the magazine. It was in this magazine that the classic in jokes about young May Woolley first came out. Question: "Who was the first woman?" Answer: "Miss Woolley." Within three of the four years Mary Woolley was at Brown she and Anne Tillinghast completed their work for and received the degree of Bachelor of Arts—the first time in the history of Brown University that it had been given to women.

Always possessed of a phenomenal memory, Mary Woolley remembered much of what Dr. Andrews discussed during those early years—

words that he spoke such as: "All the scholars of the world get out of any system of philosophy only just as much as they put into it. The great aim of life should be in 'putting in', not in 'getting out'." Mary Woolley commented later: "Well, that applied to the successes or failures of a woman's life, too." Another student, Emogene Manning, remembered Dr. Andrews "sitting in the classroom upstairs, discussing questions of right and wrong, emphasizing that it was the motive behind the act that really counted most. It was no soft easy life that he held up as the highest good," she relates. "'Trials make a man of you,' he once said; and he urged us all to say to ourselves, 'God helping me, no one shall ever hear me whine.'"

May Woolley made the mistake in one of Dr. Andrews' classes in history of asking one of the boys who seemed little interested in the subject why he had selected the course.

"You don't suppose I'm taking it for the history, do you?" he answered scornfully. "Well, I'm not. I'm taking it for a course in manliness."

President Andrews' benefactions to the "Young Ladies", as he called them, did not end with courses in ethics and in history. Each year the President asked them to receive with him at his reception for the Brown Seniors. Stationing the girls in different parts of the room, he would bring up one man after another to introduce them. All that it is necessary to recall about an event like that is that the girls were young and hero worshippers, and that the "men" who were being brought up by Dr. Andrews to meet them were from the senior class.

In the fourth and last year at Brown while Mary Woolley was working for the Master's degree, she taught history at Wheaton for two days a week. Also, she wrote an article for the June issue of the *Brown Magazine* on "The Women's College" in which she said:

> ... The question of expediency has long since given place to one of absolute necessity; it is a "condition and not a theory" which confronts us. As some one has well said, 'It is no longer a question of the 'coming woman,' for she is already 'come'" ... There is room for them both, the cultured woman and the cultured man ... Cambridge has its Girton and Newnham already beginning to boast of illustrious scholars. Every year adds new names to the list of Universities and colleges admitting women as well as men to their opportunities for the highest and broadest culture, and it is greatly to the glory of Brown that she is in the front ranks of this movement.

Later she looked back to say of the years of struggle which followed the efforts of men and women to bring justice to women:

> Half a century since a group, hardly more than half a baker's dozen, seized the opportunity offered by the opening of Brown University examinations to women. There were no enticements appended to that offer:

no provision for class-room instruction to prepare for examinations; no reward of merit in the form of degrees if they were successfully passed. But after all, it was an entering wedge. More than that, it was a long step onward from the discussions in the late eighties (whether or not) to admit women to a limited participation in college work.

A good time? Yes, those girls—all remarkable for their achievements and their brilliance—found their greatest satisfaction in their work yet at times were as gay and as carefree as girls are everywhere. In that little wooden building at 235 Benefit Street which had once served as a paint shop, they were "at home" until several years later when Pembroke Hall was built. So crowded were their conditions on Benefit Street, that sometimes for lack of space they had to sit on the dark narrow stairs over which an uncovered gas light flickered, in order to study together. One of them recorded that "some of the younger professors used to blush when they ran this gauntlet to go to their classes on the second floor." Often the men stopped, hesitated, and then went bravely up, with some gallant remark about the ladder and the angels.

In the Benefit Street building these "angels" had a dark little room where at noontime they gathered for the lunches they had brought from home. The first one to reach this room at noontime—it was May Woolley on this day—began making cocoa for them all on a gas stove. On the shelf above the gas stove was a sturdy candle in a saucer candle stick. Another scratch of a match and this candle flame revealed the cocoa beginning to steam in the saucepan. Above the happy chatter of the girls as they were assembling came the sound from a hurdy gurdy with its grinder and red-capped monkey, who on the street beneath the window were grinding out dance music for them. One of the "young ladies"—perhaps Mary Woolley, for even then she was a "leader"—was leaning far out over the sill of their Benefit Street window, making signs and dropping something—pennies or a nickel or a dime—wrapped in a piece of white paper. At that the little monkey doffed his cap, and the hurdy gurdy man played more dance music, while the young ladies, singing, danced together. "A regular arrangement with the hurdy gurdy man," said one of the "young ladies" in a matter of fact way many, many years later. Also, they gave plays, formed a Greek letter society called Alpha Beta, and went on picnics in the beautiful sea-surrounded countryside of Providence.

At the close of those afternoons of work Mary Woolley and Nettie Serena, who had not known each other in Pawtucket but had become fast friends at Brown, dashed down Providence Hill. Taking a short-cut out to the old railroad station, they caught the train for Pawtucket.

Once in the train they exchanged confidences in a friendship which even in the freshman year had become intimate. One of these remembered confidences Nettie Serena recalled when May Woolley said "that she chose not to go to a woman's college because she 'wanted to come in contact with men's minds'." When May Woolley confided this thought to Nettie Serena just what was in her own mind? Or, in no mood to confide, the two girls settled down on the old plush train-seat to study until the brakeman shouted "*Paw*—tucket!" and they were home again.

But reaching home for May Woolley seldom meant that the day's work was over. Briskly she let herself into the house with a key, catching sight of her mother darning stockings in the living room as she waited for her children to come home for supper.

"In a hurry, May?" asked her mother.

"It's Dr. Jewett's course in Hebrew literature this time, Mama," she answered. "Where's Papa?"

"Papa's lying down in his study, resting after marrying the Fullers."

"No!" exclaimed May. "So Ora Fern *did* marry him after all. Did they . . . ?"

"Yes," answered Mary Augusta, "they did. And the fee was generous and is already in the box in my top bureau drawer."

Mary Augusta smiled happily: she knew what she would do with *that* fee!

The daughter crossed the hall and Mary Augusta continued her darning.

Rapping on her father's study door a little loudly as if he might be asleep still, May asked: "Papa, may I come in?"

Even before she had stepped inside her father's study door she began telling him that she needed his St. Elmo Bible.

"The one they gave me in Meriden?" JJ asked.

"That's it, Papa. The one with the Apocrypha translations in it."

"I thought the Apocrypha books had survived *only* in translations," he said, smiling and taking down the handsome copy.

"Yes," she answered, "a point I mean to make in my paper on Hebrew Literature."

JJ placed the Bible on the old dark walnut revolving book stand and paged through it eagerly as he said: "Here it is, here, the Second Book of Esdras." His lips moving slightly he repeated: "Yes, here is the passage I want." He began to read: "Come hither, I shall light a candle of understanding in thine heart which shall not be put out.'"

CHAPTER 6

MARY LAMB

"No one factor in the nation outside of the home has had so much to do with the shaping of human life as the teacher."

It was *not* to be the fellowship in advanced research for which she had applied through Dr. Jameson. In notes on Autobiography Mary Woolley herself tells the story of her appointment in the autumn of 1895 to the chairmanship of the Biblical Literature Department at Wellesley College:

> For the appointment I was indebted chiefly to Dr. Andrews who opened the way and through his generous support made the approach a simple one: luncheon at his house to interview President Irvine of Wellsley; then an informal afternoon gathering at the home of Ex-Governor Claflin in Boston, to meet a group of Wellesley Trustees, chief among them Alice Freeman Palmer—and the deed was done!
>
> As I look back upon my blithe acceptance of that post, I am reminded of a remark of General Howard, a guest in our Pawtucket home during my childhood. "I have often wondered," said the General, "how I dared assume such grave responsibilities during the Civil War. I never would have dared had I not been so young." Blessed be the confidence of youth! . . .

Here, then, with her love for and understanding of youth, is a suggested sketch of the young professor who became the chairman of our Biblical Literature Department at Wellesley College and the teacher of our very fresh freshman class. At that first class Miss Woolley gave us a friendly "good morning". And *mirabile dictu* we forgot the class room. Even to us, she seemed young and vigorous. Who was she, anyhow, this learned instructor with a flair for clothes? For the present all we knew was that her name was Mary Emma Woolley and that she read and wrote Hebrew, Greek and Latin. But one of the important facts was that this young chairman was the tailored woman emerging and, as one of us said of her at the time, "Par excellence IT in that well-cut tweed of hers!" The spotless blouse, the friendly eyes, "spoke" more loudly to us than any buried ancient language could speak! One of the girls exclaimed gratefully that this teacher was "a new and welcome type of college faculty". Nevertheless, we accepted our instructor with reservations on that day when she gave us our first lecture on Biblical literature, some of us hatefully counting the number of times she used the word "unique", or admiringly surveying the skilled outline which she stopped to chalk upon the board before each section of the lecture, or studying the brown eyes and the strong mouth.

With the next meeting—we came to think of these classes as "meetings"—Miss Woolley began calling each one of us by name: "Miss Cady, Miss Chandler, Miss Coonley, Miss Foote, Miss Gilson, Miss Hewett, Miss McFarland, Miss Frances Mason, Miss Ella Mason (twins as it happened), Miss Judd, Miss Phemister, Miss Sutherland, Miss Tewksbury, Miss Thomas, Miss Warren," and on and on with the names, and never once even glancing at the little black class book to identify us! How in the world did she become familiar in a first week of freshman Bible with the name and individuality behind every one of many scores of names? Nor was that all. Lydia Southard has not forgotten that early in that freshman year although she was *not* in Biblical Literature, Miss Woolley greeted her cordially by name when they met on the stairs or in the corridors of old College Hall.

Later on one of us had the temerity to ask how she did do it? She laughed and replied: "Perhaps my memory resembles that of a relative of mine—a member of the Sherman family—who wrote a history of Rhode Island and had firmly implanted in his mind the age, achievement and not infrequently the mistakes of every native—a gift which in the end did not increase his popularity!" We laughed, too, but we went on thinking. We noticed that when she listened to us, her entire attention seemed to be focussed on *us*. Perhaps, after all, this concentration and not the "relative" was the explanation.

From the windows of that lecture room on the east side of old College Hall, when one felt idle one could look off at Lake Waban, dream about forbidden swimming, think about permitted rowing, gaze at a gondola making its stately way across the lake, get ready in thought for the winter's ice hockey team. Yet it was in that room the young chairman opened the "windows" of another horizon, that of scholarship, as with no personal bias, no emphasis upon religion she talked objectively of the literature of the Bible as history. Even then among those girls there was some appreciation of the young professor's broad understanding of human relationship.

Youth has its natural depressions and despairs, but here, as she revealed the story of a Biblical past, was someone who made you proud and hopeful about being a human being. She herself never made any comment upon what must have been the elementary technique she used in work with freshmen but, as one girl said, "She deliberately trained us to follow her well-planned lectures by actually putting an outline on the blackboard and pointing with a ruler to the Roman numeral she was then discussing. Elementary, my dear Watson!" Maybe!

Mary Woolley's sense of humor many of those girls have loved in recollection even as they loved it in those freshman days when, teacher and taught, they were doubled up with laughter over some of the comments which came from their own papers. After a study of Biblical family life and monogamy, one student wrote: "Where there is monotony, there is religion." Not infrequently examination papers pointed the moral and adorned the tale of the student's lack of preparation, for instance: "Galilee received its name from Galileo, who once wrote a history of Palestine." Professor Woolley's chance remark that the desert life of the Semites gave time for reflection and bred seers and prophets, men of religious and philosophic thought, came back at the next written test as the somewhat startling declaration that "in the desert men had nothing to do, and so became philosophers." Nor have we forgotten the classroom in which one of those freshmen was asked to draw a map of Palestine on the board in order to illustrate some points in the influence of geography on culture. The young woman who went to the board drew that map with a flourish of self-confidence, for before entering college she had had some training in map-making. Now, confident, she turned to face Miss Woolley and the class. She might have been warned, but was not, by the quirk in the young teacher's mouth and the smile in her eyes as Miss Woolley said: "Yes, Miss Marks, a well-drawn map of Palestine. My only criticism is that you have drawn Palestine upside down—a position which might make a difference in the culture of a country as well as of a human being!" The class shouted with laughter. They loved not only the downfall of an over-confident member but also the standing jokes of their Biblical Literature classroom, among them a joke about Anne Judd's spelling.

As a freshman Anne always thought that the spelling of Judaea should follow that of her own name — Judd-aea; and young Mary Woolley gave her many good-natured digs on this spelling of Judaea, but without any spelling success. Years afterward at a reception, Dr. Woolley saw Anne Judd coming down the receiving line and called out: "Anne Judd, can you spell Judaea yet?" Bitterly do some of us recall a first class after freshmen mid-years and our instructor's smiling remark that she rejoiced in our devotion to mathematics—the "devotion" in this class was due in large part to an almost *en masse* failure in math and resultant conditions—but that Esdraelon was not spelled p-l-a-n-e. And she never forgot a row on Lake Waban with one of students who had brought her loose-leaf notebook along with her, thinking the row might prove to be a good opportunity to pump the instructor. Suddenly *in medias res* of the executive part of this plan, the notebook fell overboard; and the anguished girl cried out: "Oh, there goes my education!"

Perhaps better than anyone else, Mary Woolley's friend Dr. Henry Sloane Coffin has described her sense of humor: "Her humor showed itself not in quips or in any conscious effort to catch attention by introducing the comic, but in a light turn of expression. She illustrated Miss Thackeray's definition that 'humor is thinking in fun while we feel in earnest,'" and there was a constant and serious side to the joyous education available in those classrooms, for their teacher, however light she might have thought it best to make her touch on these immature women, never forgot the significance and weight of the education she tried to share with her first freshman class of which she had become the honorary member. Yes, she loved her youthful charges, those wonderful girls of '99. Even then we knew that here was a kind of impersonal love which in those days we were unable to define and did not appreciate. One student, Elvira Slack from another class, came close to one aspect of this democratic, impersonal love when she said: "There is a curious something about Miss Woolley. I don't understand it and it is difficult to get words around it." Another member explained this trait in a more usual way, saying that despite her friendliness she seemed to be "reserved, even a trifle distant."

Although she was one of the most brilliant of students, Mary Woolley was never primarily an intellectual, for her great gift was that of leadership. As Katharine Jones said, she made us feel that "we must go forward or fall behind." Her students sometimes were ashamed of the work they *didn't do* but for this reason Mary Woolley never hurt those girls or made them feel hopeless about themselves. Thus they could go to her with their confidences. Then, as forever, little things mattered so much to that youth of ours. We were always certain that Mary Woolley's friendship would with a faithful hand take our confidences

> "Keep what is worth keeping—
> And with the breath of kindness
> Blow the rest away."

When lovely Evangeline Booth came to Wellesley for a Sunday and a sermon, great was the excitement. In those days Mary Woolley was not only the head of College Hall, she was also responsible for all the ministers who preached at Wellesley. In what had then been her short lifetime, she had heard many good sermons, including those of her father; and she had heard what her father called "rousements", a form of sermon in which he himself never indulged. The old College Chapel was a straight perpendicular cut out of the northeast end of College Hall, and its three floors. Its gallery was where the freshmen had to sit and was entered from the third floor. This gallery was never adequate for the growing needs of either the College or of what might be called the unbounded vitality of the class of '99. The results of this inadequacy were noisy. It was the duty of the Dean, firm, stout, kind Miss Stratton, to prevent noise and to foresee exit blocks. When the daughter of General Booth became our guest, traffic jams were almost inevitable, argued Dean Stratton. Always a little uncertain what "those '99 freshmen" would do next and flustered for once, Dean Stratton was determined to prevent trouble and to have respectful quiet. In morning chapel the day before Evangeline Booth came, Dean Stratton gave out preventive instructions. Among other things, she said, as she gazed upward to the Freshman Gallery where '99 was in leash: "Young ladies, after Commander Booth's daughter has spoken, please pass away quietly and meet your friends below." This was about what '99 in its merriment and wild larks thought of itself but no one else had ever said it quite so plainly, and the chapel laughter was an explosion of joy as we "joined our friends below"!

Many were her friends in adjacent classes, among them: Isabelle Fisk, Frances Rousmaniere, Martha McCaulley, Winifred Augsbury, Helen Kelsey, Lucy Freeman, Mary Dewson, Edith May, Florence Painter, Bertha Trebein, Alice Childs, Mary Talulah Maine, Edith Merrill, Ruth Baker, Gerry Gordon, Pauline Sage, Eliza Newkirk, Elizabeth Manwaring, Sally Tomkins and others. In time all of these Wellesley students were to find a memorable place in the life of women.

In that golden age any attempt to call any roll of the significant women who were on the faculty would result in failure. But among those colleagues and friends of Mary Woolley's were Emily Greene Balch, fearless, slender, indomitable for justice and for peace; and as the students rejoiced to know and some to see, the performer of a marvelous Highland Fling; Katharine Lee Bates, author of one of our national hymns, *America the Beautiful*, and her friend Katherine Coman, economist; Mary Calkins, philosopher; Sophie Chantal Hart, unique, and passionate for the right; Ellen Hayes, patriot, poet and mathematician; those two beautiful friends Sophie Jewett and Margaret Sherwood with whom to work was to discover depth under depth the meaning of what it is to be a student and to love learning somewhat as the ancient Greeks must have loved it. One of the girls of '99, Maynard Force, said of Miss Scudder's class: I "was breathless for my mind had been carried to far places. It might as well have been a class in religion, art, science, history for we had touched them all in our class on Literature. It made the whole world of the past come alive for me as nothing else ever did and awakened a feeling of responsibility to play my part in this ongoing world."

Miss Scudder, aware of the greatness of some of her colleagues and of the greatness of the work which was being accomplished at Wellesley, herself thought of it as a golden age and wrote: "A special light hovers for me, too, over that period." Finally there was Ellen Fitz Pendleton of whom some students—especially those who were poor mathematicians—stood in awe, but most students loved her for her fairness and sense of justice, her warmth and for the hoops she rolled with us down the corridors of old College Hall.

It must have seemed only incidental to Miss Bates that she was one of the freshman advisors, and she took this obligation whimsically, and with unfailing good humor. An advisee, Louise Reynolds, went to her dutifully. Miss Bates looked at Louise and said: "Now what do you want to know?" Louise Reynolds answered: "Nothing as far as I know." Miss Bates replied: "That's good, for I am sure I couldn't tell you!" Miss Bates' absentmindedness was almost as well-known as her unpredictable sayings. Once, just outside the library, then in College Hall, Adeline Putnam was reading the bulletin board when she felt an arm around her shoulder in a fleeting embrace. Turning around, to her amazement she was alone except for a plump but rapidly disappearing figure at the other end of the hall. Miss Bates possessed, too, a baffling way of dangling ideas before you. As you saw fit, you could take the ideas or leave them, understand them or be puzzled. Once she told us that she had a new kitten, adding that she had "named the kitten 'Frisky Fuzzy' after Miss Woolley." More obvious was a conundrum she often asked about the young chairman of Biblical Literature: "Why is Mary Lamb like a trolley car?" After one or two guesses on the part of others, KLB would say: "Because you can never tell when she's going to stop or to start!" And, chuckling to herself, off she departed rapidly—probably for some hard work.

One day she overtook her "Mary Lamb" on the campus who, much dressed up, was carrying her golf bag.

Miss Bates exclaimed: "I thought you said you had a lecture at the Ladies' Guild in the village this afternoon?"

"So I have," replied Mary Woolley, her eyes twinkling.

"A lecture on golf?" chuckled Miss Bates.

"No doubt the Guild would enjoy that more," came the reply.

"Mary Lamb, I thought you said that talk on the prophets had more illustrative material than any lecture should ever have?"

"I did say that," was the answer.

"By any chance is it those illustrations which make your golf bag look so stuffed?"

"How did you guess?" exclaimed Mary Woolley, drawing a large Bible out of the golf bag.

For a moment the two friends faced each other, laughing. Mary Woolley realized that "Katy Lee", as she called Miss Bates, always got the better of her but she also came to know that it had been a sorry day for her when she had let the Bible out of the bag for the amusement of a College Public.

These two great women, young then, were to have need of laughter and recollected merriment. It is good to recall their laughter, and it is good to remember how simply and vulnerably human and lovable both of them were! If, as Emerson says it is, the soul's highest duty is to be of good cheer, then Katherine Lee Bates and Mary Emma Woolley were two almost perfect, as well as great, women.[1]

❖   ❖   ❖   ❖

Mary Woolley was an illustration of one truth which in her work she felt passionately: that young people could hardly do without the care, influence, and love of the right sort of older people. What she owed to her grandmother, to her father and mother, and to her Uncle Frank no one except she herself or someone who had lived in her home could know. There at home had the foundations of her character been laid; and there, first, did she learn: "Justice, compassion, friendship, goodwill, the spirit that binds man to man, that works for peace."

It was in a brief weekend vacation that for the first time JM found herself at home with the Woolleys. After supper Mrs. Woolley limped upstairs to get a dark skirt of her daughter's on the hem of which she was sewing a black braid. This she wished to finish in order that her daughter might take the skirt back with her to college. When she came down Mother Woolley sat under the gas light, the heavy tweed skirt upon her knees, a look of strain about her big dark eyes and of delicacy about the tired sweet face on which the small finely-shaped nose stood out like the profile of a bird's beak. Over all, including her dark hair, was the glare of the gas lamp. Her daughter was seeking her mother's advice concerning an unpleasant incident which had taken place. But all Mary Augusta would say as she sewed on and on was: "We have to endure a good deal from those we love."

The next day, Saturday, JM was not surprised to find that one of the most important members of the family was Sergeant Rags who like his master had a twinkle in his eye and a nose sensitive to joy and to sorrow. Even in those days there were reasons why a much-loved dog should not go downtown into the center of traffic. About those reasons there was a difference of opinion between the Sergeant and the Chaplain. If the Sergeant stated those opinions, however discreetly, he got no further than the backyard. But the years and the parish had taught Chaplain Woolley and Sergeant Rags one and the same wisdom: that you seldom regret having said too little. After breakfast, while the master was formulating his Saturday marketing plans, Rags signalled to the mistress—a look and a quiver of the tail—that he needed—very much—to go into the back yard. Mrs. Woolley let Rags out quickly. For a moment as she watched him from the window, Rags was nosing around the bushes most remote from the street and looking out for himself. That was safe, and Mother Woolley left the window and went back to her household tasks.

Then a glance up at the empty window told Rags she was gone. A black shadow, he slipped across the street and down the street to a vantage point where, observing but not observable, he could watch for the master. Rags had learned that most important factor in genuine freedom: the art of not calling attention to yourself.

Stepping delicately, stopping when the master stopped to speak to some worthless dog or to some only less worthless dog-of-a-parishioner, Rags shadowed him "down street" and to the center of the shopping district. Having reached the strategic center where in those days the beefsteaks were thick and tender, and butchers, under the pastoral eye, were generous with scraps, Rags threw aside his cloak of shadow and announced himself. As the Chaplain caught sight of him his eyes snapped, his nose moved up and down a little and he stiffened. You, Sergeant Rags, saluting with one paw, came to attention. Plainly, the master did not like what you had done. It was insubordination. Yet he liked brains and ability whether in dog or in daughter.

About half an hour later, the mistress heard the clang of the trolley bell in front of the house, and saw dog and master turn to say goodbye to the conductor and then step off the trolley. The Chaplain and Rags came towards the open home door and the Mother Woolley they loved and took advantage of who was standing framed in the doorway, waiting to welcome them. Well, this was life—and it was good—for man and dog "o' sense"! Home to welcome you, rewards for ability and hard work, abundant appreciation, and the certainty—never any doubt about that—of a big dinner.

CHAPTER 7

TRADITION OF WOMEN

"I cannot see that the sequestration so long observed was ever meant for women. A woman is a human being—before she is a woman. Just as a man is a human being before he is a man."

Early in November of 1899 Mrs. Howard Porter, a Mount Holyoke alumna whose daughter Carrie was in the Class of '99, at Wellesley, wrote Mary Woolley: "We were at Mt. Holyoke College for 'Founders Day' and I have been mentioning your name most strongly to individuals as the next president of the college. If you should be asked, I hope you will consider the subject earnestly and prayerfully, assured that one of the alumnae at least would be rejoiced to see you in that position."

"The December of 1899," said Mary Woolley, "was a critical month, the most critical, probably, in my life." Wellesley had granted her leave of absence for the academic year of 1900-1901 and she was "deep in plans" for absence from Wellesley and graduate work "when I," she wrote, "was confronted with the question of leaving Wellesley, not for a year, but for all time, and giving up teaching for administration. An even more difficult decision was involved, for almost at the same moment there came two opportunities, to be Dean of the Women's College in connection with Brown University, and President of Mount Holyoke College. . . . That I decided as I did I have never regretted."

Events followed one another swiftly. On the 4th of January, 1900, the Board of Trustees of Mount Holyoke met in Springfield to consider the recommendation of the Committee that Mary E. Woolley be appointed President to succeed Mrs. Mead. The recommendation was accepted by the Trustees.

Mary Augusta Woolley entered in her diary, January 15: "May accepted invitation to become Pres. of Mt. Holyoke College. Resigned at Wellesley." Congratulations formal and informal, personal and impersonal, literally poured in upon the President-elect. One chatty congratulation from an aunt of Katharine Lee Bates contained these lines: "I can almost say to *you* that 'I knew all about it!' for Tuesday

52

morning I had a letter from Miss Coman in which she said 'You will
hear great news from Mt. Holyoke this week', and Tuesday afternoon
in Katharine's letter she said 'Miss Woolley will have a delightful item
to tell you about herself this week'—and I am not so far gone that I
could not put *this and that* together." One large covey of these letters
of congratulation sounded like a chorus of birds on an early spring
morning in which the song repeated over and over was "You are just
the person for the place." But there was another type of congratulation
in which the message was: "The Trustees have chosen one who understands and respects the past and yet is not bound by tradition." The
intimate and informal congratulations were most dear to the heart of
the President-elect, among them loving stanzas written by President
Hazard of Wellesley, from which this is the last:

> So bid her God-speed—and we crush back a sigh—
> Today's for rejoicing—time enough by and bye
> To find how we miss our Wellesley professor
> Mt. Holyoke's president,—cheer girls—God bless her!

There were, too, some gay nonsensical stanzas by Katharine Lee
Bates with the title:

> WELLESLEY ADDRESSES MT. HOLYOKE
> (In Strict Privacy.)
> Mount Holyoke, our relation
> Perplexes pedigree.
> You are the deep foundation
> Of Vassar, Smith and me.
> Yet of our college cluster
> Are you the youngest star.
> Now tell me by your lustre,
> What curious kin we are.
> It seems almost too hard on
> My poverty, that you,
> With famous flower-garden,
> Insist upon a Zoo.
> Yet, as befits your scion,
> Of generous blood I am,
> So add to Mary Lyon
> My Mary Woolley (-lamb).

Congratulations also took the substantial form of honorary degrees:
in 1900 a Litt.D. from Brown University and an L.L.D. from Mount
Holyoke's neighbor, Amherst College.

Convinced that she should study the university system in Great
Britain and its effect upon and relation to the education of women, she
declined the advance salary offer until she could take up her work at
the College, and asked that the date of tenure begin not on July 1st,

1900, but on January 1st, 1901.   In Notes on Autobiography and even
more in the talks she gave, Mary Woolley has left a somewhat complete
record of this "interim" experience between the years of 1900 and 1901
from which the following is taken:

> The year 1900-1901 was an interim year.   The gathering in College
> Hall Centre that January morning in 1900 when all Wellesley sang to the
> new president of Mount Holyoke and then showered her with flowers,
> began a hectic semester, spent in part keeping regular appointments in
> the Wellesley classrooms, in part on the railroad, journeying to various
> sections of the country to meet the alumnae clubs of Mount Holyoke. . . .
> It was not a case of "off with the old love, on with the new"—far from it.
> Wellesley had taken deep hold on my affections . . .
>
> Wise counsellors advised an autumn studying education for women in
> the British Isles, and in September of 1900, my cousin Helen Ferris and
> I sailed for England. . . . The three months offered a striking contrast to
> my first trip of ten years before.   That was "seeing Europe" from the out-
> side; this was living in the United Kingdom.   Somerville, Lady Margaret
> and St. Hugh's, Newnham and Girton, Bedford and Royal Holloway,—
> became more than names and the residence in some of them, brief as it
> was, furnished a background for better understanding of differences be-
> tween the Halls for Women in the British Universities and the American
> College for Women . . .

At the time of Mary Woolley's visit to Newnham, Jane Harrison, a
brilliant classicist and anthropologist, was resident.   Later her essay
"Homo Sum" was to become an influence in Mary Woolley's work for
and with women.   In particular these five lines are notable:

> I share with you the feeling that a vote is unwomanly.   I add to it the
> feeling that it is unmanly.   What I mean is that, to my mind, a vote has
> nothing whatever to do with either sex quâ sex; it has everything to do
> with the humanity shared in common by two sexes. . . .   The whole
> Woman's Movement is, to my mind, just the learning of that lesson . . .

*   *   *   *

What manner of place was South Hadley in the Connecticut Valley
—called the "Garden of New England"—to which Mary Woolley was
going?   Mary Lyon had chosen this garden spot on which to found
Mount Holyoke Seminary and there she had labored for the higher
education of women.   In the early eighteenth century South Hadley
was called the "South Precinct".   Some of the buildings of those old
days still remain, including a few beautiful mansions on the northern
border of what is now Mount Holyoke's spacious and lovely campus.
The surrounding hills might be called majesty in miniature.   Flowing
between the Mount Holyoke range and the Mount Tom range is the
turbulent and mighty Connecticut River.   It was in this valley of the
Connecticut, as well as in the greater New England cities like Boston,

that Mary Lyon week after week and month after month, campaigned for funds with which to found the Seminary. One morning she started off full of hope to ask some rich people for help. Returning disappointed, when her hosts asked her about the visit she replied: "Yes, they are rich people. They have fine furniture and an imposing home. But they are little bits of folks." During these days Mary Lyon said about her educational scheme: "Many good men will fear the effect on society of so much female intelligence", but she stated she would collect a thousand dollars from women with which to start her building funds, for she was convinced that woman should have as much intellectual training as man. Mary Lyon said one day to her class: "It is often said, 'nobody but Miss Lyon can carry on this Seminary'; I expect some of you, young ladies, to do better than I have ever done.[1] Herein lay the three-fold tradition of women in the very founding of Mount Holyoke Seminary; equal opportunity with men in education, the founding of the higher education for women through donations made by women; and the continuous leadership of women—"I expect some of you, young ladies, to do better than I have ever done."

This great seminary was engaged in an early and practical form of internationalism which might be called missionary-making. A daughter of Mount Holyoke College, Louise Porter Thomas, has written:

> It was warmth of heart and brightness of hope which made missionaries. . . . Mary Lyon had listed three essentials for a female missionary. The first two were piety and a strong constitution; the last was a "merry heart." . . . Miss Lyon tried to keep . . . worldly . . . influence from being decisive. "Never teach the immortal mind for money," she said. "If your object is money-making, be milliners or dressmakers; but teaching is a sacred, not a mercenary employment." [2]

As the years deepened the power of Mount Holyoke's work and idealism, Mary Lyon's Seminary influenced schools throughout the United States and in far-off countries: Wheaton, Monticello, Beloit College, Rockford Seminary, Lake Erie, Wellesley, the Northfield and Mount Hermon Schools, Vassar, and Elmira; in foreign lands, among others, the International Institute in Spain, the Huguenot College in Africa, and many schools in China and elsewhere.

When Mary Woolley returned from England and arrived at Mount Holyoke College, on December 31st, 1900, Dr. Hooker, head of the Botany Department, sent a basket of fresh eggs from her own Buff Orpington hens. Atop the eggs was a card saying: "Nineteenth Century eggs for a Twentieth Century president." Bird-loving, kindly Mrs. Fairbanks, the housekeeper general for the College, put the eggs away, and as long as they lasted two were sent up each morning with

the President's breakfast tray.   Shortly after Dr. Hooker's welcome,
Byron Smith arrived, a great shaggy, fine-looking, elderly man who as
a young man had helped Mary Lyon "move in".   Mary Woolley wrote:
"Solemnly he took out of his pocket two big red apples and presented
them to Mary Lyon's new and untried successor."   But the welcome
on that day was not completed until the Treasurer of the College, A.
Lyman Williston, called and said: "I am glad you came at the beginning of the year and at the beginning of the Century.   It will be
so much easier to keep track of you."   Of that welcome the new president wrote later:

> All along the line it was a kindly warm-hearted reception.   I took it as
> a matter of course without realizing how easily it might have been less
> kind, less warm-hearted.   The members of the faculty living at Brigham
> Hall where the president of the College made her home, were, mainly,
> much older women, Mount Holyoke graduates who had spent practically
> all of their professional life on that campus.   A woman without Mount
> Holyoke traditions, who had never even seen the college until she was
> offered the presidency was welcomed as cordially as if she had been to
> the manor born.

That evening after dinner Mary Woolley went into the student
"parlor".   Lucia Hazen was standing next to the door as Miss Woolley
entered.   While she talked to the girls who crowded around, the "new
President" put her hand on Lucia's shoulder.   Lucia, two-fold conscious
that she herself was a "very awkward school girl" and that the woman
whose hand was upon her shoulder was "a wonderful woman", began
to blush.   The color was rising in her neck and upon her face, and she
did not dare move for fear the hand would be taken away.   Almost
fifty years later Lucia Hazen Webster, now blind and no longer strong,
wrote:

> Her touch was indicative of her whole relation with the girls—full of
> wonderful friendlyness.   (Spelling wrong but not to be corrected.)
>   Ever since leaving college Miss Woolley remembered me.   Once, when
> she had no expectation of seeing me, she greeted me with my full name
> even to the added Webster.   I feel the girls responded to her in an un-
> usual way.   No other person of my acquaintance could have persuaded
> a group of college girls to give up their beloved college yell without a
> murmur and no one else could have by any possibility have done away
> with secret societies.   And girls who [met] her father will never forget
> him.

In her diary under March 4, 1901, Mrs. Woolley wrote: "The girls
in Mary Brigham Hall gave me a spread—it being my birthday."   It
was Mrs. Woolley's sixty-ninth birthday.   The faculty and the students
lovingly conferred on Mary Augusta (Ferris) Woolley this honorary
degree:

The Faculty and Students
of
Mary Brigham Hall
do hereby confer the degree
of
"MOTHER OF US ALL"
upon
Mrs. J. J. Woolley

The greatest day of all was still before them when in the Line a
Day Book of Mrs. Woolley was written: "1901, Tuesday, May 14,
Harriet — Grace — Joseph, Frank and I went to Holyoke to May's
Inauguration", and in the diary of J. J. Woolley, 1901:
"Tues. May 14:
"Pleasant.
"Mamma, Frank, Harriet Wright and Grace Dickerman and I at
S. Hadley.   Left here at 1.49 —
"George Grant took care of the horse"
This time it was neither "Kitty sick" nor "Kitty shod".   No, not even
for the Inauguration of his daughter would JJ neglect his horse!

                        *   *   *   *

Shortly before the Inauguration took place, a member of the faculty
drew a friend of Mary Woolley's aside and said: "Now the one thing
we need here is someone with a backbone.   What I want to ask of
you is whether Miss Woolley has a backbone?"
    Quiet and caustic came the reply: "I have never noticed that she
was invertebrate."
    It was noontime and the trolley cars had been arriving all the morn-
ing to empty their gay cargoes of alumnae at Mary Lyon Hall—and
their guests and guests of honor from all the eastern and some of the
western states, among these guests little Mrs. Fannie Augur from
Meriden, Connecticut, for whom five-year-old Mary Woolley had misspelled the word "bowl".   Then Clang! Clang! Clang! again, the trolley
cars were off back to Holyoke and on to Springfield to fetch more
guests while those already arrived streamed through the campus, many
of them toward the gymnasium where a simple lunch was being served.
    In the talk and the laughter on that day the exclamation most often
heard was: "Isn't this a *beautiful* day!"   Certainly the birds thought
it was, for robins, orioles and bobolinks, bluebirds and song sparrows
warbled and sang, flitting from tree to tree.   There was silent happiness, too.   In the blooming quince bushes about Mary Lyon Hall,
unafraid, shy sparrows watched the Inauguration throngs.   On the
side of Prospect Hill by the Lower Lake where from behind the gym-

nasium came the sound of flowing water and the songs of the thrush and veery, it was Paradise on that day. A little northward by the Upper Lake even at noontime the hermit thrushes were singing their unearthly song to the horizon line of hills beyond. None of these, either bee in blossom or bird in bush, was an invited guest. Yet without them the day would have been silent and the joy of that spring vanished when on May 15, 1901, at 2 o'clock in the afternoon young Mary Woolley was to be made President of Mount Holyoke College.

In all this miracle of beauty the commonplace business of living seemed to stand still. The fact was that it was half past one and already guests were beginning to enter Mary Lyon Hall. In a few minutes along came a little woman, her dark eyes large and excited. With her were two young women, her son's fiancé Harriet Wright and her niece Grace Dickerman, and her young son Frank. The little woman was neither dancing nor laughing but

"Mary Gus feels mighty fine
I can find nothing to rhyme

"Shic shu shu le lu
After rain the sky is blue"

Leaning on the arm of the son who had been named after her brother Frank Arthur, she was smiling. People pushed a bit up and down the waiting line, and the words heard most often were: "It's Mrs. Woolley!"

"That little woman?"

"Yes, isn't her smile nice!"

"Like sunshine!"

"Lame?"

"Yes, lame."

An usher—one of the able girls from Mary Brigham Hall—signalled to another usher and disentangled herself and her baton from door responsibility. In a friendly voice the girl said as she reached the little mother: "Mrs. Woolley, your seats are waiting for you!" To the line she said: "Fall back, please, and let Mrs. Woolley and her family through!" Swiftly the group was passed along and through the great doors, down the aisle and into the seats roped off with blue ribbon.

In the distance were heard the introductory notes of the band playing a march. At the gymnasium the academic procession was forming, its various groups falling quickly into line. Leading the procession was the choir of ninety students in their new black cassocks and white surplices. Following the choir were the freshmen, the sophomores and the juniors all in white. But the seniors wore their black mortar boards and gowns, followed by the faculty. Marching with the faculty

on that day were, among others, great hearted women whose devotion
to the dreams and plans of Mary Woolley never failed: Bertha E.
Blakely, Dr. Cornelia Clapp, Louise Frances Cowles, Caroline Board-
man Greene, Frances Hazen, Dr. Ellen Hinsdale, Miss Fitz Randolph,
Miss Searles and Clara F. Stevens. At the end of this line came the
President of the Board of Trustees, Judson Smith and, marching with
him, Mary Woolley. After them followed the inauguration speakers,
President Hazard of Wellesley, handsome and friendly; Dr. Harris,
President of Amherst, Mount Holyoke's academic neighbor; Dr. Taylor
of Vassar; President Faunce of Brown University now, academically
speaking, *in loco parentis* to the "youngest of college presidents in
the youngest of colleges", for Mount Holyoke had become a college
in 1888; and finally that most splendid figure for thirty-six years among
the Mount Holyoke Trustees, Dr. Stimson. Beside him, dark-haired
and handsome, marched Chaplain Woolley. After them came the
academic guests in their bright-colored hoods. Within the chapel on
the organ bench was young William Churchill Hammond clad in black
gown and white surplice, playing Handel's Overture to the Occasional
Oratory as he waited for the signal which would tell him that the
procession was nearing the chapel entrance. The signal came as the
choir reached the chapel door and the organ with all the choir swung
into "Ancient of Days Who sittest throned in Glory".

As the inaugural program took them through Processional, Scripture
Reading and Prayer, a *Festival Te Deum,* and Dr. Smith's Address
and Presentation of the Keys to the President-elect, how did Mary
Woolley feel? What was she thinking and believing about education
for women? With all the power which charged every day to the full
for her she was believing in the supreme worthwhileness of the work
she had set out to do, and in her own words that "Nothing that is
human is foreign to it; nothing that has to do with the best development of a human being is outside its province."

In a sense the Inauguration Address which followed brought little
reply to that question. She was far too honest to pretend that she
knew what she would do or what she thought. She quoted Dr.
Andrews several times. In one of these references, Dr. Andrews said:
"Nearly all great advances in practical industry depend upon principles which have been carefully wrought out in the study or the laboratory." And she knew that in a sense it was in the study or laboratory
she, too, must work out her dream for equality and a shared leadership
for educated womanhood. Earnestly she herself asked several practical questions: What outlook is there for the college woman? What

must the college do to make a woman ready for her work in the world as homemaker, social worker, scholar or teacher? In character and culture what should this college woman be? When a few minutes later she closed her address with one of those aphorisms which were instinctive with her: "Education in its highest sense is something more than intellectual discipline; something more than culture," Mary Lyon Chapel rang with applause again and again. Finally the young President had to rise to acknowledge the applause. After the prayer by Dr. Stimson came the addresses by Miss Hazard, by Dr. Taylor of Vassar, President Harris of Amherst and Dr. Faunce of Brown University—all warm with welcome and tribute. Then followed the singing of "A Mighty Fortress is our God". On that day the complete satisfaction of the audience was almost audible as Chaplain Woolley rose to pronounce the benediction for his daughter's inauguration.

The word most often heard as the guests had poured into South Hadley on that glorious spring morning had been "Beautiful!" Now, as they marched from chapel to gymnasium, the exclamation most often heard was "Perfect!" Chaplain Woolley, saying he would join them later, slipped away and wandered off toward the apple orchard between the street and the gymnasium. There beneath one of the apple trees he sat down, still quivering with pride. He had gone there, as Minnie Dwight has said in a *Golden Memory*,[8] "to escape the emotion of his high hour of living. He came upon a child who was not excited about it—who preferred the bees in the apple trees to the noble words and the stirring music. She could hear the band as she watched the butterflies. The two found a harmony," as the "handsome, dark haired man . . . sat with [the child] on the grass under an apple tree and told of his pride in his daughter's inauguration."

In happiness and laughter at the reception there was abundance of relaxation evident everywhere. One of the most relaxed guests was Miss Woolley's younger brother Frank — the *enfant terrible* of the Woolley family — who, surrounded by friends wondering what he would say next, was asked by a Rhode Island friend: "But, Frank, aren't you proud of May?" Smilingly he answered: "Yes, I am, but she is the only one of our family to be in an institution!"

That night, as two middle-aged people in the Mary Brigham Hall guest room were preparing for bed, the students were still serenading their daughter.

"Beautiful!" said Mother Woolley.

"Perfect," agreed the Chaplain, chin in air as he wrestled with his best gold stud—one his mother had given him when he became 18.

A few minutes later Mary Augusta took from her travelling bag a little book, lavender bound, printed on its cover *A Line A Day*, pulled out its purple ribbon and wrote under "May 15": "Wednesday May's Inauguration day—bright and beautiful in every way."

Slipping the gold stud into its little box, J. J. took out a small black bound book, on its cover in gold the words *Standard Diary*, and wrote under May 15, 1901: "Beautiful at South Hadley Inauguration of May, President of Mt. Holyoke College. A great and glorious time. . . . All our family was there—"

Although there was no one in the house except Mother Woolley, Bridget the cook, and Lizzie the maid, somehow in the Woolley parsonage in Pawtucket on that day there was an atmosphere of people, pressure, haste, as well as the fragrance of roasting chicken. This year, two months after the inauguration of Mary Woolley on May 15, Chaplain Woolley's own engagements were such that the celebration of his daughter's birthday had to be held on the evening of the 12th instead of July 13th. The door bell whirred. Mrs. Woolley limped anxiously to the door, opened it, but smiled gratefully at the flower boy because he was not some guest come before she was ready. She had hardly put the flowers in water when whirr-r-r! the bell sounded off again, this time the delivery man from Carr's in Providence with an ice-packed bomb of strawberry ice cream.

Then Mrs. Woolley and Lizzie went into the dining room where weaving in and out among the chairs they set the table, Lizzie calling out the arrangements in square dance fashion: "Miss May, mum, on her mother's right, Mrs. Ervie and Mr. Ervie, and on the Pastor's left Miss Lill Wright; the Pastor himself, Miss Jeannette on *his* right, Miss Harriet Wright and Mr. Frank—my how them two *do* love each other! —*and* Miss Grace! With every place set, with the flowers, mum, and that candle-lighted birthday cake, my, ain't it handsome!"

A key clicked tentatively in the front door lock followed by whispering and the wild whirring of the bell with an accompaniment of joyous laughter and greetings.

Lizzie opened the dining room door a crack, saying *sotto voce* to Bridget: "*Herself* has come with her brothers, that's all. Teasing her they are!"

Mary Woolley's 38th birthday had begun. Hours later, as her father went to bed, J. J. Woolley did not write "Our daughter has become an important person—a College President." What he wrote in his diary was: "May is 38 years today, is well, good and useful."

CHAPTER 8

MINISTRY OF EDUCATION

"Education . . . helps in the development of the whole man or woman, a result as far beyond the ability to make money as living is more than earning a livelihood."

As she settled into the harness of being a college president, Mary Woolley found that there is no time of year when the collegiate system does not need attention: from the day when the freshman enters and must be coddled, through Christmas time when the students returning from their homes begin to spread the sicknesses they have acquired as part of a "holiday", on through to the early spring of the year when the instructors flood the President's office to describe what enticing financial offers they have had from other institutions, and finally to the season of graduation with its sequel for the president in official housecleaning during the hottest weather of the year. Like woman's work, this work is never done. From every side, inside and out, college presidents see the demands crowd up on them. When the public does not want anything else the public wants to be talked to, and will not believe that speeches or addresses or "just talks" have, like breakfast foods, some history before they are served. Not content with asking for speeches, articles, letters, secretaries, teachers, social workers, it sometimes asks for wives. The writer recalls that shortly after the "new president" took up her duties at Mount Holyoke, a friend of the college said that she did hope Miss Woolley "would have the time to become personally acquainted with every single student in college" even then about seven hundred, and that she did hope "Miss Woolley would *make* time to represent the college outside!" After these "hopes" followed more. This friend of the college brightened with this afterthought and said that she *did* hope "Miss Woolley would have plenty of time to rest and keep well for her work!" [1]

Night and day, safe and unsafe, to the rich or the poor, to the crippled or the dying, Mary Woolley's father went to anyone who needed him. This was the Ministry of Christ. The daughter followed in the father's footsteps in her Ministry of Education and for her, too, there

62

were no calculations of convenience or safety, or personal advantage, or of financial reward. Her reason for going to some hill-top group in some unknown village in New England or to some forgotten hamlet along the Hudson River was simply that they "wanted" her. Perhaps Mary Woolley knew that they needed her but that she never said. Wherever she went, if she was offered a fee and compensation for her travelling expenses, she accepted them graciously. If she was not, her hostesses had no consciousness that their young and famous guest was earning her living and had to make ends meet on a small salary.

During these early years at Mount Holyoke, if it was humanly possible to keep them, Mary Woolley felt it was important not to cancel her own speaking engagements. One of these engagements was in the Connecticut Valley where she had promised to speak at a club meeting in Chicopee on a winter afternoon. The trolley was the usual means of getting about. But the day before the engagement a good old New England snowstorm settled down on Chicopee, disrupting trolley service. On the day of her talk the cars were running again but the service was very irregular. In spite of our urging her not to attempt to get to Chicopee, she was resolved not to let her public down. Dressed in a trim tailored suit with a soft blouse, she made an early start, snowshoes in hand, and determination in her manner, planning to snowshoe when and if necessary, and having not the slightest idea how near to her destination the trolley could possibly take her.

Another time—some years later when automobiles were used much more than trolleys, she had promised to speak at an evening meeting near Northampton. It had been snowing steadily for days and the roads everywhere were barely open. Nevertheless she decided to keep this engagement. The chauffeur Earl Buss had a shovel on the driving seat beside him. President Woolley sat on the back seat of the limousine, her snowshoes beside her. Much of the roadway from Amherst to Northampton had become one way traffic between high walls of snow, virtually a tunnel, and it was necessary from time to time for the "faithful Buss" to get out and shovel. But the young president, dressed in evening attire, sat undaunted in the back seat, disregarding more than hints from Buss that it might be a good idea to take the first place where they could turn around and go back home. When they arrived, practically on time, she found the audience small, but she was there and she had not failed her public. Another time, again snow was falling. But on this occasion the engagement was not away from home but an *at home* for the faculty. When Professor Florence Foss told this snowbound story she said: "I remember going to one of Miss Woolley's teas for the faculty in a heavy snowstorm. I went over the fields on my *snowshoes*, wearing a large black velvet hat suitable for formal occasions! I carried the regrets of all the other members of Faculty House who could not get through the snow. As I approached the house I saw Miss Woolley's amused face at a window watching my laborious progress, and she herself came to the door to let me in, laughing heartily and saying: 'Why Miss Foss! You came on your snowshoes!' Only a handful of the faculty were able to reach the party that day, but we had a delightful visit with Miss Woolley."

In these early days of her administration there were times when Miss Woolley's sense of humor was audacious as well as irresistible. Call this gift "merriment" or "sauciness", for it was both. Quick as a flash she was in with her witticism and off and, except for the laughter which followed, out of reach before the audience or the individual knew what had happened. No one admired M. Carey Thomas, President of Bryn Mawr, more than did Mary Woolley. But this admiration included awareness of the fact of Miss Thomas's fixed conviction that no other woman's college could offer opportunities equal to those of Bryn Mawr.

Speaking at the twenty-fifth anniversary of Bryn Mawr, Mary Woolley said:

> It is seldom, if ever, true that an institution is the achievement of one person. Some members of this audience know better than the speaker to how many men and women this College owes much, not only in its inception, in the largeness of view and generosity of gifts and of spirit which made it possible, but also in the devoted service of this quarter century. Yet it is not less true that the progress of Bryn Mawr College, its place in the educational world, is, to an unusual degree, the work of the woman whose name has been identified with it from the beginning. One can hardly think of the College without its President, or of its President without a vision of the College. I should like to except one person from this generalization and to tell a story which I have never had the temerity to repeat to Miss Thomas, but to which, on this auspicious occasion, it seems safe to refer. At the time of my own inauguration, several years ago, a note of regret was received from a distinguished professor in Oxford University, who evidently suffered from absentmindedness, and, quite as evidently, had not consulted his invitation before declining it, for the note ran thus—
>
> "Dear Miss Thomas:
>
> "I am so sorry that I cannot be present at your inauguration as President of Mount Holyoke College. And so you are going to leave dear Bryn Mawr? Well, I suppose it is to enter upon a wider field of usefulness!" [2]

No one who has watched college wheels "go round", seeing committee within committee and the endless ramifications of courses all revolving together but not always singing like Milton's angels, and who has been conscious of the sound backing of essential work and essential money down to the least important man or woman and the fraction of a cent's difference figured out in the cost of table napkins—no one can have seen all this daily commonplace of college life, invisible to the casual observer, and for the most part uninteresting to the lookers-on, without acknowledging what a smooth-running machine the corporate college has to become in order to be successful and how symbolically indicative of its economy a college president, its students and faculty are.

In 1901 the College Entrance Examination Board had invited the New England colleges to join. During the ensuing ten years Mount Holyoke took an active part in shaping the policy of the Board, and from 1924-1927 Mary Woolley, president of Mount Holyoke, was its chairman. The New England College Entrance Certificate Board had been organized in 1903 and from its inception Mount Holyoke was connected with this Board.

The Carnegie Foundation honored Mount Holyoke under Mary Woolley by making it its first selection as a beneficiary. With this help fellowships were established to stimulate graduate study on the part of students and members of the faculty. Ten such fellowships and scholarships were granted between 1911 and 1912.

From the beginning of her presidency of the college in 1901, she had set up an Appointment Committee—the logical and essential "follow-up" in the development of graduate scholarships and their resultant need for adequate teaching and/or research appointments. The first dean was appointed in 1907, Florence Purington, together with an assistant registrar and four secretaries. The curriculum advance kept pace with that of the administrative offices, several departments virtually doubling the number of courses given; and a new curriculum together with a change of requirements went into effect in 1907.

In so far as the rapidly increasing demands upon Mary Woolley made it possible, she entered into the lives of the students. Sometimes she did this in her office, sometimes by a chapel talk and not infrequently at a reception. In those early days when nobody else could do anything, the president untangled many a classroom snarl. One day one of these "cases" said to her: "I worked so hard for Mr. ——— in the preparation of a paper for his course in ——— and then he said that I had altogether missed the main point and given him something that had no connection with the main subject,"—all this tattling punctuated by tears.

"Yes, Sadie," said the president, "students often do have their troubles in the classroom. I know that from my own experience. But have you ever stopped to think how *much more often* it is the instructor who has the trouble!"

But Mary Woolley did far more than interpret instructors to some students. She gave students the chance to see that she had entered into their lives and cared about their problems—as she did with the life of a distinguished, sensitive-looking dark-skinned American Negro girl, Frances Williams. Some years after Miss Williams had graduated she went back to Mount Holyoke and found that Mary Woolley had just sent a check for the defense of the Scottsboro boys. For the record Frances Williams added:

> She suggested that I should tell her from time to time about things that were important to which one should give money but I never did, I felt sure she had enough contacts already to exhaust her gift budget. But I loved the thought of her sending the Scottsboro boys a check. There was something so fine about that—these sad, under-privileged lads—that she could see as I did that they and their trial were important. This was good. This was what I knew she would do when long ago I sat in the chapel and heard her say, "Now are we the sons of God and it doth not yet appear . . ." These were not idle words to her—that is why they had power when she spoke them and as I remember them . . . But the [Chapel] services were something far more significant than the mere sharing of knowledge and insight—they were the occasion upon which the student body had an opportunity to become acquainted with a great personality.
>
> To my mind nothing in the educational process is more important than the acquaintance with a great personality. For it is only in the person that you see and experience the value of knowledge, for it is only here that you see knowledge function in terms of a real life situation. Now to become acquainted takes time and here is where the value of the daily chapel services contributed so much . . .

Years afterwards another student said of these talks: "I have only to think of Miss Woolley to feel a strengthening of my backbone." Some of the students "listened" to her voice, rather than to the meaning of what she said—to the timbre of that strong, clear voice, whether she was talking about keeping off the grass—the "down-trodden family" she called it—until it, too, had a chance to bloom with the spring, or was talking about "walking under the stars". For Mary Woolley, it may be that the most important of all the questions she asked and attempted to answer was this: "Has not our whole relationship towards life something to do with our contribution to life?" This, too, she answered by another query:

> What is my contribution to the sum total of happiness? That is a question that no one of us can escape. We are answering it whether we wish to answer or not. As we live, day by day, we are *adding to* or

subtracting from that sum total. May God grant to each one of you the joy of adding to the happiness of the world, save you from the tragedy of subtracting from it!

Of all college events seemingly the most useless to the lives of students is the big freshman reception at the opening of the college year. Felicia Gressitt had left her home and family in far away Japan, travelling many miles and visiting many relatives before reaching college. An aunt and uncle from Baltimore, who drove her up to South Hadley, stayed for the president's reception for freshmen and their parents because they were eager to shake hands with the eminent Dr. Woolley. This, as they learned, meant shuffling along in an endless line which wound from the back door of Student Alumnae Hall toward the front, up the stairs, around the upper hall, and finally into the New York Room. After the better part of an hour they reached the receiving line, to be greeted by Harriet Newhall, who in turn introduced them to the president. As Mary Woolley took Felicia Gressitt's hand, she asked: "How is your mother?"

"Fine, thank you," replied Felicia, flustered by the unexpectedness of the question. "She is in Japan, of course . . ."

Felicia wished to go on to explain that with her were her aunt and uncle, but Mary Woolley continued: "Yes, I knew your mother very well."

The mention of her mother brought tears to Felicia's eyes, but the president's friendliness, and evident clear recollection of her mother, helped to make her feel secure in the strange, new place.

Harvard has defined a college faculty as a group of mutually repellent particles. How did Mary Woolley handle conflict among "mutually repellent particles"? One of these contentions covered in time several unhappy years and arose in part out of the president's eagerness to develop a department to its fullest possibility and yet restrain one member who was capitalizing at the expense of others. To this end she wrote to the person she wished to assume the chairmanship:

> The case is really this—here is a chance to make a very strong department; it is not at present realizing its full possibilities. The duty of the president of the college is to see that it is put in charge of some one who has the power to realize that end; such a change can be made without the slightest unfairness to those now in charge, will be made without sensitiveness on their part, if possible, but must be made. It is not fair to save the feelings of one or two people at the expense of the students, other members of the staff and the college . . . I think that you will see what I mean, that the question must be considered impersonally and "in the large" . . . At the most, it will involve only the administration.

By adroit management and patient work the administration brought about an almost complete change of personnel and quietly solved a problem which might have split the college wide open. However, it took Mary Woolley years of hard, nerve-racking work to achieve this miracle of readjustment which resulted in the new chairman's not only directing her whole energy toward saving the department from the devastating experience of an intradepartmental split but also in her bringing worldwide distinction to the department and to the college.

At other times when differences in faculty opinion threatened serious disagreement, no matter how strongly she herself might agree or disagree, complete freedom of expression was allowed. Ann Morgan, later to become chairman of the Zoology Department, said of the president:

> She gave me freedom in selecting candidates to do the work with which I was concerned . . . She examined the credentials of candidates, discussed them with care and was concerned as to their *character* and *ability*. She was an excellent listener and remembered what she heard. When she felt it necessary she took notes and she did not lose them . . . She expected that those who secured candidates would know the particular professional fields involved . . .

The freedom she gave to members of the faculty might have become Mary Woolley's undoing, yet it remained, almost invariably, a point of strength, appealing especially to some of the brilliant women on the faculty, such as Dr. Laird, Dr. Nellie Neilson, Dr. Bertha Putnam and Dr. Helen Thompson Woolley, and to many of the more independent members such as Dr. Viola Barnes, Dr. Alzada Comstock, Dr. Emilie Martin, Dr. Ada Snell, and Dr. John Warbeke. In an endeavor such as her second founding of Mount Holyoke had become, "the adventuring of a little astronomical observatory", said Dr. Young, "could have been crowded virtually out of existence"—a fact equally possible with other small departments. But under Mary Woolley's administration such crowding-out never happened to the Little-Great-Departments.

*   *   *   *

If Mary Woolley had seemed immature when her father decided she was to go to Wheaton, nevertheless as the pattern of her life began to appear, maturity came early—first as shadows of eager desire for a wider education for women in general, then for equality of rights for them, and finally aspiration that women should share with men in the leadership of policy-making and in work for peace. From the time of her inauguration as president of Mount Holyoke College up to 1919 the mosaic of her life became as definite as the tessellation on a pavement. This pattern of her life was made even more distinct by the abilities and character of the acquaintances and friends with whom she was associated during the earlier years of her administration. Among those women were Jane Addams, Alice Stone Blackwell, Carrie Chapman Catt, Madame Curie, Kathleen Courtney, Winifred Cullis, Mary E. Garrett, Lida Shaw King, Lucia Ames Mead, Ellen Fitz Pendleton, May Wright Sewall, Anna Howard Shaw, Ida Tarbell and M. Carey Thomas. It was one of these friends, Mrs. Sewall, a guest of the college, who wrote in the President's Guest Book on March 5, 1908: "It is by virtue of the expansion of consciousness, not by territorial expansion that the individual may possess the world." During these years, too, other women of distinction came and went at Mount Holyoke, among them President Hazard of Wellesley, Helen Miller Gould, Laura Gill, Katharine Lee Bates, Madame Breshkovsky, Baroness von Suttner and her friend Andrea Höfer Proudfoot. Among the men who came again and yet again to Mount Holyoke and whose experience and friendship were influential in shaping the young president's early executive years were Lyman Abbott, Clarence A. Barbour, Raymond Calkins, Dr. Henry Sloane Coffin, Dr. Faunce, Albert Parker Fitch, Colonel Thomas Wentworth Higginson, President William DeWitt Hyde of Bowdoin, Rufus Jones, David Starr Jordan of Leland Stanford, Bishop Lawrence, Bishop McConnell, William Pierson Merrill, Dr. Stimson of the Mount Holyoke Board of Trustees, Dr. Leighton Stuart, Henry H. Tweedy and others.

The President's House had come into being in the spring of 1909—the gift of the Secretary to the Board of Trustees, Joseph Skinner. Its first guest was Edward L. Moore of Cambridge, Massachusetts. Its first presidential tenant was Mary E. Woolley. To us a more important fact was that its first collie inmate was Lord Wellesley, a gift of Eloise Robinson. His Lordship had arrived in a basket, like a small *bon voyage*. But the size of that puppy's brains was anything but small. Guests alternately marvelled at him and adored him. An English woman, Ethel Arnold, who shared the fame of the Arnold family from Rugby through Oxford University, was relaxing one day in the president's living room with its wide view of the Mount Tom range, by eating some chocolate creams—a treat since chocolate creams were not then available in England. Lord Wellesley—Old Mannie as he was lovingly called—was asleep on the window seat. Whether or not some puppy dream pushed him off the edge, I do not know. Anyhow he fell from the comfortable window seat onto a hardwood floor. Loud were his cries. Miss Arnold rushed to Mannie's assistance, bag of chocolate creams and all, picked him up, put him on his window seat again, gave him a chocolate cream and returned to her chair. As she sat down she saw Mannie lick his chops, roll his eyes at her and fall off the seat again, looking expectantly at her as he struck the floor. The end of this story is that puppy and bag of chocolate creams finished together in Miss Arnold's lap. A few minutes later there were no chocolate creams. This amazing cleverness of Mannie made Miss Woolley keep him with her every possible moment.

One day the president was out walking with Mannie when she met a faculty wife, Mrs. Gale, and her two children.

"It is nice," Mary Woolley said, "to be out with your children on such a day as this, Mrs. Gale." Then the president looked at Mannie walking beside her and continued: "It is nice being out with the dog."

Mrs. Gale replied proudly: "I suppose it is if you haven't any children." Then she paused to look at Mannie: "Is he intelligent?"

A young doctor on the faculty, puzzled by some of Mannie's performances, asked: "How did he get started *not* being a dog?" That's it: how did he? We do not know. For one thing Mannie had the habit, when he wished to come in, of buzzing the front door bell. If no one answered the buzz promptly he would run around to the back door and ring there. The second maid, Anna, thought she knew why Mannie was different—deviltry. Anna was provoked with Mannie too often for the president's peace of mind. Even in those days much ivory hunting had to be done before a good maid could be found. One day the president was jotting down notes at her desk in the living room on the first floor when she heard the front door buzzer ring loudly.

"Oh, dear!" thought Mary Woolley, "it's Mannie and it was only a little while ago Anna let him out!"

She got up quickly and went towards the front door. Hearing Anna on the way from the back hall the president called: "Never mind, Anna, I will let Mannie in!"

Reaching the front door in haste the president jerked it open, saying cheerfully: "Come in, Old Man!"

There she stopped speechless, for it was not Mannie she faced but the handsome and impressive Mount Holyoke trustee Charles Bulkely Hubbell, who was distinctly startled, if not intimidated by this welcome. There was an instant of complete silence, then laughter and an explanation. There was very little that big, sensitive mountain of a man did not understand. He smiled as he replied: "I think I saw Mannie out there by the barberry hedge, peering around the corner at me as I came along. Let's have him in so I can meet him!"

Excitement over the new President's House was greatest among the old ladies—the emeritus group of the faculty. This was before the day of geriatrics. In some cases the pathos of those aged women was heart-breaking—"the desolate hath many more children than she which hath a husband." One year at a New Year's party for these retired ones, Miss A., looking like an old witch, black hair, strange gray eyes, heavy mouth all puckered up, voice suppressed, remarked that she liked to study the different tree branches against the sky—"as different as different kinds of lace work". Miss Bowers wanted to write a story about witchhazel embodying its qualities: "perversity and —" but she could get no further and fairly shook with excitement when she asked Mary Woolley if she knew that she had never been inside the President's House? She was invited for lunch the next day.

On Sundays after the service in the Mount Holyoke chapel came dinner at the President's House. With Mary Woolley in that house and a good preacher who was tired and needed to relax, the dinner table with its surrounding happy dogs was likely to be one of the merriest places in the Connecticut Valley.

One Sunday afternoon president and Mrs. Hadley of Yale were with us at dinner. The older waitress, with vision that was never perfect and excited by the honor of serving such distinguished guests, ticked the back of Mary Woolley's chair with a serving dish. Some of the juice from the peas spilled on the floor, and from the waitress there followed an agonized exclamation: "Oh, Miss Woolley!" Smiling re-assuringly, Mary Woolley started a ball of good stories rolling by describing one of her own nervous moments during her first money-raising campaign. She recalled how her wealthy host and his family were faultlessly correct, including an over-done table service and a footman behind each chair. The main course of the luncheon con-sisted of lamb chops, peas and olives. The young president found her-self increasingly nervous in the midst of all the pompous strain. Seek-ing firm ground, she brought her fork and knife to bear too decisively upon the lamb chop on her plate. The pinioned chop skidded and started a shower of peas and olives. In silent horror at what had happened Mary Woolley *heard* the olives striking against the base board of the dining room. But her hosts, still faultlessly "correct", heard and saw exactly *nothing*! Later one of the footmen moved cor-rectly towards the escaped peas and olives.

Mr. Hadley followed this tale with one about Mrs. Hadley and him-self. Unable to find time to prepare a talk he was to give away from Yale University, he thought he would be less liable to interruptions as he worked on the train if he and Mrs. Hadley travelled in the regular day coach. President Hadley was to sit on the inside of the seat where he could use the window sill for the notes of his speech and Mrs. Hadley on the aisle side to protect him from possible interruptions. When they entered the coach they noticed, gratefully, that in the seat behind them was a quiet, motherly-looking soul dressed in black. As the train moved out of the New Haven station, President Hadley got out his papers and pencils and set to work. Those who knew him will remember that he had a nervous handicap in the occasional jerking motion of his head. More and more deeply absorbed in his notes, Mr. Hadley's motions increased. Suddenly Mrs. Hadley felt herself tapped on the shoulder. Over the back of the seat and looking compassionately towards Mr. Hadley, the motherly woman whispered in Mrs. Hadley's ear: "You poor dear, I have one like that myself at home!"

Another Sunday, Bishop William Lawrence told a story at his own expense. There was little in the robust but homely physique of this eminent churchman to suggest clerical sanctity—to quote Chaucer, "A manly man, to been an abbot able". Called abroad by an unexpected demand, Bishop Lawrence took passage on the first available ship and found himself possessed of an unknown roommate. After sizing up said roommate with some uneasiness, he went down to the Purser's Office to leave his valuables. As he was handing over his money belt and papers to the Purser, he remarked: "Since you can never tell what is going to happen in this life, I think it might be safer to leave my valuables here with you!"

"*Isn't that interesting!*" exclaimed the Purser. "Your roommate has just been in to leave *his* valuables and *he* made the same statement."

There were many famous men and women who left a good memory as well as a good sermon among the recollections of those Sunday dinners at the President's House, among them William Lyon Phelps who in his bread and butter note to Mary Woolley wrote: "Please pat the blind doggie." Certainly with Mary Woolley, as well as with William Lyon Phelps, the Ministry of Education was not without its dogs.

CHAPTER 9

BIRD OF HAPPINESS

"Feminism is not a prejudice; it is a principle."

The earliest and strongest of Mary Woolley's memories came from her father and mother and their belief in women. In those early days her mother had written: "Do you think I love May too much?" Beyond what the daughter knew about herself, her father had perceived something of what her future might be. It was Chaplain Woolley who had taken his daughter out of and away from her dream of a life of pleasure and had placed her first at Wheaton, later giving her into the care of E. Benjamin Andrews at Brown University. Perhaps even before she entered Brown her wish was to work for the betterment of women in order that educated women might create peace in a better world.

Mary Woolley's emphasis on "women as human beings" did not begin with any conviction of hers about the equality of men and women but with an attempt on her part to understand the motivation of men's thinking. Was this in her thought when she confided to Nettie Serena that she wanted to "see how men's minds work?" An indirect answer to what she found was that as early as 1884 she was *not* writing about "our Grandsires"—supposedly the superior sex— not a bit of it! She had been writing about "Our Grandmothers" under the title of "Portraits of Our Grandmothers" and was thinking, seemingly, about women's place and plight as human beings.

It seemed as if Mary Woolley had hardly stepped over into the great career which was to be hers when her mother fell ill. On March 2, 1905—two days before Mrs. Woolley's birthday—her daughter came home for a long weekend. On the following day Mrs. Woolley entered in her diary: "Friday. Ervie was home for the night. May paid Catharine four dollars." On Saturday, Sunday and Monday she set down only the day of the week, for she was not feeling well. On March 28th, Mary Augusta Ferris Woolley died. Her gay, loving, patient life was over. She had been married forty-four years to the man she loved. Among the precious family secrets shared only among themselves there was one put away in the family strong box for Mother

73

Woolley which would not "mature" until December 11, 1911. The tiny envelope containing gold pieces in denominations of two and one half and five dollars had been pinned and repinned with the large heavy pins of those days until there were almost as many pin holes in it as there were square inches. On the face of that envelope all the names of the family had been written and on the back of the envelope had been inscribed:

> "Mother's — 50th Anniversary
> present from the Woolley family
> to be saved for Mamie"

A short time after Mrs. Woolley's death, J. J. Woolley became very ill. When he was strong enough to acknowledge the gift of an old friend, he wrote:

> I have been quite ill, which will account for my not writing sooner and thanking you for the three pairs of delightful and most acceptable socks you sent me. I am living in our former home on Summit Street, and some of the children come every week to see me. My sickness was a severe attack of indigestion which gave me great pain. But I am well now, with less strength, and am about my work, as usual. I think often of you, Sarah, and Ralph. I shall never forget your coming, all of you, to the R.R. station when we went for the last time with Mrs. Woolley to Norwalk. I thank you all, with all my heart.

On June 12, 1905, he entered in his diary: "May & Jeannette Marks came," and on the day following: "May leaves for college. Jeannette Marks leaves for Boston to sail for Europe." As we stood on the lower steps of the Summit Street House, J. J. Woolley loomed above us on the top step, erect and seemingly robust, his face twitching a little, his figure clad in a linen suit, outlined against the dark green shutters of the door. By the curb the cab waited and we had to go. For the first part of a long sea voyage customary in those days, it was restful. Then anxiety began to overtake JM, about *what* she did not know. This anxiety increased to illness. As soon as the ship docked she went to the cable office and sent this message to Mary Woolley: "What is the trouble?" The reply reached London within a few hours: "Papa died July First." While visiting with his daughter at the college, J. J. Woolley became violently ill and was taken to the Holyoke Hospital; his trouble was diagnosed as ruptured appendix. On July 1st they knew that he was dying and so did Chaplain Woolley. Like the brave soldier he was, he began quietly repeating the Twenty-third Psalm: "The Lord is my Shepherd; I shall not want. He maketh me to lie down in green pastures; He leadeth me beside the still waters. . . .

Yea, though I walk through the valley of the shadow of death, I will
fear no evil."

        ❋   ❋   ❋   ❋

One of Robert Owen's first memories was of a room in which he and
his brothers were at a moment when his mother entered that room
and set free a bird with these words: "You must take care of it." That
bird became in the mind and heart of Robert Owen the bird of happiness. True, the words of Mary Woolley's mother and father had not
been literally "You must take care of it," yet they had given over
into their daughter's hands a great conception of the purpose of life.
There were times when the evil of the world seemed insoluble to her
but there was never a time when she was not confident that women,
set free from an age-old bondage—a bondage in which their very privileges were at times oppressive—could scarcely fail to make a better
world than is associated with the phrase "a man's world". This dream
of the development of women as human beings—the thought and the
work of which she "took care" virtually all her life—now became Mary
Woolley's bird of happiness—happiness which integrated and bound
together her life with her work. Added to this great conception of the
purpose of life was the strength of sorrow driving her forward, whatever the discomfort, whatever the distance—in the work she was to do
for education, for peace and for justice to women.

On the night of February 8, 1906, Mary Woolley was in Baltimore
for an evening in honor of Susan B. Anthony. Sitting on the platform
in the center of the speakers was Miss Anthony, hands quiet and relaxed, her white hair smooth and parted, her eyes thoughtful, her
features worn by time, and, although this was the year in which she
was to die, still seemingly ageless in her strength. A few years before,
when someone had asked Miss Anthony whether she prayed, her reply
had been: "I pray every single second of my life; not on my knees but
with my work. My prayer is to lift women to equality with men."
And she had said again and yet again in public: "Equality, civil and
political, should be the demand of every self-respecting woman." She
did not say the "hope" or the "wish" or the "desire" of every self-
especting woman, but the "demand".

That evening Dr. Ira Remsen of Johns Hopkins presided and the
ushers were in academic dress. The speakers seated about Miss
Anthony were Mary E. Woolley, Lucy M. Salmon of Vassar College,
Mary A. Jordan of Smith College, Mary W. Calkins of Wellesley, Eva
Perry Moore, trustee of Vassar and President of the Association of
Collegiate Alumnae, Maud Wood Park, founder of the Equal Suffrage

League of Women's Colleges and President of its Boston Branch, and President M. Carey Thomas of Bryn Mawr. There was also Dr. Anna Howard Shaw, at that time President of the National American Woman Suffrage Association, and Julia Ward Howe. It was on that evening it was decided there should be a national suffrage association of college women.

Young Mary Woolley was the first speaker. For many years she had seemed to be oblivious of the differences between the laws which governed the male and those which governed the female. She had not written or spoken a word about women's legal position under the law. Nor did she on this evening. What she did say was:

> The emphasis upon woman as an individual, *as well as a member of a sex having the power and the rights of a human being*, means that the same reasoning which would hold for the education of her brother applies to her. In other words, if education is desirable for a man to prepare him for his life, it is equally desirable for a woman to prepare her for her life.

By this banner phrase—"the power and the rights of a human being" —Mary Woolley was pointing to the inception of a great movement in history, for she went on to say:

> Some movements in history have been brought about by a stroke of the pen or a sudden uprising of the people, like a great tidal wave, sweeping everything before it; others have come slowly as the result of the cumulative force of years of effort and represent the gradual growth of conviction. The time will come when some of us will look back upon the arguments against the granting of the suffrage to women with as much incredulity as that with which we now read those against their education.

These are different utterances from those of her inaugural speech on May 15, 1901. They reveal Mary Woolley's growth in feminism. And, as she had in her inaugural at Mount Holyoke, she said nothing about "the sacrifice of gracious womanhood [being] too high a price to pay for the vote."

That night, as the meeting was closing, M. Carey Thomas stated with Quaker directness and with eloquence:

> If, then, women need the ballot to protect their labor—and they do need it beyond all question—it seems to me in the highest degree ungenerous for women like the women in this audience who are cared for and protected in every way, not to desire equal suffrage for the sake of other less fortunate women. And it is not only ungenerous but shortsighted of such women not to desire it for their own sakes.

All who were present on that evening in Baltimore sensed that "Aunt Susan" knew that the flame of her life would soon go out—sensed that

they were indeed paying a "last tribute" to this great leader of women.
Dr. Shaw wrote:

> . . . when the final address had been made by Miss Thomas, Miss Anthony
> rose and in a few words expressed her feeling that her life-work was
> done, and her consciousness of the near approach of the end. After that
> night she was unable to appear, and was indeed so ill that she was con-
> fined to her bed in Miss Garrett's most hospitable home. Nothing could
> have been more thoughtful or more beautiful than the care Miss Garrett
> and Miss Thomas bestowed on her. They engaged for her one of the
> best physicians in Baltimore, who, in turn, consulted with the leading
> specialists of Johns Hopkins, and they also secured a trained nurse. This
> final attention required special tact, for Miss Anthony's fear of "giving"
> trouble" was so great that she was not willing to have a nurse. The
> nurse, therefore, wore a housemaid's uniform, and "Aunt Susan" remained
> wholly unconscious that she was being cared for by one of the best
> nurses in the famous hospital.[1]

About a year later, on April 16, 1907, there were headlines in the
news sheets of New York about Mary Woolley and the Peace Congress
of Women being held at Carnegie Hall at which women denounced
the war glorification then in evidence at the Jamestown Exposition,
and at Norfolk, Virginia. Of the Carnegie Hall meeting the *Evening
Mail* said:

> It was Mary E. Woolley, president of the Mount Holyoke college, who
> created the excitement . . . Miss Woolley . . . announced that the "new
> woman" had come to stay. Here is what she had to say about James-
> town: "If we would substitute arbitration for brute force, peace for war,
> an ideal of world unity for national and racial antagonisms, the reasonable
> hope of permanent accomplishment of those ends lies in the education
> of the children and the youth of today, the men and women of tomorrow.
> 'Imitation enters into the very fastnesses of character,' and the ideals held
> before the child determine to a great extent what the man will be." . . .
> From Warships Miss Woolley switched to the "new woman", whom she
> declared to be different from the women of other ages, saying: "The
> achievement, the distinction of the representative womanhood of today,
> is that it unites the intellectual and the emotional for some larger social
> end than the world has ever known before. Her opportunity extends from
> neighborhood nursing to world organization in the cause of peace."

Here is found, six years after she became President of Mount Holyoke
College and thirty-eight years before the founding of the United
Nations, the three-word directive for her work of a lifetime—education,
women, peace. It was her conviction, as she said, that women, because they *are* women, "have a peculiar contribution to add to the
contribution of men, including especially the problem of international
understanding, of the substitution of reason for armed force." Finally,
in one of those brief unforgettable statements of Mary Woolley's

about war, she said: "No amount of sophistry can define love and hate as synonyms."

On October 6, 1914, five years after the publication of *Homo Sum*, Mary Woolley spoke at the centenary exercises of the Emma Willard School, and she and all American women were still without the right to the ballot:

> A hundred years ago, to many of my audience, must seem like the Dark Ages. And it was, as far as the education of women was concerned. It was not far removed from the days when the little girls of Hatfield, Massachusetts, sat on the doorstep of the schoolhouse to gather what crumbs they might from the feast of reason spread for their little brothers inside the aforesaid house; when the town fathers of Northampton, now the home of Smith College, the largest woman's college in the world, voted, first "not to be of any expense for schooling girls," and then, with a softening of heart, four years later, opened the doors to them from May first to October thirty-first, when there would not be enough boys to fill them.

She was eager that women should have this right and eager to set the feet of women on the upward path of leadership. Although she had not yet become fully conscious of the brutal legal discriminations still in force against women, she knew that laughter as a tool is irreplaceable and from a large and hilarious repertory of stories used that tool frequently. Speaking to Sorosis, she recounted the following:

> Recently I saw reference to regulations in the Boston Athenaeum, a little earlier in the century than the birth of Sorosis — which excluded "females"—we were females in those days—from the library part of the building, on the ground that "a decent female would shrink from the narrow galleries and steep stairways," and that her presence "might embarrass modest men."

In those days two American girls, Alice Paul, a Quaker, and Lucy Burns, a Catholic, were sharing with English women all the hardships, insults, assaults and prison terms of the British Militant campaign. The hub of the British Militant struggle for equality was in London. In the United States the hub of the struggle centered around the Susan B. Anthony Amendment in Washington. At that time the American movement for equality was in the hands of such women as Maud Wood Park, Alice Paul and Carrie Chapman Catt and their organization The National American Woman Suffrage Association. From this movement later came the National Women's Party; and it was a great day when equality for women was championed by the Business and Professional Women's Clubs.

Mary Woolley had never been present at a street scene or suffrage parade nor had she ever seen the prison vans swoop down upon suffrage

pickets whose only offense was that they were standing quietly outside
the White House holding up their pennants on which were inscribed
such slogans as the following:

LINCOLN STOOD FOR WOMAN SUFFRAGE 60 YEARS AGO

PERFECT EQUALITY OF RIGHTS CIVIL AND POLITICAL IS AND MUST

CONTINUE TO BE THE DEMAND OF EVERY SELF-RESPECTING WOMAN

DEMOCRACY SHOULD BEGIN AT HOME

Had she seen even one of the brutal events which women had had
to endure in their militancy and had she known the inside of even one
prison, had she heard Inez Milholland, as she fell dying, cry out: "Mr.
President, how long will women have to wait for freedom?", would she
have thought their "sacrifice of gracious womanhood [was] too high a
price to pay for" the vote? She was much more at home with the
National American Woman Suffrage Association and women like Alice
Stone Blackwell, Anna Howard Shaw, Maud Wood Park, Carrie Chapman Catt than with any type of militant. As did others, she resented
Alice Paul's handling of some of the suffrage work. Even among pro-
nounced suffragists there was wide difference of opinion concerning
militancy. The Equal Suffrage League of Women's Colleges, for which
Mary Woolley had spoken in 1906 in Baltimore, had never advocated
militancy. The National American Woman Suffrage Association was
opposed to militancy but for the National Woman's Party militancy
had proved to be a useful tool and it was used frequently until women
won the right to vote on March 22, 1920.

Time and again in these earlier years of her administration of Mount
Holyoke College, as well as in later years, Mary Woolley wrote and
spoke on women, on feminism, on evolution in the feminine world, on
world understanding from the point of view of women and on women's
part in the settlement of international problems. Gradually, beginning
with the year 1911, Mary Woolley's conscious work for the advancement of women was to crystallize into a life-long use of Jane Harrison's
phrase "women as human beings". To this phrase Mary Woolley
added a precept of her own: "Feminism is not a prejudice; it is a
principle."

In 1906, she had said at Baltimore: "The emphasis upon woman as
an individual, as well as a member of a sex having the power and the
rights of a human being, means that the same reasoning which would
hold for the education of her brother applies to her." Five years later
she wrote: "Civilization has been hard upon woman . . . [The] new

privileged class [represents] a privilege based not upon birth, but on education and opportunity . . . The ideal of womanhood . . . is rather that of a woman who is, first of all, a human being."

And in 1919, when she was fifty-six years old, Mary Woolley made this statement on the status of women: "The higher education of women is a feministic movement, the natural expression of a fundamental principle, that is, that women being first of all human beings, even before they are *feminine*, have a share in the inalienable right of human beings to self-development."

Even after she had ceased to be able to write, these sayings were often on her lips as she continued to use them to the close of her life —abiding expressions of her hope for the liberation of the moral capacities and powers of women.

CHAPTER 10

CENTER OF THE WORLD: LETTERS HOME

*"Truly China is in the centre of the world and bound up with
her destiny is the destiny of the world. That her educated
women will play a significant part in the shaping of that destiny, no one who knows the China of today can doubt."*

On August 13, 1921, Mary Woolley reached the station from the
Blackstone Hotel in Chicago only to find the sleepers already jammed
with human beings and with luggage.

Turning back from the train steps to say goodbye, she laughingly
exclaimed: "Oh Miss Cratty! I suppose you, too, are going somewhere?"

They both laughed, for they were old friends and Miss Cratty was
being sent to China and Japan by the National Board of the Y.W.C.A.,
whose General Secretary she was.

In 1915 the China Christian Educational Commission had taken the
position that there should be "a careful study of the higher institutions
of learning [in China] by a commission of experts," expressing the wish
that Dr. Burton would be chairman of the body.[1] The first world war
over at last, Dr. Burton (later to become president of the University
of Chicago) agreed to serve as chairman in 1920. With Dr. and Mrs.
Burton was their daughter Margaret, who was serving without salary
as secretary to the Commission.

Together Mary Woolley and Miss Cratty boarded the train and
were soon out in the observation car, side by side.

"I am anticipating a chance to relax," said Miss Cratty as she sat
down.

"I am looking forward to the same chance," agreed Mary Woolley,
smiling.

"Mr. Burton's secretary is on board," explained Miss Cratty, "ready
to help us if we need help."

On the first day out from Chicago, Mary Woolley wrote home: "I
have just filled out a blank for the Canadian Immigration officials,

which states, among other facts, that I am physically and mentally 'all there'. What would you have said? . . ."

After they left St. Paul, Mary Woolley was to have a small compartment to herself. The first morning out, however, she had risen early in order to be alone in the dressing-room. She wrote home:

> I arose early this morning for there is a little two-by-four dressing-room in a car filled with women, most of them going to China: I am glad that I change to a compartment car at St. Paul for I do like room in which to wash, as you know and after all Lake Champlain, a sleeper dressing-room affords somewhat close quarters.
>
> Early as I was, I found another member of the feminine persuasion inspired by the same bright idea and she told me that a third had already departed. A little "Chinese lady" who has been a year at the Y.W.C.A. training school and is going back to her work as Y.W.C.A. Secretary in Shanghai, soon appeared, as she too did "not like a crowd"! She hooked my guimpe and observed that she did "not like American clothes, too many hooks and buttons." She added—"I have an Japanese kimono. I don't like it—makes people think I am Japanese!"

Two days out from Chicago, she reported:

> There is a cosmopolitan company in the observation car, Chinese students going home, missionaries and Christian Association workers, Mr. Monroe, whom I know, and his daughter, the former appointed by the Chinese government to examine their schools, people from Washington going home after a trip to the East, tourists both "Americans" and Canadians going from place to place in the Rockies . . .

Upon arriving in Vancouver, she wrote:

> We were in at eight this morning, just on time. It is pouring and as we do not sail until afternoon tomorrow, I have left the two or three little errands that have accumulated, such as oranges and soap (not to be taken together) until tomorrow morning. . . . Miss Cratty and Miss Burton have gone "shopping"—I will finish repacking and follow suit. It has been such a comfort to have a day here, in fact, almost two, for we do not sail until late this afternoon. . . .
>
> My passport has not yet arrived! There are still two mails and—
>
> Later—I had written so far when I was interrupted and now my passport *has* come.

And so the question of her being "physically and mentally" all there was settled and Mary Woolley was allowed to proceed to China.

Never undignified but, like her father, sometimes absurd in her tenderness of heart, the last letter written on board ship, or call it the first letter posted in Japan, could have been said to have been the letter she sent the dogs(!). Here it is:

> My darling doggies—Thank you for that beautiful present. I am going to buy something in Japan or China with it and will show it to you when I come home.

I have not seen any Doggies as handsome or dear as you are. Here is a hug for each one of you . . .

For Mary Woolley, never a good sailor, this was a surprisingly fortunate voyage, free as she was for once from *mal de mer*. It was, too, a happy voyage in the midst of men and women who shared a high regard for one another. Among her letters were the following:

> The Pacific
> 8.19.1921
> When I look at my watch about nine o'clock just after breakfast and realize that you are probably at dinner, between twelve-thirty and one, it makes me feel far away. But in other respects I do not feel far and I hope that that feeling will continue. I have a suspicion that Japan and China will not seem so distant after this journey.
> We reached Victoria about half after ten last night and I stayed on deck until after that. I am out again this morning soon after breakfast and am not exactly warm in my blue winter coat . . . My room-mate is a Mrs. Robertson, a Canadian, who is going to Tokio to do Christian Association work as a dietitian opening a cafeteria, etc. She worked in Serbia and Czecho-Slovakia during the war and says she knew well some Yovanovitch family in Belgrade, tell Marya.
> I suspect that she is rather homesick, poor girl, and she tells me that she is not a good sailor. . . . Wednesday afternoon Mrs. Rockefeller gave a tea at the "Vancouver" for members of their party and ours and a few others, so there is no lack of "speaking acquaintances" on board.

> Saturday, the 20th
> I spent an hour or two last night watching the informal dancing, in fact, was actually asked to renew my youth by Theodore Green of Providence, who was in the High School with me! He and Mr. Rockefeller did their duty by the rows of feminines waiting to be asked to dance!

> Sunday morning—21st
> I have had an unique experience this morning—left my roommate on the couch when I went to breakfast! . . . I just heard a steward speak to a stewardess about three people sick in one stateroom — "Ought to be ashamed of themselves"—she sputtered—"Will come soon." But she is still sitting outside of the Lounge, while two passengers stand and talk with her. There is the greatest difference between the English stewardesses, as far as I have seen them, and the Chinese stewards.

The China to which Mary Woolley went and in which she was to work unceasingly for six months on the educational problems of Chinese women was, to quote Wellington Sun, "enjoying . . . practically a millennium." True, there were civil wars among the war lords, but as a rule these did not disturb "the way of life for a majority of people." Middle class income groups had independent means or steady jobs, there was no inflation and social unrest was negligible. However, in this comparative prosperity there was vast illiteracy. Of the China she studied Mary Woolley set down in her note books: "No near hope of Central & Stable gov't; Old ways for 4000 years, sudden change upsets everything. China like big loaf of bread, outside burns, inside undone." Regarding the educational system she jotted down: "Ed. at present time, top-heavy. Upper suffers because lower not well done." But Mary Woolley loved this China; she felt and was at home even to the extent of having a Chinese calling card.

Her note books record that Mary Woolley asked herself many questions as she worked. "How build up on old basis without destroying it, the Xtian Ethic?" Or she jotted down records of her meetings with Bishop Welch at the Chosen Hotel and descriptions of the beauty of Korean mountains. She made entries such as this: "Motor drive with Mr. Brockman. Wonderful view of Seoul among the mts. Reminder of Canadian Rockies—Less grand—Tea with Prince & Princess Pak." And she recorded the fact that Japanese police were standing guard by the window at the entrance when the visitors entered the Palace. She was surprised to find that only one year after American women had won the right to vote in the United States, Chinese women were already far advanced in their demands for equality with men. In speaking of their organizations she went out of her way to reproduce the exact facts of what Chinese women *were* doing. Of this there are many pointed illustrations, among them this:

> The Woman's Rights League calls for these things:
> 1. All educational institutions shall be open to women.
> 2. Women shall have the same constitutional rights as men.
> 3. The relation between man and wife, parents and children, rights of inheritance, property and conduct laws shall be based upon the principle of equality.
> 4. Marriage laws based upon equality between men and women shall be enacted.
> 5. For the protection of girls the "age of consent" shall be incorporated in the criminal law, and a law shall be enacted whereby the taking of concubines shall be considered as bigamy.
> 6. Licensed prostitution, the slave trade, and foot-binding shall be prohibited.
> 7. Protective labor legislation based upon the principle of "equal pay for equal work" and "protection of motherhood" shall be enacted.

Again and again throughout her five note books these three words are set down: "Ask Dr. Stuart"—meaning "Ambassador Stuart", then president of Peking University. Sometimes she set down what he had said while chairing a meeting—for example: "Value is adaptation to a purpose." Two or three pages further along in her notes she wrote: "What is the purpose of these schools & how are they adapted to this purpose?" Sometimes against some notes she would write: "Mrs. Thurston"; and once she set down the query: "Education is the question one of women even more than men." And frequently: "Miss Law". At that time Yau Tsit Law and Mrs. Thurston, both Mount Holyoke alumnae, were eminent women in China.

On September 25, 1921, twelve days after the mission reached China, Mary Woolley made a notable address at a vesper service in Peking University, where she had been in conference with Dr. Stuart, and closed with these words: "Humanity strikes its roots down into the same Mother Earth. We must satisfy the same great human needs, grapple with the same great human problems. . . .Never did the world need as it needs today what education *may* give. What, alas, it does not always give. . . . 'None liveth to himself' should be written on the heart of every student."

After Mary Woolley had spent six months in the hardest sort of work studying Chinese education and women, she cited an article written by a Chinese student in the *Weekly Review*:

> My opportunities for education have been rather limited, but my desire to prosecute further studies is above the boiling point. And I found many a girl whose desire to prosecute further studies was above the boiling point.

Then Mary Woolley added:

> Even more encouraging is the character of the Chinese woman herself, her deep earnestness, mitigated by a keen sense of humor, which prevents her from taking herself too seriously, and her capacity for hard work. Again and again we were told by the teachers in the girls' schools that they had to drive the girls away from their books to take needed recreation and amusement, a necessity, may I add, under which we do not always labor in the Connecticut Valley.

While she was hard at work in China one of the privileged earnest students she met was Mayling Soong (Madame Chiang Kai-shek) of whom and her sister, Mrs. Sun Yat Sen, Mary Woolley wrote:

> Again, in the social and industrial life of China, the need of the trained Chinese woman is felt. One day in Shanghai Miss Burton and I went with a sister of Mrs. Sun Yat Sen, both of them Wellesley graduates, down to the Yangtze settlement, and I was much interested in the questions of that young Chinese woman. Miss Soong, serving on the Committee on Social Questions, which reported at the Shanghai Christian Conference last May, was alive to the implications of the changed industrial and social conditions in China today and the necessity of a new attitude on the part of the leaders among the Chinese women as well as among the Chinese men. The need of women trained in social questions is a very real one in the China of today and tomorrow!

All the while Mary Woolley was fearlessly asking herself and other women what still remains one of the most important questions in our world today: "What can we hope for from the educated woman? . . . I am one of the group of hopeful optimists who believe that we can hope for a great deal. And for no less, in proportion to their numbers, from the women of China."

In Shanghai, aside from her immediate and heavy work as the Commission brought together its report, for Mary Woolley there were two outstanding events: one the giving of an address, the other the reading of a book. Of her Armistice Day in Shanghai she wrote:

> More like an Armistice Day was the union Thanksgiving service in Shanghai, the church filled with Americans, among them rows of "boys" in khaki, very quiet and reverent on that day around which clustered so many associations. The crowning feature of the afternoon was the singing of "America the Beautiful". Can you imagine the significance of those words in that city on the other side of the world:
> "America! America!
> God shed His grace on thee,
> And crown thy good with brotherhood,
> From sea to shining sea"

Two years later Mary Woolley wrote:

> Last Armistice Day was celebrated in a great audience of teachers and school children. Again we sang "America the Beautiful" and again I thought what joy it must bring to Miss Bates to think of the inspiration of her words, far across the Pacific, far across our own great continent.

For Mary Woolley the second event in Shanghai was the reading of a book. On November 28, 1921, she wrote home:

> . . . a rainy day followed by a rainy evening . . . When I reached home at tea time I was aweary—so had a nice nap before dinner. At quarter before eight I was in my room in a kimono, before my grate fire, a-reading Kidd's "Science of Power".

Of this room in Shanghai where she was sitting by her grate fire on that night, she had written:

> A Miss Brown, a Washington woman, and her cousin are here for two years investigating some Christian Association possibilities and have taken a large, old fashioned house down in the city. Having a "spare" room, they offered to take me in, fortunately for me—for abiding places are as difficult to find in Shanghai as the traditional needle in a hay-stack. The rooms are big, attractively—and not too much—furnished with Chinese rugs and brasses etc, and I suspect I shall be both comfortable and independent. The only way of heating is by open grates, about as big as the English ones . . .

As she read on in Kidd's *Science of Power* she came upon facts and ideas which had haunted her even as a child:

For in the darkest recesses of their hearts . . . "women live altogether more in the race than in the individual" . . . It is this kind of capacity which enables even delicate women to maintain constancy to an ideal for a prolonged period in the face of the greatest difficulties and persecutions. Women in such circumstances have the same capacity for devotion to causes as they have in other circumstances to persons even through a long succession of mental and bodily tortures. J. S. Mill described the type of mind from which this quality proceeds either in man or woman as always closely associated with the power of leadership of mankind . . . It is one of the most pregnant facts in the upward progress of the race that the emotion of the ideal in its relation to Power has *always* had its chief and deepest expressions in the mind of woman . . .

In these letters she sent home from Japan, Korea and China Mary Woolley tells the story of the expedition with all her characteristic wit, loving-kindness, and records of hard work. Included are some of the shopping expeditions which she and Margaret Burton shared together, the three silver teapots she, Miss Burton and Miss Cratty received from Prince and Princess Pak and other gala affairs, together with anecdotes about her rickshaw boys, including the classic downfall of one rickshaw boy who fell upon Mary Woolley herself! And despite the fact that her engagements were legion—engagements beyond the scope of this biography—she did not forget that back home there was a little girl who was getting together a collection of dolls, for Mary Woolley sent a Chinese doll home to that child. From Tokyo Mary Woolley wrote:

Imperial Hotel, Tokyo
8.29.1921

. . . From the time we landed this morning, there has been such a combination of the usual and the unusual—I climbed into a jinrikisha, and dashed madly through the streets dodging bicycles and automobiles whose chauffeurs looked as if they might have just arrived from Boston to the station where we took an interurban trolley for Tokio. Then another jinrikisha whose "boy" looked rather fagged when he dropped me at the Imperial Hotel. He did not know that he should have given thanks that I had just had a week of living on orange juice!

Wednesday morning

I had written so far when I had to stop for a "conference" which lasted all the morning followed by a brief one, after lunch. Then we packed again, Miss Cratty, Miss Burton and I, and came to Dr. Nitobe's house, where we expect to stay until we leave for Kyoto Sunday night . . . You would love it here in my room with its soft deep cream walls and deeper woodwork, the lattice on the side near the hall and over the door, the sliding doors leading to clothes press and bath, covered with a gold grass paper, with blue and gold leaves scattered over it, its matting with an occasional soft pink flower. The minute I came into the room I said— "This is just the kind of a room Jeannette would like."

Dr. Nitobe is one of Japan's representatives to the League of Nations, in fact, Secretary to Sir Eric Drummond and while he and his wife are in Geneva, they have let the Secretaries of the Y.W.C.A. here, live in their house at a nominal rent . . . I can see nothing but trees all about my room, although I hear voices from other houses.

Thursday 9.1.1921

I hope that today will not be quite so crowded as yesterday. When I reached the house from Miss Tsuda's school, I found Mrs. Ebina, wife of the President of Doshisha, here and when she went we started at once for "Gyu-nabe". Do you know what Gyu-nabe is, Dear? I did not until this week. It is really meat (Gyu) cooked in a little pan (Nabe) over a fire—charcoal in this case. We went to a Japanese restaurant where we had a little room opening onto a garden with rocks, and ferns and fountains and real storks, going to sleep with their heads reposing on the back of their necks, three low tables, and cushions on which we sat a la Japanese, while two members of our party of seven cooked the meat and bamboo sprouts and onions, etc., over the charcoal eaten (not the charcoal) in tiny bowls with rice, supplemented by small cups of lemon colored tea, sans cream or sugar. It is surprising how good it was, and how *full* one felt after two bowls of rice and this "stew" . . .

Tokyo, 9.2.1921

It is very hot in Tokyo and very damp—so damp that the mistiest mornings on Lake Champlain and in the Connecticut Valley rolled together would stand no chance by comparison. As I look from my window— again before breakfast, everything is heavy with moisture. There is little grass in the garden but soft green moss everywhere, on the stones and under the trees.

Yesterday afternoon was a "day off". Most of the party adjourned to Yokohama to shop—one can get more characteristically Japanese things there—but I went motoring with Shigeyo, first to see the more imposing parts of Tokyo, the broad avenues around the Imperial Palace section, the "Ginza", the Fifth Avenue, and along one of the moats, where it is parklike and spacious. One of the Imperial Palaces is modelled after Versailles, as Shigeyo said: "Wherever it is very cool in summer or warm in winter or particularly beautiful that spot the Emperor chooses for a palace or a park." When I inquired how the people liked it, she said, "They used to think it all right. Now discontent is beginning to be with them." Even Shigeyo slips up a bit, not like the tailor down town who advertised "Tailor of the resistant wet coat", or the one who states alluringly "upstairs ladies has fits". Another merchant cheerfully says "Come in, all customers promptly executed." . . .

It has been an awfully hot day and also a very interesting one. First we visited Waseta University, founded in 1862 by Count Okuma as a protest against the rigidity of the state institutions, with "Liberty of thought and freedom of expression" as its slogan. Then we had an hour and a half with Count Okuma himself in a beautiful big room opening by sliding doors onto a lovely garden. The covering of the walls was shaded gold, deep at the bottom, lighter at the top, and a corner of the corridor had purple and white Fleur de Lys on it. First bouquets were given to the ladies, then tea and little cakes were served. As the Count does not speak English the conversation through an interpreter was leisurely and gave abundance of time for studying the interior of the room and the exterior of this astute gentleman.

This noon a luncheon was given here for us, at which the guests were progressive Japanese women, heads of schools, the editor of the leading woman's magazine and so forth. All but one spoke English well and from their points of view regarding social, educational and international questions, were as like a similar group in America as peas from the same pod! We were one even on the League of Nations and the folly of Militarism! An exclusion act when one comes into contact with such people seems insanity and seeing their pride and real dignity of bearing makes one realize how delicately that question should be handled, not entrusted to cheap politicians.

Kyoto, Sept. 5. 1921

We arrived in Kyoto this morning, after a night on a queer little Japanese sleeping car and have had a third full and interesting day. We go on to Kobe in the morning, where it is said that there is very little that is interesting except the Woman's College so I am hoping for a little time to myself . . .

The Oriental Hotel
The Bund. Kobe
Kobe, 9.6.1921

. . . The enclosed "Schedule" which was handed to us on our arrival in Kobe this morning, is an indication of the kind of days we are spending. We take a night train reaching Miyajima tomorrow morning, having a day there for sight-seeing and going on to Shiminoseki in the evening where we take a night boat for Pusan, Korea, then an all day train Thursday to Seoul, where we spend twenty-four hours! We "struck" yesterday morning in Kyoto, so after seeing one of the largest and most beautiful Buddhist Temples, we all went "home" and after a cup of tea and an hour on my back, I revived sufficiently for the Luncheon given us at Doshisha.

Well, to go back and take up the thread of my narrative, Saturday was the day the Crown Prince arrived after his months tour, and we started early for one of the down town hotels where places had been reserved for us to see the "Clown Prince" as the Japanese say it and his procession, but alas! the trains were packed and jammed to the suffocation point, also delayed so that we reached the station plaza in time to hear the "Bansais" and see the crowds but not see over them.

The Miyajima Hotel, Ltd.
Miyajima, Japan
Sept. 7, 1921

We reached Miyajima this morning, leave this afternoon. It is beautifully located on Japan Inland Sea . . . with mountains around the sea, making me think of Lake Champlain. I was homesick when I stepped onto the motor-boat, somewhat larger than the Fleur de Lys, to be brought to the hotel, in fact, I am not infrequently homesick . . .

To return to Saturday—we lunched with the Fosdicks and then at quarter before five, went to the Imperial Theatre for a very interesting evening.

Between the first and second plays we went to the theatre restaurant in the same big, beautiful building—and while dining, watched from the balcony some of the many "processions of lanterns" in honor of the Prince. We stayed through three of the plays and then at half-after ten went home, through the brilliant, crowded streets, with processions of lanterns everywhere.

Sunday night we took a train for Kyoto, and had from Monday morning until Tuesday morning in that most fascinating city. Monday afternoon we visited temples, gardens, a modern exposition, pottery, cloisonne and antique shops, the last three sufficient to tempt the last penny out of one's pockets! Then hurriedly back to Doshisha for Gyu-nabe and at a later hour, bed. So much I shall have to tell you at home. I cannot put it all on to paper, even if I had the time. I seize every possible moment for writing, but some days—like the last four—have no moments to seize.

> The Chosen Hotel
> Keijo (Seoul), Chosen
> 9.8.1921

. . . Miyajima used to be a sacred island and the temple is conspicuous there. All along the shore are temple lights of stone, there is a long street, lined with quaint little shops—and some charming walks, in addition to its beautiful setting on the Inland Sea surrounded by mountains.

Tomorrow promises to be a busy day—automobile ride at nine, schools to be visited, a tea which Bishop Welch gives in the afternoon and leaving for Mukden on the night train. . . .

> Keijo, 9.9.1921

. . . Today has been interesting. Again there are such contrasts. This is a very good hotel and as I look from my window, it is onto a brilliant electric lighted city, yet as we motored through the side streets, we passed between low thatched huts, with mud floors, one or two rooms and almost no furniture. The scale of life among the "people" being much lower than in Japan. Then again the faces of the girls in the girls school where I spoke this morning were sweet and intelligent, pathetic in their earnestness and their quaint costumes of white linen, with long full skirts, were immaculate. Most of the men appear to have been recently laundered. They wear the most absurd costumes, of white linen, trousers sticking out in the back bustle-like, short jackets and over all, a coat down to their heels like the old-fashioned duster. But their hats are, in truth, a crowning feature, like abbreviated stove-pipes, of black gauze, tied under the chin, giving them the appearance of horses, with tiny hats on their heads, in the fly season!

> Saturday—10th

We have been this morning with two Japanese, a man & a woman, to see a government high school for Korean girls and one for Japanese. We also visited two Kindergartens. The little Koreans are too quaint for words, with their little tight linen waists of white or yellow and long full skirts of the brightest colors imaginable, pink, red, green, purple, blue.

Tonight we—Miss Cratty, Miss Burton and I—dine with Jessie Willis Brockman, 1908 . . . They are coming early for us, in order to see some Korean homes of the better sort. It will be a comfort to know that not all live in the poor little thatched huts that we pass in the side roads.

A little dog, lying on his mistress's desk in one of the school-rooms, attached himself to us and was quite inconsolable when taken back. How I would hug my Doggies, if I had a chance! I dreamt last night that I was at home and then awoke to look out on the hills of Seoul! . . . We had tea with a Korean prince and princess, watched by Japanese police ensconced in a room at the entrance as we entered and left . . . Well, almost one sixth of the time away has gone.

Grand Hotel des Wagons-Lits. Ltd.
Peking
9.13.1921

It seems very strange to realize that I am actually in Peking. We arrived this evening, so I have not, as yet, formed many impressions, except that it seems good to look forward to bath and bed after two nights on the train.

Yesterday we spent at Mukden, strange city and strange history. China is not as clear as Japan. When the coolies crowded into the train for our luggage, it—the odor—nearly knocked me over! As we drove in our droshky —(have I spelled that right?) through more narrow streets, big black pigs, sometimes several of them, lay in the doorways or just outside sleeping as comfortably as the dogs. On our way to a Scotch-Presbyterian hospital which we visited, Mrs. Burton and I had a narrow escape from being landed not in a mud puddle, but in a mud *lake*! Inside the mission compound, the houses are cool and comfortable, as they should be. Surely these missionaries have sights and sounds and *smells* enough outside to deserve comfort and something attractive when they reach their homes.

9.14.1921

I am just back from a garden party given at the Summer Palace by the Chamber of Commerce & the Bankers' Association of Peking, a part of the ceremonies in connection with the Dedication of the Medical College. We motored from the college, a long procession of automobiles with police every few yards to show the way and keep the road clear, through wide streets, in many cases lined with trees, quite unlike anything I have seen on this side of the ocean. The palace, a favorite resort of the Dowager Empress, is situated on the side of a mountain, with an artificial lake at least a mile long on the grounds. We climbed many steps to her temple above the palace rooms and had one of the loveliest views I have ever seen, of the great plain of North China around Peking. The whole thing, the setting of the palace, the colonnades, the different state rooms with their Chinese paintings and wonderful carvings, made a picture I shall never forget. People who have lived for years in Peking, told me that they went into some rooms for the first time today, that generally all that they could do was to peep in through dusty windows. There were no dusty windows today. The summer palace had sure had a housecleaning . . .

You will be interested to know that the *third* cake of Dot chocolate served as dessert for seventeen hungry members of our party on the train yesterday. Little Jimmy Russell, aged five, said: "When you come to China again, please bring your trunk *full* of that chocolate."

9.15.1921

A long conference this morning, so that I felt like a mummy at noon. But I took a bit of a nap and by three o'clock was ready to be escorted by Helen Russell, of 1906, to the reception at the Medical College buildings. Such wonderful buildings as they are, grey stone with the decoration in Chinese style, green roof, and blue painting of eaves and pillars. Inside, the most perfect fitting and equipment of college and hospital and nurses home. It does one's heart good to see the most perfect thing of its kind brought right here to China. Aside from the physical good which it will do, is the great help to inter-national friendship . . .

But the thing that you would have enjoyed was a picnic supper at the Temple Heaven. We escaped from the tea and took rickshaws — Miss Cratty, Miss Burton and I, with a group of Association Secretaries and after a half hour of "rickshawing", reached the Temple . . . What would I not have given to put you down there tonight, to see the Temple with its wonderful roofs of blue in the sunset, and then the uncovered altar of marble in the moonlight. That was built before America was discovered! It takes away—or at least reduces a tendency to spreadeagleism. I think we all felt that we had been in a place of worship, as well as of beauty.

Friday afternoon

I am on the program committee and what we must put in before the thirteenth of September is staggering. It is like a three ring circus, doubled. Commission Conferences; interviews with educators; visiting institutions; "seeing Peking"; accepting social invitations, and, I hope, shopping. At "Tiffin" today Margaret Burton expressed my sentiments when she said to her father: "I am so tired, I don't care whether China is educated or not!"

Sunday A.M. 9.18.1921

. . . It is a clear fresh morning cooler and more invigorating. Yesterday afternoon was spent at the Presidential Garden Party with a lot of walking and standing. The President is a pathetic figure when one realizes how shaky the pinnacle which he occupies. Everyone says that the fall of this government is inevitable. The various military governors of provinces are lining their pockets, the central government has absolutely no money, fighting is going on all the time in certain parts of China, bandits are as numerous as mosquitoes . . . and yet everything moves on as calmly, orchestras play, rickshaws careen madly about the streets, teas, dances, receptions and dinners are in full swing, discussion as to amber & amethyst beads alternate with politics—and there you are! A funny old world. Yesterday afternoon while "The party" was waiting for the President to receive Mr. Rockefeller, it was inferred—from the length of the "wait", that the former was trying to borrow a few millions . . . Write as you did —about all the little things at home. There is no place like it.

Hug my dear doggies. Chinese doggies can't *compare*.

9.19.1921

Today has been beautiful almost cold, quite making me forget the heat through which we have passed. This afternoon was the formal dedication of the Medical College buildings, and the academic procession passing from one court to another with the gray buildings and their green tile roofs as a background, was a brilliant sight. The exercises were very impressive, the Chinese minister of foreign affairs and the Director of a Chinese hospital spoke perfect English and made good addresses. Mr. Rockefeller also spoke exceedingly well.

The procession was very interesting to all the Chinese attendants in the hospital, who crowded the windows—and to the rickshaw boys!

This morning an American brought from Seoul a big box containing three silver teapots, gifts to Miss Cratty, Miss Burton and me, from the Prince and Princess Pak. I felt quite like Mr. Wilson!

Peking, 9.28.1921

Did I tell you that I have been "adopted" by a rickshaw coolie? Every time I appear in the hotel door, he starts up from somewhere.

10.1.1921

The evolution of my rickshaw boy is an interesting study. First, he wore a clean jacket, then some new trousers, to match the jacket, after that new shoes & stockings and today, literally to crown all, a cap. The first one I have seen on a rickshaw boy's head. I must be adding rapidly to the family wealth.

Tomorrow four of us are going to the Great Wall. I rather long for a day of entire rest, but if I did not go I should regret it, I suspect, the rest of my life. Everyone says it is one of *the* things in the world to see.

10.2.1921

The Great Wall is a wonder and I am glad that I did not yield to my lazy self and stay at home.

The trip meant a train ride of three hours, much of it up-grade among the mountains. This is the only road in China, I believe, built and operated entirely by Chinese and it certainly is well done.

The Great Wall is built along the sides of the mountains, zigzagging from peak to peak for thirteen hundred miles. We climbed to the highest peak in the region where we were and looked out to mountains as far as the eye could reach. It is certainly wonderful. One of the two diminutive Chinese coolies who insisted upon assisting me, exclaimed "wonderful" when we reached the summit. I suppose it is the English word which he has heard most often.

The day was beautifully clear with deep blue sky and we could see for many miles. Incidentally, I had good stiff exercise, the best that I have had for some time. There were diminutive donkeys to be hired, but I prefer two legs to six!

10.7.1921

Founder's Day—and I suppose that now—eleven p.m. here—you are all rushing around in academic costume, preparatory to escorting M. Carey [Thomas] to the Chapel. What would I not give to look in upon you.

The Mt. Holyoke girls were here for tea this afternoon. It is such a nice group here in Peking.

I have dined this evening in a charming Chinese home. (You should see, by the way, how adept I am becoming with chop-sticks!) The mistress of the house, the aunt of one of my hostesses, is one of the Red Cross officers here, on the Board of Directors of the home for aged women and quite like American middle-aged women of leisure and philanthropic instincts. Of the six younger women—I being the only foreigner present— two are American college graduates, one of them spending five years at Wellesley in the regular college course and the physical training department, and two are graduates of Ginling. We sat long over the nuts and sweetmeats, discussing international questions. (The League of Nations trots out often here!) Not only did they speak perfect English, but two or three of them could easily be taken for attractive American college women. Alert, witty, earnest—one cannot despair of China's future with a group of this sort. I like the Chinese, immensely. Even the coolies— some of them—attract me; the cultivated class seem more like the same type of Americans than any other eastern nation that I have seen—especially the women. Their sense of humor, their quick perception, their directness, are very likable. They looked so nice tonight in their light brocaded silks, mainly blue, made in their coat style. The Chinese houses with their several courts, are very attractive, I suspect more so now, than in cold bleak January or February . . .

10.9.1921

. . . I am just back from the Western Hills, where the first anniversary of the opening of the Orphanage new buildings and the opening of the Red Cross Hospital, have been celebrated.

. . . Yesterday morning, I had a nice quiet time all by myself. After speaking at the Methodist Girls School, I went to the Imperial Palace and wandered about the courts and state rooms with no one to disturb me except placid guards—who didn't disturb—and a few coolies, digging weeds out from between the cobble stones. Then I went to the museum, equally unmolested, and feasted my eyes on the exquisite colorings of the potteries—reds like a fading sunset, blues as intense as the deepest blue sky, soft violets and greens—colors that cannot be reproduced today. One room is filled with cloisonne, some of it exquisite; another has only bronzes with indefinable green and red in the bronze. A Chinese gentleman told me that the potteries gained their colors largely from the clay, not to be found today.

Tomorrow will be the tenth anniversary of the establishment of the Republic and I passed many gay decorations as well as flags . . . One cannot help wondering what the next ten years will bring to the Republic. The man to whom I was entrusted today, a member of the Ministry of Communications, returning last summer after eight years of study in America, seemed very cheerful about it, said that China must be given time to find herself, in this entirely new kind of government, after her thousands of years of something totally different—of course that is true. If only her officials thought more of their country and less of their pocketbooks! Every time I meet an official, I feel like asking him to which class *he* belongs—but I refrain.

I passed also many camels. The way they hold their heads and their lofty expressions remind me of Arrow, only where his expression is one of gentle superiority, theirs is mild superciliousness. I understand that they can bite—hence a sort of straw muzzle adorns many of them. I never grow tired of watching the way in which they hold their heads and their stately steppings.

10.10.1921 7 p.m.

All packed and ready to start south on the 10:15 train this evening. In some ways I am sorry to leave Peking; I doubt whether I shall enjoy any other city as well . . . If you could see me, as I start off tonight, with a thermos bottle of drinking water slung over my shoulder, two boxes of lunch, as I am not "partial" to Chinese diners, and two boxes of belated gifts from Chinese friends, in addition to my regular luggage!

Wuchang, 10.13.1921

I am really in a Chinese city in Central China, quite different from Peking. We crossed the Yangtze in a launch yesterday afternoon. Then were at least twenty minutes coming in a rickshaw to the Boone University Compound, through narrow streets—some of them so narrow, that I could easily touch the walls on each side—thronged with Chinese, and lined by open shops of every conceivable variety—tailors, carpenters, wood splitters, barbers, food vendors—ad infiinitum. I am staying with Mrs. Miller, a Mt. Holyoke girl of '96 and wife of a member of the Boone faculty—in a charming house. My room is big and airy, opening by French windows onto a screened porch—(I mention screens as mosquitoes are still with us) looking into a garden, and beyond the garden only a few roofs of low Chinese houses before the city wall. The city gates are closed every night at dark, a regulation strictly enforced since the looting and burning and shooting by the Northern troops one night last June . . . It was hard to realize in that drawing-room that I was in China, but not difficult to realize it when crossing the Yangtze in a Sanpan . . .

10.14.1921—10 p.m.

. . . tonight dined at the house of the president of Boone University and then spoke for an hour, with an interpreter to the students of Boone, men, on "Higher Education for Women"—in which men students, it is said, are much interested.

It has rained all day, the first all day rain since reaching China.

This afternoon the Trustees cable reached me by mail from Shanghai and pleased me greatly. Please tell Mr. Skinner.

On the Yangtsze
Central China
10.19.'21

. . . we are going farther into the interior and when we turn back on Monday the skies will look bluer! Then every step will mean nearer home and in Shanghai I shall feel that I can just step on board a ship, and lo and behold! will be there!

Yesterday was one of the full days, conferences morning and afternoon at Boone, followed by a tea, then a trip to Hankow, a late dinner at Bishop Root's and arrival at the steamer just before it sailed at midnight.

. . . This is a British steamer, with only a few passengers in each cabin. Our party of seven almost fills the first "foreign" cabin. We are running very close to the shore, flat and marshy, and where there are homes, they are such miserable little mud or stucco huts, a contrast to the beautiful, "Western style" house of a Chinese business man where we were for a few minutes last evening. The contrasts in China are more striking than in

America—I suspect that I shall realize for myself what a Mt. Holyoke girl felt when she came home, that "every one looked so well-dressed." I shall also realize, without doubt, that it is not possible always to find someone ready for a few coppers, to do any service that may be desired. Which reminds me, of what I often think, to hope that the service end is running smoothly and that you are being made comfortable . . .

It is much warmer and damper here in the Yangtsze valley than in Peking.

There are many Chinese junks along the river—yesterday we crossed from Wuchang in one.

10.20.1921

We have passed several pagodas this morning—one of them apparently rising out of the water. It is difficult to realize that in a month navigation will stop during the dry season and that the lake itself will be a narrow stream through a marsh.

We had a conference yesterday afternoon and evening and again this morning. We are making out such a beautiful educational scheme for China—if only Boards and Missionaries agree to it . . .

En route to Nanchang, 11.28.'21

. . . We have left the Wu-Nan cities and have started on another "lap" toward Shanghai . . . We are travelling by a little "one-horse railway", quite a contrast to the fine river steamer by which we came from Hankow last night to Kiukiang. There is only one train a day and so many soldiers seize all the places in the cars, that only the baggage car was found, but the windows are wide open and we are making ourselves quite comfortable for a six hour journey with bananas, sweet chocolate and Episcopal caramels—very good ones too—for lunch. I have a new respect for the banana—it is always available and since it wears a jacket, always presumably clean!

Sunday morning—Nanchang
October 30, 1921, Kiansi

. . . I am ensconced in a steamer chair in front of a grate-fire, having had breakfast in bed—the first lazy morning in China! You cannot know what this means without the background of the days we are living. I am staying in the home of the foreign staff of the Baldwin School, a Middle School for Girls connected with the Methodist Mission and fortunately have as hostess a Miss McDade, a thoughtful Goucher woman, who by the way, knows Miss Hewes & Miss Morriss.

We left Hankow Thursday night by one of the fine Yangtsze steamers, reaching Kiukiang Friday morning and coming to Nanchang by the one daily train. Yesterday morning we had one of our usual conferences, in the afternoon an unusual entertainment and garden party at Dr. Kahn's, one of the Chinese women who are doing such splendid service as physicians. Besides running a hospital for women, she "runs" a wonderful rose garden full of roses that blossom until Christmas and after—and a chrysanthemum show. After the Chinese conjurer had finished the garden party and before the Chinese dinner was served, we had an hour in the gardens.

You cannot know what these gardens and mission compounds, brilliant now with chrysanthemums mean, except as you place them in contrast with these thronged, narrow, walled streets. Nanchang has a population of 750,000 on an area of seven square miles, "the most densely inhabited seven miles on the face of the globe" says an English geographer. I could quite imagine it this afternoon, as my rickshaw boy shouted and elbowed his way through the midst of pigs and chickens, dogs and cats, an occasional cow, rickshaws, wheel barrows—a favorite vehicle here—babies and indefinable humans. And yet nature has done her best to make Nanchang attractive, with the river Kan and the beautiful mountains. It *is* lovely on the compound. My room looks toward the city walls and the sunset, just as the room in Wuchang looked toward the walls. There we were just *in*side the walls and here we are just *out*side.

I have had quite an experience with rickshaw boys. Returning to Wuchang last week, I knocked down a man the first day—and ran into a water carrier the second, thereby "dousing" all the bystanders and leaving an atmosphere surcharged with irate remarks! But I—or rather, my rickshaw boy—capped the climax in Nanchang last Friday, on my way to "tiffin" at a house which neither he nor I knew. He had passed the gate at a rather brisk pace, when one of the men riding behind me called him to stop, which he did so suddenly that he fell flat on his face, and I on top of him! A rickshaw coolie is not a landing place which one would choose but, being soft, it has advantages. I was not hurt, not even lame, but after reaching my hostess's—on foot—I discovered that my glasses were not on my nose. Diligent search, aided by the police, resulted in nothing except the conclusion that they are probably now in some "curio" shop, deposited there by an enterprising coolie!

November 2, 1921, 3 p.m.
Kiukiang

We are on the steamer for Nanking, scheduled to sail at two, but not yet started. It is a wonderful day, like early September at Fleur de Lys and the Yangtsze is beautiful in the sunlight.

We have started. It is wonderfully beautiful, mountains and river flooded with sunshine.

18, Yuen Ming Tuen Road
Shanghai, 11.6.1921

. . . my first letter from Shanghai I am writing to you. We arrived late last evening from Soochow and this morning, Sunday, I have been putting "things" away with a sense of relief that they—some of them—could stay "put" for a season!

But the great thing was the letters. Five from you, ranging in date from September 15-October 9. I suspect that some came by fast ship and some by slow and that the cautious Dr. Gamewell or his equally cautious secretary thought it better to hold them than to run the risk of losing them. Five weeks tomorrow night with no mail from home except one letter from Harriet. You can imagine how I devoured them. I reached the house about half after ten and retired at one, after reading and re-reading . . .

Hangchow, Chekiang, 11.10.1921

Shanghai is unlike anything that I have seen. As Mr. Burton says—

"Shanghai is not China; it is Shanghai." In many ways it is more New York than China—but in New York the police do not wear red turbans, nor rickshaws dash in and out among automobiles, nor the crowd look quite so Oriental. It is fascinating with its broad streets, and fine Bund and color. I am glad we are to have six weeks there . . . Our little group has had a good time and is easier to move around, in opinion, as well as physically! Now for the report, in some ways, the hardest work of all . . .

Nanking, 11.14.1921

. . . I only wish that I could reproduce all that I have seen. I like China very much. Much better than I had supposed I should. It is a land of the greatest contrasts—wonderful scenery—and then miles of streets of people, huddled together between gray walls.

Nanking, 11.20.1921

Thursday we spent at South Eastern University, Dr. Kuo, the president, being one of our Commission . . . In the afternoon there was a "reception", which here almost inevitably means speech-making, but it was worth being a victim to look into that sea of earnest faces, the hope of China. It takes hold of one increasingly realizing the possibilities and the difficulties more and more. If only the Washington Conference will do the right and wise thing by China. America's "throwing her cards on the table" with regard to disarmament, is received very favorably here. I see by yesterday's "North China Daily News" that the Conference has decided to consider China's case before proceeding to other points. Certainly world welfare is very closely bound up with what is done regarding China. If only the rest of the world will give her a chance to find herself. And interfere only by the helping hand! . . . Politics, religion and education, fight for preeminence at all the tiffins and dinners and we talk interminably.

18 Yuen-Ming-Yuen
Shanghai, 11.22.1921

. . . We arrived at midnight yesterday and at nine this morning held our first session of the final gathering for the next six weeks. Not all the members of the Commission have come so we adjourned early and I wandered around Shanghai, doing various errands. . . . The date of sailing of the "Hoosier State" from Yokohama is January 20th, which, I suppose, means arrival in San Francisco about February 14.

Mr. Burton is better and hopes to meet with us in ten days. He has had a serious intestinal infection which, for a day or two, acted like cholera.

12.4.1921

Seven o'clock Sunday evening and time to begin my letter before dinner. I have worked all day on my talk for the "Returned Students Service" at five o'clock this afternoon, for the week past has not given "margins" for preparation.

A meeting like the one this afternoon gives one hope for the future. Grace Yang presided beautifully—a duet was sung in English by a Barnard and a Wellesley graduate, with really lovely voices. Such attractive Chinese women, in their soft colored silks and up-to-date furs, Chinese men, in European clothes for the most part, lawyers, business men, doctors, teachers, Christian Association Secretaries, preachers—I should just like to put some of our Americans who judge of China from the coolies they see "over there", down in such a gathering, where the English spoken is much better than in most American gatherings! I have grown very fond of these Chinese women—they are so earnest and yet so full of fun. They give one "heart" for the future . . .

12.10.1921

I have "dined out" three nights in succession and been late every night; Wednesday evening, Mrs. Raven's chauffeur (it may be superfluous to remark that Mr. R. is a banker, not a missionary!) made a mistake in the house. Thursday night the taxi broke down on its way to us; and last night I surveyed Shanghai for an hour and a quarter, while my ricsha coolie found my hostess's house, arriving at ten minutes before nine for an eight o'clock dinner! It was worthwhile, for it was so interesting. My hostess, Mrs. Mei, is a Barnard graduate, and her husband, a leading lawyer here, a Columbia man, Drs. Mary and Phoebe Stone, two Chinese physicians, who have a hospital here, were at the dinner—and four "foreigners" including myself. The combination of east and west, in the homes of these returned students is most interesting. Incidentally, we had a most delicious dinner. When Chinese food is good, it is *very* good indeed. I thought of you when eating little fritters made of sweet potato and served in a sauce concocted from orange and sage. The food was Cantonese, Yau Tsit Law told me with great satisfaction, the Meis coming originally from Canton and importing their cook from that metropolis.

Yau Tsit stands up valiantly for Sun Yat Sen—and for his wife, whose sister I met at the College Club. Both of them, I think, are Wellesley graduates . . . the registered parcel came this morning, but I have put it resolutely away, not to be opened before Christmas Eve. I do hope that my little package will reach you. To be perfectly frank, I shall be glad when Christmas is over! . . .

12.17.1921

This afternoon I went to the "Commercial Press" to buy some toys for the little Russells and then up Nanking Road hunting for some Chinese shoes for Eleanor and Janet. In Canton I could find them on every corner —in Shanghai they are like the traditional needle in a haystack. The Chinese ladies are buying more up-to-date satin slippers, even with heels! In the toy shop, it was interesting to see the Chinese mothers and children, the latter wide-eyed over the mechanical toys. At one window on Nanking Road filled with "foreign" dolls, a novelty to Chinese children, there was a crowd, largely little boys, with their faces *glued* to the glass. I longed to buy a doll for every one of them. My Christmas shopping here is very mild, some candy for the children in Changsha and Wuchang, and for the grown-up children who were so good to me at Soochow and Nanking . . .

Christmas Day, 1921

. . . it is Christmas morning, before breakfast, and I am saying my first greetings to you. I shall go with you in thought every step of the way and one month from now I shall be turning my steps—(any-how wavy watery ones!) homeward.

If you could look in upon me this morning you would see me cozily
ensconced in bed, a bright fire and lots of flowers, poinsettia, violets,
oleanders, to make my room cheerful. I decided yesterday that my cold
had lasted long enough, two *weeks,* so I had an osteopath and strong advice to spend my "holiday" in bed, so here I am, having given up Mrs.
Raven's tiffin, and Christmas services.

January 5, 1922

This noon I had tiffin with Mrs. Arthur Curtiss James, who with her
husband and four friends, is sailing around the world on their yacht. After
tiffin at the "Astor", we put on our coats, Mrs. Thurston and I, to go back
to Quinsan Gardens, they to sail for Manila, Hong Kong and Singapore
on their way to India, and one seemed as much "in the day's work" as
the other! Sailing to or from the ends of the earth is such an everyday
occurrence at Shanghai that no one is much excited over it.

❖   ❖   ❖   ❖

So ended for Mary Woolley one of the happiest years of her life. As
her letters show, she loved China; she admired and loved Chinese
women. She was never to go to China again. But she was to travel
eastward, once in 1925 and once in 1927 as a member of the Institute
of Pacific Relations to conventions in Hawaii.

A wire on arrival sent home from San Francisco; another from Chicago; and the day following Mary Woolley's train had reached Springfield and the Connecticut Valley. That crisp, winter day of February
20, 1922, was overcast. The noise outside the President's House was
like millions of bees about to swarm. It was oddly punctuated, however, by muffled barks and muffled voices from the inside of the house
where wide orange bows were being tied around the necks of our
collies, Old Mannie, and Ladybird Holyoke, Arrow and Tuttle. Outside, crowded close up to the front stoop, and lining the driveway and
College Street beyond that on either side, were many hundreds of
students and of younger members of the faculty. They were waiting
for the president's car which was bringing her on the last lap of the
journey home from China.

When the humming began again a voice close to the stoop said
clearly: "No, I was registered for Wellesley but we both came to
Mount Holyoke."

"What made you do that, Rebecca?"

"Well, the year before we entered we had some letters from a friend
who was here at Mount Holyoke and she couldn't say enough about
Miss Woolley—all our discussion about Wellesley and Mount Holyoke
ended with the fact that Mount Holyoke has Miss Woolley. That was
the unanswerable argument: we came here, Sally."

"Well, maybe, Rebecca. But it wasn't later than Freshman Week before I wanted to go home to stay. I was so homesick, my father came and got me. As we were going out of the President's Office, what do you think Miss Woolley said to me?"

"What?"

"'Sarah, I will hold your place open for you for a week. You don't look like a girl who would give up just because a thing was hard.'"

"I came back, and I'll never forget what she said to me then."

Suddenly down College Street a shrill voice cried out: "Oh boy, *she is coming!*"

After that pandemonium broke loose and the whole college clapped, waved, shouted its welcome.

"Doesn't she look nice!" yelled one student.

Smiling, the president was waving to the students from the car window. Before the car could reach the front door, the door of the President's House opened and out stepped four collies decorated with oriental bows. After that Old Mannie and Ladybird Holyoke and Arrow and Tuttle despite protests of "Kee-eep still!" and "Stop—that barking!" and "Bee-have!" went right on adding their joyous barks and yelps to the bedlam of welcome as the president's car came slowly down the drive.

Amused, Earl Buss opened the car door swiftly and Mary Woolley stepped out. In their happiness the dogs flung themselves upon her: their Missus had come home! The girls who saw this welcome from the collies laughed and clapped; and the cheer leader, Peggy Shane, already encircled by a group of her best and strongest voices, got down to business. For an instant their heads were together as they tuned into the melody of their welcome:

> May we sing a song or two
> To say we think it's fine of you
> To leave the folks in China
> And come back to us.

This doggerel was followed by more wild cheers and handclapping until the cheer leader swung them back into singing:

> Do you miss the atmosphere
> Now you've come back home?
> Do you want your jinricksha,
> Does Buss's car seem queer?
> You may ask, Miss Woolley, then
> Us to be your coolie men
> We won't charge a single yen
> Now you've come home again!

Silly stuff but warm and true like the youth of those girls on that

February winter day when Mary Woolley, tears of happiness in her eyes, reached home again. Fifteen years later, also in the morning but in the summertime, Earl Buss drove the President of Mount Holyoke College out of that driveway. Walking beside the car were only one Mount Holyoke "girl", two alumnae of other colleges, and Rosalie Calkins, the head maid of the President's House, as Mary Woolley left the College never again to return.

CHAPTER 11

BRICKS

"What women have done in the way of material provision for this education, no statistics can cover . . . the "bricks" for their own institutions and for others, have been accumulated largely by their indefatigable efforts."

Sir Phillip Gibbs stood one night on the platform of Chapin Auditorium at Mount Holyoke College lecturing about American life. Suddenly, and to the delight of at least some of the members of that audience, he shouted: "Damn your dollars!" Mary Woolley's way of making approximately the same statement to a world-wide audience lay in this message: "Too often it has seen supreme value in dollars and cents; in the acquisition of power; in mechanical progress; in physical comfort; even in amusement. *But seeing supreme value in human beings,*" she went on to quote Bishop Oxnam, *"is what must be, if civilization is to endure."* Hers was what Beatrice Forbes-Robertson Hale has called "collective motherhood" in which the "supreme value" for Mary Woolley lay not in buildings but in the thousands of college women for whom the foundations had been and were being laid towards the education of women and their training for leadership.

Mary Woolley knew that the pawns for the "bricks" of the great college for women of which she had been dreaming since 1901 and which, with the cooperation of others, she was building, were adequate financial funds. From the point of view of what was to be done, money seemed a large problem. Yet even the funds already collected shrank as she tried to stretch them to meet the requisites of the college being built. She made herself look upon this money-getting as a game of hide and seek or of chess and the next move to be made on the board. Also, as a skilled executive she made it the rule to find the right person, if possible, to do the work under her direction. If, however, at the time the right person could not be found, she herself went about the business and the amount she raised ran into millions.[1]

Sometimes the "bricks" she was making were made in China as well as in New England or California, Iowa or New York State, for "bricks" to build the college followed wherever she shared her power to inspire others to do their utmost for the education of women.

Problems were many. One, a music building, would bring with it unavoidable noisiness. The trustee member of the committee of four which included the president and Julia Dickinson was determined the music building should be located at the rear of the chapel in Mary Lyon Hall, and housing also the executive offices. A generous miser abhorring waste, the trustee intended to cut the cost of this erection by making use of the already established water and sewer systems of the executive building. He could not be persuaded that the day-long crashing of arpeggios and running of scales in a music building would be a hindrance both to the executive work and to the religion of the college. This situation remained an impasse until Dr. Woolley tactfully intimated that the use of *"some waste land"* on the very boundary of the campus would be an economy. At once the thrifty trustee sprang to attention, asking the president indignantly how it happened that there *was* any waste land? Mary Woolley's reply was that this plot had seemed useless for most purposes. Suggesting that the committee take a look at the waste land, they all walked down together. No one was more eager than this trustee to get there, and when he arrived he thought the place ideal for the music building.

"It was the slickest piece of diplomacy I have ever seen!" said Julia Dickinson.

Another lusty problem was created by a fire which destroyed Williston Hall with much of the research work of several professors, including that of Dr. Ann Morgan, and Mignon Talbot's baby dinosaur. Among other losses were some of Dr. Hayes' manuscripts, including a revealing collection of dreams contributed by a psychology major about her romance with an Amherst boy. The fire's destructiveness of the professors' researches was rather complete but the psychology major turned dream into fact and married the Amherst boy in June! The baby dinosaur, however, never recovered! In a crisis like this what did Mary Woolley *do*? First she secured some of the badly needed temporary comforts and facilities, then went on to plan and to work for the raising of funds and the construction of a science building to be called Clapp Laboratory, a structure many times superior to what some of the science departments had had.

Of the college and its phenomenal growth she herself said: "No one person can ever be responsible for its growth." In these campaigns, first she awakened the interest of the college itself. She was always definite about the objective for which money was to be raised. Among these objectives, buildings never had entire right of way. Her favorite purpose was the endowment of teaching chairs and the purchasing of the best available equipments for the teaching staff. Mary Woolley's position in the Seven College Conference, whether as member or as chairman, was important, a nucleus for invaluable influence, for many strictly academic matters were related to this fact, including the adjustments of a new curriculum and the status of the faculty.[2]

What else did this "brick-making" involve for Mary Woolley? Whether it is or is not possible to answer the question, the following letters will at least suggest in her own words *how* she did it:

> Mount Holyoke College
> June 9, 1915
>
> . . . This morning I was up at five, to finish the talk for the Chamber of Commerce Dinner at the new hotel tonight and I must rest this afternoon.

> June 15, 1915
>
> I spoke to the Alumnae this morning; at eleven, began Trustee Committee Meeting, which lasted until one, then luncheon at Mead, and the Trustee meeting at two-thirty, adjourning between five and six. The bull was taken by the horns, as far as the Treasurership is concerned, the trustees voting to establish a resident treasurership . . . There is a relief in having it over, but it has taken a lot "out of" me.

> The College Club, Boston
> June 22, 1915
>
> After speaking in Worcester this morning, I came here and am having a few quiet hours before going to the Radcliffe Dinner tomorrow night. I was up at half-after four yesterday morning, so you can imagine that a little extra sleep will not be bad!

> Hotel St. Francis,
> San Francisco
> July 28, 1915
>
> My train was due at Oakland Pier at 8.20 last evening, and the Ferry at San Francisco at 8.50 and we were in on the moment.
>
> San Francisco looked very beautiful as we sailed into it last evening— even the Ferry house is a thing of beauty outlined like a great jewel with electric lights and a great electric welcome "California Welcomes the World to the Panama-Pacific Exposition" across its "front".
>
> It is a most hospitable place, so hospitable that I had one caller before I had my breakfast—which isn't saying much after all, as I did not arise with the chickens, if there are any. I did not omit my breakfast, however, which was fortunate as my next meal was dinner at seven-thirty this evening. I am becoming quite addicted to the no lunch habit and really do not feel hungry at noon. There is a fifty-cent breakfast in the grill-room, another fortunate circumstance, as my room takes all my available pennies.

July 29, 1915

I have said my say at the "Lord's Day Congress", now tomorrow I must go to work on one for the alumnae reception in the Massachusetts Building on Saturday. I am afraid I am lazy—for I should like just to *loaf* in the California sunshine, instead of speaking every other day . . .

I went to dinner tonight, although I did not feel hungry before and did feel uncomfortably full afterward—I think I shall soon get down to *one* meal a day! I was not sorry to escape from the hubbub down stairs to my nice, quiet room. Every one and his wife are here, including J. P. Morgan's grandson and bride, who arrived yesterday and Billy Sunday, who comes tomorrow, as the guest of the management. I wish that I were the "guest of the management"—it would be much better for my pocketbook!

Los Angeles
August 4, 1915

The people in California seem to have a genius for doing things well. The luncheon was at a charming Club House. I spoke *before* luncheon —not afterward, when I was fagged, then they gave me a rest-hour, shut in a room by myself, before the general reception from three to five.

August 7, 1915

After tomorrow morning I shall be somewhat more free. Trying to finish my talk and keep pace with these enterprising Californians has been a problem, as perhaps yesterday's schedule will indicate.

1.45 A.M.   retired;
5.45 A.M.   arose;
8 A.M.   started by motor for Claremont (50 miles)
10.30 A.M.   arrived and was shown campus of Pomona College
12.15 P.M.   luncheon Mount Holyoke Alumnae
2-3 P.M.   informal reception, Pomona Faculty and Alumnae
3.40 P.M.   started by trolley for Redlands, 54 miles
5 or thereabouts—arrived
6 P.M.   started by motor for Smiley Heights and outdoor supper overlooking mountains
10 P.M.   Retired

Hotel St. Francis,
San Francisco
August 12, 1915

. . . I leave for Portland next Wednesday afternoon, speaking at the A.C.A. Tuesday evening, my last effort. Tommy Tucker has surely sung for his supper this trip!

Mount Holyoke College
September 16, 1915

. . . it has seemed as if everybody and everything had to be attended to, at once. To cap the climax, Brainerd and Leeds, architects for the proposed Residence Hall, appeared, and that meant an hour and an half in the middle of the afternoon.

Chicago, Illinois
November 14, 1915

I forgot that my watch was Eastern time yesterday morning and arose at *four* instead of five! At six I was on the train—until nine o'clock at night, dividing my day between reading "Monarchical Socialism in Germany" and taking much needed naps. I went to church this morning—but did not stay for Sunday school and as all the rest of the family did, am having a quiet afternoon for writing and resting. It is just as well, for this will be a strenuous week, speaking eight times and doing no end of other things.

Chicago
November 5, 1916

I am having two hours of quiet—all the others having gone to Sunday School. I really need it, after my strenuous visit in Des Moines, finished by a call on the Grinnell pupil of Mary Lyon, between ten thirty and eleven fifty-five last evening. I will tell you all about it when I come home.

Another pupil of Mary Lyon, a wealthy woman of Cedar Rapids, the Iowa alumnae are anxious to have me see, hoping to interest her in the endowment, so I take a midnight train back to Iowa tonight returning in time for another midnight train to Pittsburgh tomorrow night! Well, it is all in the day's work.

Youngstown, Ohio
June 20, 1922

I reached Pittsburgh at 9.20, was taken by my hosts for breakfast; then to the house, where I changed my gown; then to the church, where I spoke; then to the Alumnae luncheon, where I spoke again; then to the College Club, where the Mt. Holyoke Alumnae gave a tea, at which I spoke a third time; then back to the house where I changed back into my travel togs again; then to the train! And all on a hot June day.

Seal Harbor, Maine
8.24.1922

It is just after breakfast and before I begin my work, I am going to have a little talk with you . . . My window looks out onto the water, over clumps of bushes and through the trees. It is lovely here, but nothing seems quite like Fleur de Lys to me.

I have just heard Mrs. Hoe say to Tammas "Why, what's the matter, Lovey Dear?" Sounds like home!

8.25.1922

The fog is drifting in again this morning but the sun is trying to come out. It was like this all day yesterday, but it didn't matter. In the morning we motored to a church fair that Mrs. Hoe likes to help and I bought you another apron. They work all the winter making aprons, hemstitching towels etc, so one of the women told me. The children looked so pasty in this beautiful out-of-doors, which I suppose they shut out all winter!

After the Gilpatrics went I lighted my fire, lay down and read stories until it was time to dress for dinner. Today promises to be less leisurely. This evening the Rockefellers have a dinner party at eight o'clock, which means no early to bed. Mr. Raymond Fosdick is with them but I suppose we shall not introduce the new residence hall as table talk! Ah me, if he only would!

The Cosmopolitan Club
New York City
9.1.1922

Tonight's & tomorrow morning's trains "sold out". A day coach by day seems preferable to one by night, so you may expect me at 4.34 (Standard) tomorrow afternoon.

Mr. Field "cannot do anything at present"—wishes we "could see the size of the mortgage on the new estate on Long Island." Will however come to the College this autumn, probably in October.

Mr. Skinner was keenly disappointed—"had expected at least $150,-00.000". I think I must be growing blase. I have had so many of these experiences I expect nothing else!

We had an hour at the General Education Board with Dr. Buttrick, could not get away. He was much interested—will do his "best to persuade Mr. Rockefeller to give a residence hall." So perhaps the trip is not wasted. I have not had such a tiring one for years as yesterday's.

C. B. & I.
Between Ottawa and Omaha
11.6.1922

. . . Before I begin to work on my report this morning, I am going to send you a "jiggly" letter. Then I shall feel more like working. We are going over the Iowa prairies, in brilliant sunshine, which means that they look their best . . .

We have just passed "Albia", an hour late. I foresee sitting up most of tomorrow night and reaching Grand Junction just before breakfast.

Colorado Springs
11.9.1922

. . . You cannot imagine what a joy it was to find your Sunday note at Pueblo. A nice Mrs. Maston met me at the train—(2½ hours late, so I jumped from the car platform onto the auditorium ditto—) and after the meeting took me to her house for a quiet hour and nice luncheon. Suspecting that I might have mail at the Congress, she went there and brought me yours. How I wish you were with me! But the pace, Dear, has been terrific. My train due at Grand Junction at 1.20 Wednesday morning, arrived at 3.45 [A.M.]. At the hotel no room was reserved, so I sat in the office until 4.45, when an expected man, *not* arriving, thank the Lord, on the train from Salt Lake, I had his room, and slept from five until seven. I then arose and until the late afternoon, was on the jump, speaking four times, with the result that when I reached the hotel in the late afternoon, my head was also on the jump. Every one was cordial and kind, to the last degree, and if Tuesday night had been a sane one, I would have been all right. Today has been much easier, despite the late arrival. The Denver and Rio Grande has not settled the trouble with the strikers and the result is broken down engines on the highest mountain route in the country!

The Cosmopolitan Club
January 11, 1923

I have spoken my little piece at Bethlehem. Now at Gloversville tomorrow and for the Albany Alumnae Saturday and then home. I am glad that I have few "little pieces" to speak after this.

I am tired tonight but I think my cold is a little better.

Lindores, Ormond Beach,
Florida
March 24, 1923

Again it is before breakfast but not quite so early as yesterday. I am lazier this morning, perhaps due to a long motor drive yesterday afternoon. The beach drive when the tide is out is wonderful twenty miles of hard, smooth, broad boulevard . . . This afternoon it will be a shorter drive as Mr. and Mrs. John D. Jr. and Frank Chapman, the naturalist, are coming for dinner.

March 25, 1923

Mr. Chapman last evening told so many interesting things about birds and natural life here. The air is full of birds . . . Sunshine, birds and flowers are the things that impress me here.

Also the fact that apparently everyone goes to church! The little church was full this morning and we had a good sermon. After the service I met John D. Senior. He is a childlike bland old gentleman, eyes still a bright blue! What a mystery human nature is. John D. Jr. told me last evening it was Dr. Andrews who took him to Brown and that he was the one teacher who had left a marked and permanent impression upon his life. I wonder whether Dr. Andrews ever suspected the influence he exerted upon the life of his day!

The Cosmopolitan Club
June 14, 1923

I started early this morning and rested all that I could on the train, so that I am feeling not quite as much like a punctured tire as I did. I hope that I shall not feel more like one after this evening! . . . back at the Club at ten-thirty is not so bad. Everybody was very thoughtful but I am glad this evening is over. I dreaded speaking in the Opera House, with its balconies to the ceiling.

President's House
June 17, 1923

Tomorrow I go to Princeton for the graduation Tuesday morning, then to Yale for the exercises Wednesday morning—and immediately following those, to Radcliffe for the dinner to Dean Briggs. Thursday morning I am to see Mr. Kendall, Mr. Plimpton's nephew, to ask whether he will join our Board of Trustees. I hope that that means an end of functions!

Cambridge
June 20, 1923

. . . It has been a terrible day. It seems to me that I was never so hot as when I reached here at seven o'clock this evening and tried to dress for the Radcliffe dinner. Today I hurried from the exercises to catch the train for Boston.

President's House
July 18, 1923

. . . After supper with Mary Atwell Moore at the College Inn, I sat on the Faculty House porches for a time, conversing amiably with the ladies.

Miss Cushing says that Mrs. Adams has a horsewhip and is trying to break Bulbo of his bad automobile habits. Here's luck to her! And also scepticism!

8.31.1923

Yesterday afternoon I spent at the new dormitory with Mr. Skinner, Mr. Cox, Mr. Ranger, the "clerk of the works", and the man who made many of the architect's drawings. We went carefully over the building [Mandell], which will be practically complete at the end of this week, some puttering "last jobs" excepted. That will eventually be the "beauty-spot" of the campus, with its broad grassy terrace and lovely outlook. It will be somewhat unfinished-looking this autumn around the house. I am sure you will like it. It is really lovely, simple, dignified and in good taste.

September 4, 1923

I corralled Mr. Skinner this afternoon and we "ascended" to the dor-mitory, to find that Amy had corralled the painter and the country had been saved from the combination of wisteria hangings and mustard walls . . . I am having continuous seances regarding the new dormitory. It was promised us the middle of July; it is actually not yet finished and Amy is trying to finish with workmen and cleaners under foot. Most serious of all, the walls of the principal rooms are "off color" as far as her scheme is concerned. This afternoon I am going to pull Mr. Skinner into the seance, to have his backing that it must be made right. This is only to show you that I have a fellow-feeling; that I too am not sailing on the smoothest of seas.

Cleveland, Ohio
1.21.1924

I welcomed yesterday's quiet on the train for either an "after-math" of my cold or a new one struck me the last of the week. Today at the Clinic an X Ray was taken to see whether my sinuses are responsible.

I had three interviews this morning, one for money—which I did not get!—one with a reporter and one with a business woman. Tomorrow and Wednesday promise to be "full up" and I hope to feel up to par to meet them.

The Cosmopolitan Club
April 14, 1924

I lunched with Harriet and Gertrude then went down to the rooms of the General Education Board, where Mr. Skinner and I spent two hours with Mr. Arnett. He was very nice, no one could have been more so, but it is evident that we must "pitch in" and raise the half million lacking on the million dollar fund, to complete the Biological building and also pay for the new fire mains, electric equipment, etc., that we may not be in debt to ourselves. I will tell you the situation more in detail when I re-turn. Mr. Arnett will come to our meeting and lunch tomorrow . . . To-morrow night Mr. Stuart will dine with me. He is leaving soon for Peking.

New York
December 18, 1924

Mr. Duke is reported saying that he did not care for money, only the power it gave. I have thought of that remark many times the last two

days. I am wasting half hours, waiting to see people. When this last
quarter million is raised, no more campaigns for me.

New York
1.19.1927

. . . before I begin my day's activities, a little talk with you. Then I
must look over the "life history" of "The Women's Foundation for
Health," before I go to a two or three hour conference. That is bound
to be wearisome for it is like beating the air. We get no where, from
the financial point of view. I stay *in*, because I feel that I have no right
to get *out*, when the work they are doing is good and the workers so devoted. But they are operating on a shoe-string and for some reason, seem
unable to secure any financial assistance. We will try once more today
and see what happens.

Then tonight a lengthy dinner of the Seven Colleges with a group of
lawyers, to secure their advice as to the way in which to secure bequests
for our seven worthy institutions and, incidentally, secure their cooperation. I am tired of trying to interest "wealth" in worthy causes! Today's
"jobs" are not particularly to my liking.

11 East 71st Street,
New York
April 2, 1928

I talked with Mrs. Hoe about the "Little Theatre" and she will give
one thousand dollars toward it. If you can find time this week to send
her a note, I know she will appreciate it.

Tell Chuckie I dreamed about him last night—saw him just as distinctly, standing with his little head thrown back—the darling . . . Please
express my regrets to Lord Dunsany. I hope that you will enjoy him and
I hope that everything will go well with you.

Whether or not these "jobs" were to her liking, she continued to
tackle them as in her brick-making she obtained a thousand dollars
toward a laboratory or one hundred thousand toward a library. Even
this handful of quotations from her letters reveals the fact that summer
and winter, weekends and holidays, she was never free from responsibility. She had not only to travel to raise funds but afterwards within
the college there was the follow-up of funds whether applied to a
building or a scholarship—not merely the plans for building but, later,
the very colors upon the walls of that building.

During Mary Woolley's travels there are records of the inadequacy
of the funds which were to support her. Nor was life any smoother or
more carefree for her when she travelled than it is for others—in fact
less so because of the pressure of responsibility and the distances which
were part of travelling for Mary Woolley. Sometimes the "bricks"
were made regardless of personal financial struggle to make the ends
of her small salary meet, and again and again she refused offers of a
post elsewhere which would have brought her a salary many times

as large as her college salary. Also, the so-called "financial" work included paying her own travelling expenses in the receiving of honorary degrees—a form of *kudos* which widened her sphere of influence and therefore her power to influence others to give to the college for the education of women. Nor is it a negligible fact that Mary Woolley met personally all expenses involved in the entertainment of college guests at the President's House. In all financial matters she was scrupulous, independent and generous.

About the time that her work in college-building was reaching the zenith of its success, during the years 1919-1925 when the president and the alumnae were making plans to raise three millions, she said:

> When I went to Wellesley from Brown, Dr. Andrews gave me some good advice—"Do not tell Wellesley how they do things at Brown." I often thought of that advice and, I hope, profited by it. I am, however, about to tell you how they do this at Mount Holyoke: of the total three million dollar fund, two million for endowment, one million for buildings, of which there has been pledged $2,711,918, the alumnae pledged $1,467,668, and the outside gifts amounted to $1,244,250.

Fortunately her sense of humor never deserted her. Concerning the aftermath of merely one of the twenty-one honorary degrees awarded her, she wrote: "My right eye has been growing 'puffier and puffier' the last three or four days. The result possibly of the Yale degree."

As she travelled about brick-making she gladdened herself with quaint observations and even quainter messages such as: "The canary and I are alone in the apartment—two nice little birdies, you see. He sings occasionally—I am glad to keep my mouth shut, for a season."

Or ". . . a little dog is half-way out of a fourth story window on the other side of Lexington [Avenue], engrossed in what is going on in the street. I am somewhat engrossed in him, lest his interest be followed by a tumble. He *is* cute . . . The little dog has been standing on the window sill. Now a maid has come and reasoned with him and he has retired to the room:—No, here he is again!"

Or she sent messages to the collies at home: " . . . Tell doggies I miss 'em! Tell yourself too" and ". . . Tell Chuckie breakfast will be a doleful meal without him."

What is found in these excerpts? An appreciative attitude toward others; a good tempered acceptance of difficulties and, when she met it, a well-balanced acceptance of failure; early and late hours of work, including all the years during which the discomforts of night-travel after a day's hard work were taken for granted; a clear schedule and a persistent follow-up of any project she had set in motion. Not only did her sense of humor support her, so also did the affection of others

She was able to build up the college in so many different parts of the world and in such uncomplex ways—because she herself was more lovable and uncomplex than any college or cause can ever be.   To a wide public within and without the college it must have seemed that President Woolley had made the college what it was.   At least that is the way it seemed to President James B. Angell when he wrote Mary Woolley: "You have really made another institution since I first knew it." [8]

CHAPTER 12

LEADERSHIP

"It will not be without effort—we are not wafted to a mountain top on beds of ease—we climb!"

Wherever Mary Woolley was speaking usually there were two facts about her talks not always found together: purpose and laughter. When at the Twenty-fifth Anniversary of the Women's College in Brown University Mary Woolley spoke, her purpose was honoring the memory of Dr. Andrews and appreciation for the work at the Women's College of Dean Lida King. As she continued speaking her audience relaxed in laughter over the stories she told, among them this one:

> Yesterday . . . a student with that genius for remembering facts without correlation which students sometimes possess, remarked with enthusiasm, "Oh, Miss Woolley, so you are going back to help celebrate the anniversary of the College of which you were one of the first members! It's the one hundred and fiftieth anniversary, isn't it?"

During the year of 1930 she had been here, there and everywhere, speaking on education, on women as research workers, on peace and on religion; and the speeches this year included the dinner discussion on November 20th at the White House, with Mr. Hoover as host. With her that night at the discussion dinner in the White House, Mary Woolley had a few rough pencilled notes—the writer is now holding in her hand these pencilled notes — on points which Dr. Woolley thought it might be important to discuss. She had received what was called an "intimation" that her expected contribution would be to take part in the discussion about "the School of Tomorrow". To her amazement she heard Chairman Sutton introducing her as one of the speakers. Clutching the now useless notes, Mary Woolley had time to see the amused look on Mr. Hoover's face as she rose and began spontaneously:

> Mr. Chairman and members of this informal group (laughter) to which we were invited *not* to speak but simply to start the discussion: There was in New England for a long generation a man who became eventually the Grand Old Man, who was equally grand after he had reached his 90th

birthday, Dr. Charles Eliot, for so long a time the President of Harvard University. I was reminded last night of something he said at an inter-collegiate affair, that among the nice things of being a college president was that of meeting delightful people. I was reminded of it last night because I heard of the remark of a Washington taxi driver that one of the nicest things connected with his job was the pleasant people he ran into. I share his feeling this evening.

This program, as it has been outlined, the program of this great conference, is impressive from many points of view. I think that to some of us who as yet have had little contact with it, the fact that it has been emphasizing principles rather than purely progress, has made a great appeal. I have been thinking of that in connection with the school of tomorrow—and it was intimated to me that I should speak along that line and I want to touch upon it. You see, we all have different intimations.

Her friends, colleagues and relatives felt that they meant something —something warm and human, something "special"—in her life. They did, whether they were cousins or students, AAUW associates, the editor of the *Herald Tribune* or a group of her presidential colleagues among the colleges. In any battle of the wits, gay, frank yet subtle, she never tried to over-reach others though sometimes in jest and with laughter she got the better of them before they realized what she was about. The place of the following episode was the Cosmopolitan Club. The others present were the presidents of six colleges for women: Dr. Ada Comstock of Radcliffe, Miss Gildersleeve of Barnard, Dr. Mac-Cracken of Vassar, Dr. Neilson of Smith, Dr. Marion Park of Bryn Mawr and Miss Pendleton of Wellesley. Fellow-sufferers in academic fund-raising, as well as friends, Mary Woolley in the chair, they were planning their joint effort as Miss Comstock explained, "to give the American public a realization of [their] usefulness and [their] need." Under the merciless light which beats upon presidential fund-campaigners they were getting what joy they could out of hard work when this bit of characteristic repartee took place between President Neilson and President Woolley. With mock deference Dr. Neilson referred the problem under discussion to the chairman, declaring that he was "by nature a shy and retiring man." At which Mary Woolley retorted: "Mr. Neilson, if you were any more 'shy' than you are, I should be afraid of you!"

In Mary Woolley's great art, the art of public speaking, not only during the earlier years of her work but even in 1931 something of the cumulative happiness and confidence of her phenomenal success expressed itself. Often she was merriest when she found herself speaking in the midst of "her own people"—her college kind. At home in Mount Holyoke College a few months later but in that same year of 1930, she was presiding at a dinner for the Alumni Council—an intercollegiate advisory group which was meeting at Mount Holyoke. After a gracious greeting she began her speech as follows:

> This is a remarkable valley . . . We have the advantage of colleges for men, colleges for women, and colleges for men and women; we also have the advantage of being very near one to another . . . I hesitate about telling an experience of one of the presidents of Amherst. However, years ago when President Harris went out to the Pacific Coast to give a course of lectures at the University of California, he said: "I come from a college in the far east, not a very large college, a college which is for men only. But it is only five miles from Smith College, the largest college for women in the world, and about nine miles from Mount Holyoke College, another great college for women; and it is connected with both by trolley." Before the words were out of his mouth, one of the men jumped to his seat, and called for three cheers for the trolley.
>
> Now to the trolley we have added the automobile. I remember one night, several years ago, an Amherst professor speaking at our vesper service, seemed a little restless, not quite at ease, an entirely new experience of mine, as far as Amherst professors were concerned. Afterward I learned the secret. He said: "You know I gave a talk tonight that I used at Amherst last Sunday night, and by Jove, there were more Amherst men in the congregation than I had the other side of the mountain." Presumably they were not the same ones. I think he hadn't thought it through to that extent.
>
> We are grateful to you who constitute this organization, as well as glad to have you here. I had some enlightenment this morning as to one reason why we college executives feel so grateful to you. I was in my study, with my mind occupied by various things as you can imagine, when I heard a knock at the door, and a voice with something of a brogue, saying: "Miss Woolley, they can't fix it." Wondering which one of the college problems was insoluble, I said, "Pat, they can't fix what?" "The floor mop, ma'am." And I breathed a deep sigh of relief that it was only the floor mop that they couldn't fix.
>
> May I digress for a moment to say that in these four colleges, as far as the executives are concerned, I am the only one of my kind. However the others may impress upon you the fact that they are overburdened, you must remember that they are not interrupted in the midst of their meditations with accounts of the status of the floor mop. But I am grateful to that floor mop for its reminder that one reason why we appreciate you is that as an organization and as individuals, you are helpful in "fixing" many of the "its" which appear as difficulties on the horizon of the college executive.
>
> I would not, by any means, disparage other members of the college faculties and staffs. There are a few of my own within hearing this evening, and therefore I tread gently. But it is true that as a group, you do not belong to that particular section to which the professor belonged, whose little boy was brought to him by the nurse. "Professor, here is Frederick." "All right," the busy professor answered, "just put him in the file under F."

By this time her audience was with her in other ways as well as laughter, and Mary Woolley went on to the main business of her speech, and then concluded:

> Of course, the conclusion of the whole matter is that it is the alumni themselves who really make or unmake an institution; and for that, as I said, neither you nor we are absolutely responsible.
>
> I came across something in the New York Times, yesterday. (I say "I came across"—I looked for it, as I do every day) that Will Rogers said. I understand from the conversation at the table tonight that some of you listen to Amos 'n' Andy. I occasionally hear Amos 'n' Andy: I always look for Will Rogers.
>
> He said yesterday, "Half our life (speaking of Americans) is spent trying to find something to do with the time we have rushed through life trying to save. Two hundred years from now history will record :'America, a nation that flourished from 1900 to 1942'" (I don't know just why he uses that date) "'conceived many odd inventions for getting somewhere, but could think of nothing to do when they got there.'"
>
> I have quoted that saying because it is just the opposite of that for which you stand. You are spending your lives in trying to get somewhere; but you *do* know what to do when you get there; and I congratulate you upon your success.

Mary Woolley could match good stories with anyone yet never failed to give credit for their sources, as in the following story told at a Phi Beta Kappa meeting:

> President Park, of Bryn Mawr College, tells of an historic occasion at Radcliffe, when Dean Briggs was one of the speakers. There had been special preparations for this important banquet, even the chairs coming in for attention, to the extent of a new coat of varnish. The evening was hot, as Commencement evenings are likely to be, and when the speakers arose to speak, they arose with difficulty, Dean Briggs proving no exception to the rule. Those of you who are so happy as to know Dean Briggs, will at once infer that he was equal to the occasion, as he was. "Ladies and gentlemen," he began, with a sidelong glance at his evening coat, "I had expected to bring you this evening an unvarnished tale, but circumstances make it impossible to fulfill my expectations."

Because she was herself a person of power, Mary Woolley did enjoy the comradeship of her equals—the men and women of power among whom she moved. Aware of her personal success, she was neither self-conscious about it nor self-content. *Frequently she was troubled.* In the social life which was part of her work, was Mary Woolley worldly? Yes, delightfully so at times! With a child's frankness she loved things that glittered—in one sense "toys"—beautiful appointments, silver, attractive clothes, a nice looking car. And, too, she enjoyed the glitter of some social experience: association with the important, and sometimes with the rich. But in her worldliness there was never any wish to under-rate others—no political techniques that defamed or lowered others in order that she herself might be elevated.

As she had developed her credo for the education and leadership of women, besides mountain-climbing, hard work had been her only form of "climbing". She never worshipped the seats of the mighty or thought of her own "seat" as "mighty". And in her credo, again and again throughout the years did Mary Woolley stress the sharing by men and women of responsibility for the solving of the world's "tremendous problems". Again and again throughout the years in her speaking and in her writing did she return to the need and the justice of admitting women to community of public guidance with men in education and in government and to a shared leadership in all human affairs.

When she was asked: "What do you see for women in the future?" her reply was: "That first of all they will be human beings, with brains the same as men, with the opportunity to develop their highest capabilities." In the title of an organization she was to found in 1941 the first words were "Participation of Women". And she went on to speak these words: "It is only as human relations are shaped by women—as well as by men—with the thinking of both directed by the good heart, that we shall ever achieve the better world."

❖   ❖   ❖   ❖

To Westport on August 7, 1930, from Mount Holyoke College a wire was forwarded informing her that she had been voted by the *Good Housekeeping Magazine* Board of Distinguished Judges "one of America's twelve foremost women" and asking her until further notice to keep this information confidential. Then followed a letter from the editor. In a first vote, limited to three selections, the judges had agreed upon Mary Woolley's name "as unquestionably belonging in their roll."

After reading the telegram came the gay exclamation: "So this is what we have to live with! Now our dogs, our little accomplishments, our own wonderful personalities will be swallowed up altogether by one of the Twelve Greatest Women!" The others were Jane Addams, Ernestine Schumann-Heink, Helen Keller, Grace Abbott, Dr. Sabin, Mrs. Coolidge, Martha Berry, Willa Cather, Carrie Chapman Catt, Minnie Maddern Fiske and Cecilia Beaux.

In March of 1931 Alice Booth's article about Mary Woolley came out in *Good Housekeeping.* And perhaps this paragraph by one who was not even an acquaintance will balance the honors account:

> . . . Most valuable of all its [Mount Holyoke's] possessions—more valuable than its newest and best building—more valuable even than that distant sweep of rugged hills against the western sky—is a woman, Mary E. Woolley—who has been its president for thirty years . . . Like the hills, too, she seems perennially young. Her keen eyes and her smooth cheeks flushed with January's own rouge, her soft brown hair, her easy swinging step . . . are a flat contradiction of the birth date she and *Who's Who* have agreed upon as authentic . . . Somehow Miss Woolley always manages to create the atmosphere of leisure, yet in thirty years she has accomplished a work stunning in its magnitude . . . Through sheer force of personality and character—a life lived quietly and beautifully—Mary Woolley's name has become famous.

In something over a year and a half from the publication of the *Good Housekeeping* award, Mary Woolley was to receive a similar but a more extensive honor. An open poll was held by the Council of Women and the *Ladies Home Journal* in order to decide upon who were the twelve greatest women leaders in the United States during the *previous one hundred years*. Conducted from the middle of October 1931 to the middle of December 1932, the poll was designed to determine the "greatest" women for the Hall of Fame at the Chicago Century of Progress Exposition. The resultant balloting became of interest not only for its implicit definition of greatness as leadership and its selection of eminent women but also, and more important, for the following qualities of character which the voters emphasized: attaining a purpose, overcoming insuperable difficulties, service to humanity, whether in founding a church, establishing settlements for the underprivileged, care of the war-wounded, or working for peace, the political and social emancipation of women and the intellectual emancipation of women.

The last woman ever to claim for herself either precedence or fame, Mary Woolley was the last name on the resultant list; Mary Lyon was next to the last. Of these two the *Schenectady Union Star* wrote: "Mary Lyon and Mary E. Woolley represent the intellectual emancipation of woman-kind." In this poll those selected by number of votes and in their order included Mary Baker Eddy, Jane Addams, Clara Barton, Frances E. Willard, Susan B. Anthony, Helen Keller, Harriet Beecher Stowe, Julia Ward Howe, Carrie Chapman Catt and Amelia Earhart Putnam. One male editor said patronizingly, "a pretty good list". Another editor admitted: "It is a good list, of course. It is a typical 'woman's list' . . . these selected lists for this and that leave us cold."

Different people in the public Mary Woolley had built, thought of her in different ways: some thought of her as an educator and the president of Mount Holyoke College; others as one who stood for equal opportunity among men and women; and still others as the intrepid woman who, in whatever way she could, was working for peace. When she spoke of her work at all, what she said disclosed a modest and unspoiled estimate of all she was doing. Often she said at home: "Some women receive more honors than they should have and all too many women do not receive the honors they deserve."

In Notes on Autobiography Mary Woolley jotted down with characteristic modesty these words: "Feel somewhat guilty as I look back. Opportunities seemed to come my way and I took advantage of them! Possibly I should take some credit for that, but [not] as I see the effort which human beings put into the search *for* opportunity." So wrote one who never thrust herself forward but in time had come quietly to accept the eminent place endowments made hers by natural right. In her Notes at times her simplicity is amazing as well as refreshing:

Friends. Two for over seventy years—Martha Kunhardt and E. C. T.
My home on Lake Champlain. J.M.—fifty year friend.
My canine friends.
People whom I have known—five of them Presidents of the United States:
President Taft, President Wilson, President Coolidge, President Hoover,
President Roosevelt.

At the height of her success in 1931 Mary Woolley was asked what
her religion meant to her. Despite all the gaiety and laughter that
companionship with Mary Woolley brought, hers is one of the saddest
of replies to the question which most human beings ask sooner or later.
As she tried to think through this question it became a twofold inquiry
and she asked:

What *is* character? What *is* religion? Have they relationship or are
they independent one of the other? . . . Character of some kind is ines-
capable. We can no more get away from character than we can get away
from our bodies. It is a part of us, intangible but more real than the
tangible. The question is not "Has a human being character?" but "What
kind of character has he?"

In *What My Religion Means to Me* she wrote: "'I shall pass this
way but once—how can I make it a better way for others?' . . . [by]
the acquirement of habits, everything that adds to [our] strength . . ."
After that she went on to another question: "You may be willing to
follow to this point, to say 'I grant the importance of character, the
fact that it develops and all the rest, but what has that to do with
religion?' Well, what has it?" Her reply was:

My religion means to me *courage*. It takes courage to live today, courage to face the uncertainties, to meet the unexpected, to stand for the unpopular. The very breathlessness of our lives calls for this quality . . .
Unless I believed that . . . some way, some how, some time, all will be
right with the world, I wonder whether I could find the courage to live
at all.
Religion means to me strength to "stand against the drift". A "drift"
presents the most insidious of temptations: to be loyal to one's convictions; to hold a position on the unpopular side; to stand squarely on one's
own two heels, and not sidestep . . . I do not enjoy recalling the times
when I should have been outspoken and when I said nothing, the coward's
method of assent, standing aside "Till the multitude make virtue of the
faith they had denied."
My religion means to me comfort. "As one whom his mother comforteth,
so will I comfort you." How can we live without that assurance? We are
very like children, we grownups, so self-assured, so confident of ourselves
—until the deep waters sweep over us.
Lastly my religion means to me confidence, confident during the life
that now is, in the life that is to be. Do you remember the story of
Augustine's mission to Britain and the reception of the embassy in the

Kingdom of Northumbria . . . [when] one of the aged counselors . . . arose in the assembly, and said: "O King, man's life is like a bird, that, driven by the storm, flees from the darkness without and flying in by the open door flits for a few moments in the warmth and light of the dwelling, where the fire is glowing, and then hastily darts out again into the cold and darkness. Whence it comes, whither it goes, no one can tell. Such is the life of man . . ."

What does my religion mean to me? It means a blessed memory; a steadying power and a truer perspective; the courage that I sorely need and the comfort when even courage fails; assurance in the life that now is and of the life that is to come.

❋   ❋   ❋   ❋

Mary Woolley believed that opportunities for women in leadership must follow their education, for otherwise neither women's education nor their experience could ever come of age. The good and just people in her background and what might be called the spiritual habitat of her family were the sources of her unbreakable faith that human nature would work for justice to women as well as to men. If the soundness of her conviction was challenged, all she would ever say— and she said it often — was: "Human attitudes can and must be changed."

Believing as Mary Woolley did in the right of women to guide their own educational work and that the awakened and shared leadership of women with men in education and in government would increase knowledge, clean up government and find in internationalism the possibilities of world-wide peace, she labored as few men or women have ever worked for an equality of opportunity of women with men. It was in part because of her trained and wide historic vision that she was able to step with amazing swiftness out of old ruts and that, however catastrophic some of the events of her life were to be, she never huddled for protection from a headlong progress. In her work toward co-equal leadership among men and women and its resultant struggles, the conduct of Mary Woolley is itself an interesting comment on the behavior under pressure of some women.

Perhaps it can be said that the part which the American Association of University Women—this greatest of organizations in the educational progress of women—played in Mary Woolley's life was pivotal to her career.[1] In April of 1931 as president of the AAUW she opened its fiftieth anniversary celebration in Boston. After telling a good story about Alice Freeman Palmer, she went forward from picture to picture of the development of the AAUW from November 27, 1788, when Dr. Marion Talbot and sixteen other women founded the Association

of Collegiate Alumnae, up to 1931. And she closed with these sanguine
and dauntless words:

> As a result of this birthday party we may carry back to our respective
> groups all along the line inspiration from what has been accomplished,
> an even greater inspiration in the thought of what the future holds for
> the Association. What may we not do? Perhaps we have come to the
> world for such a time as this, to raise the whole plane of life of thinking
> human beings on the side of understanding not only among ourselves but
> among the women of the world.

It was characteristic of Mary Woolley, while in session with the
AAUW, to feel the need and find the time to write this note home:

> . . . before I start on the morning's work, a moment's chat.
> You can imagine what this week is like as I can imagine yours. Several
> people have inquired for you but it is hopeless to try to remember "who"!
> Last night's reception, following the pageant, was a mass of humanity.
> The program yesterday was well worth while but long and the evening
> of lightness was a welcome "let up".

In the evening of the day (April 10th) the *Springfield Republican*
called her by long distance, the editor saying there was a rumor she
was resigning the presidency of Mount Holyoke College. Was this
true? The "story" published in the *Republican* the next day included
her reply:

> How the report of a possible retirement got about is hard to say. When
> reached last night in Boston, . . . Miss Woolley said simply that she had
> made no public announcement to any effect and was not prepared to
> make any. Several trustees of the college, when interviewed, although
> they did not wish to be quoted personally, declared that they had re-
> ceived no resignation or intimation of a resignation to take effect in 1933,
> and that no action had been taken in the matter by the trustees.

But the rumors continued to be printed and discussed. As the third
decade of phenomenal achievement and increasing fame was closing
for Mary Woolley, the cry of "old fogey" was raised against one who
was always abreast and often ahead of her times. It was natural that
there should be widespread discussion about the "next president", but
for some obscure reason this discussion threatened to turn into con-
troversy. At the first meeting of the Board of Trustees in that new
academic year a proposal was made by the alumnae representatives
that a committee be appointed consisting of representatives of the
trustees, of the alumnae, and the faculty to secure a new president, a
procedure which would, of course, have led to "political chaos within
the body of the Alumnae." Unfortunately this proposal was based
upon an informal statement Mary Woolley herself had made when
plans were being discussed with regard to raising funds, and was

simply a statement of her plan to retire at seventy. Although it was
not then her *personal* wish to retire in the full-tide of her powers,
nevertheless the newspapers continued to carry reports to the effect
that she was resigning the presidency. All she herself said was that
she was not resigning, and the Board of Trustees said no resignation
had been received. But when Mary Woolley received from the Board
of Trustees the draft of a letter which they proposed to send out to
the alumnae, she realized that this little cloud no bigger than a man's
hand had not been imaginary. Twice in her letter of reply to the
trustees she wrote that she had *not* repeatedly expressed her wish to
retire, the second time in these words: "There has not been a repeated
expression of a desire to retire," and without expressed resentment
she suggested other alterations.[2]

Some of the local alumnae in close touch with the college were as
puzzled as Mary Woolley. The president of the Springfield Alumnae
Club, Mrs. Beatty, left no doubt about the position which local alumnae took when she said they felt "that if Mount Holyoke were to lose
President Woolley just at the time when it is about to celebrate a
century of pioneering in the field of higher education for women it
would be disastrous . . ." The only conclusion to be drawn was that
an attempt was being made to "edit" into public consciousness the
thought of Mary Woolley's retirement, and to force her to retire by
creating an impression that she was "leaving" because she wanted to
leave. Hurt and incredulous, Mary Woolley continued to ask herself
why this attempt was being made? By whom was it being led? And
for what reasons?[3]

CHAPTER 13

MR. HOOVER APPOINTS

"What can be done to limit this human wastage, to restore, to rebuild, in short, to substitute merciful construction for merciless destruction?"

The deadened sound of long distance telephoning was heard, followed by Mary Woolley's audible: "Oh yes, Miss Detzer, how are you? . . . You ask has Mr. Hoover called me—no, there has been no call from the White House."

Except for the continued low cluck-clucking of long distance while Miss Detzer talked, there was silence in the President's office. As Mary Woolley listened, the color in her cheeks deepened.

Finally she spoke: "Miss Detzer, this has come so without warning that I hardly know what to think or what to say except that I *do* thank you and the Women's International League for Peace and Freedom for your confidence in me. You say Secretary Stimson will call up from Washington in an hour or two?"

Again muted telephone sounds from Washington, and the message was finished. For a minute Mary Woolley sat on, motionless, looking out her office windows to the bare December elm trees of College Street. Then her right hand moved something on the desk but did not touch the buzzer of the outer office.

Instead she called a little helplessly: "Olive!"

"Yes, Miss Woolley," came the reply as Olive Copeland stepped in.

"What do you think Miss Detzer of the Women's International League has just said to me?"

"What did she say, Miss Woolley?"

"She said, 'If you are appointed by President Hoover to the Disarmament Conference at Geneva, we hope that you will accept the appointment.' Also Miss Detzer said that in an hour or so the Secretary of State would call from Washington to give the official invitation from the President."

"Oh, Miss Woolley!" Olive exclaimed.

"But, Olive, for the present this is strictly confidential."

Later, while engaged in dictation as the afternoon was closing, the telephone rang harshly.

"Oh, Miss Woolley!" exclaimed Olive—by this time even her New England calm a bit tossed about—"that must be the Secretary of State! . . . Just a minute, please," she continued, her hand over the receiver. "It isn't the Secretary of State, Miss Woolley, it's the Washington press."

"The Washington press? But . . .!" came the exclamation. Checking herself in the midst of a sentence, Miss Woolley spoke into the telephone: "Yes, this is Miss Woolley."

There was silence as long distance spoke, followed by Mary Woolley's reply: "No, I have had no invitation as yet to join the delegation to the conference, in fact, I have not even received any definite word that I am being considered."

At half past four that afternoon the list of American delegates to the Disarmament Conference was made public. Except for Dorothy Detzer's inquiry Mary Woolley had received no word from Washington, but already the news was on the street. In the to and fro of news pounding on their quiet doors tranquility was maintained because both the President and her Executive Secretary were New Englanders. As yet no official word had come—only the newsmen and women calling.

The story behind this story lay in the struggle of a brave and witty member of the Women's International League for Peace and Freedom. It was the morning of December 23, 1931, when she learned that President Hoover had decided not to appoint a woman—although the State Department had agreed to accept any woman all the women's organizations agreed upon and they had all agreed upon Mary Woolley. Through the noted newscaster, Drew Pearson, Mr. Hoover's decision became known to the League and Dorothy Detzer. The latter immediately went to see an Assistant Secretary of State. There followed a heated discussion about the State Department's "breaking faith with the women's organizations." But Miss Detzer had no success in getting the high official's interest until she raised the political implications in the Administration's failure to carry out its promises. When she reminded him of the coming elections and "that women and elephants never forget"—the Assistant Secretary decided to call the President. About half past one that same day he telephoned to say that the Delegation would be announced at 4:30 as originally planned and that Dr. Woolley's name would be among them.

When at the close of that afternoon Secretary of State Henry L. Stimson telephoned, Olive Copeland exclaimed: "Miss Woolley, this *is* the State Department calling now!"

On the following day, December 24th, the press from all parts of the country, despite Christmas pressures, beat its way by telegram, telephone and personal calls into Mary Woolley's office. To an early caller she replied: "I have been interested for a great many years in the whole subject of international relations, and in the substitution of international understanding and cooperation for the old theory of international brute force. But my participation in the conference will *not* mean my resignation as president of Mount Holyoke." For about a week to ten days every day had its "story", and Mary Woolley had a good press. Weeks before she had even packed her luggage for the ocean voyage to Geneva, annoyed by one reporter's curiosity about what she would say at the Geneva Conference, her brief reply was: "I shall be neither dumb nor garrulous."

Great was the rejoicing of the alumnae of the women's colleges over the appointment. No doubt there were partisans for a different appointment—there always are—but to use the words of the press the universal reaction was that if President Hoover was "trying to represent the enlightened will to peace among women throughout the country, he probably could not have made a more accurate choice," and that if it was the woman's point of view that was wanted, Mary Woolley could give it readily, for it was "bone of her bone and flesh of her flesh." Caroline McCormick Slade, peace worker and feminist, said in an interview that this was the biggest honor that had ever come to a woman in the United States. The excitement and satisfaction included not only Mount Holyoke College cubs, kittens and alumnae, but many of the great women and men of that decade. In her biography of Carey Thomas, President of Bryn Mawr College, Edith Finch recorded: "By 1931 a new note of something like despair about the international situation creeps into her letters; she had hoped, she said wistfully, that she would not have to see the world crumble though she had long realized that crumble it must." [1] For Miss Thomas the appointment of Mary Woolley to the Disarmament Conference was a "bright ray"; she at once urged Dr. Woolley to "recommend 'to the Nine Power Pact Nations and to the League of Nations' that they enforce economic boycott—above all in the matter of war supplies—upon all nations using force rather than arbitration to settle an international dispute."

Excitement among the Mount Holyoke alumnae—still in ignorance of the trustee-alumnae officer attack on Mary Woolley—rose to an all-time high as they basked in their leader's new international importance. Even the little cubs and kittens who would some day enter Mount

Holyoke took part in this excitement. Among those cubs and kittens were the two daughters, Jane and Lucy, of Lucy Jennings Dickinson, an alumna of Mount Holyoke, and to become President of the Federation of Women's Clubs. Both aunt and great-aunt of Mrs. LaFell Dickinson were alumnae. It was in Lucy Jennings' first years out as a Mount Holyoke alumna that the great-aunt came back for a fiftieth reunion and her aunt for the thirty-fifth, and it was then Mary Woolley had asked Lucy Jennings Dickinson to take charge of the fifty-year people—a group which proved to be so lively that Mrs. Dickinson was exhausted to the point of collapse. Now in all the excitement, her own Dickinson daughters had also become "lively".

On the morning the news of Mary Woolley's appointment came out, little daughter Jane had as usual gone downstairs early to read the newspaper. When she saw that the very leader of what might be called their family college tradition had been appointed by President Hoover to the Disarmament Conference, Jane tore through the rest of the article hastily.

Rushing upstairs to her mother who was still in bed and asleep, she banged violently on her mother's door, shouting: "Mr. Hoover has appointed Miss Woolley to the Disarmament Conference and the newspaper says she is eighty-six years old!"

At the first pound on her door Mrs. Dickinson woke with a start. Sharing Jane's enthusiasm for the appointment as she came out from sleep, Mrs. Dickinson knew there was something wrong in the child's statement.

"Jane," she asked, "what did you say?"

"I said," shouted Jane, "Mr. Hoover has appointed Miss Woolley to the Disarmament Conference and he says she's eighty-six years old!"

At that point Mrs. Dickinson objected: "'Eighty-six years old?' But, Jane, I'm sure Mr. Hoover didn't say any such thing. You must have made a mistake; I'm sure Miss Woolley is only sixty-eight."

"Well," Jane yelled defiantly through the door, "eighty-six or sixty-eight what is the difference!"

The "rouge" on Mary Woolley's cheeks at "eighty-six or sixty-eight what is the difference" was the rouge of health as she stepped about briskly, looking as if her maximum age was somewhere between forty and fifty. In her sixty-ninth year she was not tired, she was not flustered but relaxed and on excellent terms with herself; she was interested in all the to-do about the appointment. In an office in which now the telephone rang all day and telegrams and mail and state documents filled all the corners, Olive Copeland, too, stepped about briskly checking the work of additional assistant secretaries, while Mary Woolley calmly welcomed photographers and Klieg lights and reporters and their questions with no suggestion of anything but unhurried time and attention for all of the men and women of the press.

But unintentionally Mary Woolley's reticence sometimes gave rise to false impressions, as it did in one of the best of the "stories" about this first woman in our American democracy to represent Disarmament. This was the story by Eunice Fuller Barnard in the *New York Times* magazine section for January 3, 1932. Mrs. Barnard wrote: "Quite naturally and honestly, in spite of her self-effacing personality, she has a success complex, the outcome of what to the observer's eye seems a singularly smooth and triumphant life." This was written about a woman whose parental home life had been a never ending struggle to make ends meet; who in 1930, through no fault of her own and as she was nearing the close of her active academic life, had lost the savings of a lifetime; who had been blacklisted many times, including at that time by the Daughters of the American Revolution of which she was a member, and for her liberal and fearless advocacy of various forms of peace work and of justice. At the beginning of the very year in which Mr. Hoover's appointment was winning world-wide acclaim, in the college her leadership had built up from seminary status to one of the foremost colleges for women in the United States, an attack was launched against her by a powerful minority of the trustees.

Of the blacklisting by the Daughters of the American Revolution, Dr. Woolley had said at the beginning of the interview: "I can truthfully say that the woman who is not in favor of some new and more pacific basis for international relationship is an exception. Of course you may say," she added with a twinkle, "that the women who are not in favor keep away from me. But I don't think that is the case. . . . Moreover, I believe that part of women's strength and their effectiveness as peace advocates lies in the very fact that they have *not* had the experience in directing affairs that men have had. . . . Here, as many times before, women may rush successfully in where masculine angels fear to tread."

As Mrs. Barnard was taking her leave in the darkness of that late December afternoon, she was asking herself: "How much after all . . . could the diplomats of Europe and all their realism shake the serenity and faith of a Mary Woolley in the evolving good in human nature?"

"Faith in the evolving good in human nature?" Yes, just that; for Mary Woolley still had her unshakable faith in the good in human beings, and as Mrs. Barnard wrote: "an optimism at once serene and shrewd—that invincible New England conviction of the final victory of the right whether on the material or the spiritual plane."

Eight days later, when Dr. Woolley was interviewed by Harold Butcher of the New York Herald-Tribune, she again emphasized the part of women in the prevention of war: "There are pessimists who say, even before the delegates have met, that the Conference will be a failure. . . . I will not think of failure. The way in which one approaches a subject has a psychological effect. . . . Hundreds of thousands of women in the United States are taking the keenest interest in international affairs. They are studying international problems through such groups as the League of Women Voters, the Federation of Women's Clubs and the Association of University Women . . .

"In a group of men and women, hating war and wishing it could be eliminated, you will generally find that the men will agree that war is wrong without being able to show how it can be abolished. The women in the same group will say war is wrong; therefore it *must* be abolished . . . We ought to approach these international problems not as men or women but as human beings."

In the few weeks between her appointment on December 23rd and the sailing of the "President Harding" on January 20th, Mary Woolley was present in Washington at some of the preparatory meetings for the Geneva Disarmament Conference. For one week her headquarters were in Washington at the Club House of the A.A.U.W. On January 6th she wrote: "I have discovered that the 'President Harding' sails at three o'clock on the afternoon of the twentieth; that we land at Cherbourg; and that there will probably be an Easter recess early in April, giving the delegates a chance to talk with their home governments. Beyond that, no one's information seems to go, except that the Conference will reconvene early in May, and, I suspect, go on into the summer!

"Yesterday afternoon and this morning were devoted to generals and admirals and their 'experts'. . . . A Mrs. Roberts of the Secretary of State's office has been detailed to me. She is competent, I am told, and seems very nice."

On the evening of January 19th, the night before the ship sailed for Cherbourg, at the dinner arranged by the A.A.U.W. of which Mary Woolley was president, and with delegations and guests from many organizations, hundreds of women were assembled to do her honor at the Hotel Roosevelt. With Mary Woolley was Dr. Ethel B. Dietrich, an ardent feminist and economist who lived at the President's House. In her speech of gratitude for their confidence in her, Mary Woolley stressed these words: "There may be times when it will be necessary to remember that in the definition of 'achievement' the direction in which we are moving is as important as the point reached."

The day following, signed petitions for Geneva were taken aboard ship by three delegates of the Women's International League for Peace and Freedom—Katharine Devereux Blake, Hannah Clothier Hull and Mrs. Victor L. Berger. And still another unofficial delegation had as its leaders Mrs. Frank Day Tuttle, chairman of the board of directors of the League of Nations Association; Mrs. Ben Hooper of Oshkosh, of the General Federation of Women's Clubs; and Elvira Fradkin. All-told, in the care of these delegations were sixteen bundles of petitions bearing 618,415 signatures representing eleven national women's groups.

As Mary Woolley was leaving on the "President Harding" that afternoon of January 20th, delegations went out on the boat to Quarantine. Then Ruth Nichols, dipping the wings of her plane in salute, flew out to the vessel with flowers for Dr. Woolley from Mrs. Roosevelt and the Women's International League. Making a spectacular landing, Miss Nichols boarded the ship with this message from the League: "We trust you not to allow technicalities to involve or mislead you. You have been chosen for a great mission at a critical time. You carry with you 400,000 signatures of American citizens who demand genuine disarmament now. They express their confidence in you. They send you out with Godspeed. When you come home victorious, you will have inaugurated a new era upon a stricken earth."

❂   ❂   ❂   ❂

Les Bergues, Geneva
January 31, 1932

. . . When I finished my letter Tuesday, it looked like a late arrival but the sea calmed down and we were only a few hours behind time at Cherbourg. There we were met by the mayor, the president of the Chamber of Commerce and a few other functionaries, who presented Mrs. Swanson and me with big bunches of yellow mimosa and deep pink carnations; treated us to tea and a polite conversation of mingled French and English.

The ride to Paris was in a European Pullman, very comfortable; Admiral and Mrs. Hepburn, with her sister and one other person and I had a big compartment with chairs and tables, where our dinner was served.

We reached Paris just before midnight, where we were met not only by a group of cameras, taking ferocious pictures, but also a group of attaches who conveyed Senator and Mrs. Swanson and me to the Embassy for the night. The Ambassador and Mrs. Edge had delicious lemonade and sandwiches for us and after an hour's talk, I found bed just as comfortable as it always is after a voyage. My room, by the way, was next to the one they call "Lindbergh's", occupied after his flight.

I had breakfast in my room and at 10:15 we left for the train, accompanied by a large section of the Embassy, led by their Chief, and met by the inevitable cameras. The journey to Geneva was, on the whole, restful, the Swansons and I in a compartment and everybody, apparently, content to "stay put".

Pessimists grow on every bush over here—the Chinese-Japanese situation not adding to the cheerfulness—and the cultivation of a pollyanna disposition clearly is one's bounden duty. When we said goodbye to the nice old mayor of Cherbourg, he said: "Good luck to you at the Conference. Disarm everybody—except France!" Last evening on the train talking to M. Julienne, one of the leading journalists of France, I said: "Disarmament would help in this financial depression." "Armaments are not responsible for that," he answered, "Germany's failure to pay her debts is the cause of the world depression!"

After landing at Cherbourg and being welcomed by its mayor, the United States Delegation left for Paris, where they spent less than twelve hours. With the Delegation were thirteen trunks full of petitions which were to be presented to the Geneva Conference. Mary Woolley, the only woman of the United States Delegation, reported the Paris edition of the *New York Herald-Tribune*, "beamed her enthusiasm as the express pulled out" from the Gare Saint Lazare for Geneva with a few dogs belonging to the Delegation, tons of personal luggage and the thirteen petition trunks. . . . As Mary Woolley wrote: "For years 'Geneva' had been for me a magic word." When she reached Geneva and Les Bergues on that first night of January 29th, she set down excitedly: "Arrival Geneva in late evening. Met by large group, *cameras everywhere*! Introduced to delightful suite at Hotel Les Bergues." The quotation marks had vanished from the "magic word" as she made herself at home.

How did Mary Woolley impress others and what did they say about her? So far as she was concerned, dignity had little to do with honors or with office and everything to do with the value of human nature itself—her own and that of others. To her colleagues at the Disarmament Conference how did she seem? Early and late there was considerable enthusiasm about her presence, her personality, her symbolic importance. In her clipping books she treasured the following absurd lines written about her by Laurence Willson of New Hampshire:

> Whilst walking down the street one day,
> I overheard another say,
> "Herb's sending Claude among the Swiss
> To guarantee our foreign bliss.
> He's going to make them hock their rifles,
> And maybe dicker over trifles,
> Herb couldn't 'a' picked a better guy,

> The European hash to fry—
> With Mary to wash the cups and sassers,
> He'll sagely counsel his harassers;
> From what he wants you can't budge Claude
> A whit more than proverbial Maude."

Metaphorically speaking, Mary Woolley did indeed "wash the cups and sassers". A niece said of John Dewey that no one "knew Uncle John" until he helped them wash the dishes. In Dr. Woolley's "dish washing" she had—even as President Hoover had—the greatest admiration for Hugh Gibson. These two had much in common—including a sense of humor! When Ambassador Dawes described diplomacy as "easy on the head but Hell on the feet," Hugh Gibson retorted: "Well it depends which you use most."

It was recorded somewhat later by the *Washington Post* that when the cynical males of the Washington peace front heard of Mary Woolley's female intrusion upon their group, their faculties were confounded and desperate. Reportedly they said to one another "that perhaps they could use her to pacify the peace organizations; and that unless you had survived the London Naval Conference, no one would believe 'how exigent these women can be.' "

They expected a "frail old lady, the faded voice of the scholar, the pedant's stoop," but from the train on that day of arrival of the Delegation in Paris, "stepped a sturdy figure, upright, vigorous. Her eyes were cheerful, but piercing. She answered the correspondents in a quiet tone as efficient as any sword; she learned more about her interviewers than they learned about her, and she never forgot.

The Russian Church at Geneva to which Mary Woolley refers in her letters had a famous choir and the ticket-demands for its Easter midnight service exceeded the supply. Nevertheless, a friend secured places for her and Theodore Marriner. The latter, a State Department official, remembered that people don't sit down in an Orthodox Church and cautioned the other men: "We mustn't overtax her strength." In this connection the *Washington Post* reported:

Unostentatiously, a chair was tucked behind her; she, standing, shook her head to her host's urging that she use the chair. At the end of the first half-hour she shook her head. An hour: Marriner was pale, his 170 pounds swaying—she shook her head.

She stood through the whole two hours' service, went to bed at 3 a.m. At 9, she attended a committee meeting, fresh as Easter lilies.

"But I'm afraid she'll be finicky," Hugh Wilson, United States Minister to Switzerland, worried. "She doesn't smoke; she'll object to our nicotinized caucuses."

"This Doctress American," wailed a prominent Pole, "she is prohibitionist. She will give teas without whisky-soda; teas with tea?"

After a week, Wilson cheered: "She insists on sitting between Swanson's cigar and my pipe."

The Pole reported: "Actually tea—and non-alcoholic cider, which, after five Geneva years, I did not know could be found here. I inquired would it be a breach of good manners should I insert into that delicious cider the cognac by physicians' orders carried with me. And she said: "Monsieur, even in America are invalids who carry pocket-flasks."

In their delegations when men find themselves with a woman in their midst, they always hope that she will be a "yes-woman". But this time what had they? Their answer was: "If we protest," an old school diplomat complained, "she just closes her eyes and says, 'You don't understand; there is a new spirit in the world. Besides, the President told me to work for the maximum of reduction, and I propose to work for that'."

At the convening in Geneva the individual who had had the first "say" about Mr. Hoover's appointment of a woman was not a delegate but none other than Will Rogers. While unofficially engaged with the Disarmament Conference in hoisting one folly after another with a petard, and as for several weeks Will Rogers kept up his running fire of witty comment, he wrote home: "You would like her," And in the following letter to the *New York Times* on February 1: "Our female delegate, Miss Woolley, is the outstanding novelty. I had an hour and a half's chat with her this afternoon. Didn't know whether to call her Miss, Mrs., Professor, Doctor or what, so I called her 'Doc', and 'Doc' and I got along ɡ eat. I had taken an interpreter, but I didn't need him . . . Thirty million women of the world have hope and faith in her common sense versus diplomacy. It's no joking matter getting the world to disarm. Maybe a woman can do it. It's a cinch men can't. So good luck to you 'Doc'." On February 2nd, Will Rogers wrote: "Went into another huddle today with Doc Woolley. I am strong for Doc."

❋   ❋   ❋   ❋

How did things begin at Geneva? It is possible to reply in Mary Woolley's own words:

> They began in the great Hall of the Reformation the afternoon of February the second, 1932, at four o'clock instead of three, the hour's delay caused by the emergency session of the Council of the League of Nations, to consider the acute Sino-Japanese situation at Shanghai.
> There were . . . blinding lights from the movie picture cameras that afternoon . . . In [the pictures] were included not only delegates and the group of attaches, experts, secretaries, accompanying the delegates, but also "the press"—newspaper correspondents from all over the world, with

camera men and "sketchers" innumerable; unofficial groups, representing the peace organizations of the world, national and international; I was told repeatedly, although it was not possible to corroborate it, some representatives of groups that were distinctly *not* for peace, in other words, the great munitions interests; and last, but by no means least, "just people", an endless procession limited only by the impossibility of securing tickets.

Delegation of the   GENERAL DISARMAMENT CONFERENCE
United States of America   Geneva
.February 6.32

The Conference opened an hour late, Tuesday, in order to have a meeting of the Council, which was most impressive. Mr. Thomas of Great Britain, reading the statement with regard to Japan, adding that the United States would act in conjunction with G. Britain. The representatives of France, Italy and Germany followed and the meeting was a most solemn one, Japan's representative stated that Japan was pleased that the Western Powers had taken this action on her, Japan's, initiative and were coming to *her* defense! Everyone hoped that that was the beginning of the end, but I think that they are not now so sure. Mr. Gibson told me this noon that he had given up going to the mountains for the week-end, since the situation was "too jumpy". He also said that Matsudaira, formerly Minister to Washington and an old friend, is very distressed—but helpless, as the military are in control. Well, everybody hopes that Japan will soon cease being "quite mad".

The opening session was solemn. Mr. Henderson is not well and his speech lacked "rousements" although solid in substance and fine in spirit.

I was put on the Committee on petitions and a long meeting was held Wednesday. The representative from Chile was not in favor of a public and formal meeting, so I had a chance to make my maiden speech! The Committee voted down Mobaldes-Mandeville and this morning there was a great gathering and presentation. When I reached my room, I found an orchid and maiden hair, tied with the ribbon of which I am sending a sample and an exquisite little traveling clock, dull blue with gold tooling and a gold face . . .

Tardieu's statement, which we will probably discuss Monday, is causing excitement only second to the Sino-Japanese situation. Mr. Gibson thinks that he is trying to do one of two things, either throw a monkey-wrench into the machinery and thus disrupt the Conference or be able to say to the Left before the election that he had proposed to the Conference their plan and "it" would have none of it.

February 13.1932

. . . The week has been one of speeches, you know that, and I am not going into them in detail. The last was Dr. Yen's at the close of the session this morning, and I must confess it has struck my deepest note of depression — during the week. Very moderate, in perfect English, he stated what the Chinese attitude toward disarmament would naturally be —but if the sanctity of contracts and the restraint of a belligerent nation could not be accomplished, what was there for China to do but arm to

protect her rights. I can only hope that the solemnity of his address &
the seriousness of the situation will have an effect.

It is disheartening that the League has not taken effective action. The
reason is evidently in the attitude of the governments comprising the
League—but the Council should act with strong recommendations, even if
the governments fail to put them into effect.

Every day from ten to one has been spent at the Plenary Session. The
desks of the Etats Unis D'Amerique are six rows back, just in front of
France, Tardieu sitting behind Mr. Gibson. In front of us is Denmark
and at my left, Finland. Yes . . . I wore my purple gown the first day!

All Monday afternoon the Delegation worked on making changes in
the speech and telephoning to Washington for authorization. If you will
"cross your heart" and not tell anyone, I suggested an *absolute* prohibition
of lethal gas and bacteriological warfare—which the State Department approved. Mr. Gibson gave the speech well. I liked also Escolando's
(Spain), Grandi's, Litvinoff's—etc.

The Delegation is fine to work with—gentlemen from start to finish.
Speaking of delegations, the women were fine. On shipboard, most careful not to take time. The one conference was called at Senator Swanson's
suggestion. Probably the press on board did not have much to say and,
as you inferred, "played that up".

What was the opening day of the Disarmament Conference like?

The very simplicity of that opening day, [February second] helped to
make it impressive; even more, the great audience, representing almost all
the peoples on earth; and most of all the significance, the realization of
the hopes and the possibilities centered in that gathering, gave to it a
dignity and a solemnity not easy to put into words.

Confident from the very beginning that women would win the peace
in the end, she was certain too that the influence of women and their
peace work would make themselves felt in this conference: "Women
rush in where diplomats fear to tread and do a lot to make this world
a better place to live in." But shortly after her arrival in Geneva so
insoluble had the problem of presentation or "staging" of the world-
wide signed petitions for peace seemed to the Committee on Petitions—
except for Mary Woolley, who was the only woman member on that
committee—that they had almost decided, because of the immensity
of the problem, to drop the issue of presentations altogether. How,
on one of the first days of the Disarmament Conference, was it possible
for any committee to handle petitions which in the aggregate represented not millions but hundreds of millions of human beings? No, the
men agreed, it was virtually impossible! Whereupon Mary Woolley,
who had quietly listened to the men, took up the struggle on behalf
of a hearing for the petitioners, and carried the majority of the committee with her.

Early on that morning of February 6, 1932, one tractor-drawn truck of petitions signed by the representatives of forty-five million human beings had drawn up outside the League of Nations building. With the boxes and bundles of signatures were fifteen women—including Amy Woods and Anne Zueblin—carrying blue and white banners "for peace" from the twelve organizations which formed the Disarmament Committee of the Women's International Organizations. On this day the plans by Rosa Manus of Holland, as secretary of the Committee, for the forty-five million women they represented, were being carried into action.

An hour or so later, in the center of the great Geneva Hall, four hundred women marchers representing international organizations were standing at ease, two by two, their coats crossed by silk bands giving the countries they represented. Mary Dingman, chairman of the Disarmament Committee of the Women's International Organizations, was speaking. The marchers stood at attention as she spoke. Facing the delegates, her voice was carrying to the furthest corners of the great hall:

> . . . we declare that the will of the people is for peace . . . We are weary of the unending sacrifices expected of us for purposes of destruction . . . [we] are determined that a way . . . must somehow be found; [we] are knocking at the doors and [our] call must be answered . . . [The] mighty . . . force of public opinion . . .

As Mary Dingman closed, the waiting delegates took up their orderly march; right, left, right, left, firm and even in step they marched down the hall to the Tribune where Kathleen Courtney and Rosa Manus received the bundles, announcing first in English, then in French the country from which the petitions came.

In *Vox Populi* it was written: "They could bring only a few bundles from each country, as a symbol: for instance, the 2,100,000 petitions from Great Britain had to be represented by a few sample packets. Even so, the pile on the table mounted higher and higher, till it began to topple over. Again and again the bundles were carried away in baskets, to make room for more. The President leaned over from his seat to watch. Everyone stirred. At last the pile was complete."[2]

Next came the International Union of Catholic Women Organizations, Madame Steenbergher-Engerings speaking as president. Then in the name of all churches Dr. Joachim Mueller. For the students' organizations two young men spoke: James Frederick Green and Jean Dupuy. As one of these young men was speaking, Count Apponyi, 84 years old and Europe's grand old man, leaned forward attentively to hear young Green say: "Organized slaughter does not settle a dispute. It merely silences an argument."

As the marchers passed Mary Woolley her shoulders were erect, lips quiet, eyes shining, face relaxed and happy. The presentation of petitions by four hundred marching women with their white and green arm bands, carrying their ribbon and flag-decorated bundles of eight million signatures for peace, was her dream of peace coming ever closer to fulfillment. At the Tribune as the speeches and the presentations were being completed on that day "delegates, spectators, and participants" were "caught up in one great irresistible force" for peace, and a European writer said afterwards: "We have often heard of public opinion; today we saw it." Even as the event was proceeding and after it was over, the names of millions of other women demanding reduction in armaments and expenditure were still pouring into the headquarters offices.

At Geneva there was a strong if small international group of officially appointed women: Margery Corbett-Ashby, representing Great Britain; Miss Winnifred Kydd, Canada; Mme. Anne Paradowska-Szelagowska, Poland; Dr. Paulina Luisi, Uruguay, and Mary Woolley. They were all women of experience accustomed to face and to deal with facts. Together these and other leaders fought for disarmament with a weapon it takes more courage and skill to use than does the trigger finger on a gun; unwavering faith in the essential decency, kindness and generosity of human beings. In meeting after meeting of the Disarmament Conference these four women spoke out, and there what Mary Woolley had stated she would be, she was—"neither dumb nor garrulous".

CHAPTER 14

LETTERS HOME FROM GENEVA

*"For this new city of hopes—this city of understanding and good
will among the nations, we must exercise patience."*

In the following letters Mary Woolley continues to tell her story
intimately on the Disarmament Conference. Again and again in these
letters what she writes is like a quizzical smile, direct and warm-
hearted, and without a word of cynicism or a line of expediency.
There are a few exclamations such as: "My, human nature is queer!"
And definitely there are shrewd appraisals of human character as well
as unbroken loyalty to women and their work. Also in these letters
are many pictures of value in contemporary history: among others,
President Hoover, Secretary of State Stimson, Hugh Gibson, Ambassador Yen (once Premier of China), Dr. Beneš, and a young man named
John Foster Dulles, then earning his shoulder straps in internationalism.
Mary Woolley wrote home:

February 14.32
Walter Lippmann is to be here two or three weeks writing for the Herald-
Tribune. He is a close friend of Mr. Davis, who tells me that he thinks
his articles will help by their influence over the American people.

February 21, 1932
This is to be an "entre nous" for the household paragraph. Mrs. Corbett Ashby lunched with me in my room yesterday that we might really
talk. She feels that Great Britain and the United States ought to pull
together for a real gain, even at sacrifices. This afternoon Mr. Davis and
I are having tea with Mrs. Corbett Ashby, and Lord Snowdenderry, heading the British delegation while Sir John Simon is in London on the Far
East problem. As you probably know, Ramsay MacDonald is not yet sufficiently recovered to be here . . . Tuesday evening Mr. & Mrs. Davis invited the Delegation to dine with Walter Lippmann, and a similar evening
followed. Tuesday at Madame D'Arcis' lovely home, it was a feminine
talking "fest"—all on big questions. Thursday, at the International Club
luncheon, when Count Apponyi spoke, I sat next to Professor Rappard and
Friday night at the disarmament dinner next to Dr. Beneš. Friday noon,
Mr. Tuck, First Secretary of our Embassy, gave a luncheon for Count and
Countess Apponyi and asked me to be hostess, which gave me a chance to

sit next to the Count, who is the "grand old man" of Europe—next to Briand.

March 6, 1932

It has been—and is— a tense week. I did not go out until Wednesday when I motored for an hour, but since Thursday morning I have *lived* at the Assembly! That afternoon Dr. Yen spoke for over an hour. During the French translation Mrs. Davis, Mrs. Swanson and I "slipped out" to a little tea room and then returned for Matsudaira's answer — weak as water! . . . Yesterday I sat from ten o'clock until half after one, from three until six-thirty listening to the smaller powers—Norway, Colombia, Mexico, Sweden, Finland, the Netherlands, Denmark, Switzerland, Spain, Estonia, Czechoslovakia, Greece, Persia, Uruguay, Portugal—speaking, in no uncertain terms in support of League action . . .

March 11, 1932

Mr. and Mrs. Davis and I drove back together and we agreed that it was a great moral victory for the League. For a week, I have sat "glued" to the chairs in the Assembly, listening to endless speeches, being stirred by the small powers—last week Saturday and Tuesday—and depressed— Monday—by the "big" ones. What I am about to say, is for "the family" only—that is, Mr. Davis and Mr. Wilson have had more to do with the drafting of a resolution that should say something, than the outside world is likely to know. Sir John Simon has been eager to "play with" the United States, and today, after the resolution was passed, came up to our Delegation and said: "Well, we crossed all the 't's' and dotted all the 'i's' didn't we?", as pleased as punch! Tonight, he and Lady Simon are having a private dinner—guests, Dr. Yen, Matsudaira, and Mr. and Mrs. Davis! I think it shows pluck and I must confess "Sir John" has gone up in my estimation.

The week has been a solemn one. Monday afternoon Briand's death was announced and the entire assemblage stood while tributes were paid by M. Hymans, the Chairman, and Paul Boncour. Many, including Mr. Gibson, have gone tonight, for the funeral. I am glad that the action came today, a dramatic coincidence.

This morning while our Delegation filled the front row "behind the rope", next to Senator Swanson sat Litvinoff! I would give a great deal to have a movie, to show the United States Senate!

I am glad that I planned to stay here for a week of the recess. Membership on the Budgetary Commission is no sinecure. I can appreciate the feeling of Solomon's baby! On one side my army advisor, Major Ord, not enthusiastic; the state advisor, Mr. Reber, somewhat sceptical; Captain van Keuren, of the Navy, whom I have not yet seen on the subject. On the other side, my friend, Sydney Strong, who has no use for anyone who does not embrace Litvinoff's views—without question!

Walter Lippmann came in for an half hour before leaving, Thursday night and gave me some good suggestions . . . The four members of the Delegation represent four types; Mr. Gibson, friendly, witty, somewhat cynical; Mr. Wilson, thoughtful, quiet, hard-working, not over optimistic; Senator Swanson, genial, warm-hearted, *extremely nationalistic*; Mr. Davis, eager to go all the way, but realizing that it is a condition, not a theory, which confronts us, bringing all his international experience, which is great, to bear on these questions, caring only for accomplishment, not an iota for recognition.

March 17th. (St. Patrick's)

Well, as you probably know, our recess has been extended until Monday the 11th to cover the German elections, with the hope that Hindenburg will be elected. Hitler would surely throw a monkey-wrench into the international machinery . . . Mr. Gibson's resolution on "speeding up" after return, was passed and we have hopes that three months—from April 11 to the middle of July, may see something accomplished . . .

Mr. Davis sails tomorrow by the "Bremen", getting back on the eleventh, in order to take Mrs. Davis, who is expecting a grandchild, but primarily (entre nous) to confer with the administration. The delegation wishes to go further than it is authorized . . . Mrs. D. told me that one of their relatives said: "When Norman once gets his teeth in, he never lets go!" You can visualize the scene in the White House about next week, Thursday! Here's good luck to Mr. D.'s dental efforts!

The Lindberghs are constantly in the thoughts of people here. Every day my first glance at the "Herald" is with the hope of good news.

Grand Hotel Bellevue, Monnetier-Mornex
(Haute-Savoie)
3.19.32

. . . it is four o'clock Saturday afternoon. Mrs. Roberts and I motored out—three quarters of an hour drive from Geneva—then took quite a walk, on "route du Grand Saleve" and now are sitting in the sun-parlor.

This is a simple, clean hotel—over the border in France, with a lovely view, which is somewhat to be taken on faith this afternoon. We are hoping that the clouds will lift by tomorrow morning. In the afternoon we motor back.

There goes the radio That and the talking of some French children playing are the only sounds. A Frenchman near us is having tea and his wife is knitting; in the corner a young woman is reading and having tea at the same time. I suspect the few hours of quiet will be good for me. Next week I "aim" to do a lot of work before going to Paris.

Since I have been writing, Sato and I suppose, his wife and two young daughters, have come in for tea and are at the next table. He does not look very happy. The children are absorbed in honey and jam and oblivious to the woes of the world.

Sunday Noon—Les Bergues

Back again in time for lunch in front of an open fire in my room, which seemed more appealing than the Bellevue. It was a lovely drive down, only half an hour, with the sun shining on the snow-caps of the lower mountains. Mt. Blanc refused to show herself this morning.

My conscience smites a bit when I recall Sir John Simon, whose weakness, Mr. Davis thinks, is lack of moral courage. Not strange with a Parliament that the progressive British do not hesitate to call "Conservative, mainly nit-wit". I do not need to add that these "Observations" are confidential! Sir John certainly did his best in the Sino-Japanese affair.

Friday evening

It has been a lovely day. This noon we—Mrs. Roberts and I—motored
to a restaurant up in the mountains, with a lovely view, for luncheon.
The rest of the day we worked hard. I have prepared two talks for Paris
and dictated a lot of letters . . .

Do not pin your faith to . . . He said to Mr. Medofsky, one of our staff:
"You can't tell the truth. You have to say what people want to hear!"

Reid Hall
The American University Women's Paris Centre
4, Rue de Chevreuse, Paris (6')
Easter Monday, 3.28.32

I left Geneva at two-eighteen, arrived at eleven-thirty, Paris time; had
a compartment to myself—and apparently, the whole car, spoke only to
guards and waiter, in my "special" lingo part French, mainly English—
and had more absolute quiet than for the last two months. At the station
I was met by Miss Leet, Mary Virginia Horner and Mr. Pell, the last-
named bringing us over in his car.

Reid Hall is lovely . . . a rambling French mansion, around three sides
of an open court. My rooms and the little "salon" in which I am writing
—"reserved" for me this week as is a compartment—open onto the paved
court, where ivy and some red blossoming plants, give the impression of
summer. I have been awakened some mornings by the birds, although
right in Paris. Already I feel rested. There is, inevitably, a strain at
Geneva, which I realize more when away from it . . .

Yesterday was a nice day—beginning with breakfast, which had two
Easter eggs on the tray, one "hard-boiled" with dyed red shell. The other,
chocolate. When I came back from Church, I found a *big* chocolate egg
—with a little yellow chicken on top—which the chef had made.

March 31, 1932

. . . I am sad over little Cecco's going. I love that Birdie and I cannot
bear to think of not seeing and hearing him again. Only yesterday noon
I was talking about him to Madame Geraux—the wife of "Pertinax" who
travels about with two birds and three dogs! I am constantly meeting
dog-lovers over here. Miss Leet has a cunning little one "Gillie", given
her by Miss Gildersleeve.

Les Bergues
Geneva
April 8, 1932

We are all glad that Mr. Stimson is coming. Mr. Gibson is going to
speak, probably on Monday, making several concrete proposals for action
and there are some other proposals "up the sleeve" of the Delegation.
He read me his speech this morning and I lunched with him and Mr.
Wilson, talking over things in general.

Sunday, April 10.32

The Church bells are ringing, but I have time to talk with you before
I start . . . I have been very busy since returning from Paris. Dictation
takes much time. Official letters keep up and the cables increase. *Six*
under my door when I arose this morning.

Delegation of the   GENERAL DISARMAMENT CONFERENCE
United States of America   Geneva
April 16.32

Saturday evening and the end of a full week. The papers have probably given a resume of the events, but the "side shows" do not always figure—although that is not the fault of the reporters!

Mr. Gibson's speech Monday afternoon was fine. He talked it over with us before recess, and read it the morning of the day it was given, so I was fairly familiar with it, but it sounded even better when delivered. It was warmly received by every one except our friend M. Tardieu. During the giving, Mr. Marriner said to me: "Our French friends are about to expire from wrath" and that was almost literally true of their leader, not of Paul Boncour and some of the others, however. Sir John Simon delivered a gallant "second" as did President Molta of Switzerland, and several others, including Nadolny of Germany, Madariaga, the representatives of Brazil and Turkey; when the representative of Brazil was speaking, Tardieu, who sits next to Mr. Gibson at the Commission Meetings, inquired: "What have you done for coffee, in Brazil?" He certainly was mad, M.T., but he has calmed down somewhat . . .

Mr. Stimson came in to see me this morning; we had a meeting of the Delegation and tomorrow night we dine with him and Mrs. Stimson at the charming Chateau taken for them.

It is good to have Mr. Davis back again. He is enthusiastic about Mr. Stimson, rather fine for a former Under-Secretary of State in a Democratic administration.

. . . Today I have had a lot of official mail . . . I have had by mail and cable 1261 petitions—some of them representing hundreds, even thousands . . .

4.22.32

. . . can you suggest a synonym for "patience". The thing of which we need the most? The other day at a Delegation Meeting, Mr. Stimson said: "Tomorrow Ramsay MacDonald will arrive, chock full of fears, and the next day Tardieu, chock full of politics." I thought of a remark when I was in the Far East: "Japan is the France of the East." They, France and Japan, have certainly made the difficulties for this Conference.

You are right in thinking that there are difficulties even in being a woman: I must be effective, but not aggressive; womanly but not womanish; equal to social obligations but always on hand for the business ones; informed, but unable to take my pipe and join other "pipers" in the corridors during translations—et cetera, et cetera! However, all the males are good to me and so are the females . . .

Mr. and Mrs. Henderson gave a luncheon Tuesday. I sat between Mr. H. and Dr. Yen, the latter rather blue about Manchuria, poor man. Last evening, Countess Kreiberg, whom I often see as a Correspondent, came in to tell me about a visit to Munich and the way her old acquaintances —royalty as well as nobility—were living in small apartments with a fire part of the day, to save fuel. Anyway, Litvinoff looks plump enough. I am sure he is not living on half rations!

4.29.32

It has been a somewhat hectic week. As you probably know from the papers, the stage was set for a Conference of the five powers at Bessinge; MacDonald and Bruening were here, Grandi was ready to come on call, and Tardieu had promised to be present when word came that he had laryngitis! . . . The Prussian elections have not simplified the situation and the French are enough to try the patience of Job! Well, it is a wheel within a wheel and that quality beginning with "p" [patience] which I am under bonds *not* to mention, is increasingly needed.

Last evening Mr. Davis gave a brilliant dinner here for the Secretary and Mrs. Stimson. Among the guests were Dr. Bruening and von Bulow and the latter, with whom I had a little talk, was manifestly troubled because the conference had to be called off . . .

I sat next to Sir Eric Drummond who said: "You know, I should like to see this question handled by a conference of women. How do you think that they would do it?"—And I said "Of one thing I am sure; they would cut off some of the corners." I am sure they would. The General Commission approved the principle of "qualitative disarmament" and referred to the technical commission on land, sea and air, the listing of "weapons of aggression". Those commissions have been "sitting" all the week and are gradually transferring everything from "aggression" to "defense" columns! Commander Kinkaid spent two hours in my room this morning, along similar lines of argument. It took only a short time at Versailles to remove from Germany what the allies considered "aggressive weapons"! I think that a conference of women would say: "In order to have 'qualitative disarmament,' all we have to do is to apply to other nations, the German restrictions."

5.5.32

In spite of no meetings of the General Commission, I am busy all the time, working on reports, dictating, and seeing people. Every "tea hour" this week has been devoted to the last pursuit: one day "Dorothy Thompson" (Mrs. Sinclair Lewis) another, Mrs. Moorhead, of the Foreign Policy Association; this afternoon Mrs. Morgan and Miss Howard, of the American Committee; tonight Princess Radziwill. Do not imagine that these are purely "social engagements", far from it! I lunched with Mr. Davis yesterday and he said that one of the most important things is "keeping up the morale". I cannot understand this attitude of going down into one's boots whenever things fail to be on the crest of the wave. One does not give up in time of war because there are difficulties; why do it in this crusade? . . .

There are lighter sides. This is the Geneva tale of the gathering of the Powers. Mr. Stimson: "Mr. Bruening, Germany will have equality; Mr. Grandi, Italy will have parity; Mr. MacDonald, Great Britain will have freedom from giving guarantees." Tardieu: "And what will France have, Mr. Secretary?" "Nothing." "Well then, I will have a sore throat."

The poor leaders of the Powers have certainly had "sore throats" or their equivalent. Mr. Stimson was "shaky" from the effects of the grippe all the time he was here and Dr. Bruening was on the ragged edge. Only

Grandi seems hale and husky. I hope that the last named is just as nice and frank as he seems.

5.10.32

The swing to the Left in the French elections will have nobody knows *what* effect upon the Disarmament Conference. Yesterday noon I lunched with Mr. Wilson and Mr. Dulles, and they thought it would be uncertain, probably unfavorable; last night I dined at Mr. Gerig's and the guests there thought it would be favorable; tonight I had coffee with Mr. and Mrs. Tuck and he thought "favorable". But the last-named would take anyone in preference to Tardieu! So would I.

Wednesday p.m. May 11

. . . It sometimes looks as if we might spend the remainder of our lives discussing technicalities! When the Soviet representatives "spun a long spiel" this afternoon on the necessity of accurate reports on all that private industries are doing in the line of "War Potentials", I gave up! . . . However, I think now it is as certain as one can be of anything, that the Conference will adjourn in July, probably the middle . . .

Sunday evening, May 15.32

The drives to and from Grenoble yesterday and today, were lovely. Mountains all the way, often snow-capped; the fields green as emeralds; horse chestnuts, lilacs, wisteria, apple, pear and cherry trees, in full bloom; radiant sunshine and clear air, which made the highest peaks visible—the word "ravishing" is not extravagant. The road went through Annecy, Aix-les-Bains, Chamberg and innumerable French villages, a three hour drive, at a pretty brisk pace. Mrs. Morgan went up with me, but I came home alone, and had nothing to do except feast my eyes.

May 20.32

At six tonight I meet "The Press" to talk more in detail along the same line, the foreign as well as our home correspondents. I have received in the neighborhood of two thousand letters and cables, representing millions, and it is a really marvelous collection of "human documents". I read a few of them to our Delegation the other day, including a paragraph from your letter concerning "appalling depression" et cetera. *Between us,* I sent last week a hundred or more, with a letter, to Mr. Hoover. I thought that the poor man should know what the American people are thinking and not simply what the politicians "choose" to pour into his ears!

One of the nicest luncheons imaginable was Wednesday, at the Sweetsers', in honor of Viscount and Lady Cecil. There were only six other guests— among them two of our nice correspondents, Stewart Brown—of the United Press—and Mr. Whittaker of the Herald-Tribune, and Lord Robert talked freely of what he thought the Conference might do. We had coffee out of doors and sat for a long time, in the radiant sunshine looking out toward Mt. Blanc and the Lake. Again *entre nous*—Lord Robert thinks it absolutely essential that Great Britain and the United States should stand firmly on the suggestion of abolition of aggressive weapons, and that Italy, Germany—of course—Spain and many of the small powers, would follow. Then, with some concession to France, she would fall into line.

Last evening I dined with Mr. and Mrs. Davis, Mr. Wilson and Mr. Dulles, on the balcony and we talked at the table until after ten; then Mr. Davis came up stairs and told me in detail about his and Mr. Gibson's conversations with Baldwin and MacDonald. If only our government will allow us to go as far as *they*, the British will: I have absolute confidence in our Administration but I think it is awfully *cautious* . . . There are many well-meaning leaders here—but they seem to lack that quality which sends one confidently and swiftly over the thin ice necessary to cross instead of stopping in the middle to meditate on its "thinness": I speak as if I were an expert skater. To speak frankly, there seems to be in the world today, no outstanding leader of men. Well, perhaps we shall "arrive" with one. There is a quiet, determined effort by men like Mr. Davis which does not figure in the press reports, but which is going steadily forward . . .

May 28.32

. . . What is hoped is this, that Great Britain and the United States will suggest a real cut to France, with the realization that Italy and Germany will accede and many of the smaller powers fall into line. Just hope for us. Count Apponyi said to me at lunch Thursday: "We shall not go out of this as we came in. If we accomplish something, things will be better; if we accomplish nothing, infinitely worse."

All the afternoon, I have been working on a proposed speech of Mr. Gibson's concerning a "cut" in "effectives" which he must send first to the Administration for approval. If only Washington will not be "*cautious*". This is not the time for *caution* but for *daring*. Mr. Gibson, Mr. Davis and Mr. Wilson, are all for a *big* thing, and Mr. Davis is delegated to bring Senator Swanson "across"! Do you think this delegation is doing nothing but the social stint? It is a kind of work which cannot appear in the head lines . . .

I am enclosing a note from Count Apponyi in answer to my congratulations on his eighty-sixth birthday, which comes tomorrow. I have seen him and his wife often this spring and like them very much . . .

Hug the dear Doggies for me and tell Turvey that I hope she enjoys my room—including my bed—as well as my company. I so fear that Flag will forget me. Tell them that I love them "lots", those darling doggies. The Gibsons have two little dogs, cunning things, but not like "our four"!

June 2, 1932

The situation is this. For two days the combined brains of the Delegation have been at work on a cable to the Administration, trying to make it clear that we have a program that we should be "pleased" to submit if they would to see it! Now, we are "holding our thumbs" hoping that they will accept our modest suggestion. It is a fine program and certainly has nothing to suggest being "beaten".

I cannot understand the Administration Attitude, (the capital A in "attitude" was inadvertent but significant!). Mr. Gibson, Republican, Mr. Davis, Democrat, have the greatest confidence in the President and the Secretary. The Senator some times growls about "not having enough confidence in a Delegation to give them a free hand"; Mr. Marriner murmurs imprecations on "back seat driving"; and Mr. Wilson discreetly says nothing. "Me too"—but I think a lot! I spent most of the morning writing down my "thoughts".

"Here's hoping" that we shall be allowed off the leash; that Great Britain will be as liberal as Baldwin apparently was two or three weeks ago; that Herriot will be cooperative; that Grandi will live up to his professions. If all this happens, then I can send a cable that will say something.

June 10 '32

. . . I have a feeling intensified that June will determine whether anything is to be accomplished before the summer adjournment, which, for the United States contingent of our Delegation, will probably mean the close. We *could* stretch the appropriation through August—but not beyond that and Congress, in its present mood, is not likely to add to it.

Another bright morning. I am hoping for a quiet day—writing, reading, resting—for the week, I suspect, will be anything *but* quiet.

Sunday morning, June 12

MacDonald is in Paris today—if plans are carried out—and he and Herriot will arrive here tomorrow night or Tuesday morning. A long cable went to the Secretary Friday afternoon and if a "liberal" answer comes, it will help out. I shall send for my "code-book" tomorrow morning, with fingers crossed!

When you receive this, Commencement will be over. I so hope that it will go well. If only the gods have in store for me a *few* hours listening to the wind in the trees at Fleur de Lys, the barking of Doggies and the chirping of birds, Becky et cetera. Hug them for me—the Doggies—I suspect Becky would object . . .

6.13.32

This is principally to say that I have just read *such* a fine cable from the Secretary, so frank and warm-hearted . . . In it he speaks of the tension at home making the "April atmosphere at Geneva seem like a balmy Elysium". The "balmy Elysium" had some "tension" . . .

My fear is that MacDonald and Herriot are not being quite as liberal as was hoped—but after all, that is just conjecture. I will write you when I know—or there is anything *to* know! Of one thing you may feel certain and that is that your own delegation is "all wool and a yard wide". At least, it does not say one thing and do another. There are times when I feel as narrow as my friends the "Nationalists" and as profane as—Well, enough to enable me to say "Let Europe go hang"—herself, if she wants to! But I know that we shall all "hang separately" unless we learn to "hang together" and that there will have to be an abundance of those "ps" that you dislike, for years to come.

Saturday, June 18th

The "conversations" are going on, but not without "hitches"—Yesterday morning I had a long talk with Mr. Gibson, who reported in detail, up-to-date. I cannot begin to give you an adequate idea of the situation but here are a few "entre-nous" hints with regard to the British-French constituencies: Sir John Simon "handling the truth mighty 'keerless-like' ";

Mr. MacDonald saying frankly that since his operation, he "cannot remember accurately"; Herriot—"Weak"; Paul Boncour "not to be trusted". The one personality in the combined group commanding entire confidence is M. Massigli, a "French protestant of deep religious convictions", says Mr. Gibson adding "and there is no finer type."

I saw Mr. Henderson at Madame de Rosales and he said—as he has said before: "We look to your country to save the situation." But our delegation proposed the beginning of "equalitative disarmament" and the French jumped on it with both feet; had a scheme for the reduction of "effectives" and again our French friends, followed by others, began to pick flaws. They want only "internationalization" of armaments. The British forget from one day to another, what they *do* want. Well, "Here's hopin' ": And we are not going to give up hope or effort to realize it.

A note from Mr. Hoover thanking me for petitions that I forwarded to him and hoping that I am "finding some enjoyment in Geneva".

Sunday A.M. June 19

. . . while at luncheon Mr. Gibson came up to me, with a beaming countenance, to say that a cable had just come from the President, granting all that we want—and more! I went right up to his office and read it— feeling transported to the Seventh Heaven! It is great, as Mr. Gibson says—"The President has taken the bit in his teeth and gone as far as he wanted to go." It is better than our best hopes . . .

Three o'clock   Entre Nous

Mr. Gibson has just been up to talk over the cable. Now he has gone to his office to await a telephone call from Washington. He feels that the President—for whom he has great admiration—has broken loose from advice or "caution" and has asserted himself. Thank the Lord!

June 23, 1932

. . . The "conversations" have not been easy. Mr. Gibson and Mr. Davis, the principal "conversers" being somewhat "wore out" today. To take representatives of other groups into confidence and be sure that they will respect the confidence, is a trying experience. As Mr. MacDonald says of Herriot . . . "His head is all right and his heart is all right. The trouble is with his feet." Apparently they insist upon carrying him to someone to whom he can tell what he has been told!

As for Sir John! "He resembles nothing so nearly as he resembles a cork screw," says Mr. . . . Well, he wrote himself down in the estimation of everyone, judging by reports. Mrs. Morgan says that the unanimous verdict of the press of all nationalities was: "The one tragedy of the afternoon, Sir John's failure to take advantage of his opportunity." Following is my

"Summary":

1. Sir John Simon, long, windy, indirect:

2. Paul Boncour, long, harping, on the old French string of "security", with variations on "Sanctions";

3. Litvinoff, since "total disarmament" apparently not possible, this a tolerable substitute. Grace of manner is not the Soviet "long-suit";

4. Nadolny, good, could not refrain, keep his hands altogether off Ger-

many's "harpstring" of "equality";

5. Matsudaira—courteous, implication that when London treaty expires, Japan will demand *more* not less!

6. Grandi, the belle of the ball. Simply great. A storm of applause, indicative of sympathy with proposals, as well as admiration for him. Mr. Gibson cabled Washington that he had never seen such enthusiasm at an international gathering. Grandi himself was quite overcome, pretended he had a cold in his head in order to bury said head in his handkerchief! He sits almost in front of me, so I had a chance to note effect. He is *the* man of Europe today, I think, simple, direct, sincere. For once I say "Blessed be the dictator!" He received Mr. Hoover's statement from Mr. Gibson late that morning, "called up" Mussolini, and presto! it was decided to reduce Italy's forces one third: As Mr. Gibson said, "Grandi could afford to 'sit pretty' with no council or parliament to fear."

7. Madariaga, absolutely flat—the most striking example of an anticlimax.

I am sorry to say that Mr. Henderson also missed his opportunity. I do not know why he has been "prodding us" to take the lead. Several European gentlemen have been meditating on "lost opportunities" the last thirty-six hours, I suspect. To quote Mr. . . . again: "They all love applause!"

June 26, '32

. . . My principal forte at present seems to be in the line of conferences with members of our own delegation, Mrs. Corbett Ashby and Mrs. Morgan, the Chairman of the Inter-organization Council in Geneva. We had an enthusiastic meeting of the last-named on Friday when the cable from Chicago was presented to Mr. Gibson.

. . . the sun has come out this Saturday afternoon and I should like to be "out" too, but "Stanley High" comes at four o'clock; Professor Philip Marshall Brown of Princeton at quarter after five; and a dinner engagement at Mrs. Gregory's at half after seven. The days are bound to be more and more hectic as they draw to a close. I have a feeling that adjournment will come within the next fortnight, although no action has been taken as yet.

This morning I sent copies of yesterday's and today's "journal" giving abstracts of the discussions of the Hoover plan Thursday and yesterday. Mr. Gibson and Mr. Davis are conferring with the British on a "resolution" approving the "principle", taking action on some parts and referring others to a committee for attempted "adjustment" before the Conference re-convenes. If it were not for British, French and Japanese—a fairly big "if"—I think it could be adopted without much delay. However, agreement must be reached and that calls for no end of negotiation.

The dinner in honor of Ex-Secretary Kellogg was a brilliant affair, thirty or more at a long table, gay with pink sweet peas, the manager's favorite flowers! I had Lord Londonderry on my right, M. Russo, the Italian Minister—plenipotentiary, on my left, and a "talkative" evening! Grandi was on Mr. Gibson's right.

This coming Friday evening the British Delegation gives a dinner. It is difficult to "rise to" these social functions when anxious about the real things, but I suppose that they help. I had a chance to tell my right-hand neighbor Wednesday evening about public opinion in his own "United Kingdom", of which he was apparently in blissful ignorance!

Sunday, July 10

I had written so far when Mr. High arrived; he went in time for me to collect my thoughts before Philip Marshall Brown appeared bringing Mrs. Whyte, the Mother of "Sir Frederick"; they had hardly "cleared their skirts"—and trousers—when the concierge telephoned that "Miss Mary Lee of Westport, New York" would like to see me. I had a nice call with her here for a few days. She expects to be in Westport next month but I may see you before she does! It looks as if the Conference would adjourn within the next fortnight . . .

Miss Ball of the "Republican" is in Geneva for a few days and is dining with me tonight.

July 11, 1932

. . . Almost as soon as we had sat down—at the Pells' dinner—M. Comert —head of the Information Section at the League, said: "I am glad to be next to you, for I am disturbed over a situation of which I wish to speak confidentially." Then he told me in substance that he was sure that a group in the English and French Delegations were trying to "block" the Hoover proposals, "although two thirds of the French Delegation—including Herriot and Jouvenal, are in favor of them." Boncour, as I knew, is opposed. Although he mentioned no names, I am certain that Sir John Simon is behind the manoeuvre. Well, without M. Comert's name, I am to give Mr. Gibson the information! As Mr. Pell, with his reportorial eye, sat opposite and Mr. Reber next to M. Comert, it will not be difficult to gain information, if Mr. Gibson wishes it!

These are anxious and difficult days. The "conversations" are being carried largely by Mr. Gibson and Mr. Davis, but I find that there are opportunities for all of us, in one way or another.

Tuesday, Mrs. Morgan, Miss Dingman, Miss Heneker, of the International Office of the Business and Professional Women, and I, lunched with Madame D'Arcis to discuss ways in which the various organizations could help in strengthening public opinion in the countries represented. As a result, the Women's Committee met that afternoon, formulated the enclosed, which went out that evening, and other international organizations —League of Nations, Religious, Students, Labor—followed suit. Public opinion is strong and stronger every day, even in France, but too often the "Statesmen"(?) act as if they had never heard of it!

I am enclosing a note from Countess Apponyi, to whom I sent my "Times" article on "Women in World Affairs". She uses your expression about the work of men!

Les Troiselles was lovely Tuesday. The rose garden a dream of beauty, and it was easy to feel that only man is vile! . . .

In re-reading my letter, it sounds as if I were a "man-hater". There are splendid men here, idealists, courageous, doing their best—but there are also men thinking only of their own nationalistic or personal interests and blind as bats, as to what those "interests" really are. Well, I suppose that has always been true.

Tuesday, July 15, 1932

Yesterday was a gorgeous "Fourth". When I looked out in the morning and saw a big "Old Glory" floating from the "Russia" I actually had cold chills up and down my spine and legs, I was so thrilled! At luncheon the American tables had, each of them, a flag in the center and little flags at each place . . .

Ex-Secretary Kellogg is coming from Paris for a few days and Mr. Gibson is giving tomorrow evening an official dinner, at which I am to be "the only one of your kind" as Mr. Gibson expressed it! You should know in advance in order to hold your thumbs for me, one lone female with thirty "official males" of various nationalities.

July 16.32

. . . it was dear of "you all" to send the [birthday] cable. To tell the truth, I felt a little "down" that morning, which did not seem very "birth-dayish"—a rainy, muggy day, no one who knew, apparently that the day meant anything more to me than any other and a distinct under-current of anxiety about the "resolution" to be presented before the Conference adjourns. Then the cable arrived and I felt cheered! . . .

In the evening the Marquis and Marquise Paulucci—(I will omit the rest!) gave a very charming party, which I felt was in the nature of a birthday celebration, as I was on the Marquis' right. I told the Marquise and last evening, at the British dinner, I heard her say that here was *my* birthday party! . . .

The papers give a somewhat distorted view of the situation, I fancy. It is this: when the General Commission meets this coming week before adjournment, a resolution is to be presented about the Hoover plan. The one "in the works" finally "emanating" from Dr. Benês, the "Rapporteur", seems to us—and to public opinion—not strong enough, due to the fact that neither Great Britain nor France has been willing to "come out" for the Hoover plan, the former held back by Navy considerations, the latter, by effectives. Our "negotiators" are to make another attempt with Sir John Simon and Herriot and Boncour, the last two arriving from Paris Monday morning. If they do not succeed, the present plan is for the Delegation to present an amendment, which would make it necessary for the powers to "show their hand" to their own Public, which, in the case particularly of Great Britain, is strong for the Hoover proposal . . . If all goes well, I shall not mind. Two weeks from tonight, I shall probably be on the "Leviathan" homeward bound!

July 24.32

. . . Mr. Henderson was great yesterday, in "summing up", when he said that the "Resolution" did not go as far as many of us would like, but laid down a great program which must be fulfilled at the next session. I will not try to analyze it on paper—but you must prepare your ears for that when I return with an account—and the hours of "negotiation" lying behind it. Although I have not been in the actual negotiations, I have had many opportunities. Last Monday evening, at Ambassador Matsu-daira's dinner, I sat between the British Secretary for Foreign Affairs and ditto for Home Affairs—Sir John Simon and Sir Herbert Samuel . . . and we "talked shop" the entire time. As I was leaving the Conference Friday

I ran into Nadolny, the head of the German delegation, who is a good friend, and tried to persuade him not to harp on "equality" when we are 'headed" in that direction—but it is vain to plead! With all their ability, the Germans are almost destitute of the art of getting along with people who do not see through their eyes.

We adjourned just before one, in an atmosphere of happy speeches and good feeling, in spite of the fact that the day before Italians and French at a meeting of the Inter-Parliamentary Union in the next room, had come to blows! . . .

I go to Paris Friday afternoon, stay at Reid Hall that night and at three o'clock Saturday take the boat train for Cherbourg . . . A large part of the group will be on the "Leviathan" but Mrs. Swanson suggests a "taboo" on "Disarmament".

        ✿   ✿   ✿   ✿

Whether in Rhode Island or Switzerland, Will Rogers, children and dogs liked her. The average dog took one look at her and, just like Will Rogers, wagged his tail. After that the dog settled down to a lifetime of happiness and disobedience. Dogs had been that way with her father, and with her, as with him, if you were a dog you could hope to do as you pleased. But if you were a human being and met with confidence in that fact, the probability is you did less of what you pleased and more of what it was right to do. Besides the letters she wrote in general, during the Geneva half year, Mary Woolley wrote to the birds and dogs individually. These were letters and postcards with tempting pictures of things to eat and such messages as this on them: "Wouldn't you enjoy an hour here, with the counters of candies and little cakes within easy reach. I can just see you now, Mlle. Flag leading, but the rest of you not far behind!" And in the two picture postcards which followed in March, one a picture of the League of Nations where the Delegates were meeting: "This is where I have been going 'in & out' for the last month, dear Doggies . . . Canines Gibson, Bullard & Turner, are nice but none as nice as you . . . Commander Turner's dog is looking out of the window at the 'Russie' on the other side of the road. I wish you were all here to look out of my window at him!" She was most certainly laughing at them when she wrote: "I forgot to tell you that in my room at Monnetier was this announcement: 'Dogs pay for their board.'" Then: "I miss you all 'turrible'. Will you be glad to see me when I come home?"

Finishing and folding her letter home, Mary Woolley looked out her window again. Commander Turner's dog was gone but the little bird hanging in his cage was singing on and on. She had said elsewhere he "bolstered" her courage; on that day she slipped out quietly from Les Bergues and into the Geneva shopping district. Walking with rapid youthfulness, she did not enter a Geneva pet shop but at a spot where the shop windows were glittering in the sunlight she went in through the door of a jeweler's shop. For reasons of economy—nobody knew this fact better—she had no business to be there. Yes, there—having seen it once—was the jeweled Geneva Bird she had not been able to get out of her mind; and she wanted something—something special— to take to those who were waiting for her.

The jeweler stood respectfully beside her as in a lingo of mixed French and English, guiltily she asked him to "play" it for her. Enraptured, Mary Woolley listened to the song that followed. The Geneva Bird's breast was rose and gold and as it sang it fluttered shining green wings, holding its proud little scarlet tail motionless as its beak trembled with song. Was she thinking of her father bending over the cage of his birds, pursing his lips, whispering, whistling, cooing, until the birds sang with him?

And then, at last, she was homeward bound on the ship "Leviathan" —with her the Geneva Bird. A long time afterwards, Mrs. Roberts, Geneva Secretary, writing a letter from Washington, asked this question: "Did Miss Marks like the bird?"

CHAPTER 15

FRATERNAL PEACE?

"There is emphasis today upon the influence of public opinion, all to the good if an intelligent public opinion. But what about unintelligent public opinion and its influence upon the future of the human race?"

Shortly after landing, Mary Woolley wrote to Mr. Hoover that the "Hoover Plan" had been the salvation of the Conference, that his delegation had worked hard for its acceptance but that in spite of their inability to accomplish that, the resolution which they had adopted represented a real achievement. The President, receiving this letter, thanked Mary Woolley informally for her kind note, and nine days later wrote formally:

> I wish to convey to you my most cordial congratulations on the part you played as one of the few women delegates to the General Disarmament Conference. Your tact and understanding in dealing with delicate situations and your clear presentation of this country's peace policies when occasion arose have aroused universal praise. You were successful in striking a just balance, expressing on the one hand the determination of this Government to do away with war, and on the other showing that pacifism need not be synonymous with unrealistic dreams and disregard of actual possibilities. This country is justly proud of having sent you to Geneva and I wish to add a message of personal thanks for your participation.

It is not difficult to imagine how much pleasure and encouragement she continued to derive from President Hoover's letters.

After a brief vacation at Fleur de Lys, Mary Woolley went back to Mount Holyoke College. There she made an excursion up onto the hillside of Mary Lyon's birthplace in Buckland with Mr. Hyde, president of the Board of Trustees, Mrs. Hyde and Harriet Newhall. As they climbed the Buckland hill on that late summer afternoon of September 12th—clear and with a touch of autumn in the air—these New Englanders were all having a good deal of fun jesting at one another's expense. Mrs. Hyde found the hillside difficult to get up. She climbed slowly and sat down frequently to rest. Whereas Mary Woolley, climbing briskly and without hesitation, consoled Mrs. Hyde by saying: "In the Adirondack Mountains my trouble begins with the coming down. I'm always afraid of falling. Coming down I shall have to stop and rest oftener than you are doing going up.

"Yes, Mrs. Hyde, just wait and see," Harriet agreed, laughing. "Up there in the North Country I have seen Miss Woolley as she tried to get down safely on the steep trail of Hurricane. That's something!"

When they reached the top they found that of Mary Lyon's birth-place only the cellar hole was left. As they stood about the cellar hole looking off onto the Massachusetts hills and talking about Mary Lyon's vision in her work for the education of women there flew over them a big silvery airplane, and somehow on the summit of that little hill on that day there was glory.

Then Mrs. Hyde found a place where she could sit down to rest and Mr. Hyde joined the president by the foundations of Mary Lyon's home. Quietly he informed Mary Woolley that the trustees were unanimously requesting her to continue in the presidency until the one hundredth anniversary of Mount Holyoke—the centennial in 1937. Mr. Hyde had become a member of the Board of Trustees in 1929; and in March of 1931, at the time of Joseph Skinner's resignation, Henry K. Hyde had been elected President of the Board. Presumably "whatever there was to know", he knew on that September day—among other things that the group fighting Mary Woolley had been clever enough to fold up temporarily following Mr. Hoover's appointment. A Christian gentleman, remarkable for his business success and good judgment, honest and fair, modest and unselfseeking, a loyal friend to Mary Woolley, Henry K. Hyde had the courage to support any conviction he held—even against the background of the fact that in 1931 one of the trustees had offered the presidency of the college to Frances Perkins, saying if she would accept it they would "get rid of Miss Woolley." At that time two other members of the Board—one an alumna trustee —privately asked President Woolley to resign before the Centennial. By a few quiet words spoken by Mr. Hyde on the Buckland hilltop of Mary Lyon's home, Mary Woolley believed the difficulty with the trustees — whatever it was — had been ended. This hour with the Hydes and Harriet Newhall was the happiest hour she had known since the covert attempt had begun in 1931 or earlier to force her resignation.

About twelve days later, Mary Woolley, seated at her desk in the living room of the President's House, was alternately chopping a cake of Dot chocolate with a fruit knife and with her pen writing a letter to Fleur de Lys. The chocolate chips she did not let fall where they would. Not at all; she fed them to Turvey beside her! Doing well with the chocolate and contentedly nibbling at the piece she had just chopped off, she was writing on this evening of September 25, 1932 that she had preparation to make for the *New York Herald Tribune* afternoon at the Waldorf Thursday, and that if only she could "Just open her mouth and let the Lord fill it," she could save time! For once, the humor of the situation did not disturb her.

Among "the good and the great" who were to speak on that September 29th—only four days distant—were Mrs. Belmont, Dr. Damrosch, Lillian Gilbreth, Miss Gildersleeve, Mr. Hoover, Fannie Hurst, Walter Lippmann, Dr. Shotwell, Mrs. Sporborg, Irita Van Doren, Dr. W. A. White, Governor Winant, Mary E. Woolley, and Owen D. Young. The day came and Mrs. Meloney—affectionately called "Missy Meloney"—launched what was to become her annual *Herald-Tribune* Forum. Not one but two women were the source and the inspiration of this forum: Helen Rogers Reid and Mrs. Meloney. Ishbel Ross has called these two friends "breath-taking ladies of the press"—both tiny in stature, both mighty in abilities, and devoted to each other. "Missy" Meloney was one of the great newspaper women of her time, witty and dashing; Mrs. Reid, fearless and loyal as a feminist, believes that no position is too large for an able woman, and she exemplifies that fact as Editor of the *New York Herald-Tribune*. In the talk which followed, Mary Woolley's whole message centered about the opportunity and responsibility of women.

As a leader Mary Woolley had been a "headliner" for many years. As a human being she was becoming more and more interesting to the public. Now this public began to want to know how long she slept at night, and whether she dreamed when she slept, what she drank at mealtime and how she voted. Her brief and candid replies to questions like these were that she needed eight hours of sleep and she wasted none of the public's time by saying that frequently she did not get eight hours. Yes, sometimes she dreamed and "generally these dreams" were connected with something she had been doing or talking about. About beverages at mealtime she wrote: "Tea I drink very seldom; coffee generally only at breakfast time; I never take alcohol in any form; as a rule I eat a rather light evening meal, in my own home supper instead of dinner . . ." She mentioned no chocolate, "Dot" or otherwise! About it all she was good natured and obliging. But how she voted: that was a bird of a different feather, and a difficult bird! Her reply was straight-forward: "I am a registered Republican, but the type of Republican which is qualified as 'independent' and on that account not always appreciated by party leaders!" Having set down an exclamation mark—not a period—she smiled and went on to discuss splitting her ticket. She was an ardent member of the League of Women Votes and an admirer of our old friend Belle Sherwin, with Maud Wood Park, one of its founders.

It seemed as if no sooner had she reached home from Geneva than Mary Woolley began working heart and soul for peace in her leadership of The Peoples Mandate to End War, formerly a committee of the Women's International League fo Peace and Freedom. The Quakers have a saying: "Eternity is now," and then do or do not live up to it. When the devoted, hard-working director of the Mandate, Mabel Vernon was asked: "In your experience in the Peoples Mandate what has been the outstanding event for you?", without an instant's pause she replied:

> When the decision had to be made whether to make the Mandate an independent Committee, for me the outstanding event of all these years was hearing Dr. Woolley say: "Now we have to make this decision today because the opportunity is now. I am sure this is the right thing to do and I will go along with you."

Mary Woolley seldom thought of her personal comfort. One illustration of this fact occurred when members of the committee and the director, Mabel Vernon, were talking with a potential donor. Mary Woolley said: "Mr. ——, I cannot give much money to the Mandate but I give as liberally as I can of my time and my strength. The only way I can do this in addition to my college duties is to rise early and stay up late. Yesterday I was dictating to my secretary at five o'clock in the morning in order to make the trip to see you possible." With this simple directness and sincerity Mr. —— fell promptly in love and became a generous friend, later in his will a testator. When a member present at that meeting told Mrs. Zilboorg, who could not be there, that "Mr. —— had fallen in love with Dr. Woolley," Mrs. Zilboorg's reply was: "Who wouldn't!" With her fellow workers Mary Woolley was quick to praise, never failing to give encouragement when the way was difficult. No matter what results were secured she had a word of commendation for the effort that had been made, and in this work covering twelve years of her life she showed no discouragement and remained confident that women were slowly bringing to the fight for peace the zeal and determination they had exhibited in winning educational and political rights for women. Some of the distinguished women associated with her in the Peoples Mandate campaigns were Grace Abbott, Judge Florence Allen, Jane Addams, Katharine Devereux Blake, Sophonisba Breckinridge, Pearl Buck, Carrie Chapman

Catt, Dorothy Canfield Fisher, Hannah Clothier Hull, Congresswoman Caroline O'Day, Ellen Fitz Pendleton, Mrs. Gerard Swope, Lillian Wald. Some people have implied that the Geneva 1932 Disarmament Conference began with high hopes and ended with low failures, but MEW believed such a conclusion untrue. Granting there was an element which could be called "failure" in the Disarmament Conference of 1932, the only comment on this "failure" Mary Woolley ever made lay not in words but lay in the phenomenal work done by the Peoples Mandate under her Chairmanship.

In her first public speech (not committee speaking) at the Disarmament Conference on June 4, 1932, Mary Woolley had said: "We need moral leadership rather than moral disarmament. We must recognize that changes in human nature come from within as a result of a long-continued intellectual process, not from without by legislation." In her heart of hearts she believed that Countess Apponyi was right when she wrote Mary Woolley that men had made a mess of the world.

*   *   *   *

Candle-lighted, lamp-lighted Fleur de Lys for safety reasons was no longer to be so peacefully lighted. Electricity had been installed throughout the house in the old wrought-iron lamps and lanterns. Between the library and the dining room the candlesticks and wax candles, except for parties and blackouts, were to stand unused on the candle mantle shelf.

Early that July at Mount Holyoke, two weeks before Mary Woolley began packing to leave for Fleur de Lys, she sent off a special delivery letter in which she said: "The following hope to start not later than nine A.M. Friday: 1 bottle of vanilla, 1 can baking powder, 1 Turvey, 1 Portia—and a few other things." "Other things" being herself. The vanilla had come from S. S. Pierce's in Boston. The baking powder was an inseparable specialty of Portia's; Turvey was Mary Woolley's devoted and beautiful collie; and as for the fourth item, Portia was a large item in bottled-up humanity and not always corked. During the summer of 1953 we enjoyed the quiet of lake and mountains and the good food Portia prepared.

All that we ever asked of Fate was innocuous desuetude. But that summer innocuous desuetude was not to be, for this was the village announcement: "Dr. Mary E. Woolley, President of Mount Holyoke College, will speak in Westport, N.Y., Sunday morning, August 27th, at 10:45 a.m. Her subject will be "The World We Live In."

When the Sunday morning came, great was the uproar as sound traveled from the old stone church over Lee Park, across Hoisington

Brook and to Fleur de Lys where Portia stood on the south bankside, shading her eyes with one long, sensitive hand, and looking off towards another hillside and its stone church. The old woman could hear the roar of the motorcycles of many State Police directing traffic and finding parking space for those who, in the jam of traffic, could not find it for themselves, and the sound from hundreds of cars coming into Westport and the strange bee-like noise of multitudinous human voices. Among those who had to find a parking space was Harriet Newhall, who had driven niece Mary Emily Woolley and nephew Bill Bacon over to hear their aunt speak.

On this glorious North Woods morning with its invigorating air and sunshine, even before the speaker reached the church with Dr. Noel Merrihew, the church was already crowded and hundreds of men and women, shepherded by the State Police, stood quietly outside waiting to hear over the amplifying system the first woman delegate sent by their country to a peace conference speak on "The World We Live In".

Again the roar of the motorcycles of the State Police, the hum of voices talking excitedly, the honking of cars as the largest audience Westport had ever known made its way back home and to Sunday dinner.

About that time while Mary Woolley was *en tour* she wrote home: "Tell the Doggies that Mrs. Eisenhart's nice police dog had a nap in my room while I was dressing this morning. He is *nice* but not *as* nice as they!" Or she would add a light touch at a hard moment to one of her *en tour* letters. These were the moments when one seemed to hear her saying: "Hard?" Yes!" But with a toss of the head she would go on, as she did in a letter from Chicago: "Had a two hour nap —consecutively not simultaneously!" Then she edited this sentence laughingly: "Did an errand and had a two hour nap—consecutively not simultaneously!" While *en tour* she was never happier than when somebody asked her about the dogs. And in these memoranda in affection it is not unimportant that Mary Woolley wrote home from Pittsburgh: "Tell Doggies that at the alumnae meeting in Pittsburgh, during the 'question hour,' one loyal friend and well-wisher said: 'And how are the Dogs?'"

On September 15, 1935, at a dinner at the Hotel Commodore in New York, before Secretary of State Cordell Hull got up to speak, Mary Woolley had spoken, giving a program which provided for "a return to sound economic principles" in the entire Western Hemisphere as well as peace. And it was this Western Hemisphere work of the Peoples Mandate, not Geneva, which in the closing years of her life was to take much of her time, for her chairmanship of the Peoples Mandate stemmed from her work with the peace groups and in particular from work with the Women's International League for Peace and Freedom in which the Mandate had been a committee. There were conferences, too, with Secretary Hull, as well as with President Roosevelt. At one of the interviews with Mr. Hull, his desk was piled high with stuff when he said: "It looks like the desk of a country newspaper editor, doesn't it?" They agreed that it did.

About half a year later, at the White House on March 12th, Franklin Delano Roosevelt was telling one good story after another. From time to time the President's handsome head was thrown back in laughter in which the women who stood around him and behind him on that day joined. Despite this "encirclement" of eminent women, the committee of the Peoples Mandate was unable to stop the President in order to present their problem. As precious moment after precious moment of the time allowed the committee slipped away, not for an instant did these women forget the reason for which they had come, yet courtesy made them helpless. Just as the committee was beginning to despair, without discourtesy Mary Woolley made lightning use of a chance to introduce their subject. After she had taken up this address to the President, not for an instant did Mary Woolley pause, but, without haste and with appreciation expressed for what President Roosevelt had already done, she proceeded quietly to the close, and the fact that they had not come to present the Peoples Mandate because they were going on to secure 50,000,000 signatures, but that they had come at a time when over a million Americans had signed to urge upon the President the first point of the Mandate, that is, "stop immediately all increase in armaments and armed forces . . ."

During this time the Director was standing a little back of Mr. Roosevelt's chair and desk, saying *sotto voce* to Mrs. O'Day: "As soon as Dr. Woolley finishes, you begin." Passing from one woman to another just as each finished, she repeated the magic phrase: "As soon as Mrs. O'Day finishes, you begin!"[1] And each of them *did* begin! What chance had one United States President with eight of the ablest women in the United States?

It was in 1935 that Mary Woolley's little book, *Internationalism and Disarmament* was published.[2] In this work she outlined the action of the Disarmament Conference in 1932, analyzed the political assets and liabilities of Europe during the winter of 1933-34, and discussed the problems of progress towards international amity based on reason rather than force. She wrote an eloquent chapter on "Education and the Disarmament of the Mind". In describing what she calls the "five classes" of fellow citizens in their reactions to disarmament, she said of one group:

> The first class is the group that does not want disarmament, or any form of international relationship based on reason instead of armed force, and is working against it. Why? The answer came to me with startling force during the War by way of the most inhuman remark that ever fell upon my ears. It was made by a woman, a woman of unchallenged respectability, of high social standing, the wife of a man of large business interests. "I do not know that I ought to say it, but as long as my husband is making as much money as he is making now, I do not care how long the war lasts."

*   *   *   *

Two years before, suddenly, in her college work the sky had darkened again. Unexpectedly on November 18, 1933, Henry K. Hyde had died—a grave misfortune in Mary Woolley's career. Another successful businessman, but of a wholly different type, had become acting chairman, and in March 1934 he was elected president of the Board of Trustees. It was in that year that the trustees appointed a Committee on the Succession to the Presidency, made up of five members, consisting of three men and two women. Of these appointments only one woman, an alumna, was in favor of a woman—a position soon altered to preference for a man.

About this time Dr. Woolley pointed out to the secretary of this Committee the importance of choosing a woman as her successor.[3] A few months later, in the fall of 1934, one of the men from this Committee called privately on Mary Woolley and asked her to resign. And in October of 1935 the Board sent out a questionnaire to alumnae which did not definitely raise the issue of the choice of a man for president.[4] On July 1 of this year Mary Woolley had written to each trustee, stating the following reasons for wishing to have a woman as her successor:

> The choice of a woman for the post seems to me most important from every point of view. I should feel that the celebration of the Centennial of Mary Lyon's effort to open opportunities to women as human beings on an equal basis with men would better be omitted, if a part of that celebration is the installation of a man as President of Mount Holyoke. The importance of this action is not limited to Mount Holyoke. All over the country men and women interested in the recognition of women are taking a keen interest in this matter and realize that Mount Holyoke's action would count for or against the progress of women more than the action of any other college possibly could. I cannot over-estimate the intensity of the feeling which has already been expressed along this line.

This letter she followed in a few days by letters to a small list of men and women who were heads of other colleges; in these letters she asked about or for recommendations of other women, usually pointing out that several people were being considered. She continued: "I am eager that the decision should be in favor of a woman— peculiarly important, I think, in the case of Mount Holyoke opened in 1837 with the intention of giving to women opportunities equal to those given to men." And to President Wilbur she added: "It would seem to me a curious way of celebrating the Centennial to depart from that purpose!"

This entire year had been and was to remain torn not only by college problems but also by personal sorrows. Hearing of the losses overtaking us among our dogs—Flag had been bred by Mrs. Shields in her Vermont kennel—she and Colonel Shields drove fifty miles up into the hills of West Stockbridge, Massachusetts, and brought down to us from the Faraway Kennels a little fellow who had been whelped on February 14, 1935. His legs were so straight it seemed as if the joints might work both ways (and did when he became old), his brush was as straight as his legs, and hung without a quirk, his coat—sable and white—was heavy and perfectly marked even as a puppy, his eyes were large and kind. "Bummy" we called him and his kennel name became Blue Flag Heron Master after our Heron and Old Mannie. Of the changes small or large which were taking place that summer and of the cruel problems if at all we spoke little. It was in the autumn of this year, on Tuesday, November 12, 1935, that Mary Woolley's brother Erving Yale Woolley died. Although following the crash of Lee Higginson's he had been less and less well, his death from cerebro spinal meningitis was sudden and unexepcted and came at a time when his sister was least able to bear the accumulation of sorrows, large and small, which came upon her.

One early morning that fall JM was at work in her unfinished attic study of the President's House—a place with one window, two chairs and a table. Under the table on this morning lay Chuckie Chuckles, quiet but not asleep, when a knock sounded on the inner door and Mary Woolley's voice was heard asking to come in.

Getting up JM gave her the morris chair. Mary Woolley opened a manila folder, on it written in her large clear handwriting: "Succession to the President", and said: "When I came home last night I found some of these letters waiting for me."

She took out a carbon of her letter to the President of the Alumnae Association in which she had listed six outstanding possible candidates —candidates any college would have been lucky to have.[5] Then she

said: "Here is her reply. You see what the Alumnae President says?" *
JM read: "'Personally, I want first what is best for Mount Holyoke,
and then what is best for women in general'," and exploded with "What
poppycock! As if any college in the universe could be as important
as 'women in general'! If the alumnae as a whole knew about this,
they would be with you."

"Oh, don't be so impatient;" objected Mary Woolley, "but perhaps
you are right. However, my relationship to the Board of Trustees
makes it impossible for me to become the person giving such information. The source of the whole difficulty seems to be some of the
alumnae officers, a few of the alumnae trustees on the Board and the
men who have joined them or who started this—I do not know which."

Puzzled, Mary Woolley was silent a moment. At that time, despite
the evidence, she believed, as others had believed before her and still
believe, that in reputable institutions boards of trustees and faculties
are above taking advantage of a weak law and above the use of
chicanery, lies and slander.

Then, sighing, she continued: "But in the end, they will not dare
appoint a man."

"In Chicago," commented JM, "they have 'known for several years'
that the trustees were 'hunting a man'. To be specific Sophonisba
Breckinridge and Miss Abbott have known and their University of
Chicago group believes that the Mount Holyoke trustees are doing
just that! And there is the man Carolyn Smiley knows. Not so long
ago Carolyn Smiley and others knew that a member of the Board of
Trustees said to a man of academic distinction they were looking for a
man as president of Mount Holyoke, and the man's reply was: 'That
would be a crime!'"

"But there are so many trustees on the Board who *are* trustworthy,"
objected Mary Woolley.

"Yes, splendid men and women like Boyd Edwards, Frances Perkins
and others, but they, too, are having a hard time."

In the light of past experience it was difficult for Mary Woolley to
believe that there were men and women on the Board who had no
intention of making peace with her—fraternal or otherwise. Mary
Woolley had not as yet perceived—few academic women had—the
danger embedded in the very composition of the Board of Trustees of
the women's colleges—a danger to the leadership *by* a woman *of* wom-
en in those colleges. This jeopardy was *not* peculiar and personal to
Mount Holyoke College but existed among them all in the 1930s,
whether Barnard or Bryn Mawr, Radcliffe, Smith, Vassar, or Wellesley

and many other colleges for women. In the majority of the women's colleges this peril still exists. Yet a few women of legalistic minds and training did see the peril. One of those women was Carrie Chapman Catt.

JM broke the silence with: "If Mr. Hyde were living, this would never have happened."

"You are right, it would never have happened!"

"Aren't you a bit over-trustful as far as other people are concerned?"

"If you can't trust other people, whom are you to trust!" she exclaimed.

There was no reply. Under the table blind Chuckie Chuckles sighed, edging himself over the bare floor a little closer to those he loved.

After a moment Mary Woolley spoke, as if in explanation: "I fear I have been too successful."

CHAPTER 16

LEGEND

"Our responsibility is for today, but it does not stop there. It is also a responsibility for tomorrow."

On May 18, 1936, the Chairman of the Board of Trustees informed Mary Woolley of the decision of the trustees to propose a man for election as president of Mount Holyoke College. Two days later, on May 20th, before leaving to speak for the Federation of Women's Clubs in Greenwich, Rhode Island, she wrote to each trustee a letter of protest in which she said she had been told only two days before of the intention to appoint a man; that one hundred years ago Mary Lyon had founded Mount Holyoke for the advancement of women because she believed in women as human beings, and in the tradition of women as leaders of Mount Holyoke; finally that there had always been a woman as head and that what the trustees were planning to do would be a blow to the advancement of women. Then she closed her letter with this paragraph:

> In loyalty to Mary Lyon's vision and to her superb achievement; in loyalty to the women who have borne the heat and burden of the day, during these hundred years; in loyalty to the cause of the advancement of women, I protest against the proposed appointment of a man as President of Mount Holyoke College.[1]

A few of the trustees replied—among them James M. Speers who said that he was in "hearty accord" with all Mary Woolley had written. Stating that Wellesley had set Mount Holyoke a good example, he said that "surely there are other women of Miss McAfee's type." Frank Clayton Myers sent a telegram: "assuming an available woman can be found possessing the qualification," a woman should be chosen.

During her absence that May, Mary Woolley had found time to write home on the 12th as she jiggled along on the Southwestern Limited in the neighborhood of St. Louis where she was to speak at a Trust Officers luncheon. She did not write about what she herself hoped to accomplish by this difficult journey at a difficult time. What she wrote, as so often, was for the sake of others, and she added: "It is

165

almost midnight and soon I must start for my train. It is cool, thank a happy Providence and therefore I am not so tired as I otherwise might be, after an exceedingly full program in St. Louis. The days went well, I think, a 'Thought' which is consoling in the light of this evening, which it seemed to me, did not go well. I just felt tongue-tied!"

The social fabric of the past had been built up by men for men; and the law has followed this pattern. It was upon a basis of educational opportunities for women that women had made their first stand for the betterment of women. This they were forced to do—if it was to be done at all—under the guidance of men and with their help. Though women sought in various ways to free themselves from male dominance, they found themselves—as they do today politically—under the control of male governments directed by male principles and in education by male boards of trustees. Thus every freedom women gained was made uncertain or tentative by male autocracy.

On the Board of Trustees of Mount Holyoke College during 1936 and 1937 there were seventeen voting men and seven voting women.[1a] A two-thirds vote of the trustees was necessary for the election of a trustee and presumably a larger vote for the election of a president. In the election of a new trustee to fill any vacancy, the men, it is plain, had the necessary two-thirds to select a man to succeed a man; and, if they so desired, to elect a man to succeed a woman as president. Men and custom had made these laws, and women and justice had had little to do either with the formation of the College Charter or with the By-laws governing its Board of Trustees. As the Board was permitted to hold all the property and, apparently, make the appropriations for the conduct of the college, the men also had full and complete control of the financing of the college.

Although both Charter and By-laws were open to all who cared to read them, not a handful of the alumnae or of the faculty knew any of the facts about the Charter and By-laws of their college. The majority of the faculty and alumnae were still unaware that two years earlier (in 1934) the trustees had appointed a committee of five members on the Succession to the Presidency, and that all of the women appointed as members of the committee, except for one alumna trustee, were opposed to the election of a woman.

With the probability that the trustees as a body did not know, a trustee had appeared suddenly in South Hadley and attempted to force Mary Woolley's resignation. Not alone in those homes where the male reigns supreme but also here in a woman's college was the complete "domestic tyrant"—a buccaneer robbing women of the rights which should be theirs in a democracy. A long time ago Thomas Jefferson believed in those rights when he wrote: "Equal application of law is fundamental. Females have equal rights with males." It might be added that when the men's colleges begin sharing their boards of trustees with women—greatly to its own honor the University of Pennsylvania recently added a woman to its Board—then will be time enough to rediscuss the whole subject of justice to women. The last of several visitations had been shortly before Christmas when, descending unannounced upon her, Mary Woolley was told that she should no longer stand in the way of the "advantage" of the college, that this trustee had a candidate who would come immediately but did not care to wait, that Mary Woolley should resign at once, that if she would do so she might have a year's salary with permission to live in her house another year, and, the year after, return to be the center of the Centennial. All of this was stated in calls and, except by Mary Woolley, nothing was put down in writing.

The Committee of Five had now become a Committee of Nine, and few alumnae knew anything about the Committee of Nine or of the fact that the plans of the men and women on the Committee went back to the first year of the 1930 decade and even earlier. As rapidly as alumnae became informed of trustee intention to appoint a man to succeed the women who had been presidents of Mount Holyoke for one hundred years, Mary Woolley's file began to be filled with letters from bewildered daughters, not "ungrateful daughters", some of them believing that President Woolley herself advocated this change. Surprised, shocked, grieved, they were asking for information. It was not long before men and women outside the college began to ask about the "legend of the ungrateful daughters"—a phrase used by the Alumnae Committee of 100. About this situation Mary Woolley wrote:

> In July 1935 I sent a letter to each member of the Board, of which I am enclosing a copy, and repeatedly expressed my opinion to certain members of the committee, as for instance, the chairman, Mr. Morrison, Mrs. Maguire, Miss Keyes, Mr. Cheney, and Dr. Furniss. From time to time I sent, on my own initiative, names of women to be considered. I was not consulted in the spring of 1936 and did not know that a man was being considered, until after the choice was made.

Under protection of having sent out a questionnaire to the alumnae, the Chairman of the Board of Trustees said that the response from the alumnae did not indicate a preference for a woman. What the President of the Board and other members of the Board did not mention was that no question on their questionnaire raised the issue of the succession which was embedded in the traditions of women as presidents of Mount Holyoke College.

For two years it was barrel and blaze and one explosion after another, and not a handful of alumnae and faculty knew what had been stored in that barrel. "Hatred" they knew was the kerosene being poured upon it. Suddenly—it seemed like that—the air was filled with accusations and with conflict cutting like flying bits of shattered glass.

"It's a *fait accompli!*"

"It's too late!"

"Get this college groomed for bankers' daughters."

"Get rid of Miss Woolley!"

During these days our blind dog, like the rest of his family, had become aware of something which hurt. Psychic, like all sensitive dogs of high intelligence, he had begun to be not very well. Once in a while Chuckie, as if something jerked him, would throw his little head into the air. "Glandular disturbances," said the doctor, "probably related to the deficiency which caused his blindness. He isn't suffering too much now but when he begins to do so I will tell you, and Chuckie Chuckles will have to be put to sleep." More than ever did Heron continue to watch and follow him everywhere. November and the first two weeks in December had passed and the little fellow seemed even less well, ate less, yet would still lap malted milk from his pan when those he loved asked him to do so. But the worst had to come. For a week Heron, a healthy dog up to that time, lost ground visibly. Despite all we could do and all we did, Heron died within a week, broken-hearted over the loss of his brother Chuckie Chuckles.

Nor were our problems over. During that winter and spring Bummy sought everywhere for Chuckie Chuckles and for Heron. At each unexpected opening of a door he got up, looking eagerly. Sometimes acknowledging our presence with a nod, he would stand in the middle of a room looking towards the door or doors for those who did not return. They did not come, and by spring Bummy, too, was losing ground.

Finally, desperate conditions needing desperate remedies, when we were about to leave Westport, we wired Dr. Smead asking him on our arrival at college to bring us a young collie in the hope that this would help.

And there at the end of the journey were Blue Boy and kind Dr. Smead.

❖   ❖   ❖   ❖

The trustee who since his election to the Board had been determined to break the one hundred year precedent of a woman as president decided upon a bold plan. Failing to reckon with the fact that to the public Mary Woolley had already become a symbolic figure representing education for "women as human beings" and working for the substitution of peace for war, the Committee of Nine were soon possessed of a world-wide audience, but it was an audience hostile to them.

A member of the college administration, an alumna, returning from a trip among the alumnae, gave the president the key to the group's bold plan. The "key" was false education. This administrative officer went on to say that it was essential that the "false" education which alumnae were receiving should be quickly opposed by an education based on truth and facts. Her letters to the trustees are the best evidence of the part Mary Woolley played in building up the education based on truth and the facts.[1b]

Also, a friend in a responsible position in another college wrote several times, implying that there were rumors concerning the mistakes made by Mount Holyoke's president. Asked to send the "reasons", the following "reasons" were given. First, the president had spent a large portion of her time away from the college working for internationalism and it was difficult to get appointments for discussion of academic matters. There is accuracy in this criticism. But accuracy is not always the truth and was not in this case, for Mary Woolley could not have done for Mount Holyoke what she did—and what the majority of the trustees urged her to do—had she *not* been away frequently. The second criticism was that Mary Woolley had involved the college in unwise investments. The president was an *ex officio* member of the Trustee Finance Committee. But except for the magnetic qualities Mary Woolley had in attracting large gifts to the college, she knew little about financial matters and had nothing to do with investments. Through her brother, Erving Yale Woolley, at Lee Higginson's, the Treasurer of Mount Holyoke did buy some stocks and bonds. These matters were never referred to Mary Woolley and she was in no way responsible for any investments. Nobody need be told what happened to Lee Higginson when the Kreuger-Toll bubble burst. What some of the trustees did *not* emphasize was that Mary Woolley had been the central figure since 1901 in the collection of millions of dollars — "bricks" by means of which Mount Holyoke had become one of the great colleges for women in the United States. The third adverse comment was that she had allowed expenditures in certain departments exceeding the budget decided upon by the financial committee. With regard to this third statement, at least the teaching departments knew too well what was being done to their budgets to believe any such patent nonsense! The author, occupant of a third floor apartment in the President's House, was the chairman of one of the two largest departments in the college and the founder and director of the Laboratory Theatre. The faculty learned later that the $15,000 which they generously clipped from their own salaries for return to the financial department of the college had been given at the time when the Comptroller's salary was being raised $900, and that while the members of the faculty were taking cuts, the Treasurer had refused to have his salary reduced. And the fourth criticism was an expression of ill will towards the author.

The conflict took the usual form of suppression of freedom of speech, of undercover movements, and of false stories, including a whispering campaign—in short, character assassination. A shrewd and wealthy business woman in the Connecticut Valley had on her grand piano a large framed picture of Mary Woolley. The devotion this woman of wealth gave to the Mount Holyoke president was motivated by her admiration for a woman who "did things" and, in a sense, fulfilled her own ambitions. She offered to erect a carillon and to name it after Mary Woolley but the president thought it a mistake to put so much money in that sort of thing. Interested in music, this friend then suggested a music building, but Mary Woolley thought that, too, unnecessary, for the college already had a Music Hall! Gradually, under the President's selfless management, the chapel idea evolved. But all these facts were cleverly manipulated by the callous group, and soon made their appearance in public in the form of the statement that the chapel was being given as a mark of confidence in the trustee appointment of a man to succeed Mary Woolley. In order to direct this incident back to the facts, this misstatement was repeated to President Woolley by one of the men on the faculty, Dr. Leslie Gale Burgevin. About this misstatement Mary Woolley did not make use of the Churchillian "terminological inexactitude". She said promptly and in plain English "That is an absolute lie!" And she went quietly on to repeat the real facts. This sort of technique on the part of the men and some of the alumnae trustees soon began to work *for* and not *against* Mary Woolley in strengthening the opposition of self-respecting alumnae to the methods being used.

During these early weeks as the shadows of character assassination took shape, Dr. Helen Griffith wrote the President: "You have always been able to discount our differences of opinion, our contentiousness, and very human bickerings because you knew that at bottom we had genuine respect for one another and respect, admiration, and loyalty for our president. And you never had your faculty more solidly behind you than we are at this moment."

Throughout Mary Woolley's administration the faculty group at Mount Holyoke never came under the Harvard definition of a college faculty: "a group of mutually repellent particles." There were some rivalries but the dominant atmosphere was one of admiration for the notable work being done virtually in all departments. On the Mount Holyoke College Faculty at that time there were men and women of eminence in their field, recognized as scholars, the winners of awards and of widespread commendation. Also, there were men and women who should be known in every household—as, for example, Dr. Nellie E. Goldthwaite, who invented pectin for jelly. The great majority of these men and women were living a confident, full life because of Mary Woolley's experience as a department head at Wellesley and because of her trustworthiness in and understanding of the problems of departments, and inter-relationship among departments and salaries. Of this faculty Dr. A. Elizabeth Adams wrote: "The education given at Mount Holyoke equals that given to women in any other college or university. Her curriculum is sound and progressive. The record of Mount Holyoke women commands admiration and respect. The achievement of her faculty is distinguished."

To the president herself in this crisis the position taken by her faculty was of outstanding importance, and no doubt in part because of this fact members of the faculty had been excluded by the trustees from any part in the choice of a new president, for the president of the college, as well as faculty representation, had from the beginning been shut out from any participation in the choice of a new president.

As the Conference Committee of the Faculty was preparing a ballot to be based on faculty preference, there were unsubstantiated rumors that the president, if not supported by the trustees, would resign. The president, neither confirming nor denying the rumor, began to receive letters from the faculty begging her not to do this. On May 21st the Faculty Conference Committee sent out a communication to every member of the faculty asking each one if he or she preferred to have a woman as president; 87 answered "Yes", 11 answered "No".[2]

It began to be evident to the majority that something nearer than Denmark called for purification. There had been women heads of colleges, women who had won honor for themselves, fame for their colleges, glory for their sex—women in whom women took pride. But the trustees of Mount Holyoke countered the selection of a woman for president with the statement that despite the vote and preference of the faculty, the "supply" had run out. That is, having asked three women, there was no woman to be found to head Mount Holyoke College. For Mount Holyoke only three efforts to find a candidate would do! At Wellesley the choice of one woman, Mildred McAfee, out of a promising list of one hundred women, resulted in enlarged distinction for Wellesley. At Mount Holyoke the trustee leading the opposition to women intimated that the three women asked had said there were problems at Mount Holyoke that a man was better equipped to handle than a woman. In the Wellesley succession the trustees had about a hundred men and a hundred women on their lists. They accepted the votes of the college constituencies as a mandate, ran a pencil through the one hundred men and proceeded with the list of women. Interpreted in one sentence: Wellesley had the good fortune of a board of trustees possessed of good will and a sense of justice to women.³ The Mount Holyoke trustees in power refused to receive and act upon suggestions even from the president for the succession to the presidency, and they "covered" themselves by going through the motions of asking three successful women deeply imbedded in their own posts. Their refusal was a foregone conclusion.⁴

Because of the provisions of the Charter and By-laws, it is doubtful whether the action taken by the Board of Trustees could have been proved illegal. But unquestionably their action was unethical in that the trustees' committee on the succession to the presidency repudiated the wishes and votes of all constituencies of the college: administration, faculty, and alumnae. On paper written in ink in her own handwriting, in the files of Mary Woolley, is the sentence: "Dangerous business to outrage practically a whole college."

❋ ❋ ❋ ❋

For Mary Woolley that spring of 1936 from May 18th to the middle of June was a hard-pressed, critical three weeks in which she gave the Commencement addresses in places as far apart as Bradford Junior College, the Masters School at Dobbs Ferry, and Berea College in Kentucky, and the address at the Inauguration of John Edgar Park at Wheaton College. On May 16th the notice of the June 6th meeting of the Board of Trustees had been sent out by Harriet Newhall, secretary of the Board of Trustees. When electing a trustee it had been customary, as long as she and Olive Copeland, the secretary to the President, could remember, to have the nomination made at the meeting previous to the one at which the vote was to be taken. But the Chairman *gave no order to Harriet Newhall to send with the notice the announcement that the election of either college president or trus-*

tee would take place at the June 6th Board Meeting. The trustees themselves were notified only by a multigraphed sheet, whereas formal notification is required for the election of even a trustee.

At the grimmest Commencement time Mount Holyoke had ever had, the Executive Meeting of the Board of Trustees was set for eleven o'clock Saturday morning, June 6th. The Conference Committee of the Faculty and Mary Woolley were to be allowed to plead that the opportunity as president of the college should be kept open for a woman: and the Board was thereafter to place its so-called vote on a successor.

What neither the Faculty Conference Committee nor Mary Woolley knew was that something over two weeks before this June 6th a man had been asked by the Committee of Nine and had accepted; that two weeks before June 6th the publicity connected with this man's election had been placed from the Atlantic to the Pacific; and that about nine o'clock this Saturday morning of June 6th, two hours before the Trustee Meeting opened, the president of the Board of Trustees had confidentially given the releases to the College Press Bureau. This "official" election day—and Mary Woolley still believed it was that—was beginning when, dressed in a familiar black gown, she left her house a few minutes before eleven, stopped in her office in Mary Lyon for a moment, then walked up College Street a few steps and into Williston Library. She went up one flight of stairs and into the Cleveland Room adjacent to the Stimson Room where the Conference Committee of the faculty was pleading with the trustees to defer their decision until women had received adequate consideration. Their liege lady, the president, had been directed by the trustees to remain in the Cleveland Room until the Conference Committee had been heard. Sitting there alone, Mary Woolley had ample time to do what she had been doing over and over again: reflect upon the causes which had brought about the conditions in the midst of which she found herself. She was beginning to see clearly—not as a student of law would see it but as a student of history could see it—*that if the laws governing the appointment and powers of a trustee were as favorable to women as they were to men, this could not have happened.* She saw also that from the legal point of view this disparity in equality was true in virtually all the aspects of a woman's life.[5]

Present with the conference group of the faculty on this day were the chairman of the committee, Doctor Emma Perry Carr, distinguished for her work in chemistry and the winner of medals and of honorary degrees, and the members of her committee, Caroline M. Galt, Amy

Hewes, Elizabeth Adams, substituting for Helen Patch who was away on leave of absence, Abby Turner and David Adams. After being introduced by Doctor Carr, in turn each member of the committee presented briefly a particular argument why the decision should be delayed. Some weeks before, two of the members of the Conference Committee, Emma Carr and Caroline Galt, had met with the chairman of the Board of Trustees. They had driven down to Cambridge to see him, and had been told that "the matter was entirely out of his hands at that time and the only thing the Conference Committee could do would be to present the matter to the Board of Trustees when they met to take final action on the recommendation of the Nominating Committee."

Each member of the Conference Committee said his or her little speech, most of them conscious of their helplessness and that the president was being kept waiting in the Cleveland Room. When these members of the committee had finished speaking, they were not asked any questions. The committee lingered a moment, expecting something to happen. As they lingered a member of the Conference Committee said that upon the faces of a few of the trustees was an expression of smug achievement and condescension toward these little people, these women, who, representing almost every honor the academic world could give, were trying to stop them from appointing a man. Then the Conference Committee filed out, passing as they did so the Cleveland Room and in it Mary Woolley waiting. Greeting her as they walked past, the hearts of some of them were filled with resentment that she should have been kept waiting in an ante-room before being called by her own trustees to confer with them on one of the most important issues of her whole administration of a college of which she had been called the "second founder".

When they were gone, Mary Woolley entered the Stimson Room and was permitted to speak. Wearing neither her heart upon her sleeve for daws to peck at, nor seeking any escape in emotion, businesslike, at the moment pale, the hand which held her notes trembling, she stood behind the table desk and began speaking without notes: "Mr. Chairman: The letter which I wrote to each member of the Board of Trustees, under date of May the twentieth, gives the reasons for my strong feeling with regard to the appointment of a woman as my successor in the presidency . . . Those reasons, as you may recall, are as follows: first, the principle upon which Mount Holyoke was founded, that women as human beings have an equal right with men for the development of their powers and an equal right to opportunities for service; second, that the progress of Mount Holyoke throughout the last one hundred years has been under the leadership of women, to whom recognition is due; third, that a change in policy with regard to the presidency of Mount Holyoke would mean striking a blow to the advancement of women, the seriousness of which can hardly be over-estimated . . ."

All the while this honest woman had a curious sensation that she was struggling with invisible forces and suffering began to show in the heightened color of her face. The fingers of her left hand just touching the table became unsteady. Nevertheless, her voice remained steady, low and commanding as she dwelt upon the blow which would be given to the advancement of women if there were such a change in policy; and upon the wishes of 87 members of the teaching faculty out of 106 that it should be a woman.

"Surely," she continued, "no expression of opinion should have greater weight than that of the faculty to whom is due in large measure the progress of an institution. No opportunity has been given for an alumnae vote on the question of choice between a man and a woman, but judging from the individual comments from all sections of the country, it is reasonable to assume that a large majority of alumnae prefer a woman as president of the College . . ."

Again feeling as if she were beating the air in a struggle with invisible forces and conscious that her voice had begun to show agitation, she paused an instant. Had she known that these invisible forces were actual facts such as the two-week-old acceptance by a man as president-elect, the two-week-old placing of the publicity, and the publicity release early this very morning of June 6th *before* the meeting at which she was speaking, her plea would have been neither begun nor concluded. Ignorant of trickery, she went on to her conclusion: "To sum up, I can imagine no greater blow to the advancement of women than the announcement that Mount Holyoke celebrates its Centennial by departing from the ideal which inspired the founding of the institution and which has been responsible in large measure for its progress."

As she closed, brow-beating by certain members of the Board began. Nevertheless, because of the insistence of two of the alumnae trustees, Frances Perkins and Harriet Love Thompson, it was decided that the president was to be admitted a second time at four o'clock in the afternoon to plead again for the traditions of Mount Holyoke and the opportunities of women.

CHAPTER 17

WHAT PRICE SUCCESS?

"Civilization has been hard upon women."

Silent and without appetite Mary Woolley had eaten her lunch at home, and then lain down for a short time. That afternoon before the second meeting she was at her desk for a few minutes. "This morning," she wrote, "following a protest by the faculty, I also presented a protest against the change of policy involved in choosing a man in place of a woman for the presidency of Mount Holyoke. Since the Board of Trustees by this action has not sustained that protest I hereby present my resignation to take effect September 1, 1936." Then she placed her resignation in the folder designated "Succession to the President" to wait until the afternoon meeting in the New York Room was over. At least there was to be that second meeting and ignorant of the facts she believed that she could still hope as she prepared to make her last plea for a woman as president.

That afternoon the tension increased as Mary Woolley rose to say: "It was on July first, 1935, I wrote to every member of the Board of Trustees and again on May 20th, 1936. You will notice that in these letters I make several points, among them that all over the country men and women interested in the recognition of women are taking a keen interest in this matter. I realized the 'intensity of feeling' that would be aroused but I under-estimated its extent. I have been to no gathering, public or private, since last Commencement, when the subject has not been introduced by men and women having no connection with Mount Holyoke College.

"I have a file of protests written to me personally by individuals and groups including both alumnae and men and women having no connection with Mount Holyoke. It is unnecessary to add that these protests are spontaneous . . . Your statement that 'it is only a small minority of alumnae and students who make objection' is not borne out by my own experience."

For the time being, she closed by repeating the words from her letter of May 20th: "In loyalty to Mary Lyon's vision and to her superb achievement; in loyalty to the women who have borne the heat and burden of the day during these hundred years; in loyalty to the cause of the advancement of women, I make this plea and I protest against the proposed appointment of a man as President of Mount Holyoke College."

As Mary Woolley finished speaking, one of the men trustees stood up quickly and said: "I have been disturbed by the way in which the Board seems to have been precipitated into action."

And another man rose, saying: "There are several members of this Board, more than one I am sure, who would like to have a delay in the voting on the succession to the Presidency."

At that up jumped one of the alumnae trustees who began sneering at Mary Woolley—words best forgotten now. Her face flushed, another alumna trustee sprang to her feet, crying out angrily: "*Stop that sneering at Miss Woolley at once and sit down!*"

Startled by this unconventional outburst, for an instant all were silent, and the unfriendly alumna sat down as the voice of Mary Woolley rang out with these words: "This Board of Trustees should know that the way in which this action towards the election of a man is being taken is more worthy of Hitler than of the United States of America!"

Then in a voice which continued to be under control she went on to give facts which some of the trustees will never forget. The sound of her voice, the words she spoke, the aspect of her face, all confirmed the truth of Mary Woolley's final judgment on what had been done to women by the methods of a few trustees, women as well as men. Even then she did not know all the facts but she knew somehow that her sensation of battling with unseen forces was valid.

As she finished speaking, the trustee who had led the fight to put in a man leaned over, placing his hand on that of an alumna trustee, and, with an outworn facetiousness of the male sex, joked at the expense of the aspirations and sorrows of a modern woman as he whispered with a sneer for Mary Woolley: "*Now* shall we have tears!" She snatched away her hand and one trustee realized too late that it was not *always* possible to count on the disloyalty of women to women, for there are women great and small upon whose unbreakable loyalty to other women it *is* possible to depend.

Towards the close of that afternoon session, when the vote for a woman as president of Mount Holyoke—a vote which would have honored the work of Mary Woolley's lifetime—was lost, Frances Perkins took Mary Woolley home. Summoned, JM found them in the dining room, the heavy curtains drawn to shut off the hallway. Mary Woolley had sunk down at the dining room table with her head resting on her hands. Her breath was coming heavily and she was trembling and silent.

Despite the fact that she knew it would take more than the U.S. Department of Labor plus a doctor, plus a nurse to persuade Mary Woolley to "take" anything, Frances Perkins was trying to persuade the president to take a bracer of whiskey. Before she left to return to the meeting she said over and over in a tone of pleading: "But, Miss Woolley, at times like these this is what a stimulant is for."

It was becoming dusk and there was the sound of a car coming down the driveway towards the President's House. The door bell rang, followed by the well-known voice of a member of the faculty.

Dr. Emma Perry Carr said a rumor had reached her that Miss Woolley had lost her plea for the succession of women as presidents at Mount Holyoke. Was that true?

It was true! Mary Woolley had lost. To quote one word from Mary Woolley's July 1, 1935, letter to the trustees, the Board was "celebrating" the Centennial by electing a man as president.

"If only I had fully realized the situation earlier," Emma Carr explained, "I might have been able to do something."

"I know, Emma, but you see Miss Woolley would not believe this could happen."

"And I can't believe," came impulsively, "that such stupidity exists in a world of intelligent human beings. I find that most men condemn even more vigorously than the women what these trustees have been doing."

As she got up to go she said: "My father used to say that it's not enough to do your best but it must be the best that could be done, and there I'm a fair target for criticism."

"Emma, we're all 'fair targets', and I think Miss Woolley, too, feels that way about herself. But her deepest grief is for her faculty and for other women."

Going out together, Emma Carr opened the door to get into her coupe but before she could do so she broke into tears. Clinging to the door handle, she wept for this loss to women.

That night in June, Mary Woolley sat alone at her desk in her bedroom. Did she hear the sneering whisper: "Now shall we have tears?" It may be she did but with Father Bernard she knew that "ridicule answers no questions."

It was three minutes before eleven. Thinking of her faculty—friends who, more than ever, were counting upon her—she stood up and took down from the top of her desk the folder "Succession to the President", removed from it her resignation, and reading it again, wrote across it, "Not presented", underlining these two words with her red pencil.

The clock in the hall below was striking eleven when by radio announcement came a statement obviously intended for the information of Mount Holyoke alumnae, faculty, students, as well as for the general public, that a man had been elected to succeed President Woolley. On the floor lay her dog Blue Boy. Mary Woolley got up and leaning down patted him, saying over and over absentmindedly: "Boydie, darling! Boydie, darling! You know I love you, Boydie?" Yes, he knew, and lifting his head looked up at her, rubbing his muzzle against her hand. In the loss which had come to Bummy, Boy had comforted him and the healing had begun. In Mary Woolley's "loss" Boy was a comfort to her, but there was to be no healing for her and she was never again to be her buoyant self.

* * * *

No criers were out on the night of June 6th hawking the sheet printed by the Alumnae Committee for the Investigation, for none were needed. Under big headlines covering the top of the flyer, eager readers had found among other items the following startling statements:

"THE CASE OF MOUNT HOLYOKE vs.
THE COMMITTEE OF NINE, JUNE 6, '36
WAS THE COMMITTEE OF NINE PACKED?
RUSHING IT INTO THE NEWS"
"PRECIPITATED THROUGH THE BOARD"
"*Rejected*: ('70 women disqualified')"

Headline after headline, packed with carefully checked information —and signed for the Alumnae Committee for the Investigation by Amy F. Rowland, Chairman, and Carolyn D. Smiley, secretary.

On the following day it was an alumna, Charlotte Parker, who asked: "As far as Miss Woolley herself is concerned would there be any honor which would seem to her greater than the succession should lie where she wishes it to lie; in the traditional leadership of a woman at Mount Holyoke?" And on the next day an editorial in the *Holyoke Daily Transcript* closed with this paragraph: "Today . . . one of the greatest doors ever opened for women in the whole history of education . . . has been closed to women's mastery. A great opportunity has been taken away from women in American education." Yet the students of that generation seemed, as a whole, to understand little or nothing about what was being done to their eminent leader and to women.

Some of them were satisfied to complain that they were tired of hearing about Geneva and they didn't want to hear any more about peace. With the hydrogen bomb pendant over Mother Earth or husband or son lost in war, it would be interesting today to know whether those students would feel quite so bored by work for women and for peace? The fact of this student inexperience is all the more sad, for if the Class of 1937 had said "*Stop!*", the decision of the trustees would certainly have had to be different. When all is said and done, what a college has to "sell"—even in a crude world "groomed for bankers' daughters" —is "bought" by the students and their parents.

In the center of this whirling public opinion Mary Woolley wrote home on June 17th that the trustee meeting at the college "went smoothly yesterday noon, with no reference to 'the succession'—and all recommendations approved. I felt that I had a steel-rod in place of my normal spine, but I suspect that that feeling will continue." In this letter, as she passed on to happier subjects, laughingly she gave the trustees an inverted thrust: "The 'woods are full' of Congregationalists and 'Christians'—I reached home in time to dress hurriedly and welcome them at Chapin, an audience the size of the Commencement one, and they are not yet all there." When, finally, they were "all there" this convocation made Mary Woolley the first woman moderator of the Congregational Churches of America—not for her wit but because her fame had never tripped her principles. Rufus Jones, the Quaker, knew, and hundreds of the clergy of the Congregational Church knew, what was being done to Mary Woolley and her life work. At this time it was about Rufus Jones in a moment of lovable off-guardedness, Mary Woolley wrote home: "I shall have a 'sheaf' of letters to bring with me. So many members of the Council—the majority men—spoke to me. Dr. Cadman said: 'It is an outrage', and although Rufus Jones did not use 'swear words' he came as near to it as a good friend could!" A little later, while she was at Harvard speaking to the Summer School, she said in another letter home: "Several men spoke to me with *dis*approval of the sex of my successor—one of them a member of the Harvard faculty—one of the 'extreme feminists' so numerous at Harvard!"

In the unceasing pressure upon her to reverse her position, contumely more subtle than slander was used in various forms. With a few alumnae this form of threat ran something like this: "Now, Miss Woolley, you have had our 'profound respect' and that of all our family but *if . . .*" etc. Or: "We think your work and that of your predecessors is being irretrievably harmed by the 'improper activities' of the alumnae who support you!" To this Mary Woolley would reply:

"It is hardly necessary for me to tell you how I appreciate your letter. The position which a group of alumnae has taken is based, however, on a principle, and I think is a question between the alumnae and the trustees." When some alumnae wired that the *Boston Herald* stated Carolyn Smiley would discuss at the Susan B. Anthony dinner the naming of a man as president of Mount Holyoke, and would Miss Woolley please stop her, Mary Woolley answered: "Your telegram of the fifteenth reached me but I took no action. In the first place, I am a firm believer in freedom of speech, and in the second, I think the principle involved in the change has become an issue far beyond the limits of the alumnae."

Urged repeatedly to publish a statement about the reasons for her opposition, Mary Woolley's invariable reply was: "If I do I am convinced that my statement should be printed in the *Alumnae Quarterly*." As she saw more doors closing upon women, again she wrote in reply: "I feel that the '*Alumnae Quarterly*'—not the newspaper—is the place for my statement." Finally, she yielded to the insistence of some of the alumnae groups supporting her and sent for the editor of the *Alumnae Quarterly*, and for her assistant. To them she explained that she had written a statement of her position and asked that it be published in the *Alumnae Quarterly*. To one who, under all circumstances as a woman and as president of Mount Holyoke had stood for free speech, it came as a shock when the editor refused to accept any statement from her, even as the editor refused to accept an article by Dr. Helen Griffith urging the need of immediate reorganization of the Board of Trustees.

Mary Woolley said: "Do you not think it is going rather far to refuse admission to the *Alumnae Quarterly* to the President of the College?"

The editor continued to refuse.

When Harriet Newhall heard of this she went to the editor, and in a stormy interview made it plain that if the editor continued to refuse to admit Miss Woolley's statement, she would be criticized by all groups of responsible men and women for such a refusal to the President of the College.

Although July and "vacation" time had come and Mary Woolley was on Lake Champlain, that terrible "June" of 1936 was not over. When the summer issue of the *Quarterly* containing her statement reached her, anxiously Mary Woolley glanced through twenty-nine pages of the *Alumnae Quarterly*. On the thirtieth page she found her statement printed in fine type in an inconspicuous place, and thus had her protest been buried. But that was not all, for the introductory words she had written for the article in order that the alumnae might understand her position, the editor, a Mount Holyoke alumna, had "edited", inserting the words "at her request", thus absolving the *Quarterly* from any responsibility for the statement and from any seeming expression of agreement with it. All this had been done without reference to Mary Woolley herself and without her knowledge. Even if it is not new, the experience of being buried alive is rare. On that summer day when the *Alumnae Quarterly* reached Fleur de Lys, its effect on Mary Woolley, once seen, could never be forgotten.

When she returned to the house, she took down from the top of her desk the folder containing the papers for the Mount Holyoke College Fund Campaign which she had been leading to raise money. Steadily she read over the names of the members of the Fund Committee, thinking that Elizabeth Wyckoff as Chairman had worked a miracle in bringing such conflicting forces together, the just and the unjust among the alumnae united for the purpose of raising in the name of Mary Woolley a fund to increase faculty salaries and for the care of Student-Alumnae Hall. The wry twist of her mouth became a faint smile of amusement, the fingers of her left hand—tap—tap—tapping on the desk.

Still she did not believe that the trustees' action, prejudicial to the future of women, as well as cruel to her, was the wish of the alumnae as a whole. But of some of them, she now asked herself, why she had ever trusted them?

She put down the folder, thought a minute, got up again from her chair and went over to the mantle piece of her fireplace, taking down a volume by James Russell Lowell. Going back to her desk she began copying this message in her large, firm hand:

> The only conclusive evidence of a man's sincerity is that he gives himself for a principle. Words, money, all things else, are comparatively easy to give away; but when a man makes a gift of his daily life and practice, it is plain that the truth, whatever it may be, has taken possession of him.

Then she clipped the two half sheets of her copying to the Fund Folder. Reaching down and opening the bottom drawer of her desk, she took out the strong box which had once been her father's and laid the Fund Folder in the strong box with other papers of value. There, eleven years later, after the anguish and sorrow of 1936 and 1937 had done their ultimate work, these clipped papers were found.

❖   ❖   ❖   ❖

Definitely, there was always in her thought a nice point of exactness in punctilio in the situations which followed one another swiftly. To an alumna: "I have felt keenly that this question was a question between alumnae and trustees and that any action on my part would be a mistake." Again, in a similar connection, she wrote: "Anything to be really effective must come from without—not from me." Any organizing of the alumnae under her leadership to oppose the action the trustees had taken was in the mind of Mary Woolley an untenable position ethically, for in the leadership of the college the primary relationship was between the Board of Trustees and herself. "Adamant" some called Mary Woolley, others "implacable". Perhaps! But, as Mary Lyon had said, you cannot polish a piece of sponge but you can polish a piece of steel.

Elizabeth Adams on request to the President was not permitted to speak and felt herself obliged to issue her statement on June 10th as an *Open Letter to the Trustees of Mount Holyoke*. In one paragraph she wrote: "The expressed preference of the alumnae is for a woman . . . Sixty per cent of the replies indicated that the president should be a woman or suggested only women as candidates . . ." It is important to remember Mary Woolley's refusal to permit Dr. Adams to speak, not so much for reasons of rightness or wrongness, but because of the light this refusal throws on one of the aspects of Mary Woolley's plan of "action". The president had little of the knowledge and none of the experience of the industrial woman—and for her the militant methods of the suffragists had always been anathema. Fight? Undignified. Scratch? She could not even imagine doing such a thing! Yet there was a group of alumnae—distinguished women whose importance in their work and to other women cannot be exaggerated— who advocated militancy, believing in it as a tool of last resort. About five weeks after June 6th one of these women, Dr. Esther Richards of Johns Hopkins, wrote Mary Woolley: "I felt then and I know now that our overtures are useless. When a group of men in power make up their minds that it is necessary to the perpetuation of their own ego to establish a male line, nothing can stop them."

In short, the "lady-like" among women were the traitors to the race —*not* militancy. In the same year of 1936 that great leader Carrie Chapman Catt had said that in fifty years of continued labor in the woman movement she had never come upon a case of any kind, whatever, where a woman or women, collectively, lost status, when it had not happened wholly because men in positions of authority believed women inferior in everything. And Mrs. Catt had found that when women surrendered to this view, and shared in it, it was because they suffered from an inferiority complex. The logical and dignified approach having failed, the group of distinguished women believed that a specific selection of militant representatives of other organizations should be encouraged to carry out militant plans. "Scratching" in its various forms should be the object of such a militant group. Some women should be "chained to the gates of Mount Holyoke College as the Woman's Party might dramatically and justifiably behave." In short, these eminent academic women had reached the conclusion that it was futile to use peaceful and dignified methods. Kid gloves and good manners would no longer help. When they wrote Mary Woolley about this plan to overcome the trustees and control any alumnae who continued to rationalize about "harmony" and nurse inferiority complexes, Mary Woolley's reply after a week's deliberation was as follows: "I must confess that I do not like the idea of the National Woman's Party taking up the subject." Following this letter, the alumnae dropped their plans. Another eminent woman emphasized the fact that "the tragedy of Mount Holyoke's succession was not an isolated incident connected with one college but a symbol of what the world is doing to women's education and advancement." And she was aghast to hear at that time that one of the hostile trustees, who had married a Mount Holyoke alumna, voluntarily stated: "No woman has ever been a scholar or ever can be a scholar!" It is difficult to know how he would have pigeon-holed several women at that time on the faculty — among them Dr. Mary Inda Hussey who could read the Hebrew, Arabic, Assyrian, Babylonian, Sumerian, Ethiopic and Egyptian languages, and who had published books and articles on the Sumerian tablets, Babylonian life and art, and comparative religions.

For the president, letters poured in from high and low, weak and strong, and all were acknowledged. Sometimes Mary Woolley wrote a two or three line note of friendly appreciation. To some bewildered college student who wanted to "stand by" but did not know what to say, the president replied: "It has been a hard year and I am most grateful to those who, like yourself, have 'stood by'." To an alumna who did not know what to do: "Your 'very best wishes' are the most helpful thing that you can do!" signing herself: "affectionately, your friend." To the daughter of Rufus Jones, Mary Hoxie Jones, she wrote: "Your letter of the twenty-third 'warmed the cockles of my heart'. As your mother and father know and you will know some day, a hard experience has a bright side in that it makes one realize and depend upon one's friends. Certainly I never appreciated them as I do today!"

In many letters of acknowledgment to the Mount Holyoke alumnae, she spoke her mind without reservation—always, whenever possible, with the emphasis upon principle. To two alumnae she wrote:

> I do not need to remind you that I am standing for a principle. May I add that if the alumnae choose to indulge in personalities, that is their own affair. The principle for which I stand remains unchanged no matter what personalities are indulged in . . . However much you and I may hope that the committee can be effectively implemented, it is still to be proved that the committee as organized can become a working committee.

Not once but insistently did Mary Woolley push aside or ignore "personalities" and emphasize principle. To a member of her family she wrote:

> Several alumnae at the Council Meeting,—Lydia Sanderson Capen, Sallie Allen Medlicott and others, feel deeply on the subject of the Trustee action and express themselves in no uncertain tones. "A wicked thing has been done"—was Mrs. Capen's greeting. The Executive Board of the Alumnae Association, however, is taking the position that "for the sake of the College, everything must be done to preserve harmony" and I think any "action" against the Alumnae Trustees, is just not going to happen.[1]

To Mr. Sherman, editor of the *Hartford Courant,* she wrote: "I am finding that only the minority have been able to 'see through' to the principle involved. I am proud that you belong to that group." To Mrs. Dwight, editor of the *Holyoke Transcript,* she confided: "Last evening's editorial in the *Transcript,* which I know you wrote, brought strength to my soul and joy to my heart. You are one of the minority who see the principle at stake and take your position fearlessly upon it."

Significantly, Mary Woolley never fortified her statement by the statements of others in her own group: as for example the president of Wellesley, Ellen Fitz Pendleton, who wrote that she was stunned by the action of the trustees, that she did not believe all the rumors she had heard, and that her sympathy was matched only by her indignation that all that Mary Woolley had "done and been for Mount Holyoke and women's education should seem . . . to be set at naught." Mary Woolley, as well as President Pendleton, was well aware of what had happened and was still happening to other women who attempted to express their moral power and ability by means of pacifism or through work for peace and through internationalism.

A letter which in this crisis brought her personally much comfort, among the many hundreds still on file, was from her nephew, Reverend Paul Woolley of the Westminster Theological School.[2] This she answered by hand, explicitly and without reservation:

The President's House
June 27, 1936

My dear Paul:—

Your letter did me much good and I am grateful to you.

Aside from the personal grief this is the hardest blow that I have ever received. You strike the nail right on the head, in your diagnosis. The vote of the Trustees in favor of the Committee report was less than two-thirds,—the vote required to elect a trustee. The By-Laws say nothing about the election of a president.

I think often of you and the way in which you stand without flinching for what you think is right.

Much love for you and for Lenny and the boys.

Your loving
Aunt May.

For reasons that she did not wholly understand, Mary Woolley began to be conscious that she was making mistakes in a hitherto successful leadership of women. Later, as she saw this fact clearly, her personal suffering was tragic. It was her inability to undo the harm of her faith in others and in their sense of justice which helped to break her superb health. It was not alone to her friend Professor Whitney of Vassar but over and over in her own thought she "wrote" these words: "I thought that I had done all that I could, but as I look back I wish I had done nothing except arouse public opinion!" And perhaps even harder for her to bear was not the "fraternal" decision of the trustees, but the knowledge that it was the disloyalty of women to other women which had brought about decisions inimical to the progress of women.

An exhausted and bewildered faculty, an uninformed body of alumnae, a star chamber committee which had done its work diabolically well, and a morally unintimidated Mary Woolley express the conditions which lay behind the tumult of these years. In that struggle for freedom for and justice to women, two women were the leaders: Carolyn Smiley, impetuous and forthright, and with limited regard for punctilio, and Mary Woolley. Of both it might have been said, "We may be personally defeated but our principles never."

❂   ❂   ❂   ❂

During these hard years it seemed as if Mary Woolley had omitted few parts of the country in her talks about education and peace. Besides formal speeches and addresses she was threading to and fro, leading a committee meeting here, present at a committee meeting there, in Washington with the A.A.U.W. or the Peoples Mandate, in New York with the Federal Council of Churches or the Near East Relief, or just taking an added honorary degree or so! From Washington at a meeting of the A.A.U.W., of which she was president, she wrote home that although they had more executive meetings than they could well take care of, there was, nevertheless, time for people to speak to her about the Mount Holyoke situation. Then she added: "And I am ashamed that it should be Mount Holyoke."

In Indianapolis on October 22, 1936, in Cadle Auditorium she spoke on "The Old Order Changeth" to thousands of men and women—ten thousand, to be exact—of the Indiana State Teachers Association. Talking with her family about the journey and its experiences, she said:

> It was a large audience, at Indianapolis, ten thousand, and my talk went well, I think. But afterward there was a small reception, only a few hundred and limited to teachers—chiefly teachers from the public schools of the city. The women showed their efficiency in the way in which that reception line moved along steadily for over an hour. But there was one woman, a teacher, such a little woman in size.
>
> When she shook hands with me she looked up straight into my eyes and said: "Miss Woolley, because of the men, we women have been having a hard time keeping our posts in the schools, and it is becoming harder for us every day. If what has happened at Mount Holyoke could happen to you, what will happen to us women now?"
>
> At a moment like that with the line of guests moving past steadily there was nothing I could say to her. But ever since her "what will happen to us women now?" has haunted me.

She had become profoundly tired, not definitely ill as yet but heavy with the sorrow of all that was happening both in education and in peace to her life's work in training women for leadership. Over and over she heard the voice of the little teacher asking, "What will happen to us women now?". As she became too depressed to get away from memories she spoke often of that little teacher. She was asking herself: "What *can* I do now?"

Well, one more thing! Despite the weariness and pressure of the college work and strife, it was only a few days after she left Indianapolis before she was writing to the treasurer, a member of the Board of Trustees of Mount Holyoke College, about her Indianapolis experience:

> I realized the "intensity of feeling" that would be aroused but I underestimated its extent. I have been to no gathering, public or private, since last Commencement, when the subject has not been introduced by men and women having no connection with Mount Holyoke College. A week ago at the State Teachers' Association of Indiana, where the attendance at the main address numbered ten thousand persons, it was repeatedly brought up. The Dean of Women of the University of Indiana told me that the Association of Deans of the State was sending a protest to the President of our Board of Trustees, and a member of the State Federation

of Business and Professional Women said that a similar protest had been sent to the Board a year ago.

Although crass egotism in the end might have done more "good" she did not say in this letter: "at which I was the chief speaker." When one of the trustees, Boyd Edwards, received a copy of this letter to the treasurer, he wrote: "Your letter to Mr. Harvey is just like you —sound, courteous, modest with that strong note of simple integrity and candor in it which is so characteristic."

And about that time Mary Woolley received a letter from her friend Dr. Marion Park of Bryn Mawr, in which President Park said that she must be feeling "sad, angry, incredulous".

At the November meeting of the trustees, Mary Woolley was a silent auditor. Despite the fact that it was the close of a campaign and that a shipping strike was crippling transportation, Frances Perkins was there and also Harriet Love Thompson, for both were working to have the decision of June 6th reversed. The so-called discussion was taken up. With the outside public the Committee of Nine knew that they could make no headway; these "papers", then, were not actually petitions from alumnae, said the Committee of Nine, for it was the alumnae who wished a man appointed to the succession of women. Following these and similar statements, a dean of other years—not Harriett Allyn, the dean of recent years—made a speech for the appointment of a man and was applauded by the trustees.[3]

Knowing as Mary Woolley did by this time some of the facts behind what was being done, she had ceased the attempt to conciliate. Under the power of her moral understanding and with the phenomenal memory characteristic of her, she moved into what was to be her last speech on behalf of women at Mount Holyoke. By the time she had finished she had given the trustees such facts as she could with dignity concerning the past three years, and they were not pleasant facts. No report of the petitions and of her "discussion" was ever shown and this despite the fact the college had published and paid for an edition of ten thousand copies of a trustee's article about the President-elect. A servant of futility Mary Woolley had never been. Except at the small conference on February 16, 1937, *to* the trustees officially she never spoke again. ..*With* the trustees she continued to speak pleasantly and courteously about the incidental affairs of the college.

❖   ❖   ❖   ❖

On February 1, 1937, the *Bedford Times* carried this news headline: "COMMITTEE FIGHTS TO OUST MAN AS MOUNT HOLYOKE PRESIDENT." This battle of the headlines continued throughout New England—Massachusetts, New York, Maine, Rhode Island—as well as in Alabama, Missouri, and elsewhere; headlines appeared in such papers as the *Boston Transcript*, the *Christian Science Monitor*, the *New York Times*—all telling essentially the same story: SAY MOUNT HOLYOKE COLLEGE PRESIDENT WAS "RAILROADED"; PRESIDENT WOOLLEY RAPS TRUSTEES; MT. HOLYOKE SHIFT ALARMS DR. WOOLLEY; MARY WOOLLEY BACKS PROTEST AT MT. HOLYOKE.

Amidst this uproar, Mary Woolley was staying at the College Club in Boston, ready to give at the Mount Vernon Church her Dwight L. Moody Centenary talk "I Knew Moody." True to her loyalty to women she said the morning following her talk: "I feel that in the celebration some mention should have been made of Mr. Moody's wife. May I say that Mrs. Moody was one of the very great influences in Mr. Moody's life."

It was at the time of the Boston engagements that two areas of high pressure in problem and emotion began to come together: the campaign of the Committee of 100 to keep the leadership of Mount Holyoke for women, followed by the one and only interview which Mary Woolley gave after her Moody address. In this interview with the *Boston Transcript* she declared the Mount Holyoke College administration could have nothing to do with the strife among the alumnae which had broken out over the election of a man as president of Mount Holyoke: "It really is a question which rests with the alumnae body itself. I can't see it in any other way."

Then unexpectedly and suddenly she found herself in the midst of a raging storm of headlines, words, people, insults and slander. The storm seemed to center around a letter she had sent to the secretary of the Committee of 100 and which without her approval or consent had been given to the press. This is what Mary Woolley had written:

> Through the interest of an alumna disturbed by the flier, I received a copy on Sunday, Jan. 31. One day later the committee sent me a copy of this sheet which Miss Amy Rowland of the Cleveland Clinic and a former alumna trustee, Miss Carolyn Smiley of Boston, Dr. Esther Richards of Johns Hopkins and others are sponsoring.
>
> To the extent of my knowledge the statements on the fliers are accurate. They are not only accurate, but they also suggest a trend which has been markedly unfortunate for women in European countries and in England.
>
> Although the women of America have been somewhat more fortunate, nevertheless there are many instances even in this country today of "fraternal" decisions to replace women by men. For the sake of other women, if not for one's own, noblesse oblige dictates that these evidences should not be ignored.

In addition to this letter, what had she actually done? And what had she said? Perhaps the most disturbing act was one that is never put into words but which in the age-old battle for freedom is always an affront to those bi-valve human beings who open the shells of their minds for locomotion and eating only: *She had dared to call her soul her own.* She did *not* say: "The case is moral, not legal." It was the flier issued by the Committee of 100 which had printed that pertinent and true statement. But she *did* say in the one interview given: "*My feeling is that so radical a change should not have been made without gaining an opinion from the alumnae and faculty . . . Presidents are not elected in other colleges without determining the opinion of all concerned, both the alumnae and the faculty . . . I think that the implication that there was no woman available to head the college is a serious side of the whole question. Haven't women succeeded, after a century of training in higher education, in bringing forth women fitted to handle the administration of a woman's college as well as men? . . . I believe that we have. For haven't we brought Mount Holyoke through the years with a woman as president . . ."*

In all the accumulation of publicity, a phrase about Mary Woolley used again and again was "leading the fight". That was exactly what Mary Woolley had *not* done and was never to do! She was constitutionally incapable of leading *any* fight; and had she been able to lead a fight, because of punctilio she would not have done so. Not once but several times she failed even those who were capable of fighting and who were trying to win the fight. Told what "tools" they were about to use and troubled by her sense of fitness she asked the committee not to use them.

Deeply shaken by the storm of publicity, she left Boston for home and on February 4th wrote this statement:

> Recent reports in the public press concerning the presidency of Mount Holyoke College have attributed remarks to me which I have not made.
>
> I have consistently maintained the position of favoring a woman, culminating in my statement to the trustees under date of June 6, 1936, but I have made no statements to the public and, with the exception of a single interview concerning the principle involved in changing the presidency from a woman to a man, I have given no interview.

After that Mary Woolley collapsed. "Home" and one of the college physicians saw to it that not by a word should it be known that she had had an acute dilatation of the heart. On the day of her heart attack, Sophie Chantal Hart, Professor of English at Wellesley College, was writing to Carolyn Smiley:

> If it is possible, would you kindly send me two copies of the statement about the Mt. Holyoke presidency issued by a Committee of One Hundred.

I admire so much the fine, courageous stand your Committee has taken and the cogent presentation. You have helped the cause of women everywhere by not keeping to the pussy-footing quiet which gives up while the fascist group among the Trustees goes on in triumph.

I am a Radcliffe alumna but deeply interested in Mt. Holyoke. I enclose a stamped envelope.

Since Miss Woolley continued to be in danger of death at any moment, the doctor, as she left the house, said: "Miss Woolley might have another heart attack. In that case you should—"

"Please write it out on a piece of paper," interrupted JM.

Dr. Groves paused a moment, wrote out her instructions, and handed over the "prescription" sheet. Through two days everything was cut off, including the telephone, for the tone of Mary Woolley's heart remained bad.

CHAPTER 18

FLYING GLASS

"One of the greatest—I think I would say the greatest, gift a human being can give to another is confidence."

For a short time Mary Woolley was in danger of death at any moment. Then her naturally superb health brought her part-way back to life. But in that coming back she was never to know the extent of damage which had been done to her heart. On the second day, as Dr. Groves was leaving the house to put in a call for Dr. Barrett of Springfield, she said: "I have never before seen anyone age so. In twenty-four hours Miss Woolley has aged ten years!

When Chaplain Woolley's church work was broken in two, he had all the resilience of youth. Chronologically, when this shock came to his daughter, she was an old woman, to be exact, seventy-four. Now she lay quietly and without complaint in bed for several days, the comforting collies about her as she did what she was asked to do by the doctors. However, her Day Book was beside her and from time to time she picked it up, making such entries as these:

"No appts. today"—"Roses for Mrs. Hoe"—"Lamb for dogs".

On the following day she wrote in a trembling hand: "Rosalie C. Monday $10. 8th"—"Withheld letters?"—"Miss Park".

These entries meant that she wanted to remember to pay the head maid on Monday, that she was worrying about some alumnae protest letters she knew had been withheld by the trustees, and that she was hoping eagerly to be able to be present at a dinner the president of Bryn Mawr was giving in her honor.

On February 7th Dr. Barrett of Springfield as well as Dr. Groves had called on her. She greeted them warmly, said little, and seemed a little amused by all their testing and tapping, as only a woman who had had, except for occasional colds, perfect health for seventy years, could be. When they left, she listened, smiling, for the closing of the heavy front door, then picked up her diary and jotted down "Invitations et cetera." She would "show them", and she did!

To JM as she came back into the room, the patient said: "I must talk with Harriet about the preparation of the invitation lists for the Cen-

tennial—only three months off now. Following the 8th of May and in
less than a month comes Commencement week . . . These three days
of quiet have helped me to see clearly that when my work at Mount
Holyoke is over I shall not be able to go back to the College until this
injustice done to women has been undone."

What is more, these days had helped the decision she made to go to
the Bryn Mawr dinner being given by President Park in her honor.
She did go, accompanied every step of the way by Harriet Newhall.

❀   ❀   ❀   ❀

How far "not quite daring to do right" is part of their inferiority
complex with women or part of the human nature women share with
men is a discussible question. In the month following there occurred
on the part of *certain official alumnae* an act which was not aggression
with all its ugly weapons but capitulation with all its weakness. As
this group of alumnae fled from the beachhead they had won, they
took with them all hopes of a reversal of trustee action. On that Saturday of the meeting, while Carolyn Smiley was on duty elsewhere, the
Opposition allowed one alumna to capture the Graduate Council
Meeting with an appeal which all commended as "statesmanlike". It
was a plea for "harmony" filled with kind words, a so-called "noble"
speech of appeasement. On that day of March, 1937, the changes had
been rung on four words: 'entirely free from emotion". Literally interpreted, this means that you are to see the democracy of your beloved
country or your home or the ideals and aspirations of your mother or
of your alma mater being pounded to pieces by some ruthless men and
women and yet remain "entirely free from emotion"! At that meeting
one who *should* have spoken for the opposition did not speak, and
one who was *not* a member of that committee took over control of the
committee and its policies. These two—one not a member of the committee— signed for the Committee of 100, without the knowledge of its
secretary Carolyn Smiley, on duty elsewhere, and of other members
of the Opposition. Then the Council issued this statement: "The
Committee of 100 is very well satisfied with the action of the alumnae
council today."

The "story" unwittingly told in this recorded report of the meeting
is clear: where officially the alumnae should have continued resistance,
they had indulged in appeasement. Some months earlier, Mary Woolley had written a letter to the two alumnae who were in part repsonsi-
ble for the capitulation in which she said: "However much you and I
may hope that the committee can be effectively implemented, it is *still
to be proved* that the Committee as organized can become a working

Committee." She had believed that the alumnae as a body cared for the principles for which she stood and that in their affection and loyalty there would be no separation between herself and those principles. This she believed no longer.

Less than a month later, after several attempts had been made by the trustees to make Mary Woolley confer an honorary degree on her successor, and in reply to a last endeavor, made within one month of the Centennial, to have her successor present at the luncheon for delegates, Mary Woolley wrote on April 4th:

> . . . My immediate reaction was that under the circumstances I could not preside at the luncheon. Upon further consideration I have decided that I must not be present.
>
> Last summer, when it was suggested that the Centennial should be held in May, I finally consented on the basis of the understanding that my successor would not be present. In the autumn I received letters of which I am enclosing copies.
>
> This is not a personal matter, as I have repeatedly stated. My presence at the luncheon would indicate that I acquiesce in the action of the Board with regard to my successor.

Meeting these efforts with invariable courtesy, she had made each time the statement that such action on her part would indicate that she acquiesced in the appointment of a man. Every attempt then and later to make her acquiesce in the action taken by the trustees on June 6th with its injustice to women failed. The last attempt of the trustees, too, having failed to force the president-elect upon the luncheon, she herself presided at the luncheon for the delegates.

Quietly, and without either recrimination or retaliation, Mary Woolley continued her work. The hands which put on the first clips and marked in large firm script "Letters Concerning the Succession to President" began to tremble a little as she reviewed for the last time the steps taken, and the notes she was making. Replacing the clips and filing the folder into place, she knew that the dream of her life had been shattered like broken glass.

❖   ❖   ❖   ❖

The decision reached on June 6th to break the succession of women as presidents of Mount Holyoke was one which outraged natural right and was followed by a crash, flying bits of glass with their cutting edges and loud calls of protest and anger from all over the world; men and women speaking, shouting, crying, writing, telegraphing; friends, alumnae and strangers; individuals, groups, colleges and universities, magazines, fliers, leaflets, newspapers high and low, important and unimportant—the real words—the actual words of men and women.

And all over the world these flying bits of shattered glass driven by a tempest of indignation caught the light—and for a moment held the light as, among men, lawyers, actors, editors, librarians, doctors, office workers, teachers, research workers, professors, undergraduates, executives, authors, merchants, spoke their minds, protested what was being done to Mary Woolley and to women.

"The century passes," cried out a librarian. "The torch—it falters! In God's name, why?" He listens. There is no answer except his own voice as he shouts again: "Because in the last firm hand its light has shone too steadily, too far across the world!"

Another man, angry blue eyes catching the light, his handsome face tense, protested: "To my poor brain this male stuff of those Trustees does not make sense! Why don't you men try settling the Negro question by going back to slavery?"

"Just what they're doing!" a voice put in.

"Anyhow," said the blue-eyed scientist, "what a marvelous illustration the whole thing is of woman's ability to adjust, to conform, to compromise, as she does in marriage and motherhood!"

"Maybe," said another man, "but I call this an insult to efficient womanhood! That's what it is, insult!"

"Yes," agreed the actor, "and that's why they are staging this clumsy attempt to humiliate Miss Woolley and the work of women!"

"No," answered the man president of a woman's college, "no, this is martyrdom for peace!"

"I thought," said the professor, "Mount Holyoke was founded not only to educate women but to prepare them for places of leadership in thought and action—am I right or am I wrong?"

"You are right, Old Boy," answered the youth from Harvard, "and here's some good reading in this Report of the Yale Prexy!"

"What's that?"

"In this report Prexy says that in giving a man as president to Mount Holyoke, it was more blessed to give than to receive!"

"Ha! Ha! Ha! 'more blessed to give than to receive'!" laughed the Yale student.

"What about the sportsmanship of this man taking a place which has belonged to women by natural right and tradition for one hundred years?" asked the author.

"Oh, God, that man—how could he do it!" retorted a youth from Providence.

Then the deep voice of authority speaking from Johns Hopkins: "College presidencies? Why should great women educators be deprived of these few educational prizes? . . . No man, let alone a woman, could be expected to do distinguished work under such discouraging conditions."

"Yeah, but wasn't it four of those *women* trustees who did more than anybody else to elect a man?" the student asked scoffingly.

"And women of that sort will continue to do it," snapped the lawyer, "if the better women continue to let men control their college boards of trustees!"

And this was followed by a man's voice giggling: "Women got their due this time when those old gentlemen elected a man!"

Followed by the stern, bitter voice of a man shouting across the chasm which separates men and women: "I call upon every self-respecting woman everywhere to join in a movement of open revolt!"

Driven by this storm the words of women, brittle flying glass, caught and held light everywhere: women from China, Australia, Hungary, Austria; women from New Zealand, Norway, Sweden, Poland; women from Czechoslovakia, Brazil, India, Great Britain, speaking, crying, pleading in pain.

"In Japan we are indignant beyond expression," cried a missionary. "This is momentous for the women of the world, and an insult to us all."

"Few leaders in China but in America so different," sadly reflected the head of a great Chinese school for girls. "This is surprise, shock, sorrow all in one."

"To hand the torch of a life's work to the right woman is one thing," spoke a learned woman, "but to have it given to the wrong man—My thoughts and my prayers are with Mary Woolley."

To a university woman traveling in Poland, Polish women said: "We have heard of what has been done. How does this happen?"

From the land of Gandhi and Madam Pandit came the voice of a woman saying: "Women of every nation and clime, let us join our hands and rise to meet the challenge in one body!"

"We in Australia hold that your Board of Trustees should have sought Mary Woolley's advice," was the matter-of-fact comment of an Australian woman. "Dr. Woolley is known and admired throughout the world."

Followed by the angry voices of university women from Hungary, speaking sudden, flaming words: "This nomination is an insult to the achievement of women!"

"We express our disapproval of your Committee of Nine," said the Austrian university women, "and the hard blow they have given women."

From a land where sheep graze peacefully upon the foothills and the sun shimmers like silk on turf, and where there is food for all and justice for all, a woman's quiet voice was heard: "We regret the trend in America to replace women by men in leading positions."

Then from Norway came a heavy voice: "The trustees ought not to have discarded the faculty vote of strong importance nor the great respect of the world for Miss Woolley!"

From Sweden categoric denial: "We do not believe it was *not* possible to find a woman of dignity and ability."

The senator from the National Council of Women in Czechoslovakia asserted: "In the interest of human rights the man should be withdrawn and the presidency filled again by a woman."

And from Brazil a beautiful voice crying for help: "American women, American women, we beg you to protest against what has been done! We are a young country, do not fail us! Do not shatter our ideals!"

A man's voice broke in: "Mary Woolley knows what she wants and she believes in it. Why don't you women follow *her*?"

"Sir, have you ever been a woman?" asked an American working woman. "Does any *man* ever know the whole story of being a woman or the whole story of jobs for women?"

"No, I—well—ah—."

"Well, Sir, I will tell you something of what it means to be a woman in a man's world. To climb even half way up in a job, you *have* to follow some man. At that, if you are too successful, the men punish you. You understand: men punish women for succeeding—sneer at her and make fun of her—not *all* men but most men do! When you have been working hard at your job for about twenty years something happens, and the men begin whispering about barriers for women. Men think we don't hear them whispering about the barrier but we do. And we *see* that barrier! We may not pass around it or over it, nor is there even a narrow crack through which we may squeeze, yet the average man alongside of us is lifted right over it. Sir, did you know that at this very moment men are trying to make laws to retire women from jobs before men? Do you know the *real* reason why they are trying to pass this retirement law? The men want more jobs and longer jobs. 'Protection for women' they call it!"

The women broke into laughter and the men and women laughed until they cried and no one could stop either their laughter or their tears.

Flying glass catching the light! America, Japan, China, Australia, Hungary, Austria, New Zealand, Norway, Sweden, Poland, Czechoslovakia, Brazil, Great Britain, speaking as many tongues as there are countries but speaking all together the "language" of Justice—women and men uniting as they struggle towards the ideal of freedom and opportunity for women.

✿   ✿   ✿   ✿

The month is March, the year 1937. The occasion is the Mary Lyon-Mary Woolley Luncheon in Lodon. The idea of this luncheon came immediately after the two minutes' silence on Armistice Day, November 11, 1936. Millions were dedicating themselves to peace. Constance Smedley Armfield decided in that two minute silence to dedicate her time and her work to a protest luncheon to be held in honor of Mary Lyon and Mary Woolley. A letter was sent to Margery Corbett-Ashby asking her to unite in the Mary Lyon celebrations that take place all over the world on her birthday, February 28th. Then the interest of Viscountess Astor was obtained.

Moving her deformed back with difficulty, this English woman with the beautiful face and beautiful voice pulls her crutches towards her, for she must get to work immediately. She calls: "Miss Auld!" There is no reply, but hearing Miss Auld at the telephone she settles back in her chair to wait while, as if stooping over her thoughts, she writes with strong shapely hand, rapidly line after line to her American friend:

> The Luncheon is going strong. The organizing secretary has started . . . I'm getting all the printing and lists done—ready for her . . . Viscountess Snowden is coming, Viscountess Rhondda, & many. Dr. Flower is the man president of the Literature—Ancient (thus bringing in classics) . . . We now have 35 *tables*, all actively moving . . . I'm doing all this with my Committee . . . The women of Britain are rallying to the side of the women of America. The American woman has helped so many women, it's perfectly glorious other women have now a chance to help the women who've done so much for liberty . . . It is a grand battle & I love to feel it's being fought with all of you!

Thus did one brave woman give confidence to other women. Constance Smedley's husband, Maxwell Armfield, R.A., wrote: ". . . She has just been a transparency for divine instructions & in no other way could this company have been gathered for she is now quite out of 'this world' & has in most cases had no direct approach to people."

A few days later, on March 18th at noon time, more than two hundred of England's most famous men and women assembled for luncheon at the Park Lane Hotel in London to do honor to Mary Lyon and Mary Woolley. Chatting, glancing at their menus, in the midst of their lunch a signal for silence is given, and as they wait voices whisper: "Ssh! They're putting on Constance Smedley's record!"

"Too bad she cannot be here to give her own speech. This luncheon
is her work, you know."

"Ssh! She's on!"

From the record a voice fresh, young, joyous, spoke: "We are here
to honor Mary Lyon as a great pioneer, administrator and educator and
as one who understood the first three great elements of dynamics:
faith, honesty and service . . . Not only are we honoring Mary Lyon
but the long chain of women presidents that have maintained the ideal
and purpose of Mount Holyoke. We are honoring all the schools and
the daughter colleges that have gone out from Mount Holyoke all over
the world, even to Asia and Africa. And we are honoring Mary Woolley
because in a modern way she has fulfilled the great purpose of Mary
Lyon's heart."

As Christine Silver, sitting next to Phyllis Bottome, listened to the
voice of Constance Smedley, she and others were comforted, conscious
that the physical presence is not essential.

The guests settled back into quiet. Dr. Winifred Cullis, one-time
president of the International Federation of University Women, was
rising to open the luncheon with a brief greeting: "It is a great privilege on the occasion of the Centennial celebration to be allowed to send
greetings and congratulations to Mount Holyoke College and to her
distinguished President, Mary Woolley . . . The fellowship of learning
is international. In the pursuit of knowledge all nations can come
together."

Lady Astor turned about in her chair to nod her head approvingly
at Dr. Cullis while with others—Ambassador Bingham and the Spanish
Ambassador, Miss Kathleen Courtney and Mrs. Pethick Lawrence;
Viscountess Snowden, the Marquis of Lothian and Phyllis Bottome; Dr.
Robin Flower from the British Museum and Rebecca West—and many
others from the 213 men and women, including many representatives
of world fairs, British Parliamentary law, the spoken word, the written
word, music, art, and architecture, the universities of America, Wales,
Scotland, Ireland; Oxford, Cambridge, London, continued their applause. There is laughter as well as discussion as they glance down at
the menu for the Mary Lyon-Mary Woolley Luncheon. Amusing, was
it not, this bill of fare. And quite apropos—especially for the Americans! Some of them might not know that "Bombe Mary Woolley"
meant ice cream. Or did they? One never knows.

In speaking, Ambassador Robert W. Bingham followed the Marquis
of Lothian with a brief address. Then with the friendliest of smiles
Margery Corbett-Ashby moved that "In gratitude to Mary Lyon and
Mary Woolley, we pledge ourselves to further the ideals for which

Mt. Holyoke College was founded," and was supported by Ma Nyen Tha. Mrs. Corbett-Ashby continued speaking: "As President of the International Alliance of Women, I have the honor to associate the women of the world in this tribute . . . we gratefully join with Mary Lyon the name of Mary Woolley . . . who has continued Mary Lyon's traditions: the leadership of women by women . . . Today new challenge is heard in many lands. Women are refused higher education, shut out of responsible posts, deprived of the right to earn . . . Today we are on trial to prove that those countries are most faithful, most learned, most happy, most prosperous, where men and women stand side by side without prejudice, or restrictions, each individual ready to serve or to rule according to their gifts. *Where liberty is everywhere challenged, women, the latest to benefit by it, must be first in its defense.*"

Following Mrs. Corbett-Ashby's resolution and speech, Dr. Cullis read to the assembled guests a letter from Mary Woolley which closed with the question: "Can we do better in this day than to rededicate ourselves to the ideals for women for which Mary Lyon lived and died?"

"Exactly what such a letter should be," were the exclamations, "not too much and not too little!"

Five days later the conservative *Scotsmen* published a glowing account of this distinguished event:

> It was an occasion remarkable in more than one sense. I doubt if any more widely representative gathering of women has ever been held. Here were scientists, doctors, research workers, barristers, and scholars, and women distinguished in every walk of public life . . . assembled not only to do honour to two famous American women—but to pledge themselves to further the ideals for which their work must stand. Representatives attended from all the Universities in Great Britain. Special tables were filled by guests representing law and Parliament, world affairs, music, drama, art and education. There were women, too, from the Universities of other countries, among them a number of Indian women in national dress. One remembers the beautifully worded speech by the Indian lady, Ma Nyen Tha. Many nations were represented at this gathering but there were no barriers between them.

In a personal letter on the day of the luncheon, Maxwell Armfield wrote:

> I took C. down to make her record yesterday but I saw that the constant labour was telling on her & that she did not architect it as well as usual—could not come to the point & clinch it. The seating afterwards was a terrific job & after supper she completely collapsed . . . It is definitely a sort of "stroke" & at present she has no sensation in her left hand & arm & is not yet normal at all, but is improving. These casualties from

the firing line make one marvel at the cruelty & bestiality of the human animal whose concentrated venom is responsible for so much of them; but C. . . . owned today she ought not to have attempted the seating direction but "I did so want the people to be happy with one another!" & I hear they certainly were & there were many expressions on the matter. Mrs. Bingham exclaimed "What a lovely lunch!" so I hear from Margery. She & Dr. Cullis could not have been more loving & kind today . . . Now don't feel regretful for one moment. Constance would not want you to, whatever is the outcome—

The "outcome" was death.

CHAPTER 19

HIGHEST HONOR

*"All education which does not soften your heart and your spirit
—all education which you keep to yourself and for yourself is
waste, just waste!"*

When the time came no candles burned for the one hundredth
birthday, reported Maxine McBride in the *New York Sun*, but sil-
houetted against the horizon at dawn on the high tower of Clapp Hall
appeared the figure of a trumpeter calling all from sleep—Mount Holyoke students, faculty, alumnae, three thousand strong—to the May
Day merry-making on May 7th and May 8th of 1937.

On the morning of May 8th, the audience in Chapin Auditorium
moved uneasily, turning their eyes away from the big empty stage or
looking at their programs. What was that sound outside? Of course,
the Goldman Band playing. But what was that swing and tap of steps
as the muffled rhythm of hundreds of marching feet came closer?
"They're coming!" ran the whisper over the audience. The band
changed to the *Tannhauser Overture*. The procession came into the
building, passing between a cordon of white-clad students who marked
the entrance route. Dr. Elizabeth Adams, chief marshal, headed the
group, followed by graduate students, assistants, faculty in order of
rank, delegates in order of the date of founding of the institutions
represented; then came the platform group—trustees, daughter college
representatives, honorary degree recipients and speakers.

"Do you suppose that handsome woman *is* the head marshal . . .?
That must be the faculty . . . Who are those women behind them? . . .
Don't know . . . Are the honorary degree recipients sitting in the front
row? . . . No, I don't think so . . . They say that celebrated sculptor
Malvina Hoffman gets one . . . and Eva Le Gallienne? . . . There, that
must be the English lady, Mrs. Corbett Ashby . . . the one that's down
to speak . . . Yes, attractive woman, isn't she? . . . Looks as if she had
a sense of humor! . . . There's Dean Gildersleeve: I recognize her . . .
Is that little woman the president of Wellesley College? Mildred
McAfee, you say? Well, she doesn't look any older than a girl . . .

202

President Woolley is coming . . . Isn't she quiet-looking, dressed in black with that bright hood! . . . You say she has the responsibility of this whole Centennial on her shoulders? . . . Well, I guess so—her eyes look sad enough for that! . . . Who's the reddish-haired, tall man walking beside her? . . . He's the Chairman of the Board of Trustees . . . You've heard? . . . Ssh, they're beginning to sit down now . . . That's Rufus Jones, the Quaker, getting up to give the Invocation."

In the top gallery the choir, clad in black and white stoles, rose in unison. William Churchill Hammond lifted his arms and gave the signal for the singing of *Saint Anne*. When the music was over, the audience settled itself with a sound like the rustling of forest leaves struck suddenly by the wind.

Covered by this swift succession of sounds, Grace Bacon, a member of the faculty, whispered to her neighbor: "Look at Miss Woolley! All she's been through and still at her incomparable best!" "Wonderful!" came the whispered reply.

The countless motions of hands and feet, programs and gowns hushed at last, Mary Woolley rose to speak. Her deep desire not to fail the thousands of men and women who were surrounding her with admiration and love had brought renewed confidence. Cordial, witty, clear-headed, she gave a warm welcome to the assembled guests and then introduced the first speaker: "It is an honor to have our program open with greetings from Harvard University. I cannot refrain from adding that Mount Holyoke has a personal interest in the first speaker of the morning, since his mother was a Mount Holyoke graduate in the Class of 1865. Perhaps from her as well as from his father, he learned the lesson of statesmanship and wise counsel. It is my pleasure to introduce to this audience Mr. Jerome Davis Greene, Secretary to the Corporation of Harvard University." After the applause was over, some of those in the audience who knew her best were still thinking: "How like her to be loyal, even in an introduction, to that mother of so long ago."

Mary Woolley rose again to introduce the next speaker: "We are fortunate in having as the speaker who brings to us a message from the United Kingdom, a woman who entered into the tradition of public service by her birth; who has worked along many lines of service in her own country; who was the one woman representing the United Kingdom at the Geneva Conference on the Reduction and Limitation of Armaments. With personal as well as official pleasure I present to you as our next speaker Mrs. Margery Corbett-Ashby, who will speak to us on 'Women in Public Affairs'."

A roar of applause greeted Mrs. Corbett-Ashby, then the most publicized woman in the United States. The newsmen came to attention and some of the resultant copy suggested nothing so much as the fact that they practically fell in love with her. During the speech that followed, one of the ablest of the reporters let his glance dwell on the facial expression of the Chairman of the Board of Trustees. "No man's face was so red," wrote this Puckish journalist. "The women were at least exercising one of women's inalienable privileges, that of having the last word."

"Absurd and senseless," continued Mrs. Corbett-Ashby, while the audience held its breath wondering what she would declare next, "to say no available woman could be found. Absurd and deplorable to appoint a man . . . an unknown man." And in the same spirit she went on jauntily to say that it had been "forced on the College by a Board of Trustees false to the spirit of their trust . . . A blow to the education of women throughout the world . . . Women are still on trial in European countries, and at a time when France names two women as Under-Secretaries of Education, it seems incredible that a man should replace a woman in a post held by successive women for a century." Then she set the audience laughing by the following lamentation: "Women are still not regarded as persons but as relatives. You can see any day in the newspapers some such sentence as: 'Sarah Brett, aged 91, daughter of Sam Brett!' Poor old lady! She had lived 91 years, probably 45 without her father—45 years of individual responsibility—but, whatever her activities and tastes, her virtues and vices, society cannot rid itself of feeling that it would be 'nicer' if she could be some man's relative."

Flying glass—all of it! Glittering and whirling and cutting, broken and blown about the earth by the wild winds of injustice, and tossed upward into the light by the thoughts of a brilliant woman.

Margery Corbett-Ashby closed her speech by demanding "fair play from man." The prize of women's service, she asserted, is opportunity. "How many women are Government executives?" she demanded. "How many are heads of great educational institutions?" The Centennial audience gasped audibly at that pointed shaft and stole covert glances at the carefully composed countenance of the Chairman of the Board of Trustees sitting beside President Woolley. "Women are now educated in most countries," she asserted, "but opportunities for responsibility and leadership are still few. Are women less capable than men when given the chance?"

She went over the list of women's notable achievements—achievements realized despite "contempt, ridicule, slander and physical violence." Accusingly she added, "The opposition is still here, but it is disguised. We believe we have equality and can gain equal leadership. This is a delusion . . . *We still need the loyalty and comradeship among women that won us the world of today."* A roar of applause broke forth. The gay defiance, the courage, the smile, had won the hearts of all. Arturo Toscanini was never more wildly applauded than Margery Corbett-Ashby; her words were music to the ears of women. When the acclaim died down, she went on. "We must break the vicious circle which denies us posts of leadership and responsibility because we have not had the experience which society has denied us . . . Speaking for all women who are near the dark shadow of tyranny and despotism, I say to you not 'Come over and help us,' but instead 'Be true to your own selves and thus help us'."

Here was the theme of the women's movement—a theme to be made more impressive by the next speaker introduced by President Woolley: "It is so common an experience to have women working together, as for example in the League of Women Voters, the American Association of University Women, and the Federation of Women's Clubs, that we have almost forgotten that there was once a disbelief in women's ability to do this very thing. Our next speaker is a woman who has done much to further the cause of unity among women in this country through the American Association of University Women, through the League of Women Voters, and in other ways. Toward the close of the war she was one of the founders of the International Federation of University Women, and for the second time is the president of that Federation. It gives me pleasure to introduce a great civic servant in our foremost city, as well as a great internationalist, Virginia Cocheron Gildersleeve, Dean of Barnard College and the President of the International Federation of University Women."

Dean Gildersleeve questioned whether women had advanced in the last twenty-five years in opportunities offered to them. She found fewer women professors in the women's colleges. In the co-educational colleges, her impression was that women were expected to stay in their place; there, she said, "no one expects a woman to become the head of the institution or the dean of a faculty and only *rarely* a full professor."

Mary Woolley brought the speeches to a graceful close with these words: "Among the good fortunes which have come to me in my life was my clergyman father with his fund of good stories. I remember the story of a brother clergyman who was bitterly opposed to having a Women's Missionary Society in his church, and when it was finally carried against his opposition, [he] said with emphasis: 'Well, anyway, I am always going to be present, for if those women are left to themselves there is no telling what they will ask the Lord for'!"

Honorary degrees were conferred upon twenty women,[1] and after a benediction by the village pastor, everyone filed out of the auditorium to the strains of the *New World Symphony.*

"Great, wasn't it!" exclaimed one alumna. "Women certainly had their innings *this* morning!" said another.

＊　＊　＊　＊

During the spring of 1937 three great universities — Chicago and Columbia, and Brown — conferred their highest honors on Miss Woolley. Dr. Hutchins gave her the degree of Doctor of Laws at Chicago, Dean Edith Abbott on March 16th making the presentation. Concerning this honorary award, Madame Adamowicz of Poland, vice-president of the International Association of University Women, wrote Mary Woolley: "I am happy to hear of the honorary degree that the University of Chicago has conveyed to you. It is once more a sign of recognition of the splendid work accomplished by you in so many fields. I beg you to accept my heartiest congratulations and best wishes for further fruitful activity." Mary Woolley replied in part: "How thoughtful you are to send me a note about the University of Chicago degree. I must confess that I was greatly pleased to be in the group with Madame Curie and Jane Addams even if I do not deserve it."

Several months later, Nicholas Murray Butler bestowed on Miss Woolley Columbia University's Doctor of Letters degree. Her own university, Brown, gave her the Susan Colver Rosenberger Medal which had previously been awarded only four other times—to Dr. William Keen, Charles Evans Hughes, John D. Rockefeller, Jr., and Dr. Charles Value Chapin. These awards were like unmistakable voices speaking against injustice to women and in loyalty to a woman's leadership during those years when, as Miss Woolley wrote her nephew Paul, Mount Holyoke's Board of Trustees had given her the hardest blow she had ever received. The honors comforted her, but they did not blind her to the fact that a few legal sentences placed in the charter of an institution founded one hundred years ago for the training of young women had given and were still giving men the right to override public opinion and natural rights. She saw at last that the work of one entire life and of many other lives could not accomplish what one well-made law in the Charter and By-laws of Mount Holyoke College could do. This fact, clearly faced by her, became a part of her new undertakings such as the founding of Women in World Affairs, her work as a speaker, the advice she gave others, and her individual decisions. And it was with a keen sense of personal pride that she awarded an LL.D. degree to her dean of residence, Mary Ashby Cheek,

who received an appointment as President of Rockford College, Ill.
It could have been said of Mary Woolley that she conferred no honorary degrees for political reasons. Perhaps in days past the degree
which had brought her most satisfaction was the degree she awarded
to Helen Frances Kimball, even then an elderly woman, President of
the New England Hospital for Women and Children, philanthropist
and benefactor of Negro schools.

A month later Miss Woolley, who had been making notes for the dis-
posal of certain articles before she left the President's House, picked
up the *New York Times*, wishing to relax in the midst of her packing.
However, her relaxation came to an end when she saw the following:

AMERICAN FEMINIST URGES DRIVE HERE

American women were chided yesterday by Miss Gordon Holmes, joint
managing director of the National Securities Corporation Ltd. of London,
for not taking the lead in the woman's movement as seriously as they
might . . . She prescribed a touch of British complacency, less shyness and
less sense of inferiority for American women if they were to take the
lead "in the proper way."

"You are the only women in the world who are taken seriously," she
said in an interview in the Biltmore Hotel offices of the International
League for Business and Professional Women.

Mary Woolley felt the sting of the unmistakable truth of Miss
Holmes' remarks. She dictated this letter to the Field Secretary in
charge of Mount Holyoke's Alumnae Fund:

The enclosed editorial bears upon the serious aspect of the situation
here. One hundred years ago Mount Holyoke had the great honor of
leading in the cause of women; today it retreats from that position, a retreat which is the more serious because it follows a century of leadership.

It will always be a mystery to me that any Mount Holyoke women could
fail to see this aspect of the situation. To me personally it is a lasting
and enduring grief, for I feel that in some way I should have foreseen and
prevented such a calamity.

I am writing you this so that you may have in a few words my exact
position. Personal considerations are as nothing compared with the great
principle itself.

May I trouble you to return the editorial, as it is my only copy?

About two weeks later Mary Woolley was sitting in the dismantled
living room of the President's House talking with Kathleen McLaughlin, a correspondent of the *New York Times*; a "string of boxes" was
in evidence everywhere. "But I shan't just be sitting on the shores of
Lake Champlain all the time," she said. "I'd like to accomplish a
great deal more than I have but I want to stop living under pressure
. . . Why shouldn't one start life at 74 as well as at 40? I shall continue

my work as chairman of the People's Mandate to End War, and as chairman of the Committee on International Relations of the American Association of University Women, and also I shall continue my work as chairman of the Cooperating Commission of Women in the Federal Council of Churches. Besides I plan to write my autobiography."

She drew the tall silver service, a parting gift from the faculty, nearer to her. Pouring out a cup of coffee for Miss McLaughlin, she went on: "I don't feel old. Perhaps that is because I have lived among young people. Not all the interests and enthusiasms of life belong to the young . . . The only regret one need have with age is the regret that would come from a life completely misspent."

Asked about the status of women, she replied: "I am a little disturbed. In the last few years there has been a retrogression. A woman is judged more critically than a man. She has to do a thing a little better than a man to get equal recognition. A man can get by just because he is a man, and a woman can't just because she is a woman." When Miss McLaughlin inquired concerning the appointment of a man as Mount Holyoke's president, Mary Woolley answered: "I have maintained consistently the position that the tradition of a hundred years at Mount Holyoke—a woman as head—should have been continued."

During the sorrowful and anxious weeks that followed Mary Woolley became unmistakably depressed. Letters posted from Westport, New York or Boston dealt with work on *The Family of the Barrett* or about renovations at Fleur de Lys but never about the college—only comments on the little, the amusing, the comforting events of everyday life; some nonsense of Boy's while in swimming, an unexpected ducking Buddy had taken while trying to push others out of his way, some roses on the dining room table.

When JM wrote: "South Hadley is like the bad dream from which one wakes and is oh! so glad to find it behind one," Mary Woolley replied:

> I cannot tell you how what you said about a home where I could be, warmed the cockles of my heart." I have felt like a man without a country and it is dear of you to want me "around" . . . How I wish some magic carpet would put me down in my room at Fleur de Lys! . . . Your letter did me lots of good . . . hugs for dear Doggies and an envelope full to bursting with love for you.

"Dear of you to want me 'around'"! Expressed in these seven words is the measure of the depression into which she had been thrown—the measure which she was gallantly trying to keep from others. For her the Bird of Happiness lived in what she could do for and with women.

She believed that her work had been destroyed. Even during the last hard week at Mount Holyoke there was never any comment on the disaster to the leadership of women; she never referred by name to her successor or to the trustees personally.

Her last day in office was painful. On June 30th she made a tour of the campus, saying her farewells and looking over large piles of material to decide what should be discarded and what should be included in the files going to Westport. On July 2nd she wrote: "A string of boxes will soon be en route to Fleur de Lys. Most of the things will come by truck, probably the day I come—*not* by truck!" On the July day the *New York Times* correspondent had had the interview with her "the string of boxes" had been impressive. Now it had become gigantic. During these final weeks of closing the President's House— "home" for some twenty-five years—her appearance of health—which somehow she had maintained even during the Centenary and Commencement ordeals—was gone. When things did not suit her as she did the final checking of boxes or put on labels, she could be heard exclaiming in a ludicrously pleasant voice, "Oh, thunder!" or "Goodness!" After her boxes were ready, she went to her desk in the southwest corner of the living room, opening first one drawer to take out something which had been overlooked, then peering into another drawer, feeling around with her hands.

On that last afternoon Meta Mallary Seaman, an alumna, called on the departing President. They had tea together outside the living room on the west porch with its panorama of the Mount Tom range. Mrs. Seaman had known that there was trouble with the Board of Trustees but when she left, despite her deep attachment and complete loyalty for Mary Woolley, she was no wiser than she had been before. Later she was to cry out: "As close as I was to that never-to-be-forgotten tragedy at Mount Holyoke, I still never knew the facts. Now I am wondering how many alumnae did know them and why we all were kept in ignorance."

After Mrs. Seaman had left, Miss Woolley settled down again to making notes. This time she was writing out memoranda for Harriet and JM. She pulled letter paper towards her and wrote:

> Are you sure that you have room for storage of my books and papers at Fleur de Lys? There will be several boxes and files, which I think should be accessible when I begin to work . . . It would be hard for me to send an indiscriminate mass of papers. There will be a great deal of sorting next winter, at the best—and there is satisfaction in knowing what I have—at least, to a certain extent.

It was just before ten on the morning of July 27th that Earl Buss reached the President's House. He was early, for he knew there would be a lot of luggage—not only suitcases and hat boxes but also a multitude of other bundles to stow away. Even for a vacation, there was always a great deal, but now Earl was thinking, "This is forever!" The Sullivan van had left some days earlier for Westport, but at the back door stood a small college truck, driven by Harold Rhoads, ready to carry the overflow of forgotten objects and articles.

As he climbed out of his big limousine Buss seemed more lame than ever. He rang the front door bell. "There's Buss!" "Earl has come!" "Buss is here!" Then a voice asking with quiet precision: "Mrs. Calkins, is that Mr. Buss?" And a sweet, respectful voice answered: "Yes, Miss Woolley, Mr. Buss has come!"

Her hat on, Mary Woolley came downstairs and looked over the stacked-up hand luggage. Just as everyone was thinking that her next step would be toward the car, she exclaimed, "Oh goodness!" and went back upstairs.

Olive Copeland called after her, "Miss Woolley, is there anything I may do to help you?" There was no reply. Harriet Newhall said: "I'll see!" and went up.

Down below Mrs. Calkins and Anna were giving Harold Rhoads some small packages for the truck at the back gate. Again Mary Woolley came downstairs, this time followed by Harriet. "The lost is found!" said Harriet, with grim non-committal humor.

They went out onto the front porch where Earl Buss and the limousine waited. At the door, Buss said, "Good morning, Miss Woolley." "Good morning, Mr. Buss," she replied as he helped her into the car.

Earl closed the door gently and went around to his driver's seat as Harriet, Olive Copeland, Mary Custis Foster and Mrs. Calkins surrounded the car. Mary Woolley did not look back at the President's House, but when they reached College Street, she caught a glimpse of the windows of her old offices glittering in the morning sunlight, of the facade of the library for which she had done yeoman's work in raising funds, of the chapel door and of the massive wrought iron college gates which had been erected early in her administration.

On College Street the car turned left and drove northward towards Amherst. As her friends watched, Mary Woolley looked back at them for the last time, waving from the rear window. When she could see them no more, she faced forward, took off her glasses, and wiped the tears from her eyes.

CHAPTER 20

HOME

"There is always the danger of seeing accomplishment only in the objective reached; the direction in which one is moving is often more important."

There are times when the power of human senses seems to be everything a magician could ask for: the world a place of wonder, with its sounds of unfolding leaves in spring and the musical notes of birds, the fragrance of lake water in early summer, the smell of the earth, the sun-warmed aroma of the leaves and the spills of pine trees, the grey trunks turning pink, even the miracle of touch, water, and warmth, and the good taste of simple food harvested from this magic land.

It was such a morning as Mary Woolley passed over the Vermont mountains to Lake Champlain. The sun rose clear and with the promise of a moderate day's warmth. Close about Fleur de Lys, the encircling border of August lilies looked strong and thick, their cluster stalks filled with lily buds which would begin to open in a month. By the little inner gate, the sentinel elm with its lofty curved branches was outlined against the lake, the Green Mountains and the sky. In the lane beyond all was order, with close-cropped grass stopping neatly at the outer gate where the cedars and the lilac hedges closed in. To the northwest was a trace of green in the sky—even in summer a sign of probable coolness.

The collies hurried out into the lane with JM on a tour of inspection. There were small bird feathers scattered over the grass under the gate elm. With significant glances at one another, Bum, Boy and Bud took a sniff, kicked with their hind legs indignantly, barked, and at top speed raced up the walk. Exactly as they thought: some intruder had been in during the night. They would settle this intruder business. Like most handsome, able young males engaged in warfare, they settled exactly nothing. But their self-importance undiminished by facts, they saluted a hostile world outside their gate angrily and were comfortably convinced that their very presence had settled everything.

In a few minutes Iva and the men would be coming to work. Portia was calling out the side door, "Miss Jeannette, Miss Jeannette, tele-phone ringin'!" As JM came through the door, Portia added, looking glumly at her old feet, "If they weren't so used up, with all this makin' ready for Miss Mary, I'd've come out to get you. Umph, there come those men and the mason with the light of mornin' in his eyes!"

"Light of *what*?" JM inquired as she passed Portia with a grin.

"Now, Miss Jeannette," Portia called upstairs after her, "that ain't like you!" There was no reply and, sighing, Portia muttered: "Guess Po'd better get busy or we won't be ready fo' Miss Mary today."

From the telephone table on the second floor JM saw the men coming down the lane, "Light-of-the-Morning" carrying in his hand a small finishing trowel with which he was to complete refacing the front stone steps. JM meant to talk with him about that, but before she could, William Sheldon waylaid her by the side door.

"Miss Marks," he said, "in the offices for Miss Woolley, I don't know where *is* best to land the stairs."

"It'll make a difference, won't it?"

"Yes, it will, and I can't do much more until you come out ."

"I'll come with you now."

It was two hours before JM was able to give the front steps another thought. When she came back from Cutwind and went around the side of the house to look at the steps, she saw with horror what had been happening there. The refacing was being done skillfully but over the big, rough stones Light-of-the-Morning had spat cuds of chewing tobacco and squirted streams of tobacco juice. Before she realized what she was saying, she exclaimed: "What *horrid* man has been spitting tobacco juice all over these steps?" Light-of-the-Morning gave the steps a whack with his trowel. Looking up at JM indignantly, he said: "I guess if you chewed tobacco you'd spit some!"

What is "home"? The picture of a good neighbor coming down hill on a Sunday morning, with a redheaded twin skipping on either side of him, the special orange marmalade Portia has made, Buddy stealing up to a closed bedroom door early in the morning to listen and sniff an inquiry: "Are you there?", as well as the silence and speech you share and have shared with loved ones, and the use and custom of all the years. This home, which JM's parents had called "Fleur de Lys" after the French lilies which grow wild all over, had become like one of those endearing people you love, who (for peccadillo reasons) will not bear too close inspection. The wonder is that it did bear inspection at all, for on the porch too many ponies had in the past shared the view —Jack the Cob enjoying an afternoon by the lakeside; Cowslip the Jersey Cow with her preference for the south side of the porch. Long

ago, also, children had roller-skated on it so constantly that it was a
wonder that the porch floor remained. And there were memories,
too, of that broad, flat railing upon which once upon a time on rainy
summer afternoons naked children raced and shouted, ducking in and
out of the rain, vaulting over onto the lawn and back with one-handed
ease.   Inside, too many dogs had scratched the door panels.   The
luggage of many people had been swung jauntily up and down both
the back and front stairs, scratching the solid beamed walls.   Given
the right wattage in lights, it was a "picturebook" home, as a friend
had called it.   Too strong a light made it become a shabby old place.
Yet within its mellow, beamed walls were many beautiful objects,
one of them a landscape over the sideboard, bringing into the dining
room, and seeming to mirror there, the outside lake and hills.

In the early afternoon of Mary Woolley's day of arrival, Iva and
JM worked in the dining room while Portia stood in the butler's pantry
doorway doing a Greek chorus with questions: "Won't they be comin'
soon, now, Miss Jeannette?"

"Yes, Portia, but if . . ."

"Miss Marks," Iva interrupted, "this table cloth has to be spread
kind o' kitteringlike to make it cover the table. There! Pull your end
turds you, Miss Marks, *turds* you, I said. Portia, you ketch that
edge on yourn side."

"Oh, my dogs," groaned Portia, trying to hobble faster in order to
"ketch" the edge. Holding on to her thigh and limping, she gave just
the right pull with her sensitive, clever hands.

"Thanks, that's the idee," said Iva, paying no attention to anyone
except that they helped get the work done as quickly as possible.

"What you an' Miss Jeannette goin' to do?" asked the Greek chorus
with a belligerent look in her eyes. "Feed those men bringin' Miss
Mary?"

"Yes," replied Iva absentmindedly, "now that cloth looks good.
Where the edge is frayed a mite it won't show much."

"If I was you, Miss Jeannette," interrupted Portia, "I'd let those men
feed theirselves on the way back home. They kin take care o' theirselves."

"Now, Portia," said Iva, "help me get the dishes and silver on."

"Good thing we got that silver polished before Miss Mary come
home," exclaimed Portia. "Miss Mary mighty pertikkeler 'bout silver."

"Portia, for pity sake," said JM, "go out and get the food ready for
the men!"

"Yaas'm," answered Portia, glad to get out of the business of hobbling about the table, "but the food *was* ready long ago."

There was a bedlam of barking, as the dogs raced up the inside fence line, giving yelp after yelp of joy.

"They're coming, Miss Marks," said Iva, "they're to the outer gate."

＊　　＊　　＊　　＊

From the dining room came contented sounds of men eating good food—Portia's best. It was late afternoon and Iva had gone home. Portia was in full charge. She had put on a big fresh cap and tied a clean, white apron around her ample waist. In the dining room she was in her element, not only enjoying the success of her own skilled cooking, but also her role as a well-bred assistant hostess.

In the library, Portia could be heard padding to and fro, her pleasant, deep voice saying occasionally, "Now won't you gent-men have some mo' of this fricassee chicken Miss Mary likes? I tell Miss Jeannette all you have to do is give Po a rabbit an' a chicken feather an' she'll serve you up the best fricassee chicken you ever ate. Hee! Hee!" And then, "Don't neglect these bakin' powder biscuits. Have some mo' with gravy, Mr. Earl, you've gotta long drive back. Just a minute while I get you mo' of that mocha and java coffee—good isn't it! We got that from S. S. Pierce for Miss Mary."

Mary Woolley looked at JM, drew up the corner of her mouth and for a moment the sombre brown eyes smiled over the talk which drifted through the lattice door separating dining room and library. Quietly, she noticed alterations in the room. She had already seen many cases of her own books in the music room and the library contained more of them. In the well-bound volumes of Emerson, Mary Woolley had set a red pencil check against many passages, among them these: "God offers to every mind its choice between truth and repose." "Nothing can bring you peace but yourself."

Buddy lay on the rug by the fireplace, Boy got as close as he could to Mary Woolley's chair and Bummy sat between Mary Woolley and JM—each dog radiating love and satisfaction in the homecoming of their Eminent Missus.

Hearing scraping of chair legs and a change in Portia's voice, Mary Woolley went into the dining room to say goodbye. Life was never too short for her to share with others and to take time for courtesy and gratitude. Earl Buss and Mr. Rhoads were her friends; they had been good to her at college and, along with many others on the campus staff, they admired and loved her. Later she took her stick from the jog under the stairway and went through the kitchen, the dogs never leaving her side. She thanked Portia for the marvelous lunch she had given the men and then walked to the office, pausing

on the way by the dogs' graves—Old Mannie, Bird, Tuttle, Flag,
Tyke, Chuckie, and Heron. Expecting a walk, the collies were disappointed to have to stand still. Then they went together on towards
Cutwind, the name of her office. Mary Woolley sat down in a little
chair and studied the rooms where her work for women and for
peace would be continued. "The string of boxes" had already found
their way there.

When she returned to the house, she laid the lavender cape she had
thrown about her across one of the chairs. Then she went over to
JM, who had been helping Portia set the table for supper, kissed her
and said: "Thank you, Jeannette, it's going to mean everything to me
to have those rooms for work. What you and Mr. Sheldon have
accomplished with that old building is a miracle, and I shall be out
there hard at it early every morning."

Portia, hobbling in with a platter of chicken and biscuits, laughed
happily when Mary Woolley said, "Portia, I'm hungry."

"Yaas'm, Miss Mary, an' you'll see I figured on that." Then Portia
looked grave. "Certainly is good, Miss Mary, to see you ladies sure
'nough home together now."

❀   ❀   ❀   ❀

As winter came on, Mary Woolley wrote that the out-of-doors "looks
like the North Pole"—"walks icy, lake . . . sounding like a winter
sea," but the house was entirely comfortable, "birds gaily singing and
Boy peacefully snoring." She walked up and down vigorously over
the ice crusted lawns, the dogs, looking a bit whipped by the wind
and the cold, following her, their heads lifted with curiosity about
this new game the Missus was playing. To most human beings a
morning temperature of 10 degrees below would be only another
sub-arctic day to be endured, but Mary Woolley put coats on the
dogs and out they went.

She called to JM, "Oh, I just love it!"

In the house Portia was calling: "Tom, is it cold?"

"Cold? No such thing!" answered Tom Scott. "It's one hundred
in the shade outside and the lawn sprinkler is going."

Throughout the winter, she led a peaceful home life, but full of
service to others. She often sent flowers and food to sick neighbors,
and on Sundays she went to church in the morning and listened to
the Philharmonic in the afternoon. She left this simple life from
time to time to carry out her important duties in education and peace,
and she was honored as never before by men and women, clubs and
organizations everywhere. Seldom, if ever, did Mary Woolley mort-

gage the future unfavorably. Gold, sometimes silver, but *never* lead in the locker of any organization she sponsored, was her continued attitude towards her public causes and her work for peace. Often when Mary Woolley was away from home, Portia wrote ridiculous and what she believed to be—and were—comforting letters. As a comic relief in a world of war nerves snapping like taut bow strings, Portia seemed to be the only one who did not seek advice from Mary Woolley but gave it to her in letter after letter of which the following is one of her classics:

> My only Miss Mary,
> . . . I dream of you all most every night. Always cooking, but never finish . . . *Now dear take care of yourself and dont worry about the war. Things will come to a head, and bust wide open and we will be sitting pretty.* God bless you is my constant pray. Your loving
> PO

Mary Woolley always found when she returned home from her travels that there was "healing in the old place"—something inexplicably happy about it. A friend, Allen Cox, had called it "the house with a personality".

A lighter aspect of the early months at Fleur de Lys was the task of "keeping up" with Portia who was, as Mary Woolley wrote, "clever in more ways than one". One night immediately after supper she heard Portia pulling herself up the back stairs and sighing: "Oh, my dogs! Oh, my dogs!" from the pain in her poor arthritic old feet. After closing up the house, Mary Woolley decided that she, too, would go upstairs to bed. It was before half past seven and she called out to Portia as she went, "I shall soon beat you!"

Portia's reply came with a chuckle: "I'm *in!*"

During the war years many incomes doubled, but at Fleur de Lys the only things that doubled were the taxes to which fixed incomes and old family homes are subject and the cost of food and service. Something was always given to good causes but Mary Woolley's cheques became smaller and smaller as checkbooks and mending baskets became more full of attempts to keep down expenses. As well as being a source of personal huimilation, relative poverty constantly hobbled her work. With illness and inflation added to the war pressure, both adequacy and margin disappeared, and the struggle to make ends meet became hopeless as we began drawing on modest capital funds. Earlier, it had been not only scarcity of service of which account had to be taken but even more important, the price of service and the supplies. With ever increasing taxes and lessening value of the dollar as well as more frequent ill health, it was not long before expenses in proportion to income became astronomical. From New York, Mary Woolley wrote that she had "been thinking on the train" how she could "save more or earn more". In the fall of 1938 she had not been able to go to Lima with the People's Mandate group for two reasons: first, she was unwilling to be out of the country when a member of her family was not well; second, she could "not afford it" and that "either one of these reasons" was "conclusive". Anyhow, she added, she would not have an appeal sent out: "Will you give five dollars for Miss Woolley to go to Lima?" (At that time the minimum fare was $900.)

Among many engaged in travel on September 21, 1938, a rainy, close day in the autumn of the following year were JM, her secretary, Evelyn Selby, and the collies Bummy and Buddy. Early in the morning they drove away from Fleur de Lys to return to college. Travel was possible during the morning hours and early afternoon. But when the tops of trees began to bend and twist in an increasing roar of sound, it was evident that it was a hurricane. In this tumult, as the hurricane absorbed all individual noises, gigantic trees twisted and fell in seemingly ghost-like silence.

When the news from radio and press reached Mary Woolley at Fleur de Lys, there followed days of desperate anxiety. She tried to telephone but got no connection. She tried to telegraph and received no reply. Not yet knowing what had happened in the Connecticut Valley, day after day Mary Woolley went on writing and wiring, "Cannot reach you by telephone or by wire." The telephone operators, conscious of her increasing anxiety, called Fleur de Lys repeatedly to tell Miss Woolley about the progress being made in restoring service. For two nights she had been lying awake, hearing sounds—the slap-slap of angry water, the hissing of wind and rain through the cat-tails, the steady drive of slant-wise rain upon the east and south windows of her bedroom, and from the floor the whistling noise of Boy's breathing. Occasionally she dropped off into a few minutes of tense sleep.

At one of these times in the early morning hours of the third day she started awake. What was that sound? She snapped on her light and listened. Yes, the telephone was ringing! She fumbled for her slippers and made her way down the hallway to the telephone stand. Boy, watching her go, sighed, pulled himself up and followed her.

Portia's light went on. "That you, Miss Mary?"

"Yes, Portia, the telephone just rang."

"I'm coming, Miss Mary!" grunted Portia, getting into her shoes.

Mary Woolley's hand was trembling a little as she steadied herself on the table and sat down, but her voice was steady as she lifted the receiver, saying, "This is Miss Woolley!" "We know how anxious you are," replied the operator. "This message just received from Miss Marks has been on the way two days. It says: 'All safe . Don't worry. Writing.'" Mary Woolley spoke gratefully, "Operator, I *do* thank you for your kindness in calling me immediately. Please thank the others for all their kindness these past two days. Good-night!"

"What she say?" asked Portia sharply. Mary Woolley repeated JM's message.

"That mean dogs an' all is safe! Now you go to bed and sleep, Miss Mary, till Po call you in the morning for yo' breakfast."

"I shall sleep better all the rest of the night as the result of this message," she said, getting up from the telephone chair. Boy pulled himself up from the floor, looked after Portia, already hobbling down the hall, looked at his Missus and followed her into her bedroom.

*   *   *   *

To a member of her family Mary Woolley wrote: "What an incredibly wicked thing has been done to Mount Holyoke. It seems more wicked to me all the time." There were some alumnae, faculty, a few students and trustees whose sense of justice and loyalty to Mary Woolley never buckled under the trustee dictum of *fait accompli*—a force of opposition which had brought about many changes including that of a new chairman for the Board of Trustees, who had attempted various devices to win over Mary Woolley. She was asked to return for the dedication of the new chapel, and refused. The year following she was asked by the graduating class to be the Commencement speaker. They received cordial replies but a refusal. Mary Woolley had been watching with anguish the increasingly unfriendly pressure on JM from the autumn of 1937 through 1940, knowing the source of it and mistakenly believing herself to be the cause of it. At first she had written: "I so hope that 'things' will be as easy as possible for you . . . I think of you all the time." When she became aware of what that pressure was she wrote mournfully: "No one can take away from you what you have accomplished."

In the continued attempt to regain her health, JM and Mary Woolley went to Florida. The outstanding event of this sojourn lay in the unexpected. They met a puppy—merely one of a litter of half-breed Belgian Shepherds—a Colleese. The puppy fell in love with Mary Woolley, and neither higher fencing nor a door on the kennel could keep him from scraping through any opening and, with his three-cornered baby head and his baggy little body intact, racing to our three-room cottage. All efforts to keep Mickey Mouse where he belonged failed, and it became more restful to have him brought to the cottage at a definite time. Never did a little dog work harder to get a good home and a "Missus" to love him.

When it became evident that JM could not recover at Fort Walton, it seemed best, in order not to interfere with Mary Woolley's engagements, for her to go alone to the Milk River Baths in Jamaica.

Writing home to Mary Woolley at Fleur de Lys about the place where Mickey Mouse was to sleep, JM said "Preferably the laundry." Where Mickey Mouse did actually sleep was in the guest room from which only the Chinese rugs had been removed, until, by industrious scratching, he removed a large part of the door and some of the sidewall finish! With no sense of the comedy in her statement, Mary Woolley kept on asserting, "Mickey is all right." At least the Mickey Mouse bulletins were happy messages in a none too happy world.

At that time Brewer's yeast with its vitamin B complex content was being given to all the dogs. However, so "high" was Mick's general condition of bounce and joy that Mary Woolley wrote that she was following Portia's advice and not even showing him the yeast can. In another letter of Mickey Mouse's there is a suggestion that his Eminent Missus had herself sampled the can of yeast:

> I am not going to church today. I could, but Missus doesn't see it that way. I would sit at the end of the pew and nip the legs as they came up the aisle. I think that it would be fun to see the different ways the owners of the legs looked. They—the "owners"—look different here. Bummy looks superior and walks off; Boy looks grieved and stares at Missus for an explanation. He is so good that I like to nip him, just to see him look in the other direction, patient-like, as if nothing had happened. Buddy—he plays—and is real forgiving, mostly; sometimes he bites back.

CHAPTER 21

HUMAN LOVE

"I wish simply to stress the truth that it is only as human relations are shaped by women—as well as by men—with the thinking of both directed by the good heart, that we shall ever realize the better world!"

Mary Woolley became itinerant again under continued and increasing demands upon her for committee work and lecturing. She threaded to and fro by train, by car, and by ship, working indefatigably. In one letter she said it had been "an enjoyable two weeks, busy, with a deal of nervous tension," and that she was "'orful glad' to get home." Ten days later she spent the day on international business: the morning at the Federal Council rooms, then luncheon at the Astor to hear Lord Cecil and an adjourned meeting of the Commission until the late afternoon.

Speaking at the Armistice Meeting in Philadelphia about that time to an audience of some two thousand "was not in the nature of a 'rest-cure'." She wrote later of the honor awarded her by the Federation of Women's Clubs when she spoke to a ballroom full of the organization's members, followed by a reception, after which she repacked and was in bed at 1:20 A.M., only to arise at 5:15. Her comment was that "the week had been a very pleasant one, but '. . . full up'."

The conditions under which Mary Woolley traveled from the time she was 75 until she was 81 would have worn down a younger woman. When she received a telegram from Paul McNutt asking her to join a committee of community leaders, she wired she would. She needed the time for work on talks and for rest, but promptly changed her plans, and left home immediately. Arriving in Washington, all she could get was an 11th floor room in the Ambassador—"no bath, hot and noisy, but a room." At least she "did not have to sleep on a park bench!" Encountering hardships during the war, Mary Woolley would not call them "hardships". There was the diner which admitted civilians only at 12 o'clock noon, so that not only did

220

she have no breakfast, but no prospect of supper. Looking at her "retired" schedule of committees and speeches gave her family the same feeling of dizziness one has when trains are moving past each other in opposite directions.

On October 20, 1937, she led another Peoples Mandate delegation to Hyde Park. This time Sumner Welles, then Under Secretary of State, made the arrangements. The committee had presented their mandate at the Buenos Aires Conference for the Maintenance of Peace in December 1936. The result was that the committee gave its attention more and more to the inter-American scene, working for popular support for the treaties. A delegation was now planned to take the Mandate on a trip around the Americas during which it would be received by the Presidents of every country. The send off was the appointment with the President at Hyde Park. Among others, the group included Mary Woolley as chairman and the four envoys called the Flying Caravan who were to go on the journey.

When previously the Mandate Delegation had seen the President, there was only one representative. This time there were several persons who had assisted in raising money and aided in other ways. The President in his library looked around at the entire delegation, saying, "Well, Dr. Woolley, I think the Peoples Mandate is growing— you are increasing in strength I should say. The last time you were here alone and now there are three!" The laughing reply was: "This is a notable increase, Mr. President!" Mary Woolley continued that the Peoples Mandate Committee was undertaking to support ratification because the Committee believed that the time was propitious to emphasize treaties.

Following this visit to Hyde Park, the Flying Caravan attempted to help speed ratification of the Buenos Aires Peace Treaties by the Republics of South and Central America. The group was dispatched on a 17,000 mile journey through 18 countries, with Gaeta Wold Boyer travelling in advance to make preparations for the meetings. The Flying Caravan members were Mrs. Burton W. Musser of Salt Lake City, Utah, former State Senator; Mrs. Ana del Pulgar de Burke, Washington, D. C., Chilean-born wife of Thomas Burke; Mrs. Rebecca Hourwich Reyher of New York, journalist, author; and Mrs. Enoch Wesley Frost, Texarkana, Arkansas, vice-president of the National Garden Club. There is a jocund touch towards the close of the particular letter in which the chairman describes the South American delegation:

Yesterday noon we all broadcasted; two — the two from Brazil and

Argentina—sailed last evening; two go next week and the fifth not until
February. I like the group very much and think the four very worth
while . . . The luncheon given by the managers of the Grace Line on
the Santa Rosa Thursday was a particularly nice one—Madame Roosevelt having her picture taken with the delegation numberless times and
being as gay as the youngest of them.

Several months later Mary Woolley started off on her birthday,
July 13, 1938, for a meeting of the International Federation of University Women in England. Her message from the S.S. Manhattan
was: "We are off and I am glad—for that means being just so much
nearer reaching home!" On the day following she wrote that no
roommate had appeared and she was luxuriating in a room "quite by
myself". She added: "Nicest of all at the next table is Hugh Gibson!
I was perfectly amazed when he walked up at luncheon yesterday.
He has been in the States for about two weeks. We are going to settle
the affairs of the world before we reach Plymouth—he says—but I shall
be content to get his point of view."

On July 25th and 26th the various committees of the Federation
were meeting to work out reports, but Mary Woolley managed to cross
the Channel for a few days. On reaching London again, she recorded
her reaction:

> I was very glad that I went to Paris but it certainly was strenuous.
> I was startled to find a note asking me to speak ten minutes Sunday
> and after a very full day Saturday sat up until midnight to prepare.
> Result, before my turn came Sunday, a minor riot in the audience on
> the part of the Communist element because their idol, a Spanish woman,
> had not been asked to speak, meant that the meeting was called off.
> And I might have gone to bed!

So much for Mary Woolley's handling of Communism.

She turned quietly back to the work in London of the I.F.U.W. In
her notes she reported: "The social crept in by various delightful avenues." On the day after the close of the meeting, in her last letter
home, she wrote that the International Federation had ended "with a
dinner at the zoo last evening". It had been a good meeting but she
was glad to omit wandering "around the illuminated Park listening to
the Band and conversing with the chimpanzee, et cetera." She and
Miss Glass escaped to a taxi, noticing that Miss Gildersleeve and a
companion had done likewise.

> Just think, next week I shall be at home! I am glad that I came but
> the nicest thing about it will be meeting the Goddess of Liberty . . .
> One week from day after tomorrow the Goddess and I should be bowing
> to each other again!

A symposium on women and contemporary life held at the Centennial Celebration of Duke University was in many ways the great educational event of 1939. Assembled for the program were such notable women as Judge Florence Allen, Mary Anderson, Anna Cox Brinton, Anna del Pulgar de Burke, Meta Glass, Georgia Harkness and Mary Woolley. The latter presided over the symposium on Women's Relation to Peace and International Good Will. The next day she spoke on Women's Leadership in Education. In learning how to live together, she stressed, "women have more interest in human relationships than men" and "have had more experience in solving problems of human relationship".

*   *   *   *

Of her proposed autobiography Mary Woolley had said repeatedly "Perhaps it will make some money for us," or "I want to get it done— that would help us financially. "However, the autobiography, for reasons not then evident, seemed to be a more or less padlocked subject. Only later was it learned that she did not begin her autobiography until 1939 was two-thirds gone. On August 30th of that year she made the following record on a used, large State Department envelope:

> " 'The History of my Life'
> Begun at 10:30 A.M. Wednesday, August 30, 1939"

This is the first formal notation on her autobiography. It was at this time that Belle Fuller, a north woods girl, took over Martha Parkhill's duties in Mary Woolley's Westport offices. She began work with the copying of some notes that Mary Woolley had made towards a sketch of her happy childhood.

The rest of the record on the State Department envelope follows:

> Resumed 10 A.M., Thursday, June 11, 1940
> Resumed again 10 a.m., Tuesday, August 26, 1941
> Resumed again summer of   1942
> Resumed again April 1,   1943
> Resumed again Autumn   1943

She included some recollections of her fortunate and joyous years at Brown University and at Pembroke-Brown and some memories of Wheaton and Wellesley days. She started on the major opus of her executive duties at Mount Holyoke, and got as far as what she called "An Interim Year"—that is, the year *before* she went to Mount Holyoke and her inauguration in 1900. But of the entire time she was President of Mount Holyoke, there were only the following three paragraphs:

Fortunately my arrival at the College which was to be my home for nearly thirty-seven years, was December thirty-first, in the year of our Lord nineteen hundred. I say "fortunately" because that judicious timing was looked upon with favor by a staunch friend of the College; for forty years its treasurer. "I am glad that you came at the beginning of the year and at the beginning of the Century," said Mr. Williston. "It will be so much easier to keep track of you."

Some of the little things warmed the cockles of my heart, as for instance the eggs which Dr. Hooker, long professor of Botany at Mount Holyoke, sent with the inscription: "Nineteenth Century eggs for a Twentieth Century breakfast." The first Saturday night after my arrival Byron Smith called, the Byron Smith who as a boy had helped to carry the furniture in to "Mary Lyon's School"   and had been known by generations of Mount Holyoke undergraduates since that time. Solemnly he took out of his pocket two big red apples and presented them to Mary Lyon's new and untried successor.

All along the line it was a kindly warm-hearted reception. I took it as a matter of course without realizing how easily it might have been less kind, less warm-hearted. The members of the Faculty living at Brigham Hall where the president of the College made her home were, mainly, much older women, Mount Holyoke graduates who had spent practically all of their professional life on that campus.

After Dr. Hooker's eggs and Byron Smith's apples, the only other comment was: "A woman without Mount Holyoke traditions, who had never seen the College until she was offered the presidency, was welcomed as cordially as if she had been to the manor born." The whole heartbreaking story of her closing years at Mount Holyoke College was left untold with not one sentence about her 37 years as its president.

＊　　＊　　＊　　＊

For a while the illness or the death of close ones came from all sides. Twice Mary Woolley went to see a friend who had become paralyzed. She remarked that if she were ever ill in that way, she would do her utmost to teach herself to speak again and to make herself understood. Suddenly Portia fell with a thrombosis. Unwilling to risk her life by having her carried up to her bedroom, she was taken into the library where she lay for a week on a large davenport. About her was all the paraphernalia of illness. It was during that week, with the front door opening into the library, that everyone we had *not* expected to see for some time decided while motoring through the Adirondacks to stop for a call!

It was in that year, too, that time, on whose ratchet all of us are moved along, brought Amy Cordoba Ransome to our home on Lake Champlain—land and house so different from the semi-tropical beauty of her own Southern California home. Although her joyous personality brought hope to everyone who worked with her, she was tragically acquainted with grief in one of its worst forms; cancer had invaded her home three times. In thanking a friend for sympathy she wrote: "Destiny (the poetic word for evolution) is great and vast. We are too insignificant to rebel but must content ourselves with making the brief moments *worthy of our true selves* and trust in the Maker of it all to know what is best. What that is may not be happiness of the individual but something unknown to us of which we are an infinitesimal part."

Unemployment was increasing steadily during the Roosevelt regime and Mary Woolley's brother Frank was out of work. With much effort, she made contacts for him which seemed to be promising. She and Harriet Newhall were in New York while he was following up some leads and they all had lunch together at the Cosmopolitan Club. Desperately discouraged by the interview he had had that morning, Frank said that there was no opening. "MEW was 'simply marvelous' in her determination to raise Frank's morale and the quiet way in which she talked to her brother," wrote Harriet. When she finished talking, Frank, turning to Harriet, said, "What a sister she is!" Shortly thereafter his health broke and he became ill of malignant cancer. After his death, Mary Woolley said in her letter to JM:

> It was blessed to have you in New York Wednesday night. When I arrived at the Roosevelt, I felt for the first time that I had reached the end of my rope and it meant everything to have you there. Blessings on you, Dear . . . I do not remember ever having such a sense of complete weariness. The realization of all the anxiety and disappointment that Frank has borne so bravely and unselfishly for four years swept over me . . .

With time the wound seemed to heal over. Yet in the deep sorrow of the loss of her "little brother" something was again lost which she never regained.

❖   ❖   ❖   ❖

Of opportunities for women, in the closing years of her life Mary Woolley said frequently: "The domain of freedom is being steadily narrowed. The belief in the unlimited value of human personality has disappeared in many places and has been supplanted by faith in an omniscient and omnipotent state."

It may be that the most important part of Mary Woolley's work for peace lay in her conviction that women should be educated for and admitted to the business of "policy shaping" or leadership, but she emphasized that women's approach to the problems of war did *not* resemble that of men. It was this conviction which led to what was possibly the most remarkable act of her life. Singlehandedly, when she was 79, she founded a new organization: "The Participation of Women in Post-War Policy, which eventually became Women in World Affairs. On September 15, 1942, she met with a group of women to whom she stated that they had been called together to discuss the question of how to secure the representation of the women's point of view in the shaping of world policy after the war. Again she expressed the conviction that women had less interest in war as a game than men have, and she recalled that during the Disarmament Conference, Sir Eric Drummond had remarked to her that he wondered what would have happened if the Conference had been composed chiefly of women. This was all that was needed to start the ball rolling. Initially the group included Dr. Gertrude Baer, Emily Greene Balch, Margaret Burton, Mary Dingman, Dorothy Canfield Fisher, Alice L. T. Parsons.

By May 3, 1943, Mary Woolley was writing Dr. Emily Hickman, who had become the chairman of Women in World Affairs, that the rapid and sound progress of the committee was "remarkable". Miraculously, almost over night, the work of this handful of women produced an interlocking organization of 4,000,000 women.

Since her retirement, to paraphrase Montaigne's words, Mary Woolley had been making defeat more triumphant than victory, not by talking about what had happened to her at Mount Holyoke College but by continuing her work with and for women and their united goals of education and of peace, and by the steadfast maintenance of her silent protest. As a councillor her advice was much sought both in interviews and letters—advice which in the course of a year must have absorbed, all told, several months' time.

Everywhere she went Mary Woolley knew she might be subjected to questions about Mount Holyoke. At a luncheon, the Chancellor of the University of Toronto inquired who was her successor at Mount Holyoke. When she told him he exclaimed, "A man? Why, under the sun, a man?" Never militant at any time in her life, she was, nevertheless, beginning to think about the relationship between opportunities for women and equality before the law. If women needed the ballot to protect their right to work during the time of Susan B. Anthony and M. Carey Thomas, was there not as the mid-century approached a need for legal equality to protect the gains women had made?

Early in 1942 Mary Woolley wrote to a cousin whose daughter had been at Mount Holyoke: "The policy which I am following is not going back to Mount Holyoke is my protest against what was done. You know me well enough to realize that I never say a word against the

present administration. The question is something bigger than the
personal . . . In the first place, the way it was done as I said to the
Board of Trustees, 'was more worthy of Hitler than of the United
States of America.'" In this letter, written in reply to her cousin's
inquiry about information for some alumnae, she went on to enumerate
the facts of her defeat and then added that in framing the by-laws she
supposed "the members of the Board never dreamed that anything
less than a unanimous, or nearly unanimous, vote of the Board would
be required for the election of the President of the College."

> The above does not, however, go to the heart of the question. One
> hundred years before, Mary Lyon had given her life to the founding of
> an institution which should prepare women for service, especially in edu-
> cation. If, after a hundred years of that service, the college could not
> produce an alumna prepared to head the institution, why continue it?
> . . . I could say much more: perhaps it is sufficient to convince you that
> I cannot give up my protest. I am sure that you will realize that this is
> not an easy decision. I gave to Mount Holyoke thirty-seven years, exactly
> one half of my life.[1]

She was also beginning to weigh the relation of privilege to the
archaic laws about women still on the statute books of most states.
She wrote: "I think many women like myself are 'thinking through' the
whole subject and are likely to come out on the side of a 'Constitu-
tional Amendment'. Mrs. Harold Milligan of New York, for whose
judgment I have great respect, said to me the other day that that was
the way her mind was working." In thought and in writing, Mary
Woolley was asking herself and others: "Are we not handicapped by
the present position of women before the law?"

A published greeting from Emma Guffey Miller to Dr. Katharine
McBride, newly appointed President of Bryn Mawr, stated what even
Mary Woolley herself was coming to recognize in her ever-widening
outlook on freedom for women:

> Again Bryn Mawr is upholding the great traditions established by M.
> Carey Thomas that women should have not only equal educational oppor-
> tunities, but equal educational responsibilities. When Dr. Mary E.
> Woolley, after years of notable service, and the Alumnae and Faculty of
> Mt. Holyoke were so flagrantly "sold out" a few years ago by the Com-
> mittee choosing a new president, every alumna of the other women's col-
> leges realized a staggering blow had been dealt to the advancement of
> women. Now all will equally rejoice that Bryn Mawr is holding fast to its
> fine standards by electing Dr. McBride to its presidency . . . May Dr.
> McBride continue to carry forward the struggle, for it is a struggle, begun
> by Miss Thomas for equal rights for women in educational opportunities,
> politics and, finally, as her last contribution to progress, Equal Rights
> within the Constitution.

Speaking in the words of another woman, Mary Woolley sent the following statement to Alma Lutz of the National Woman's Party:

> Why am I endorsing the Equal Rights Amendment? I should like to answer that question in the words of another woman with references to women and international policy. "It is time sex be forgotten and men and women become co-workers in all that concerns the destiny of the human race." We are confronting the most acute crisis in human history, a crisis to be met by human beings, men and women, on an equal basis. Anything less than absolute equality is an anachronism in the year of our Lord Nineteen Hundred and Forty-two.

What followed her endorsement of the Equal Rights Amendment? As usual, when Mary Woolley had made up her mind, a good deal happened. She joined the National Woman's Party, under the leadership of Anna Kelton Wiley, for six years editor of *Equal Rights.*[2] On September 15, 1942, she founded Women in World Affairs. On October 25, 1942, despite fatigue from over-work, she spoke at the Bellevue-Stratford in behalf of equal rights. After a gracious introduction by Emma Guffey Miller there was an uproar of welcome. Although half ill from exhaustion, she spoke clearly and quietly:

> Gigantic problems will confront humanity after the war is won, and their solution will demand the best that the human mind and the human heart and the human soul have to give—the best, *regardless of sex.*
>
> Women, as women, have much to contribute to this solution—compassion, understanding, insight, an acute realization of the cost of human life so ruthlessly squandered in the brutality of war . . . It is difficult to find a word expressing just what women as statesmen would bring to this official task of creating a better understanding among races and peoples. Perhaps "human love" is the nearest approach. Out of the depth of their conviction would come a warmth of expression that would go far toward the smoothing out of difficulties, the adjustment of misunderstandings . . . I wish simply to stress the truth that it is only as human relations are shaped by women—as well as by men—*with the thinking of both directed by the good heart,* that we shall ever realize the better world!

On the following day JM gave a memorial address on Amy Ransome to a group of Quakers and non-Quakers. Later that afternoon at a meeting of the Board, a Bryn Mawr alumna, as distinguished in her own right as Amy Ransome, crossed the room and said, "I want to thank you for your talk about Mrs. Ransome and to take this chance to tell you that in New Haven I saw that Mount Holyoke-Yale correspondence about Miss Woolley and her successor. There is just one word to describe that correspondence: rotten, plain *rotten!*"

CHAPTER 22

UNFINISHED DAY

"I have worked over thirty years in the international field and have been troubled by the individualism of people in great human problems. I have looked to women to give up personal preferences and to base their work upon the common denominator of a common cause."

On her eightieth birthday in 1943, Mary Woolley was still young in appearance, warm-hearted, witty, brisk, the well-shaped sensitive mouth unchanged by the years. Teeth white and shining, cheeks red, keen brown eyes and a jaunty slant to some of her pretty hats, it was hard to believe that she had seen more than 60 or 70 summers. Welcome everywhere in the United States, on that birthday she was speaking in Louisville, Kentucky. Her train had been three hours late. The heat was severe and she had had only the minimum of food when she wrote home: ""Well, I have turned the corner into another decade. A rather warm corner it is too, but I have an air-conditioned room, the auditorium is comfortable and I am 'getting along' all right."

She always gave the other person a chance to get along, too, for her letters were never packed with personal lamentations, problems or bad news. During these wartime years of travel and lectures, she kept her sense of humor, her love for beauty, her self-control and her love for those who meant "home" to her. From Council Bluffs, Iowa, she wrote home that the radio was giving religious songs and congratulations to various human beings in that region who had reached the advanced age of 70 and she felt that she should rise up "and say 'Me too'." "The radio," she commented, "is popular in this section: it was going all the way from St. Paul to Chicago last Wednesday. At present the cheerful beauties of the Crosby Mortuary at Omaha are being described." She no longer ran downhill in Providence with a college mate to catch a train to Pawtucket, but she knew that in the nature of things she was running downhill to "take a train" into the valley of shadows. She worked harder and harder and without complaint so that she might do all she could while she was able.

In only a handful of sentences from her letters had Mary Woolley
used the words "nervous tension", "not a rest-cure", or described types
of travelling which would have exhausted a young girl. She once
wrote of Fleur de Lys: "You are right in saying that, 'there is healing
in the old place'. I have often wondered whether I could meet the
strain if I did not have this background. I am increasingly grateful
to you."

❃   ❃   ❃   ❃

From January through September of 1944, in the course of her committee and speaking engagements, Mary Woolley was, as usual, coming
and going between Westport, New York, Boston or some city farther
afield. In one of the letters home in April 1944, there is unusual emphasis on the fact that the days, even if "tiresome" had not been
"tiring"; and from time to time in other letters there was a little too
much insistence that she was "perfectly all right". As one of the
Senators of Phi Beta Kappa, she attended a meeting held in New
York City that April. For this and other engagements she had taken
an unusual number of gowns, as the entry in her Day Book shows a
black and silver, a dark blue gown and her "new black" frock.

Two days later, her childhood playmate and lifelong friend, Edith
Conant Thornton, died when Mary Woolley was about to return home.
Pawtucket is more easily reached from New York than from the north
woods. Reached by telephone just before she was expected to leave
for Fleur de Lys, she replied unexpectedly that she was uncertain
whether she would go to Mrs. Thornton's funeral or come home the
day following, but that she would stay on at the Cosmopolitan Club
for another day. This uncertainty had the color of an attempt to make
up her mind. In her Day Book for April 19, "Westport", written in a
trembling hand, was now deleted. Both the doubt about what she
would do and the trembling handwriting revealed that all was not
well with her. In the Day Book eight days later she jotted down:
"Consideration of will." About Hillside Cemetery in Wilton, where
her grandparents, parents, little sister Gracie, and brother Frank lay
buried, she wrote on Wednesday, May 4th: "Wilton 1 lot (Room for
me!)." After this humorous if grim memorandum, she added that she
and the tentative publisher of her autobiography were planning another conference. This probably meant that she had made up her
mind after all to go on with the writing of her life. However, no one
knew at the time that Mary Woolley continued to write inquiries about
the Hillside burial plot.

In this spring of 1944 the president of the Mount Holyoke Board of

Trustees, a new and fortunate appointment, offered her an honorary degree. If she had accepted it, Mary Woolley could have rested on the laurels which she won in appointments, in honors, in achievements, and in her reputation for moral courage. Until the letters were found in the summer of 1948, nothing was known of the proffered honor and this refusal addressed to Dr. Eliot on June 12, 1944:

> Will you express to the Board of Trustees of Mount Holyoke College appreciation of their action in voting to offer me an honorary degree. I wish the members of the Board to know how deeply I appreciate this action, although it seems not possible for me to accept the honor.
> Believe me with personal regards,

Four days later, she was on her way to an honor she could accept. Alumnae Day at Pembroke College and Brown University was on June 17th and this was to be her 50th anniversary and reunion at Brown— an alumnae commencement celebration, including the founding of a scholarship bearing her name. How her academic friends in that old and unfailingly loyal alma mater felt about her is best summarized in an intended *reductio ad absurdum* sent her by the "little boy", Gorham Noble Norton, whom Mary Woolley had sat next to on that first day of classes in 1892 at Brown:

"Mary"

This is just a short story about a little Mary who didn't have a lamb. Once upon a time (very recently—it was about 1892, or was it 1492) there was a little "Mary" who didn't have a lamb (she was very Woolley herself) and she popped right onto a settee one day in a little old fashioned recitation room of a little old college named Brown University.

We little boys were surprised to see a little girl come in and sit right down aside of the young "Kid" writing this name.

The subject was Philosophy and the teacher was E. Benj. Andrews. He only had one eye—but oh boy! what he could see with that one! What he lacked in eyesight he made up in all other sight (fore, rear, future).

Now this little boy "sized up" little "Mary", with her little notebook and pencil and said (to himself) "Gee, this looks to me like a smart kid all right, and I guess I better mind my p's and q's and behave." Now this did prove to be a "smart kid" and at breakfast this little boy was told by another classmate, Marshal S. Brown, that Mary did make good use of that notebook and pencil.

Mary Woolley, I know your record. I salute you and boast often that *I* sat side of this little "Mary" who didn't have a lamb—she had many, flocks who followed her to school many days.

Well, this little boy soon "signing off" led the Mandolin Club, was cheerer for the teams, ran around a nice neighborhood in his B.V.D.'s (2 miles) and generally gave more attention to music and sports than Mary did—but he got his A.B. and I guess "they" were glad he was out.

However, we didn't get to the top of leadership of a brain factory, but we did of a woolen factory—head of the great mills of the American Woolen Co., and his own companies.

So, like George Cohan's grand song, I will sing your praises and say "So long, Mary".

Gosh, Mary, everyone is proud of you.

Gorham Noble Norton
50th Reunion

On June 17th she reached Pembroke College in time for lunch, giving everyone "an impression of continued vigor and strength and capacity". In the afternoon, seemingly vigorous, and with her gift for speaking with penetrating human warmth and frankness that did not hint her 81 years, Mary Woolley began:

A Fiftieth Anniversary! . . . It is curious how one's conception of age changes with the years. I remember a remark when I was a student at Wheaton Seminary—the forerunner of Wheaton College—a remark made by Mrs. Metcalf, principal-emeritus of the old school. While one of a line waiting at a railroad ticket-office, the ticket agent said: "Please stand aside and let the old lady buy her ticket first." Mrs. Metcalf, like the others, politely stepped aside, but no "old lady" appearing and everyone looking expectantly in her direction, the sad truth finally dawned upon her!

The climax of the ovation given their famous alumna came when a delegation of members from the Class of '94 at Brown came over to do her honor. This delegation was led by Henry Sharpe, Chancellor of the University; with him were many distinguished men, among them a famous professor from Cambridge University, England. Laughing and reminiscing, these cordial, nice "boys" of long ago acclaimed the "First Woman" as the most distinguished member of the Class of '94.

On June 18th, after reaching the Cosmopolitan Club in New York, tired despite all the happiness at Pembroke, she wrote home: "Whew!" I wonder whether the heat wave has struck Westport. It is terrific in New York." Home the afternoon of Tuesday, June 20th, Mary Woolley plunged back into hard, routine office duties and worked on a conference speech to be given at Silver Bay on June 27th. In July and August 1944, a Wellesley alumna and former student wrote several times asking for advice. In the course of her replies Mary Woolley wrote:

My home at Westport was built by Jeannette Marks's mother and father when Jeannette was a child and has been a home of mine for many years in the summers before we took it for all the year around . . . Jeannette would wish to send her warm regards. We are both busy in our "respective offices" and as we breakfast singly and alone, often do not meet until toward noon.

In that spring and summer there were two ways in which Mary
Woolley was less like herself: the character of her handwriting and
recurrent irritability.   Then, suddenly it seemed, she became frail.
Although struggling against this fact, she was conscious that she made
an impression at home quite different from the one she was still able
to make abroad.   Some of her outdoor occupations altered or were
given up altogether.   No longer did she play ball or throw sticks for
the dogs.   There was less active gardening, and for the first time in
any summer she took no notice of the dogs' grave yard and made no
comment on its condition, a spot she had tenderly cared for but now
avoided.

There was a sentence tedious to hear but which Mary Woolley was
to hear many times: "May, I think we should make some permanent
resident arrangement both in housekeeping and for a secretary."   Each
time the reply had been, "Oh no, let us keep on this way!   It is peaceful alone."   Again JM would say, "I think we should advertise or make
inquiries—at least for a resident secretary!"   The invariable reply was,
"Oh no, let us be alone!"

Troubled by the continuing evidence of Mary Woolley's lessened
energy and interest, it seemed best to say nothing but to go ahead in
the attempt to secure a dependable, well-educated assistant.   In the
middle of August 1944, Aura Roberts, a Middlebury College graduate
and the mother of four grown children, was hired as secretary.   An
impulsive, warm-hearted woman whose interests were intellectual, she
looked forward to working with and for one of the great women of
America.   Since she had had many to care for, Mrs. Roberts quickly
became familiar with "doctor's orders" regarding what Mary Woolley
should and should not do on account of her heart condition, but it
was almost impossible to prevent Mary Woolley from doing, with open
enjoyment, exactly what she had been ordered and begged not to do.

Mary Woolley and her new secretary were soon in the full swing of
office work, preparing for an autumn, winter and spring crowded with
committee meetings and speaking.   With Mick walking beside her
carrying some bag or papers in his jaws, Mary Woolley usually reached
the office early, her briefcase full of folders that she had worked on at
home.   One folder contained personal correspondence; the second
had in it letters to which she dictated replies; the third included letters
that her secretary, after brief suggestions, was to answer.   It did not
take Aura Roberts long to become acquainted with the Mary E.
Woolley style.

One morning, as she took out the third folder, Mary Woolley said,

"Mrs. Roberts, you know the sort of thing I say to these friends."

"Yes, Miss Woolley," answered Mrs. Roberts as she went to her own office. But on this day she found herself in trouble over a letter from Julia Moody. Miss Moody was a distinguished Mount Holyoke alumna and was in 1944 a professor in the biology department at Wellesley College. To Mary Woolley, Julia Moody was an old and valued name; to Mrs. Roberts it was a new name and she was puzzled. By that time Aura Roberts had come to believe that she was familiar with all who were called by their first name and to whom Miss Woolley signed herself "Affectionately yours" or "Lovingly yours, MEW". She picked up the folder and went back to Miss Woolley's office, saying, "Now, what should I do about this letter? Do I say 'Dear Doctor Moody', or 'Dear Professor Moody'?" Quick as a flash, her eyes laughing, Mary Woolley replied, "If I were you, I should just say, 'Dear Julia'."

This incident came to be a standing joke between them, for whenever there was a letter to be written in an intimate, conversational tone, Mary Woolley would say to Aura Roberts, "Now this is a 'Dear Julia' letter."

Although her books were called "Diaries", Mary Woolley's treatment turned them into what might be called "Day Books". In September 1944 at the time of her last visit to New York, the following entries were made:

Tues.   19   Fed. Council Ex. Com.
                9:00 shampoo
                11:30 Miss Shea? . . .
Wed.   20   Shopping
                New Canaan—H.W.W.
                Greenwich—Nelle Troy dress shop
                H.W.W.
                Overseas box vs check
Thurs.   21   Dulles Com.
                Parkside
                10 a.m.

For those familiar with the details of her life, some of these brief entries were full of significance for they meant that she had been active in various organizations, including the Federal Council of Churches and meetings with the Dulles Commission. The "H.W.W., overseas box vs check" entry means that Mary Woolley intended to ask her sister-in-law, Harriet Wright Woolley, whether her son, Ferris, would prefer an overseas box or a check for Christmas.

On June 26th Mary Woolley jotted down her need for a 1945 Day Book but the letter ordering it was not sent until September 2. Within a short time, as childlike in her pleasure as her father before her had been, she went to the office with the attractive "Line-a-Day" diary for the coming five years. Delighted by its format, she spent some time showing it to Mrs. Roberts. Then instead of signing letters she carefully filled in the fly leaf personal data with the size of her own gloves, shoes and stockings:

> SIZES TO REMEMBER
> Gloves 7½
> Shoes 7½
> Hosiery 10½

Still pleased, she commented: "Before we go to work I am going to jot down here in my new book the appointments I can recall." After making these entries, Mary Woolley, apologizing for keeping Mrs. Roberts waiting, said, "It's always a temptation to look at blank spaces for coming days and guess how they will be spent." Unfaltering courage to go ahead—call it faith that God has created love and "a moral universe". It had been a long pilgrimage from the days when the child trudged briskly down the road to go to grandma's until this August day as she prepared for another year of hard work.

❀   ❀   ❀   ❀

September 29 was a lovely day: warmth in the sunshine, fragrance in the air, a blue haze veiling the tapestries of scarlet maples and golden elms, the dark beauty of pines and hemlocks, and a flame of woodbine running along the fence rails at Fleur de Lys. This was a Friday with a busy morning in the office getting material ready for JM's speaking trip in western New York. At lunch JM suggested that they have "a little peace of our own" until three o'clock, then meet to drive into the mountains with Bummy and Buddy. They rode over to Wadhams for some shopping, following country roads to Elizabethtown. Traffic was heavy in Elizabethtown and no place could be found to park near the drug store. JM drove around and around, everyone merry over the parking predicament and the ice cream cones. As they rode back to Fleur de Lys, twilight was coming on. Saying that she would have to go to the cabin again to prepare for the busy days ahead, JM went down the hill with Bummy and Buddy.

That evening Mary Woolley and Mrs. Roberts had supper alone together. She asked Aura Roberts for a pot of tea with supper—an unusual request for her. With Boy and Mick lying quietly before the hearth and Chrissie singing from time to time, they had their supper, lingering at the table, relaxed in the cheerfulness and quiet warmth. Mary Woolley spoke of how well she felt. She told Mrs. Roberts that she would sit by the fire until Mrs. Roberts returned from walking the dogs and they would all go upstairs together. In the long northern twilight they got ready for bed. Mary Woolley was in one of her gay moods, calling across the hall to Aura Roberts that she had never been shown a promised picture of the mother of Miriam Brailey, a Mount Holyoke alumna.

The next day, September 30th, was hazy with smoke from the fallen and falling leaves. Pears and apples lay on the ground and the white and purple grapes by the edge of the kitchen terrace were sweet and ripe and fragrant. A few minutes before eight o'clock in the morning, Aura Roberts was eating her breakfast on the lawn when, briefcase in hand, Mary Woolley, erect and energetic, came out of the house and started towards Cutwind. Since her return from New York she had been trying to catch up.

After a greeting she said to Mrs. Roberts, "There is much to do this morning, papers and letters and one important letter which *has to go out* to Mrs. Parsons in this noon's mail. I suppose I shall have to do it longhand."

"Miss Woolley," came the emphatic reply, "why not let me type at least that one letter? Miss Marks won't mind."

"Certainly *not*," interrupted Mary Woolley. "This is Miss Marks' day and she is going away to speak and needs your help. But you could find Mick for me."

Shortly before noon, according to custom, Mary Woolley went to get dinner for the dogs. As she left Cutwind, she called across to Mrs. Roberts that she had put the longhand letter in the usual place and asked her to be certain that it was delivered to the post office in time for the outgoing noon mail.

A few minutes before twelve, when JM came up, Mary Woolley was standing on the kitchen stone terrace. Noticing her unusually swollen ankles, JM said, "May, we'd better get ourselves settled in deck chairs!" She brought around the chairs, placing them side by side. Then she went over to the arbor beyond the terrace to pick some of the white grapes. The friends sat there in the sun, eating grapes and talking about JM's plans for Buffalo and Syracuse. Mary Woolley had been working out the train schedules, and took a card out of her "Diary" with this memo on it:

> "Lv Albany 6:45 p.m.
> Due Buffalo 11:50
> sleeping cars
> get reservation
> in section—
> 'Ohio State
> Limited' "

Mrs. Roberts was starting off for the village. As she passed, MEW and JM were still talking quietly together while the dogs were eating their dinner on the lawn under the elms. Waving the mail pouch at them, the secretary went out through the gate and on up the Fleur de Lys lane.

While waiting for lunch and Mrs. Roberts' return, Mary Woolley said that when she went upstairs after lunch for her nap she would telephone for the reservations indicated on the card, then her speech faltered, blurred and stopped. Jumping up to catch her as her body began to sag, JM called for help. In less than two minutes an ice pack was on her head.

During the war the local physicians were heavily overworked. Some of them were without either assistants or receptionists, and most did not have nurses they could call upon. The housekeeper did her best over the telephone but could get no doctor.

There followed what seemed to be an endless time of waiting for Aura Roberts to return. Finally she secured a doctor from Port Henry, who with a workman, Iva, and the chore boy lifted the deck chair and carried Mary Woolley into JM's little study on the first floor, laying her on the couch there. As the doctor was leaving he said, "I do not expect Miss Woolley to live through the night. There is absolutely no hope for her recovery, and you should be prepared for the stark reality. Call me when you need me."

CHAPTER 23

GOOD SHIP

"The less we think about the destructive and the more we think about the constructive, the more we shall be able to do."

Still unaware of the fact that she was paralyzed, Mary Woolley's delirium took the form of determination to get up and go about her work. There were many incoherent words about financial anxieties, as she repeated over and over, "One thousand—five thousand—twenty thousand—no, three thousand—no—" Sometimes she would ask for our blind collie, "Is Chuckie with you?" and several times, "Where is Old Mannie?" Both dogs had been gone for many years on the long trail of eternity.

When Harriet Newhall reached Fleur de Lys that evening and heard the substitute doctor's report, she exclaimed, "They don't know Miss Woolley!" There followed a struggle to get a nurse, for the war had made nurses virtually unobtainable. But Maggie McHale, the former nurse of JM's nephew, Douglas Bacon, had become the trained nurse Margaret McKenzie, and she was secured.

It was the third day before the doctor ceased telling JM to "prepare for the stark reality". On the third day, too, came a note from Portia to JM: "I saw in the papers tonight that Miss Mary had a shock. I felt for you as well, as her illness is yours. I wish I could be some help to you if only to get supper and be company at night. Please write me as it is added sorrow to me. I am writing in the dark. Lovingly Po."

On the fourth day the puzzled doctor said, "Miss Woolley is one hundred per cent better in coming back than most people would have been!" It was possible now to carry her upstairs to her big bedroom with its windows looking out across the lake to the Green Mountains. Above the bed on which she lay hung a large picture of the Mount Holyoke gates—the gates of the college she had helped to make one of the nation's few great colleges for women, the college which for her was still the dearest place in the world.

Eleven days after Mary Woolley was carried upstairs came another crisis. She kept saying, "R—O, yes, that's it, R—O!" In her crippled thoughts, somehow conscious once again of the protection she had had as a little child, she asked, "Have you written grandma?" Occasionally she would call "Mama!" And sometimes she would reach out with her weak left hand—all she could use now—to take JM's hand, saying over and over, "Jeannettie dear, dear Jeannettie!"

In the early part of the evening of October 15th, Mary Woolley lay in a semi-coma. The nurse urged JM to go to bed, saying that if there was anything she could do she would be called. Later, Mrs. Mac said, "There is still nothing you can do but I think you should be here." Throughout the room was the rasp of Cheyne-Stokes breathing: one deep struggling breath after another, then silence continuing so long it seemed breath could never be recovered; finally a gasp, and the struggling breathing came back once more—over and over but becoming fainter.

Mrs. Mac released her patient's wrist gently, saying, "Miss Woolley is pulseless and her respiration has dropped to four. I have tried everything the doctor gave me. We can do no more." She went back to her chair, sat down and covered her eyes with her hand. JM took the nurse's place beside the bed. After the struggling breathing, this quiet was death itself. But while JM was holding Mary Woolley's paralyzed left hand, came the tap of a single pulse beat followed by another. After that the hint of catching her breath again. Whispering, JM asked Harriet for some strong coffee and orange juice. Putting one half teaspoonful of coffee between Mary Woolley's lips, then another, then a few drops of orange juice, the pulse seemed really to be coming back and with it breathing. Mrs. Mac murmured, "Yes, there *are* pulse beats; yes, Miss Woolley *is* breathing again.'

❀　　❀　　❀　　❀

With the return to life, it was not long before Mary Woolley began teaching herself to speak again. The tempo was slow, the effort evident, but the words were usually distinct even if sometimes confused.

A few days later she said, "I feel very different about the end of things. Things don't end: they last forever." She paused and then went on: "The end may not come for some time now. . . . I have made up my mind that I will be helpless all the rest of my life and that the only thing for me to do is to be as pleasant as possible about it." She smiled, her lips slightly twisted on one side where the paralysis had affected her mouth, emphasizing a quizzical expression which at times had always been natural to her.

But one day with a cry she said to JM, "I can't do anything! . . .
I can't get my togetherness." She repeated the word "togetherness"
several times as if she was turning it over in thought, and was aware
that it was not just the word she wished to use, but unaware, then
or later, that some of the words she did use in her suffering could
not have been bettered.

During the first weeks under Nurse McKenzie there was usually
quiet acceptance of conditions as they had to be, except for brief moments, as when her nurse, looking pale, came out of the sick room
and said: "Miss Woolley is behaving something awful. She's thrown
her pillow on the floor, and the things she's saying to me, why if I
told you . . . What am I to do?"

"Nothing, Mrs. Mack. This is just a flash. Already she is trying to
find her balance again."

On the whole, Mary Woolley made little effort to speak and was not
interested in hearing about anything. Yet even in the early weeks she
pulled herself together to greet the doctor and there was always a
"Thank you" when he left. What the nurse and doctor told her to do
she did, and under some of the uncomfortable and unpleasant treat-
ments she had to have she was generally patient and her sense of
humor did not desert her.

Aura Roberts now became assistant nurse as well as secretary. One
day, while she was doing what every nurse has to do, she was met
by a protest. Tears in her eyes, Mary Woolley said over and over,
"But I cannot let you do these things for me; you did not come to us
to do these things."

"Now see here, Miss Woolley," replied Mrs. Roberts. "I have had
four children. What do you suppose the nurse who took care of me
when my first baby was born said?" Silence. "Like you," continued
Mrs. Roberts, "I was objecting to what was being done for me. What
do you think she said, Miss Woolley?"

"I don't know but . . ."

"*Miss Woolley, what do you think she said?*"

"What did she say?" was the reply, for despite herself Mary Woolley
was becoming interested.

"Well, Miss Eiler said to me in reply to some of my silly objections,
'Now, young woman, you listen to me! If the Queen of England had
a baby she would take off her crown and come down from her throne
and have all these things done for her—and you, young woman, are
no better than the Queen of England'."

Mary Woolley laughed until she cried, and that settled it. From then on, all Aura Roberts had to say when trouble was in the making was, "Now, Miss Woolley, remember the Queen of England!" And again there was laughter in the room.

Through the passings days, it was becoming all too evident that one of the major problems to be solved was rebuilding self-confidence. When one of the family bulletins, emphasizing accomplishment and not failure, was read aloud to MEW, she looked surprised and happy. She said, "I did not expect it. I thought I was doing nothing."

However, gaining self-confidence remained the great problem. Where to make a beginning? It could be done only by piecing on to some life-long habit-pattern, for in them are found crutches for lame minds. Devoted to music in the past, any attempt now, even with the beloved Philharmonic Orchestra, to bring Mary Woolley some of the music she had loved, was met with troubled looks and a startled, "What is that sound?" Yet she listened eagerly to letters which came from nieces and nephews, cousins, colleagues, and friends. Noting this interest, JM urged friends to keep letters coming, and through these notes, to make Mary Woolley realize how much she had done and, as she became stronger, might still do.

* * * *

"Miss Woolley is broken in body and in mind," the doctor had said. Then he had gone on to point out that neither a mental nor a physical recovery adequate in any sense of the word was to be expected. Although at the time no comment was made, this dictum was not accepted. Had we not seen Mary Woolley begin almost immediately to train herself to speak as years before, after a visit to Martha Kunhardt, she had said she would do? Almost as quickly, with the exception of one skill, she had trained her left hand to do the work of her right hand. From the beginning, the active left hand took all the responsibility for the helpless right hand, lifting it from time to time to a more comfortable or better position—an oft-repeated gesture which soon became characteristic. The one exception was that she refused to learn to write with her left hand. This refusal focused attention on the fact that for one letter written with her own hand fifty had been dictated. Certainly, dictation had been a dominant habit pattern over many, many years. When Mary Woolley's condition warranted an experiment, dictation could be tried.

About this time the doctor began to talk about "a long-term proposition", saying that if the blood pressure could be held up where it was "the outlook would be good." One day before leaving the house he said, "Today Miss Woolley's heart is in better condition than it was for many months before this collapse." Yet despite the stronger heart she continued from time to time to be depressed. To the doctor she once said, "What is the use: I thought I was going to die and I rather preferred it that way."

A substitute nurse was brought in for a few weeks to spell exhausted Mrs. Mac. Although no one in the house had a cold at this time, Mary Woolley contracted laryngitis. This developed into atypical pneumonia. Most doctors would have said, "This is the end!" and one doctor did say it. But she recovered. What is more, both mentally and physically she began to be in better shape than before the pneumonia.

Nurse Mac was never done with telling stories about Miss Woolley's wit. One night she saw that her patient was lying awake staring at the ceiling, and she said, "Miss Woolley, why aren't you sleeping?" Quick as a flash came the reply, "Why aren't you?" And they both laughed.

Going upstairs one evening to take the dogs to their room, JM heard Mary Woolley call out, "Hello, darling!" Cautiously JM asked, "Is that endearment for the dogs or for me?" "For all of you!" she retorted, laughing.

She became quick in picking up the distinction between the conscious and unconscious mind at work. Once when JM was passing her room, Mary Woolley called out, "Hello, Mama!"

"Hello, dear!" was the reply, for no comment was ever made when the right words did not come. Continuing on down the hall, she could hear Mary Woolley laughing quietly to herself, substituting "Jeannette" for "Mama" and then laughing again.

Mary Augusta would have been proud of her daughter, for Mary Woolley's brilliant mind had somehow remained her own and so had her temperament. Another time she asked JM, "Did you tell them I have my mind still?" No one could know better than she did that contact with either reality or her own personality was never wholly lost. As the good ship of her mind was righting itself, the indestructible sanity of her nature worked to her benefit. As Will Rogers had said of her, years ago, "She has her feet on the ground." This ability in the most shattering years of her life remained intact. No alteration, either temporary or permanent, ever made her anything but Mary Woolley.

If the mind is used to advantage, it can be developed by exercise like a "muscle". Where self-confidence had become a casualty, the problem now was to restore it to life. Only the building up of a sense of independence and the ability to be useful once again could do this.

Although Mary Woolley learned to do many useful tasks, the open door was physically half-closed by paralysis. Independence, therefore, would have to come largely through mental achievement.

A few days before she had commented on the tarnished silver in the dining room. JM replied that either we must wait for the silver polishing or wait on ourselves, for at the mere suggestion of an extra task to be done, the service in the house piled up a mountain of trouble. But Mary Woolley was longing to do something with her own hands, and she was clever in getting her way. A few days later she was sitting in her wheel chair under the *porte cochere* while JM attended to a garden chore.

"Oh, Jeannettie," she called, smiling quizzically as if to say 'I'll see what she does now!', "please stop a minute. I just want to say that I love you better than anyone else in the world and I've been sitting here trying to think what I could do to help you. I could polish silver with my left hand!" They both laughed and soon Mary Woolley was polishing, as the nurse clucked anxiously about her.

In the effort to restore self-confidence and a sense of independence, her pocketbook was equipped with plenty of postage stamps, large and small bills, and silver change, for whatever she wished to buy.

On a fine sunny morning, before the crew came in to lift Mary Emma Woolley into her wheel chair beside the new high hospital bed Harriet had given her, JM remarked, "May, it is time for you to become independent again. Will you and Mrs. Cross please keep your own accounts, buy your own stationery, and why not get your own stamps? So far as you can, make your own donations and, if you like, pay Victoria Mero for your shampoos and Mrs. Cross for her bus tickets." Not unlike the sunlight without was the flash of happiness and pride in Mary Woolley's brown eyes when her hand reached out to take her pocketbook as JM left the room.

It was this unbroken power to plan and to go ahead which gave her the hope of recovery where many people under similar circumstances would have given up long since. Mary Woolley had taught herself to speak again and those who loved her gave only the negative help of setting her free from all comment.

❋   ❋   ❋   ❋

The first day of the dictation experiment, January 23, 1945, three letters were written in this order of dictation: the first to her niece, Mary Emily Woolley, another to her sister-in-law, Harriet Woolley, and the third to her nephew Paul.

The meaning of her note to Mary Emily was clear—she was aware of their relationship, she wished to send a message, but the note was evidently a "first attempt". There appears, although merely in faint outline, one of the dominant traits of Mary Woolley's letter writing: brevity. She never went one word out of the way in what she wrote. Nor did she in this first note, which was somewhat clouded by confusion. But the promises of further improvement were evident in the meaning and in this characteristic brevity. Three days later, on January 26th, she was to repeat, this time successfully, the effort to write to her sister-in-law, and the second attempt was typed and posted. The letter to her nephew Paul was sent without change.

One month from the time the dictation experiment was undertaken, the good news was that Mary Woolley was writing easily, accurately, briefly, and with characteristic graciousness. What is more, with the exercise and improvement in dictation not a little of her extraordinary memory had returned. For example, on February 21st, less than a month after the experiment was undertaken, she wrote to her friend, Mrs. Edgerton Parsons: "A letter to you was the last I wrote with my own hand! Now I have to dictate. I am launching this Valentine letter to you, though it is brief, to say I think of you often." Mary Woolley had always had time to write brief notes, and her witty brevity was returning along with something of her remarkable memory.

Without this hopeful, resolute and positive habit of mind, which made her still able to work for others and for what was worthwhile, even partial physical recovery and complete mental stability could not have become hers again. As she dictated her way through these re-education months, more than once she would say of a letter she was giving Aura Roberts: "Hold this, Mrs. Roberts, for I am sure I can do better after giving the letter more thought." Her unbroken courage included the attempt to learn how to walk again. She wrote with a touch of humor: "I walk a few steps every morning—thirty-three being my best record. They are not yet strong enough to boast about, but they *are* steps and so a gain over lying in bed. I have to be supported by two people. I sit up about two hours each day in my wheel chair which gives me a new outlook, so you see I have my little changes . . ."

It was not China, nor Europe, nor even Washington, but she did have her "little changes"! The office work on these letters did not stop with keeping the letters for further thought. After typing came corrections, slight changes, special requests, and finally the entry of letter written, date, and to whom sent—all the paraphernalia of a well-run office. It did one good to hear the daily commotion over getting off those letters and Mary Woolley's follow-up of the leather-bound Fleur de Lys post bag. It did one good, too, to see her meeting her days with the old quirk in her smile, the toss of her head, bright ribbons and perfect grooming.

"I wish I could tell you that I am gaining fast," she told a friend in a dictated letter. "However, that would not be true, for the gain is a slow one . . . But I hope that it will be secure when it is accomplished. I can talk now without difficulty . . ." Despite all this good cheer about altered or unalterable conditions, she was grieving over the fate of her autobiography.

On the ninth day of the dictation experiment she had written: "No book is yet written by me. I doubt whether I ever shall be able to write a word again." In the third month she wrote that she would never be able to "write another word with [her] own hand, or speak to any group again." Six days later: "It looks less as if I should ever walk again," and the following day: *"But I will not give up!"*

It is plain that Mary Woolley then, as always, faced facts but the contents of her letters reveal that, however unwelcome those facts were she did not dwell upon them. In a letter to Harriet Newhall in which some unhappy facts were given, she said: "I am, however, feeling much better, quite myself again." One of these "facts" was that she, as representative to the Disarmament Conference in Geneva in 1932 and the only woman delegate from the United States, had worked with all her mind and heart for a radical step away from war and towards peace by the reduction and control of armaments, only to be defeated by the male policy-makers. Now, thirteen years later, unable to help, she was aware of the formation of a new world peace structure in the United Nations which was determined to avoid the mistakes that had been made in the old League of Nations.

Mary Woolley knew that towards the close of October 1945, in San Francisco, this new organization had taken shape officially as the United Nations but she wasted no time bemoaning what she was unable to accomplish. She referred truthfully, both in health and in illness, to her disabilities. Her emphasis, however, was not upon what she could *not* do but on what she hoped to be able to do or what she was doing.

Always sensitive to music and the sounds of nature, with passionate love and observation she now followed, day after day, the life of multitudes of birds who in winter and summer made Fleur de Lys their home. She loved these living creatures even more than she loved the Geneva bird who from time to time still sang to us. Through the windows and later out of doors Mary Woolley studied the birds who found shelter in the trees and hedges and by the kitchen terrace where their food trays were. In March she wrote: "The number of birds is increasing constantly. At this moment we actually see one on my window as I write. It is a picture. I think also of the birds in other ways—*how brave they are through the long winter.*"

Conditioned by helplessness, and at times by an agony of pain, her letters are cheerful not only in the unbroken courage they reveal but because of the generous gratitude they express to the Good Samaritans who never failed to write and in whom, as she told them, she found "great comfort and much company." To her friend Dr. Henry Sloane Coffin she said in a letter on March 20, 1945: "We have had a long cold winter, but spring is coming and it rejoices us all. Last Sunday was like a summer day. It was glorious and gave me a new desire to be up and about. Today is gray, but I am not dreary."

Each day after the nurse had given Mary Woolley her morning bath, arranged her hair attractively, and dressed her in a pretty, fresh jacket, she was wheeled down the little hall to the glorious sunshine of the guest room with the rugs she had brought JM from China.

In 1945, the rain which came during March was April rain. Even in the north woods, lilacs were in leaf and daffodils were up three to five inches. Over by the old rose arbor something white glittered. It was not snow, although patches of the eight-foot-deep winter snow still lingered here and there. The white came from two snowdrops in bloom, six weeks early in arriving. JM picked the snowdrops and broke off a small lilac branch for MEW. Mary Woolley had not expected to live to see the flowers of another spring. Now her longing to get down stairs and go out of doors became almost obsessive. In April she wrote: "Jeannette is hoping to have me out in the sun one of these days. I know it will do me good to see the grass and the trees, and to hear the birds." And to her niece Mary Emily she reported: "The spring grows lovelier from my window each day. There are frogs and birds to hear, and the flowers will soon be in bloom. The Lake has lost its icy look and is now twinkling blue in the sun. There is hope that I may go downstairs one of these days. I look forward to it with great joy."

On May 11th, Mary Woolley was carried downstairs and on the following day she wrote her nephew Ferris: "Here it is very peaceful and happy and I am downstairs and out-of-doors at last. Strong friends carried me down yesterday, and I had to rest a bit before I sat in my wheel-chair on the lawn in the sun. But I had lunch with your Aunt Jeannette and the rest of the family . . . Today I have been so happy. It seems almost unbelievable after the long weeks indoors. The world is so beautiful and I rejoice in it."

Indoors or out, she went through her box of letters over and over again. This box, in which notes, cards and copies of her replies were kept, was about as big as a letter basket but deeper. In it, she herself filed with her left hand all the expressions of affection as carefully as if they represented some executive work for a cause or a college. Or with equal care she pulled out first one letter and then another, rereading the letter and thinking out her reply, and then neatly replacing it, rubber band and all, in the packet where it belonged. In this way, she prepared for the afternoon's dictation, using the routine which had developed from what had seemed at first an over-hopeful dream. The heart of all this careful work was her longing to "go about among others" as she had always done, for these letters had become her intercourse with others and in them she still had her public. Lacking only three months of three years, the experiment in dictation continued to be a dominant interest in Mary Woolley's life, filling the vacuum created by illness. Her pleasure in receiving letters and her eagerness to answer them never flagged.

The time was to come soon when her diminished powers meant only a lessening, not a relinquishment, of what she could do for others, and for herself. She was definitely happier. It was not only the bright color and the smile which had returned; it was something more. One day Mary Woolley said: "I find Sunday a very restful day." "Why is that?" "Because," came the reply, "I don't have to dictate any letters."

There it was: the satisfaction which only the good workman can have in rest!

CHAPTER 24

JOURNEY DAY BY DAY

"We shall learn how to live together as we learn to apply the Christ ideal to life."

Thanksgiving was now approaching and the wheel chair opened up many possibilities, such as having Thanksgiving dinner some other place than in the invalid's room. Like other old fashioned houses, Fleur de Lys has many mirrors, many leaded French doors and windows. But not everywhere do they reflect and reveal so much of a beautiful outside world. Just beyond Mary Woolley's door and to wards the old stairwell was a wall mirror about ten feet high and four feet wide. In the center of this upper hallway hangs an old Chinese lantern, its form and colors always patterned in the mirror. For ten days great negotiations about turkey had been under way— negotiations calling for five telephone conversations, three automobile journeys and a siege of diplomacy. Such in the north woods is the international approach to turkey!

Harriet and JM set the tables in the hallway. Outside the windows snow was falling on the balsams, hemlocks, cedars and elms. Inside, the white of damask was repeating the white of snow. Yes, it would do as a dining room—this shabby, mellow old upper hallway at Fleur de Lys.

Unconscious of what had been going on in Mary Woolley's room, JM went down to help in the kitchen, where Harriet and Aura Roberts were now busy with salad, vegetables, pumpkin pies and the all-important bird himself. A few minutes later Nurse McKenzie burst into the kitchen with, "Isn't Miss Woolley just too cute for words!" We turned from our jobs while the nurse continued: "I noticed her lying on the bed, leaning on her left elbow, and stretching out her neck kind of uneasy-like. I said, 'Miss Woolley, is your back hurting you?' 'No,' said Miss Woolley, 'my back does not hurt me.' Still she kept leaning on her left elbow and stretching out her neck and I was getting worried, so I said, 'Miss Woolley, is your right arm hurting you?' 'No,' answered Miss Woolley, 'my arm is not hurting me.' *Then I saw what she was up to*—that way, she could see Miss Marks and Miss Newhall in the mirror setting the Thanksgiving tables. Isn't that something?"

On the day following Thanksgiving these are the words Mary Woolley dictated to Harriet to be sent to her family:

> "Tell them [we] made an especially pretty dining room out of the second floor hall with pretty rugs and flowers and lamps about. There were four tables, two arranged for eating, one for serving and one for flowers. We used pretty blue and white tablecloths, my best silver and Jeannette's blue and white china, and it was very festive and gay. I sat at one end of the table in the wheel chair, and we all sat down together and we had a delicious dinner which was served early. . . . I ate some of everything. We had a gorgeous time.'

Again, as at grandma's long, long ago, Thanksgiving had become a "world of strife shut out and world of love shut in."

❉   ❉   ❉   ❉

In a trunk Mary Woolley called her Chinese trunk, she had accumulated over the years linens and other modest treasures. To provide Christmas gifts for those she loved she had for weeks been hoping to work over the contents of this trunk. Even if the nurse lifted out each article and held it up for her to see, might not the effort to decide to whom it should go involve too much strain? But believing that fatigue resulting from achievement is often better than the tedium of rest, the experiment was tried. Whether or not it was coincidence, there was a bad set-back on the night of December 12th. To keep the pulse from sinking still further she was given two hypodermics of adrenalin and four of another stimulant.

Her eyes focused on the ceiling and paying no attention to anything said to her, she asked, "How far is our trip? . . . Probably the doggies won't mind being left alone till we get home again."

All her words were clear and intelligible as she went on, "Will you stay with me, Jeannettie, dear Jeannettie? . . . You have done the most marvelous piece of work getting me safely home again over those high mountains and those icy plains through that deep snow."

Day after day the Christmas season drew closer. On December 21st there was another severe hemorrhage with blood pressure dropping from 170 to 120. Much of the afternoon of the day before Christmas, while JM was working over her bed, Mary Woolley did not know her. When she began to rally she looked up, saying twice, "Dear little girl! Dear little girl! . . ."

Christmas Eve had come. When JM went downstairs she found

Harriet standing in the kitchen by the south window, tears in her eyes, as she looked out at the dark sky and the blackening lake. Unable to think of anything helpful, JM said the first thing that came into her mind: "Hattie, we might celebrate our Christmas Eve by sitting down and having a good cry together." This dreary picture was too much for them both. They broke into laughter and Christmas Eve was at least safe from a duet in tears.

The doctor thought it best to follow routine on Christmas Day, getting Mary Woolley up as usual and into her wheel chair for dinner. But opening the Christmas presents was spread over most of a week.

It was never easy to get a lifting crew together. When the lifters were very strong it took only two. When they were not, it took three or four. One of the most willing was our milk woman, Olive Anson.

Our collies, Bummy and Buddy, had been chosen to be with us at Christmas dinner. They never touched anything uninvited, whereas Mickey, his head coming well above the height of a table, devoured instantly every object on which he could lay either paw or maw. Boy was to keep him company. As JM explained while trying to pacify Mary Woolley, Bum and Bud could be left alone with the best twenty-four point pound of butter for which you went down on your knees to the grocer and the OPA, for neither dog would ever think of taking one unrationed ounce of advantage.

Our simple holiday food filled not only the table in the upper hallway but the food and dishes overflowed onto little separate tables including two "curate's assistants"—the English nickname for those portable three-tiered arrangements.

While we were at this early Christmas dinner in came Ruth Frisbie, a former secretary, the daughter of our neighbors, the Frisbies. At once Ruth became the center of attention. Mary Woolley's speech had been confused but so great was her pleasure in seeing Ruth again that her speech cleared.

While Ruth was talking, Harriet and JM were listening to a puzzling lap-lap. We looked at each other: was something leaking somewher? There was a bathroom at the end of the hall. We raised our eyebrows and indicated that the drip might come from the bathroom. Then came one of those pauses in conversation. Definitely it was "lap-lap" and not "drip-drip" and was nearer than the bathroom. Then, horror of horrors, we saw *Bum the Perfect guzzling the Christmas pumpkin pie!* Thanks to Ruth's pleasant conversation and endearing manner, Bummy had made excellent progress through the first half of the pie! There were shouts of laughter and cries of "Why, Bummy Marks!

Why, Bummy Marks!" Nice name, isn't it? But how in the name of self-respect could any Quaker who believed in equality and simplicity go around calling even the best of dogs by the class-conscious kennel name of *Blue Flag Heron Second!* Best of all, Mary Woolley's face was crinkled with laughter, not at all at Bum but at the expense of JM! And Harriet, though it was she who had set the pie on the lower shelf, was calling out derisively her own nickname for the perfect dog, "Teacher's Pet! Teacher's Pet!"

In these days with so little left in which to have faith, neither then nor later were we able to see why it should be thought a weakness to have some confidence left in one's dog at least. Nevertheless it was a sad fact that after ten years—eighty in human life—Bum had slipped from grace into pumpkin pie!

We needed to see Ruth, and Bummy we needed to have eat the pie, for behind us lay ten days of anxiety during which neither the doctor nor the nurse had expected Mary Woolley to recover from this last cerebral accident. As bedtime on that Christmas night drew near for all of us, snow was falling as it did perhaps one thousand years ago in these North Woods and as it will perhaps one thousand years from this Christmas day of 1944. Able again to enjoy music, the radio was playing Strauss's waltzes, setting a tempo interlacing with the dancing snow. In between bites of chocolate Mary Woolley said she was going to work with JM the next day.

"No," said JM, "the doctor says no work tomorrow, for you have had a bit of a setback. After all we have had our happy Christmas together and we must be careful now." Her reply was, "Lying in bed seems so selfish."

*   *   *   *

By the spring of 1945 the dictation experiment was over. A complete success and part of the daily routine, it could no longer be considered an "experiment". Except for the handicap of partial paralysis, Mary Woolley resumed her place in normal family life. But it had been proved many times that she was still not equal to unexpected demands and it seemed to matter little whether those unexpected demands were sorrowful or joyous, and disturbing elements were the "unexpected" and the "personal". It became part of the health-building program to keep from her forms of contact and forms of responsibility which, coming upon her suddenly—such as a prolonged visit, or consciousness of a sick or wounded dog—might harm her, and all bad news. This protection was her "oxygen tent". During this period of partial health re-building it was the love of her Mount Holyoke alumnae and good news which were to bring with them the heaviest shock of the unexpected.

On the afternoon of May 19th this telegram was read to her:

WE ALUMNAE WISH TO INFORM YOU OF THE NAMING OF MARY E. WOOLLEY HALL WITH THE WISH THAT THIS MAY BE A SYMBOL TO YOUR PERPETUAL INSPIRATION TO MOUNT HOLYOKE'S DAUGHTERS.

CHRISTINE EVERTS GREENE
PRESIDENT OF ALUMNAE ASSOCIATION MOUNT HOLYOKE COLLEGE

For Mary Woolley anything from her "girls" was always personal and she trembled while the wire was being read and re-read to her. Noting this condition and hoping to find some way to balance the impact of this unexpected joy, we asked if she thought there were any words omitted from this oddly expressed telegram? If not, then why did it sound different? "Inform you"—that was an odd expression, wasn't it, and due perhaps to war regulations which forbade telegrams of greeting? To the distraction she did not reply, but held out her shaking hand for the wire so that she might read it again. Then she said, "Will you send the reply now?"

"No," I answered, "if you are able, this is something the alumnae would wish you to do. What message shall I take down?"

"Grateful for—for—tribute by Mount Holyoke alumnae. Now read it back, Jeannette."

"Is there something you wish to add about yourself?

"What is there to say about me anymore?"

"Plenty, dear."

"Let it be about women: all of us need strength these days," she replied. "Say, 'Hopeful that future—that future—will show *increased* power among women.' That's it. Now read it back again."

The wire was repeated. JM then said: "Tomorrow do you think you will be able to work out a letter to follow this wire?"

"Yes," came the reply.

When the morrow came it was plain that the shock of happiness from the group expression of alumnae love and loyalty had thrown her back into a condition resembling the first few weeks of recurrent delirium. It was not the honor that had done this. One more honor for Mary Woolley? She was accustomed to honors. It was the emotion created by the love for her "girls".

The dictation experiment and its outstanding success had made us over confident. Yet the lame mind was like the temporary inability of an over-used muscle, and the family waited patiently for improving conditions.

That was in May 1945. In early June the Field Secretary of Mount Holyoke College wrote the President Emeritus that they had a "happy project" under way raising an endowment fund to be known as the Mary E. Woolley Visiting Fellowship, which would bring visiting professors to the campus. Then the Field Secretary added, "We naturally hope that many of the lecturers will be in the field of International Relations." Knowing Mary Woolley's steadfastness in principle, they seemed to be somewhat uncertain about their plan, for the Field Secretary added this paragraph: "As yet the announcements to the public and to the alumnae have not been made nor planned; nor has the organization for raising the Fund been begun. But we want you to know of our plans at their inception." Ten days after receiving the letter, Mary Woolley wrote the Field Secretary:

> The naming of Mary E. Woolley Hall brought me genuine pleasure, for in several ways the Mary E. Woolley Hall was part of my work at Mount Holyoke College—work on which I shared with others some claim.
> The announcement of the Mary E. Woolley Visiting Professorship, however, troubles me for several reasons. The use of my name in this connection and under these auspices might suggest that I am in some way reconciled to the broken tradition of women as leaders of Mount Holyoke College. Since my position on this matter is so well known, it seems to me best that my name should not be used for this Visiting Professorship. When Mount Holyoke College again appoints a woman as President I shall be glad to have my name used for the Mary E. Woolley Visiting Professorship.
> My conviction remains that the successful leadership of women for over one hundred years at Mount Holyoke has entitled and continues to entitle women to that leadership. With time this conviction has deepened, not lessened, and the protest which I made of this action while in college will continue to the end of my life.

* * * *

Sometimes the struggle to keep Fleur de Lys running smoothly for the beloved invalid became desperate. In the midst of it all, and as day by day Mary Woolley was becoming both stronger and happier, the working housekeeper had left without a word of warning or explanation. It was an old relationship: three generations of that family had worked at Fleur de Lys. Through the gap which this act had made in our courage, poured waves of depression. But in all plans to help Mary Woolley to lead a normal life again Dr. Gray aided and betted. One of our ideas was to have her resume her place at the head of the table. It had not been long after the naming of the Mary E. Woolley Hall before Mary Woolley was carried downstairs to lead her life both indoors and outdoors in closer contacts with the family.

It was then that she took her place again at the head of the table. Opposition to this from the Nurses had to be met and overcome. The nurses were not only opposed to having her at the table but one of them said so.

As JM looked across the table on that first day, she carried a quick-beating heart. There sat Mary Woolley in her wheel chair—eager, smiling and helpful in conversation . . .

Yet by and large, and beautiful beyond words to describe were the patient goodness and motherly tenderness of the nurses to her. And tragic beyond words to describe were the tears Mary Woolley shed over some of the words she spoke to others as pain had stabbed them out of her. Some of the problems were created by illness itself and sprang out of helplessness. At such times not once but again and again we tried to warm ourselves with happier thoughts as we attempted to laugh it off. We were too sad and tired—all of us—*not* laugh, and sometimes we laughed too much in our hourly, daily tensions and were ashamed.

Nurse McKenzie, worn out by months of heavy nursing, had to leave for a long rest. A little later, lacking only a month of the first year of Mary Woolley's illness, there entered into our lives that extraordinary little nurse, Mrs. Minnie Baker: well-cut in features, minute in size, strong in muscle, deep and clear of voice, quick and young of step although age seventy, and with abundant hair and abundant heart.

Aura Roberts was gone to get herself into a long-term teaching position before it was too late, for we knew that even with the best of good fortune, the post at Fleur de Lys could not last indefinitely. In her place had come Ada Cross of Wadhams, her refinement, good education and dignity making her a valued successor to Aura Roberts.

❀   ❀   ❀   ❀

On shopping days JM went into Mary Woolley's room with: "Good-bye, Emmy, I'll be sure to bring home something nice."

Not to be sidetracked by any such superficial device, MEW would reply sternly, "How long do you expect to be gone?"

"Not a moment longer than can be helped."

"It's going to snow," said Mary Woolley.

"No, I think not. Take good care of the dogs! Goodbye, dear!"

About three or four hours later down the lane came the Studebaker, honking a salute. For some time Mary Woolley had been waiting and listening for the car. Hours before it reached the outer gate Mrs. Baker had been sent up the lane to open it.

"That," Mary Woolley explained, "will help Miss Marks."

When she heard the honking and the dogs barking, she began telling people what to do: "Mrs. Baker, have Iva let out the doggies; they are so happy to have Miss Marks back." Pound, pound, pound went Mrs. Baker's little heels down the corridor and pound, pound, pound they came back again. "Now, Mrs. Baker, you and Iva go out to the lane to help Miss Marks with all the packages."

"But Miss Woolley," Mrs. Baker objected, "you should not be left—"

"No, Mrs. Baker, I shall be quite alright until Miss Marks gets in. *Go help her please.*" The last statement was made in the best authoritative presidential manner and Mrs. Baker departed. By this time the dogs were barking wild greetings.

Iva, Mrs. Baker and JM filled their arms with oranges and bananas, dates and grapes, scallops and fragrant coffee, large green heads of lettuce, yams and mushrooms from Plattsburg, from the Welsh bakers in Keeseville: poppy seed rolls, cinnamon rolls and honey buns, feather bread and cookies and jelly roll.

Some of the specialties were carried into the dining room where Mary Woolley was sitting in her wheel chair before an open fire.

"Here we are, Emmy." Down on the table went the grapes and poppy seed rolls.

Holding out her left hand to take JM's, she said, "Oh, I should think you would be dead!"

"Well I'm not, dear, and it didn't snow. Now look at some of these things I have brought you for our tea."

As winter came on, afternoon tea became a great diversion, and as they now waited for the drink Mary Woolley took, as she often did, several looks at JM. Had she penetrated the protective covering of the home front? Its pitiful curves away from and around some subjects? Its feverish searches everywhere for amusing, brave, happy stories? Did Mary Woolley sometimes catch a glimpse of the invisible line around which was waged the battle for her protection?

Twice, off guard, JM had raised her hand to cover her cheek and an aching tooth—pain which shopping had not improved.

"Does your face hurt you?" asked Mary Woolley.

"Don't you think it should?" laughed JM.

"Don't be silly!" said Mary Woolley.

"No, Emmy, it's just a tooth aching a little. I'm not much good today."

"Yes, you are!" contradicted Mary Woolley. And then, tactfully: "Jeannette, do I speak very badly today?"

"You speak very well; much better than some other women in the

house who are well. Let's forget aches and pains, May! I'll see Dr.
Merrihew later," concluded JM, thinking not only of Mary Woolley's
resolve after seeing Martha Kunhardt but also of how beautifully she
had taught herself to speak.

Under the table near his mistress Mick lay asleep. In the fireplace,
flames danced and hardwood coals glowed. Tea came as we were
counting the fish huts out on the ice-covered lake and watching the
skaters and cars out beyond Fleur de Lys Point. "I count only 18
fish huts," said the invalid.

"I count 21. Aren't there three huts hidden behind the others?"

"When are we going to have some nice fish?" asked the invalid.

"Tomorrow for dinner," JM replied.

By this time, they were eating the poppy seed rolls buttered and
toasted. Mary Woolley put a spoonful of sugar into her cup, and
with her left hand gracefully picked up one of the rolls and took a
bite. Lifting her cup of tea she drank from it, saying: "I think these
are the very best rolls you have ever brought home." Setting the cup
down, Mary Woolley broke off two pieces of the bun. Speaking deliberately and eating the first piece as if to give pleasure, she said: "Yes,
these rolls are delicious." Then as deliberately she gave the other
piece to Mick! Again and again had we brought home poppy seed
rolls for tea. Mary Woolley gave pleasure in the very best way she
could—a way beautiful with the spirit.

Out on the frozen lake there was gaiety: men and women were
threading in and out of the fish huts, comparing their catch, chatting
a while, resting. Children and older people were skating along the
safe margins. In a shower of powdered ice, cars were speeding over
the lake, hissing around the curves of Westport Bay, and far, far out
on the glassy ice boys and girls were waltzing on the ice.

* * * *

On Sundays there was usually an atmosphere of good cheer and
bustle from those who might have lamented because there was no one
to get a dinner for them. Between the pantry and the kitchen "dining
room" table Minnie Baker ran gaily to and fro with plates, her brisk-
ness undiminished by fatigue and the fact that every once in a while
she ran in the wrong direction. Apparently she was as fond of assisting in the Sunday lunch preparations as she was of helping her
patient. Mary Woolley, groomed and attractive, looked out upon the
sunlit lake and mountains or watched with amusement the antics of
Mrs. Baker and JM, as she paged through her dictation box, taking
out first one letter, then another, saying something, asking a question.

Dinner smelled good and so did the roses sent by Alice Stevens, standing in an old silver vase on the table set with gold and white china. The fire in the huge marine range crackled; the static in the radio crackled. Indiscriminately singing his obligatos to running mountain water from a kitchen tap or to an anthem from Colorado, Chrissie—named after Dr. Christianna Smith—flitted from perch to perch whisking sunlight and shadow across the cage with him. For a while we were happy and we were glad to be alone.

The great moment had come. As JM reached the table carrying the platter set with cold sliced chicken and dressing, she said, "Mrs. Baker, please put away Miss Woolley's dictation box; dinner is ready." Off scampered Mrs. Baker, her head high and holding before her the dictation box like a large crumb in the mandibles of a small ant. JM wondered as she wheeled Mary Woolley to her seat at the head of the table if she recalled the statement that "the only way to make a League of Nations work is to have a League of Nations in your own kitchen"? Fleur de Lys had that league.

Flowers, laughter and sunshine, good food and good company—the makings of a fine dinner.

Speaking in a slow voice, MEW said, "This is the very best dinner we have ever had." We laughed, "Emmy, a while ago there were the 'best' poppy seed rolls and other 'best' affairs!"

"Yes," admitted Mary Woolley firmly, "there were other best affairs but I think we *never* had a *better* dinner. And I think this *is* the 'best'!"

When we reached the dessert our Invalid sampled it eagerly: "This ice cream is better even than the ice cream we make at home."

"It was bought from Ella Mero," replied JM.

"How *do* you suppose she makes it?" asked the Beloved Invalid.

"Mrs. Mero doesn't make it, Emmy; she buys it."

"Well, in any event it is excellent," and she dismissed the subject.

By this time the ice cream and sponge cake had disappeared and so, for a few minutes, had little Mrs. Baker. Mary Woolley looked carefully about her and then said in a low voice, "The more I know Mrs. Baker, the more I like her. I don't think we made any mistakes. And I like Mrs. Cross, too, more and more." Our little League of Nations in the kitchen was closed in confidence and appreciation.

In a medley of beauty-filled windows and sunshine, music and the song of Chrissie, old pots and pans and china, warmth, fragrant food and flowers, good will and good stories on the part of all, the dinner had been eaten and was over. The kitchen League of Nations had made the best not only of food but of misfortune.

*   *   *   *

After the first few weeks in which Mary Woolley had struggled like a bird to free herself from sudden incomprehensible imprisonment, her mind had adjusted itself to the facts of illness, and between October 1944 and June 1945 passed successfully through profoundly difficult adjustments. Whenever she reached the point where she thought she would never again "see this" or "do that", we always set about seeing or doing it! Part of the day's smoothness, and therefore the family happiness, lay in these supple plans.

Out of doors there were picnics with bonfires at the cabin and on the Point, once at Chapel Pond 20 miles back in the Adirondacks. There were visits by her handsome Ferris cousins, Helen and Belle, with whom Mary Woolley had grown up, her nieces and nephews, Paul, Mary Emily, Eleanor and Ferris and the little great niece Janet, along with calls from JM's sister and niece, Mabel Bacon and Bel, and even a carriage call on Margaret Hamilton and Vida Milholland.

Also helpful were the unexpected arrival of friends from other parts of the country: Roberta Swartz and her college president husband, Dr. Chalmers; Evelyn Selby with her husband, Eugene Stead from Duke University. Dr. Stead stood towering over Mary Woolley as she was taking a nap. Something pricking her consciousness, however, she opened her eyes just as the giant said, "Hi!" in good Southern style. For an instant her eyes fluttered, then twinkled as she broke into a broad smile of delight over this arresting bedside greeting. Another time Dorothy Stewart Albertson, supposedly busy with Red Cross executive work in Washington, drove up with some members of her family. Arriving after dark, Dorothy went into the room where the invalid was dozing. Although Mary Woolley had not seen her for several years, she opened her eyes as if she had been with her only the day before and exclaimed joyfully, "Why, Dorothy!"

We also had "gay" little affairs at home—a "coffee" at eleven for two or three friends, many lunches for members of the family and, more often, tea and music in the afternoons.

Life was full of unexpected incidents at Fleur de Lys. On the night of March 25, 1945, an official wire came from Orlo M. Brees of the New York State Legislature that the Equal Rights Resolution had just been passed unanimously by the Assembly in Albany. Mary Woolley laughed for joy. With the guidance of Mr. Brees and the cooperation of the New York State Councillors and the various branches throughout the state, we had been working for three years toward this end. There had been much delay and some disappointments but now the great moment had come. That night wire after wire went off to the branches throughout the state and to individual councillors. Aura Roberts, her hands full of copy, plodded up through the dark, ice and snow to the Western Union office and its friendly agent.

On her return, Mary Woolley sang out: "Good night, Mrs. Roberts! You're a regular walking telegraph office. Isn't it great! Isn't it wonderful!" To JM she said, "There has been a great change in my time. The time will come when men and women will work together but full equal rights won't come in my time or in yours, but it will come."

Seven weeks later Mary Woolley wrote to the President of the AAUW that she could not allow to pass unchallenged the wording and implication of "Item 15" of the Tentative and Legislative Program for 1945-47; to her this item seemed self-contradictory. How is it possible, she asked, for the members of the AAUW or for any other group of thinking individuals to "support the principle of women's fullest participation in all social, economic and political life" and at the same time to continue opposition to the proposed Equal Rights Amendment to the Constitution? Why not study the Equal Rights Amendment, she concluded.

Writing in her capacity as a vice-president of the American Civil Liberties Union, Miss Woolley sent this open letter to the *New York Herald-Tribune* in June 1945:

> As I understand it, the Union's objection to the Equal Rights Amendment is, really, based upon the abolition of protective laws. My first answer to that is that protective laws in the coming day should be made for human beings, men as well as women. My second answer is that the privileges accorded to women by our present laws are not commensurate with the lack of rights embodied in the thousand and one discriminatory laws still on the statute books of various States of the United States . . . I do wish again and again to stress the truth that it is only as human relations are shaped by women—as well as by men—*with the thinking of both directed by the good heart*, that we shall ever achieve the better world for which we are hoping and for which some of us are working.

Her friend Mrs. Helen R. Reid, President of the paper, wrote Mary Woolley: "I hope you saw that your letter was published in the *Herald-Tribune* last Sunday. I was very proud of having it in the paper . . ."

For about two years Mary Woolley's trend was upward, although sometimes conditioned by difficult periods in an irreversible disease. For a while, however, there was no pain or suffering that could not be overcome. Yet in the background of those days was a sense of deepening loneliness. One day as JM went into her room, MEW said, "You don't know how glad I am when you come in. It makes me feel warm all over."

Grief came to Mary Woolley with the news that her colleague and Connecticut Valley neighbor, William Allan Neilson, had died on the Smith College campus, February 21, 1946. They were equals in sparring wit, and she had admired President Neilson for his unfaltering belief in equal opportunities for women.

Fortunately, about this time Sarah Blanding became the President of Vassar. In her happiness over this appointment, Mary Woolley exclaimed, "Isn't that wonderful!" and for two days after the announcement her sole thought was to write an adequate letter to Miss Blanding. On February 25th she sent this note of congratulation:

> May I add my congratulations to those you are receiving from other men and women on your election to the Presidency of Vassar College. Also I wish to congratulate Vassar on its election of a woman.
>
> Mrs. Hadley's statement brings with it not only the good news of your election but also the fact that the emphasis is now on fitness for the post and not sex as the determining factor . . . You have been most fortunate in the publicity which has surrounded you, including Mrs. Ogden Reid's brilliant and loyal tribute to you as a woman both in the news column and the editorial page of the *Herald-Tribune*.
>
> With warm good wishes.

She also rejoiced in the Wellesley and Bryn Mawr appointments. Nevertheless one of these deepened the wound which had been given her.

Because of what might be called "cultural loneliness", events such as these held magnetic power. Loneliness, as well as the need for food, can be a hunger. But there was never any complaint from Mary Woolley about exile from all she had known: educators and internationalists, people, places, music, libraries, theatres. With eagerness she continued to make the best of every opportunity there was in the north woods.

CHAPTER 25

JOURNEY CONTINUED

*"The only regret one need have with age is the regret that would
come from a life completely misspent."*

The dogs' company, with their interest, devotion and good cheer,
unquestionably did almost as much health-building as the dictation
experiment. In Mary Woolley's room at breakfast time there was
usually a steady stream of dogs coming and going — a veritable
"breadline".

On the morning of February 14th the collies streamed down the
corridor led by the brilliant figure of Bummy decorated on this thirteenth Valentine birthday with roses and ribbons taken from a box of
candy sent by the Westchester alumnae girls to their president.
Amiable, plump, expectant, his legs straight and white as ever, his
brush thick and sleek despite his years, Bummy, followed by his
juniors, was on the way to a Birthday Breakfast. Usually before Mary
Woolley began giving out oaten cake and toast, she would get her
breadline in order but this morning when she saw the big roses and
wide ribbons nodding behind Bummy's ears, she burst into laughter,
saying helplessly over and over, "Oh, Bummy Marks! Oh, Bummy
Marks!" Mrs. Baker, who was standing at the other side of the bed
also began to laugh—early morning pleasure beautiful in its courage
and enjoyment of life. As for Bummy, always pleased when *he*
pleased, wriggling his body and dipping his handsome head self-
consciously, he had an inner certainty that on this morning there
would be more snacks than ever. And there were.

Sometime that winter another fight between Mick and Buddy took
place out by the barberry bushes near the kitchen terrace. Hearing
the cries and choking growls, JM ran out. Like all scenes of violence
this was repellent. But there was a brave boy, working in the office
building, who heard JM's cries for help and came running. After the
dogs were separated, JM told Mary Woolley that a new home would
have to be found for Mick who had always been an unruly and immensely powerful dog.

261

The results of this statement were catastrophic. There are times when it is useless to theorize about what even the best of human beings should do or say; this was such a time. Mary Woolley ceased not only to smile but also stopped speaking and eating. The excellent *ad interim* Negro nurse, Muriel Cheeseman, and JM became alarmed. Without too much delay a decision would have to be reached, and it must be a decision that would not be injurious to the invalid. Was not her devotion to all the dogs one of the main props for her frail re- covered health? During sleepless hours that night, JM reached a decision: a second dog pen should be built, larger than the other pen which it would adjoin, with separate gate and strong fencing. In this pen Mick could "heil Hitler" all he wished, but he could not fight anything but barbed wire.

On the way downstairs the next morning JM heard Mary Woolley calling out, "Jeannettie, you will write today, won't you?"

"Write today? About what?"

"Write to Paul about finding a good home for Mickey?"

"That won't be necessary after all, Emmy, and this is the plan."

Her left hand was trembling and her face twitching as she heard the plan which meant she need not be separated from her beloved Mickey. The fence was built and during Mary Woolley's life there were united dogs and no more war! Best of all, again there was a happy "Missus".

*   *   *   *

Mary Woolley was sitting upright in bed being made ready for supper when she said to Mrs. Baker, "Is Mickey in the house?"

In a completely reassuring voice, Mrs. Baker replied, "Yes, Miss Woolley, I believe Mick is in—yes, he surely is either in or out."

For a while peace reigned but *without* Mick who was ranging the local garbage cans in the late summer twilight while the other dogs were still confined to their pen. He had leapt his high fencing. He had the strength of a springbuck and was as good at climbing as the members of a New York City fire department. An inner barbed wire strung above the top of his inner fence presented a negligible difficulty when he wanted a good garbage can or a visit with the ladies of the neighborhood.

All this Minnie Baker knew. When he returned, she would swing his one hundred pounds like a trinket on her wrist, settling him under the high hospital bed. Tempered in the school of personal loss, year after year Mrs. Baker pounded to and fro briskly on her little heels, refusing to be downhearted. When conditions were very depressing

all Minnie Baker said to her patient was, "Miss Woolley, I tell you
nothing is so bad but what it might be worse!" Thereupon she would
frisk about the room at a great rate of speed, picking up this, adjusting
that and rattling everything so cheerfully that it would have taken a
calcified hypochondriac to think otherwise than that, no matter what
happened, life was a pleasant affair and fellow human beings, including dogs, quite perfect. Too unselfish to be shrewd in managing herself, Minnie Baker was gifted in the management of others. Whoever
went down the corridor to the invalid's room saw two lovely-looking
women sitting there together, one propped up in a modern, high hospital bed, the other knitting comfortably in a rocking chair.

When Harriet came to visit, the invalid thought, "I can get all the
news I wish." In a sense she did get just that but what she did not
get were facts which might bring anxiety or open old wounds. Often
they talked about codicils to the will Mary Woolley had drafted many
years before, for she was always clear and definite in her mind with
regard to what she wished to do with any object in her possession.
Over many years Harriet Newhall had taken down clauses and revi-
sions of Mary Woolley's will. "Things," Harriet commented, "seemed
so important to her."

By the summer of 1945 Mary Woolley's powers of observation improved phenomenally. Harriet began to be asked many questions as
Mary Woolley talked with her about the affection she felt for members
of the faculty and the alumnae of Mount Holyoke and her gratitude
for their faithfulness in writing. Early in the morning of one of these
visits there was a great to-do in Mary Woolley's room like the startled
flights of red-winged blackbirds down on the lake shore. Among other
things Harriet and Mrs. Baker were moving a small but heavy piece of
furniture when suddenly there came an indignant cry from Mrs.
Baker: "Ouch! Oh-oh-oh!" Then silence was followed by an apologetic
"Well, I didn't hurt myself after all!"

"*Didn't* hurt yourself!" exclaimed Harriet with mock indignation.
"Why *didn't* you hurt yourself, Minnetonka? There you had a perfectly good chance *to* hurt yourself and didn't even take it! It's discouraging."

This incident was followed by a reference to "dresses", the jingle
of clothes hangers and a door being banged by the nurse. Harriet
had invited them to take a drive with her back to Elizabethtown. Miss
Woolley knew exactly what she wished to wear for this occasion; Mrs.
Baker knew just as exactly that this particular dress was too thin and
not a good choice. Returning from the clothes press, her arms were
full of tempting alternate choices.

"Now, Miss Woolley, *this* dress would be warmer, and today there's a chill wind blowing."

"Yes, Mrs. Baker," she answered, "maybe this dress is warmer but Miss Newhall is taking us for a drive and I wish to look my best."

"'Looking your best' just once might mean—" she was retorting when JM stepped into the altercation with "What in the world is going on here with all this to-do! What are these references to 'dresses'?"

Mrs. Baker took a hop, skip and a jump back into the clothes press, saying as she emerged: "Why of course we mean Miss Woolley's silk pajamas and I want her to wear this handsome heavier suit for the drive today; it will be warmer. Now, Miss Marks, don't you think she should put on one of her warmer dresses—this one for example?"

"Yes, I do. It is equally important, however, that Miss Woolley should approve the selection made. Now I have to go back to the office. Suppose you re-discuss your problem, but be sure the choice you make is something Miss Woolley *does* want to wear and can wear safely."

We vanished, laughing but carrying one more incident of the pride and spirit which were making even these helpless, crippled years beautiful and natural in the life of Mary Woolley in which she relinquished neither her right to wear the dress she wished to wear nor lost the courage essential to moral leadership. To those who had known her for more than half a lifetime, the weakness and handicap of these closing years made her seem greater in her power to understand and, unself-consciously, to teach, than she had seemed in all the years of her remarkable strength and phenomenal success.

It was the late summer of 1946 when this event took place. Mary Woolley dreaded the preparation for these drives but once ready was more than content. On this day she told Harriet just where she wished to go when they reached Elizabethtown. "But first, Harriet," she added, "before we park by the Windsor Hotel let us get the ice cream cones from the drugstore near there."

All this was done and the ice cream cones were eaten where they could watch the hotel guests sunning themselves in the most up-to-date sun suits. For half an hour—all of them seemingly as light-hearted as the most frivolous—the car was full of laughter over Mary Woolley's low-voiced observations on sun suits. To this should be added Harriet's unfailing ability, whatever the sadness, to enjoy or create a good time.

*   *   *   *

One afternoon in autumn, Mary Woolley was wheeled over to Frog-mere. Beside the porch, back to the lake as she sat out of the wind, she could see the corner of the street through a hedge gap. There was a comfortable silence. Soon, however, it was plain that MEW was, with the utmost intentness, studying something through the gap in hedge on the corner of the street beyond. "What do you see, Emmy?"

"A woman who is walking with great difficulty. She must be lame."

In memory, too, did Mary Woolley see again her little mother limping across the room or pulling herself upstairs? Silence followed and, once more, came the absorbed look on her face as she watched the street beyond.

"What do you see now?"

"Two men," she replied, "one carrying a bundle under his arm."

We turned towards each other and laughed, for they saw themselves, too: Mary Woolley who had been the busiest of women as college executive, internationalist and traveller, and JM who had never been exactly idle or untravelled, were thus captivated by a little activity on the street of a north woods village.

"To be serious, May, before we came over to Frogmere I have been revising a bit of Barrett-Browning work. Stupidly I cannot remember the date of King James the First. Can you?"

"1603, I think," was the immediate reply. "That is one of the things I do remember. The date sticks in my mind. He ascended the throne in 1603."

Thoroughly grounded in ancient and modern history under Dr. Benjamin Andrews and Dr. Jameson of Brown, a great deal had "stuck" in Mary Woolley's mind—much more than ever gets lodged in many average minds of people in perfect health. This phenomenal memory still persisted—a fact due in part to powers of observation which made not only a man carrying a bundle interesting but also the name of a person or fact unforgettable.

That afternoon Mary Woolley spoke again of the appointment of Miss Blanding to Vassar. This, she thought, would be a great advantage to women coming at just the time when such an advantage was most needed. She spoke, too, of her own defeat at Mount Holyoke and ended sadly: "That was the shabbiest trick ever played on anyone. Well, now Vassar, Bryn Mawr and Wellesley all have women as presidents. At Wellesley when it was suggested that they have a man, just as soon as it was discovered that the idea met with disapproval a woman was selected. But when I suggested Miss McAfee's name with other first rate candidates, the trustees brushed her name aside with these words '—————'." She spoke the words in a low voice, then added: "But they must never be repeated. I rejoice that Miss McAfee's work shows her to be all that I *knew* she was."

Christmas had come again at Fleur de Lys and the celebration was centered before the fireplace in the dining room, the tree mounted against the leaded windows. On this Christmas the eminent one sat in her wheel chair, her gifts rising in an arching rainbow of color higher than her head. Excited? Yes, as excited as she had always been about Christmas, and for the moment fully as happy as any eager child.

But for Perceval, our gardener and chore boy, this Christmas was a new world and never before had he seen anything approaching the display of gifts about the tree. Through the open, resonant old house his "Haw! Haw! Haw!" of joy vibrated as upon a sounding board. For three hours Harriet's fusillades of wit and her management kept Perceval employed as package boy, laughing and working happily at top speed; what is more important, Harriet's management kept Mary Woolley amused at the way Perceval managed the various wrappings and boxes. As the packages were unwrapped, ribbons for winding and paper for folding were given to Minnie Baker. Folding up some of his own height, Perceval stooped to hand the gifts to Mary Woolley. Each time she thanked him. Though he was little more than a child, in his selflessness that Christmas Day the probability is that not once did he think enviously of the wealth of gift and loving thought which passed through his hands to someone else.

After sleeping for several hours in the early winter darkness of her room this last Christmas celebration closed after a seven o'clock dinner. With old porcelain and silver, flowers and damask, the lighted Christmas tree and wrought iron sconces on the walls above the wainscoting, the filigree lantern and candles, flashes of light and shadow on silver vases and crystal goblets, the old dining room glowed with a deep quiet brilliance — all the innocent pomp and circumstance Mary Woolley loved. During the entire hour of the Christmas Eve dinner there was the orchestration of great music: Bach, Hayden, Brahms, Schumann, Sibelius, Tschaikovsky—consolation and triumph above all defeat.

After dinner as JM was passing the wheel chair, Mary Woolley held held out her left hand, and looking up she said: "Oh, dearest, it has been so beautiful. I do thank you."

Later, JM, going from room to room cutting the lights, heard Mary Woolley asking, "Have the babies gone to bed?"

"You mean the dogs, Miss Woolley?" replied Mrs. Baker. "Yes, the dogs are all in."

"Where is Jeannette?"

"She's about the house turning off the lights."

Thinking of the voice JM heard asking for her, another voice came in on the wire of consciousness — the doctor's voice saying, "Miss Woolley may live for years or she may go at any minute." JM was turning off the stairway lantern when she heard still other voices from the past: the treble voices of children on another Christmas Eve, laughing and shouting, and the smack and thump of pillows being hurled at each other. Other feet, too, were going up the stairs as the children, with a leap, bounded into their beds. Now, their hands folded, they were repeating top-speed to their mother a prayer: ". . . If I should die before I wake, I pray the Lord my soul to take."

In her sleep that night JM suddenly started awake, thinking she had heard the deep voice of little Minnie Baker calling up the stairway, "Miss Marks, will you come downstairs, please?" No, all imagination! This Christmas Eve was quiet and all was as well as it could be.

*   ❖   ❖   ❖

"Jeannette!" Mary Woolley called. "Do come here!" For the last two days I've had Mrs. Baker reading aloud from the newspaper Mr. Dulles' speech on Russia. And today came a copy Mr. Dulles himself sent me, so now I can write a most gracious letter!" Her face shone with happiness as they laughed about the good fortune of a speech personally sent by Mr. Dulles and her own innocent diplomacies.

There was much reading in her little downstairs room with its leaded French windows, framed in by barberry bushes, its glimpse of the lake and its sense of nearness to the ground. Both Mrs. Baker and Mrs. Cross were tireless readers. At night after the heavy old blue silk curtains were drawn, Mrs. Baker read on ceaselessly. One of the books which held them in thrall was *Driftwood Valley* by a Mount Holyoke alumna.

As they read, Mary Woolley and her nurse left in thought the little room with its modern comforts; beyond the reach of railroads or other transportation, and with the Stanwell-Fletchers they made their way through Northwest Territories across British Columbia into the Driftwood Valley country of Alberta. If during those hours one happened to go in, they looked up from the reading as if you were a moose or a wolf, and sighed gratefully when you left them free again to forget civilization and return to the Valley.

Every night at six came the voice of Ed Murrow over the radio: "This-is-London!" Mary Woolley's depression about the possibilities of another war had been increasing steadily. Always suspicious of any sensationalism in newscasting, she knew she could trust Ed Murrow *not* to sell his soul for a mess of pottage. When the newscast was over, she said, "Sometimes I wonder whether peace is possible." It was evident, however, that she, with religious men and women everywhere, remained convinced that Christ's way of love had become the only way out from world misery and tragedy.

Evening after evening throughout the spring and early summer of 1946, after she had paged through the *Tribune* or the *Times*, Mary Woolley closed her day with the cry: "They want war!" Only someone who heard that oft-repeated cry, her eyes wide and horrified, can imagine the intensity and suffering of those words. She knew that it took a tough and athletic heart to go on beating in hopes of a good future for what seemed to be a bad humanity, and not to stop in some blind alley of world despair. In the business of living with all its enforced adjustments to treachery, broken hopes, and loss, had not the outstanding problem become how *not* to lose heart? Only the brave and the hopeful could survive—only those who when conditions are at their worst manage somehow to go ahead.

A few days later, on March 13th, Mary Woolley said that she had had Mrs. Cross reading aloud the day's UN news. She laughed, adding, "Sometimes it reminds me so much of my six months in Geneva at the Disarmament Conference: 'The Honorable Gentleman has my thanks' and bla-bla-bla! And then they adjourned until April third." Her laughter came as near to being sardonic then as JM had ever heard it.

Mary Woolley often said that "conciliation and arbitration are the basis for progress and reason." For the success of peace work, she thought it essential that there should be "willingness" to see the large issues which might and often did lead to cooperation, whereas limitation to the small issues too often led to conflict." She wrote that peace means yielding a position as well as holding one and that peace could not be made with hardened will. Finally, it was her conviction that all leadership lost something by the use of force which neither a group nor an individual could afford to lose. Mary Woolley's mind had hovered increasingly around the theme of Christ-like love. For two years she had worked on a brief Message to Women—those "women as human beings" of whom she never ceased to think. She tried repeatedly to shape up this message as she wished it to be but finally left it unfinished.

On Thursday afternoon, May 29, 1947, there was abnormal sultriness. Mary Woolley was on the north side of the porch at Frogmere, where she would be coolest. She and Mrs. Cross stayed on until about four o'clock, then crossed the lane and went indoors. Mrs. Cross went home and Mrs. Baker came on duty. JM stayed on at Frogmere until about five o'clock, putting seed packets in order. Then, noticing that a storm was coming out of the northwest, we decided before it broke to go back to the house to feed the doogs.

The storm "broke" about half past five, letting everything loose at one time: lightning, thunder, wind, cloudbursts of rain. It became dark as a black night. Crash, and all the lights were off! No longer were any individual sounds distinguishable from the general roar outside. Terrified, the dogs whined and trembled, following every step JM took as she looked for candles.

In bed in her room, Mary Woolley was in the safest place in the house, away from any possible fall of the big elm trees. Time and again, JM, still trailed by the dogs, went to tell her and Mrs. Baker that so far everything was safe; that her room was the best place to be in.

The storm continued until shortly before seven. Then JM went out towards the office and the giant elm by Cutwind, thinking that trouble might be expected there. Except for scattered branches, everything was as usual. But across the lane where they had been little more than an hour before, the immense cottage-elm had split and mushroomed over the entire roof of Frogmere. JM pushed the door, which was jammed by the pressure on the roof, part way open and crept forward into the front and middle rooms. In the bathroom beyond green foliage waved. Literally stripping the roof from the bathroom and piercing the floor, a limb had been driven like a piston shaft straight down to the cellar.

JM stood still, watching some of the two-by-fours supporting the roof cracking wider and wider open. At best, the cottage roof for only a few hours could bear the weight it was then carrying. Making her way outside she saw that up on the village street people were stirring about excitedly. Another great elm was down, carrying with it the village power and light, and blocking all exit along the road to the south. However, the road to the north was open, and JM ran down the hill to get the car out, and at top speed, was off.

Later she told Mary Woolley, "We're better off than some people, Emmy. In one section of the village, all trees are down and traffic is completely cut off. You and Mrs. Baker take good care of the doggies: they need to be reassured that whatever 'it' was, it will not come back. John Van Ornum is coming with another man to help."

At once Mary Woolley said, "Mrs. Baker, get all the collies in here, please. We'll keep them with us until the men get the work on the roof done and Miss Marks comes home."

In a crisis almost any occupation is better than doing nothing—as true for her as for little Mrs. Baker who went scurrying off to the dining room to collect the dogs.

With John Van Ornum came not one man but two: neighbors Stanley Kellas and George Reese, carrying cross-cut saws and axes, hardwood supports and ropes with block and tackle. At once the work on the roof began, and under John's expert leadership few words were spoken, no mistakes made and much accomplished. In less than two hours they had succeeded in dropping onto the ground half the weight which had been on the roof.

Drenched to the skin, about 9:30 John Van Ornum said, "I guess that'll be all for tonight. She'll be safe till morning when we'll finish the job."

Terrifying symbol of the year to be! On what threshold were we standing?

*   *   *   *

Although JM suspected what lay ahead, she tried to go forward cheerfully, welcoming the first spring months as a gate into garden work for the household. During the first week in April as they were planting early peas, Perceval said with disgust, "W'at ya plannin' to do, rot them pea seed before frost is out'n the ground?"

"If the seed should rot, Perceval, the loss would not be very great," JM replied, "for this is an experiment."

"Expuriment, huh!"

"Come on, Perceval, we're losing time! Follow along, setting those hot tents over the peas already planted while I punch the holes and drop in the seed. It won't be long before tea time."

Before the close of April, leaves had tinted green the inside of the frosted paper of the hot tents, for as the frost bubbled up out of the earth with moisture it had blessed each seed plentifully. Much of the time on those gardening afternoons Mary Woolley sat on the porch of Frogmere or on the lawn beside the vegetable garden, getting a vicarious enjoyment from the activity.

By the middle of May there were white blossoms and baby pods forming; peas were ready to be picked the first week in June. Mr. Bender of the Farm Bureau paid a visit and the news of peas up, podded and eaten was in the newspapers of the north woods. Perceval's self-esteem collapsed like a balloon as, on the porch of Frogmere, and despite all storms, the peas were shelled, Mary Woolley herself helping. In fact, she shelled the first of those miraculous peas with pride, opening it with her left hand. It was amazing what she had learned to do with that left hand, arranging her hair, folding and unfolding newspapers and napkins, eating, taking letters from their envelopes, turning the pages of books as she read to herself, and, with this "wrong hand", shaking hands warmly and graciously.

CHAPTER 26

CANDLE

*"Is it reasonable to suppose that the 'accident of death' means
an end to the nobler powers? It is far easier for me to 'believe'
than not to believe in immortality."*

It was in the late spring of 1947 that the doctor said, "Death will
come to Miss Woolley when you are not expecting it."

It would have been difficult to describe exactly what the changes
and the trouble were—simply the opposing forces of health and disease were more and more in conflict. Between Christmas and the
summer of 1947 there had been increasing loss of interest and appetite.
In swallowing food, difficulty developed and there were spells of
coughing and of choking.

On June 13th Mary Woolley became extremely ill. JM telephoned
the doctor only to find he had left for Atlantic City. A younger doctor,
Dr. Onslow Gordon, was called in. He found Mary Woolley in a critical
condition, and telephoned Atlantic City for instructions. Asked to
stay that night, he consented although he had had only seven hours
of sleep in a total of five days. Trained in the hard school of the
European battle front, he took off his coat and lay down in the music
room, falling sound asleep under the down quilt thrown over him.

Mrs. Baker, worn out by weeks of hard nursing, was sent to bed
and told that she would be called the instant she was needed. Mary
Woolley was under the influence of a sedative much of the night.
Occasionally during the hours she spoke, or a bird in the dark shelter
of the trees sang a few notes. In the stillness of dawn with lake and
mountains as sounding board, the Montreal sleeper roared to a stop
at the Westport station.

At five o'clock Mary Woolley woke and said that she was feeling
better. The night past, JM was overly eager to make the most of
any sign of hope, and concluded that the danger was over.

By June 16th the elder doctor had returned and his diagnosis was
that Mary Woolley had had "a severe heart failure". He did not believe that "she would wear out" but that sometime before long, per-

haps hours, days or weeks, she would go suddenly. He considered her "condition critical" but advised insofar as it was possible, except for lessened but not relinquished dictation, that the "usual routine" be followed.

Five days later, from 11 at night until 5:30 in the morning, JM sat on in the wheel chair by her bedside and most of the time Mary Woolley did not know she was there. Little could be done. The room became colder and colder—almost frost in June.

Taking a heavy blanket, JM laid it over Mary Woolley, asking: "Are you warm enough?"

"Warm enough," came the reply.

Exhausted by the strain of the past days the nurse lay in a deep sleep from which JM had not the heart to wake her. Mary Woolley's breathing was becoming heavier, and about every minute reached a crescendo. Then came an abrupt pause and silence, the respiration seemingly gone. After that a little gasp, and with the returning respiration followed another accession. Towards dawn her breathing quieted down. As the night closed one whippoorwill was calling "whippo-will, whippo-will!" while other birds were giving their dawn calls: the robin, the blue birds, warblers, the blackbirds on the lake shore. For Mary Woolley, too, the day had come again. She thought it was Monday and not Sunday morning as it was actually, and said, "I did not think I should live through last night." Later she added: "I wonder whether anyone ever had a dearer friend than I have — what should I have done without you, Jeannettie? Papa and Mama are as real as real can be to me now. Perhaps, dear, it will be that way for us."

In the copy of the Bible which had been given her in 1898 by her father and mother and was always beside her bed, she had placed a purple ribbon marking Psalm 17 with its "I shall be satisfied when I awake with thy likeness." After this she had written these words:

"Treading in the footsteps of the
prophets.
Fearlessness, absolute sincerity
directness, hatred of shams,
singleness of aim."

    ✿   ✿   ✿   ✿

For the first time Harriet Newhall was able to be with the family from birthday to birthday—a fact which brought immeasurable comfort. During this time Mary Woolley often assured Harriet that although she did not say much she thought a good deal. Again and again she told Harriet she wished she had adequate funds to leave and she spoke of her readiness to die. Harriet believed, however, that Mary Woolley said this without realizing that death might be imminent as she wanted suggestions for JM's Christmas gift. She spoke of her eagerness to be downstairs during the coming winter just as she had been during the past winter—being "in the midst" of everything was her happiness. In a sense, Mary Woolley clung, as she had expressed it at the time of the Disarmament Conference, "to feeling more of the real joy of being up and about."

One July day a new Enesco record which Harriet had ordered was being played.

JM said, "Harriet sent this Enesco for your birthday."

"For my birthday?" came the inquiry, followed by a flash of understanding. "Oh, so I can have it *longer*!"

On July 5th Mary Woolley woke up dazed from her afternoon's sleep. When asked how she felt she replied, "Better!" To all other questions her reply was "No" or "Yes".

Some strong coffee was made for her which she drank eagerly as it was fed to her, spoonful by spoonful.

To the inquiry, "Don't you want to hold the cup yourself?" she answered, "Yes," continuing to drink eagerly, smiling at JM, her eyes clear and confident.

After her cup was set down on the bedside table, Mary Woolley, smiling, held out her left hand. She said, "By and by—," then paused.

"By and by what, Emmy?"

"By and by I will do some work."

Later she asked, "Did I seem queer to you?"

"A little dazed," was the reply.

"I thought I seemed queer to you," said Mary Woolley. "I did not seem queer to myself."

She used no one's name in this conversation and JM thought that she did not recognize her.

The following evening at bedtime JM said to her: "The air is fresh and it's a quiet night to sleep. You'll be a good Emmy and have this window open to please me?"

"Yes, dear."

"Goodnight, Emmy, sleep well."

"Goodnight, dearest."

On July 12th, when the doctor came out of Mary Woolley's room, he remarked, "What do you think Miss Woolley just said to me—and she said it with a smile: 'Doctor, how much longer do you think I have to go on living?' "

In the early morning of her birthday on July 13th the heat was intense. Inside it was fought with electrical fans and outside with garden sprays. Her niece Eleanor and husband Lindley Franklin were expected. Before the birthday lunch JM heard the following conversation:

"Miss Woolley," asked Mrs. Baker, "shall we put on your pink flowered dress?"

"Yes, the flowered dress, but—"

"Yes, I know, I have pressed it out."

"And the blue silk jacket?" asked Mary Woolley.

"Yes, Miss Woolley, that'll be nice: the blue silk jacket with the flowered pink dress. Well, we must get busy!'

There ensued a cheerful clatter in the adjoining closet and clothes press, drawers flying open and clothes hangers rattling, in preparation for the birthday costume.

By lunch time it had become sultry and breathlessly still. In her wheel chair at the head of the table Mary Woolley sat clad in her chosen costume—her lovely face, even in pain and in old age, quiet and tranquil. Before her the birthday table shone with the silver and lustrous china she loved. At the other end JM was carving the chicken.

When Harriet and Eleanor, singing, brought the birthday cake with its lighted candles into the dining room, MEW silently watched, them. Then, still quiet, she watched the lighted candles burning down before her. All realized that she knew that this would be her last birthday on earth.

But as the candles began to flicker, she picked each up, joyously and deftly, with her left hand, one at a time, let them burn an instant longer, and blew them out thoughtfully, as if she were saying, "*That* year was good! And *this* year was good! *Even better the year I blow out now!*"

❋　　❋　　❋　　❋

At the close of August, the leaves were brittle from the terrible heat which week in and week out had covered the better part of rainless months. In the hazy atmosphere, the forests and hillsides looked more like Persian rugs than like green trees. As JM went into Miss Woolley's room, Mrs. Baker was standing by the bed with a glass poised in her hand.

The nurse waved the glass at JM: "In just a minute. We're brushing our teeth. This is the last act." She gave the glass another flourish and continued, "Now we're ready for the coffee."

Breakfast and all the routine connected with it were over and they were beginning the business of dressing for a drive when Mary Wool-

ley said to Mrs. Baker, "I am growing thin." Although Mrs. Baker
had already commented on this to JM, she replied aggressively, "*No*,
Miss Woolley, I don't think so!"

Soon after, a slight altercation took place. Mrs. Baker said twice:
"Miss Woolley, it will be cool back in the mountains, and after all the
heat here, you will need a jacket." Unbroken silence on the part of
Mary Woolley. "Now," resumed Mrs. Baker coaxingly, "you know you
said you would do anything in the world Miss Marks asked you to do.
Do you want me to call her and tell her you wouldn't put on enough
clothes to keep you from catching cold?" Silence.

"Very *well*, Miss Woolley, but *she* would want you to get into this
little jacket right away." Silence.

Something, however, seemed to be happening—a change of heart
and jacket—for in a minute Mrs. Baker said, "Now that's better and
we won't be taking any chances of catching cold. There, Miss Woolley, we have it on! The car is coming through the gate. She's waiting
out there for us. I'll call Perceval." For a few minutes Minnie Baker
was busy with the crew and the wheel chair. Then Arthur White
and Perceval lifted Mary Woolley to the car and Mrs. Baker, having
settled both the patient and the wraps, sat down on the back seat.

They made their way over the back road from Wadhams to Elizabethtown and up towards Spruce Hill, passing Hurricane Mountain.
Mrs. Baker and JM were doing most of the talking since all Perceval
contributed to the chit-chat was summed in the expletive "Huh!"

Down Spruce Hill, the longest hill road in the Adirondacks, the car
turned to the left through Keene Valley. Then a steep climb onto the
plateau over which Giant Mountain towered on a rim of the great
Adirondacks circle. Many times had the friends climbed that distant
trail up Giant! Now they looked out upon those vast rocky slopes,
and it was written in their hearts: "I will lift up mine eyes onto the
hills, from whence cometh my help."

Home by the road passing Chapel Pond, through Elizabethtown to
Westport, down the Fleur de Lys lane, through the second gate, up
to the cottage and the *porte cochere*. Home together once more.

*   *   *   *

Dr. Gray was coming frequently, and once, although it had never
happened before, Mick growled and edged towards him. For years,
when not beside Mary Woolley's chair or out of doors, under the bed
had been the dog's post of love and duty. Finally the doctor said, "I
can't work in a room where I don't know what a dog is going to do

to me." Taking hold of Mick's harness, JM pulled him out from under the bed and led him away to the enclosure.

After taking the records, Dr. Gray returned to the library where JM was waiting, saying, "I can do no more for Miss Woolley; it is in God's hands."

During the night of September 4th, Mary Woolley seemed better than she had been the night before. In the morning, as the dogs were being taken downstairs, JM heard her call to them and "answered" for the Boys, "I'll be in soon, Emmy,"—the words and routine of years.

Going in a few minutes later she asked the question asked almost every day for three years, "Feeling better?" The reply was, "Better." Up since five, JM had prepared breakfast for the others, fed the dogs and made Mary Woolley's coffee. Exhausted, she was conscious of a feeling of tenseness and apprehension. That was explicable but what was not explicable, and for which she did not excuse herself, was a feeling of irritability, together with tenseness and apprehension. While she was outdoors on the kitchen terrace eating her breakfast, Mrs. Baker came out, saying. "I wish you would come. Miss Woolley does not seem quite natural."

While Mary Woolley had been eating her breakfast the oedema in her chest had risen like a storm. It was evident that she was suddenly worse. Running down the corridor, JM said, "Please telephone the doctor that he should come at once."

As they waited for the doctor, they worked on, raising the head of the bed and giving spoonful after spoonful of black coffee. Fifteen minutes, half an hour, three quarters of an hour, and still no doctor! During that time under the effects of the coffee the action of the heart had improved, the oedema had subsided and Mary Woolley could speak a few words. At last the doctor came, took his records and gave a large dose of digitalis.

The nurse and doctor left the room. As soon as they were gone Mary Woolley said to JM, "I want to be buried from here." Then followed some words difficult to understand.

JM asked, "You mean Wilton?" Mary Woolley replied, "Yes, Wilton."[1] She kept turning her head towards the open door. JM said, "You want Mick?" "Yes, Mickey," came the answer with a smile.

The dog seemed as joyous as usual as he bounded in, licked his Mistress' left hand always held out in welcome to him, and lay down quietly under the head of the high hospital bed.

Warning the nurses not to leave their patient alone, JM went to the office but despite heavy work that morning she was in and out of the invalid's room. Each time Mary Woolley begged to get up and go out of doors. Finally, so frequent was her pleading to go outside, that JM telephoned the doctor. Thinking of the digitalis he had given, his reply was, "Yes, she may get up and go out but not until half an hour has passed."

Exactly on the half hour, at 11 o'clock, September 5th, the nurses took loving care of all the toilet affairs—a bit of powder here, a bit of powder there. They put on the dress with its delicate pattern of blue and pink roses; then the blue silk jacket. Then the invalid was lifted into her chair.

Miss Woolley looked up at Mrs. Cross and said, smiling, "Mrs. Cross, after lunch I want to dictate some letters."

"Yes, Miss Woolley," she replied as the nurses placed on the invalid's shoulders a white shawl with its scallop shells of peace. Wheeling her out under the porte cochere, they set the wheel chair beside the rough gray stone steps. Before her stood the round out-of-doors table covered with a cloth of old gold and blue. White clematis in bloom, on her left, and on the right the fragrance of the white lilies which surrounded the house, Mary Woolley sat looking across the moving waters of the lake and on to the Eternal Hills beyond.

At lunch time when JM returned to the house she was delayed by a long distance telephone call. When she came out shortly before one o'clock she put her hand on Mary Woolley's shoulder, kissing her lightly on the top of the head and sat down beside her. JM asked if lunch had tasted good. Mary Woolley, as she reached out her hand, replied that it had and took a chocolate. In a moment, however, she was evidently having trouble on the half-paralyzed side of her mouth.

JM put her arm about her, saying, "Let me have that, dear, then you won't wear yourself out trying to eat it!"

Mary Woolley did as she was asked, but as JM held her she felt the shoulders becoming limp and saw the head drooping. It was then, on the threshold of the home she loved, content and happy, Mary Woolley died.

❖   ❖   ❖   ❖

On this morning of September 7, 1947, she lies in the closed casket in the library she had loved and still loves, the early morning light the color of pearl. Before the hearth where she had warmed herself in happier days and of late years in pain and in sorrow, she is at peace. Above her rise the books row upon row to the ceiling. Beside and above her are sprays of the white home lilies, like candelabra, which two days ago were about her as she was looking eastward over the lake towards the mountains when death came.

Beneath the casket and upon the hearth are banked flowers, even as the love which had surrounded Mary Woolley all her life—roses, gladioli, cosmos, chrysanthemums, and maiden hair fern. Beyond the casement windows are the lake and the hills and, on this day, muted sunlight, voices of birds and the trees. Within, seated in the old chairs in the old room mellow with the years and use, with human joy and humor sorrow, is a reverent company of more than half a hundred men and women. They are the men and women who have been the helpers —doctors, nurses, housekeepers, secretaries, friends and members of the family—silent in prayer, or because the spirit called, speaking words of love: "Only a few weeks ago . . . privileged to see her here . . . the same sweetness, the same patience, the same great courage . . . In the welter of foreign diplomacy . . . never for one moment forgot the principles for which she came . . . could not tolerate injustice . . . Her influence lives on . . . lives of thousands of girls . . . thousands of people throughout the world . . . Means everything to us . . . Can only say: from limitations of time to the freedom . . . of eternity."

CODA: ANOTHER ROOME

"If the dead, and we, be not upon one floore, nor under one story, yet we are under one roofe. We think not a friend lost, because he is gone into another roome, nor because he is gone into another land; and into another world, no man is gone; for that heaven, which God created, and this world, is all one world." —JOHN DONNE (1573-1631)

NOTES AND REFERENCES

The basic sources used are the "papers" in the Mary E. Woolley files, including family records, genealogies, letters personal and impersonal, diaries and day books; her father's and mother's letters, their verses and their diaries; the letters of her grandmother Mary Ann Beers and her grandfather Stephen Gould Ferris; of her great-uncle Isaac Sherwood Beers and her great-grandfather Captain Samuel Beers; and the wills of the West Indian Woolleys. Among these files are other files of letters and a complete file of informal talks and formal addresses from the Wellesley days on down to the closing years of her life.

CHAPTER 1

This chapter is not "imaginary". Word for word it is based on personal letters and genealogical records.

CHAPTER 2

All the West Indian papers are the result of searches conducted by JM in the West Indies. The Valentines are in the Mary E. Woolley papers.

[1] Wills Liber 58, Folio 112, Probate January 30, 1794; L. T. Liber 34 Folio 77.

[2] Wills Liber 75, Folio 132, Proved December 27, 1805.

[3] Inventories Liber 81, Folio 147 Int'd June 30, 1794. "Pen" or "Penn" is the Jamaican word for plantation. Most of the facts were taken from Letters Testamentary recorded in the Island Record Office in Jamaica.

[4] Inventories Liber 111, Folio 67, Returned June 4, 1808.

[5] Vol. 22. Folio 267. For students of genealogy who wish to carry further the study of the English and Caribbean Woolleys, the following records in the Island Record Office of Jamaica are suggested: Vol. 2, Folio 280; Vol. 2, Folio 297; Vol. 2, Folio 314; Vol. 2, Folio 318; Wills Liber 75, Folio 132.

[6] The following line was pencilled in afterwards at the top of the letter: "Love to L., L. Carrie & all."

[7] Late in 1847 when a question sheet was sent around to the older living members of the Woolley and Ferris families—some of them over 80—not one of them knew anything at all about Mary Emma Brisco; even her existence as the first wife of Joseph J. Woolley was unknown to them.

CHAPTER 4

Unless otherwise stated, all "papers" used are in the Mary E. Woolley Papers.

CHAPTER 5

Pembroke College in Brown University sources of information: Nettie Serena Goodale Murdock letters to Jeannette Marks; Mary Louise Record, Providence Sunday Journal, September 21, 1941; Anne Tillinghast Weeden: "The Woman's College in Brown University"; Mary E. Woolley Papers, and Dean Morriss.

CHAPTER 6

[1] *Dream and Deed: The Story of Katharine Lee Bates*, by Dorothy Burgess.

CHAPTER 7

[1] *Life of Mary Lyon*, by Beth Gilchrist, p. 189.

[2] *Seminary Militant: An Account of the Missionary Movement at Mount Holyoke Seminary and College*, by Louise Porter Thomas. Printed by the Southworth-Anthoensen Press, Portland, Maine. Published in honor of Clara Frances Stevens.

[3] *Holyoke Daily Transcript*.

CHAPTER 8

[1] "What It Means to be a College President" by Jeannette Marks, *Harper's Bazaar*, June, 1913.

[2] From the *Bryn Mawr Alumnae Quarterly*, November 1910, address of President Mary E. Woolley, twenty-fifth anniversary, p. 156.

CHAPTER 9

[1] *The Story of a Pioneer*, by Anna Howard Shaw, D.D., M.D., p. 224.

CHAPTER 10

[1] See Thomas Wakefield Goodspeed in his biography of Dr. Burton.

CHAPTER 11

[1] Some figures connected with Mary E. Woolley's administration, 1901-1936:

Endowment of Mount Holyoke College (*i.e.*, "productive funds")
(Figures secured from the Comptroller's Office)

May 31, 1901	$ 568,723.39
June 1, 1936	$4,676,886.99

Student Enrollment at Mount Holyoke College
(Figures secured from Mount Holyoke College catalogues filed in the Registrar's Office)

1900-1901	550
1935-1936	1017

Number of Teaching Faculty at Mount Holyoke College
(Figures secured from Mount Holyoke College catalogues filed in the Registrar's Office)

1900-1901	54
1935-1936	123

[2] Seven College Conference: Barnard—Virginia C. Gildersleeve; Bryn Mawr—M. Carey Thomas and Marion Edwards Park; Mount Holyoke—Mary Emma Woolley (Chairman, Seven College Conference); Radcliffe — Dean LeBaron Russell Briggs, and then Ada L. Comstock; Smith—William Allan Neilson (Marion LeRoy Burton before him); Vassar—Henry Noble MacCracken (James Monroe Taylor before him); Wellesley—Ellen Fitz Pendleton and Mildred H. McAfee).

[3] At the Trustee meeting on June 8, 1931, Dr. Boyd Edwards read a letter from Dr. Stimson, a trustee and uncle of the Secretary of State. In this letter of congratulations for the achievement and distinction of thirty years, the Trustees wrote that they were "primarily conscious of the great change in the condition of the college that had taken place in these years, and also in particular of the leading and largely determining part" the President had "played in it". The letter closed with these sentences: "We simply wish to convey to her, and put on our Records, an expression of brief but heartfelt appreciation of her devotion of herself and her complete success in the service of the College. And at the same time we would assure her of our earnest desire to cooperate in every way possible, as well as to convey to her our personal regards, of which she is renewedly assured." And it was *voted* that the letter from Dr. Stimson be spread upon the Records and duly engrossed and presented to Miss Woolley.

CHAPTER 12

[1] Mary Woolley was Chairman from 1927-1933 of the American Association of University Women.

June 15, 1931

[2] Mr. Howell Cheney, South Manchester, Connecticut.

My dear Mr. Cheney:

Thank you for your note of the tenth with the enclosed statement. May I make the following suggestions:

Paragraph two, the substitution of the following for the last part of the paragraph: "The Students, Faculty, Alumnae and Trustees, wherever they have assembled in these Commencement days, have expressed their unfaltering devotion to Miss Woolley, and their personal appreciation of her work for their own lives." As you will see, I have deleted, "and their regret at her repeated expression of a desire to retire." Two or three years ago, before your return to the Board, as you will realize, I stated to the Board that it was my expectation to retire at the close of the academic year 1932-1933, preceding my seventieth birthday that summer, because the attainment of that age seemed a sufficient reason. The sentence in paragraph two indicates a reluctance on the part of the Board to accept that statement and my own insistence. As far as I know, the Board acquiesced until last March when I was informed of their action urging me to accept the invitation to act as a member of the Commission sent to the Orient, and to postpone my resignation until 1934, a suggestion which I accepted. There has not been a "repeated expression of a desire to retire."

In paragraph three, substitute "intention" for "wish", "retire" for "resign" in the second line of the paragraph, and "retirement" for "resignation" in the last line.

In paragraph four, substitute the following for the last part of the paragraph: "She has, therefore, come to feel that it is not wise for her to leave the College before January, 1932, thus reducing her absence to four months." My reason for making this change is that it is the being here in the autumn which is of equal importance with the reduction of the time away from the College. Deleting "and may give it up entirely" I suggest because I now expect to go in January, and I think the intimation of not going at all would simply confuse the issue with the Alumnae.

Believe me,

Very sincerely yours,
Mary E. Woolley.

[3] Members of Board of Trustees at Mount Holyoke College in 1932: Rockwell Harmon Potter, Frank B. Towne, William Horace Day, Edward N. White, Boyd Edwards, Richard Childs, George Dwight Pratt, James A. M. Speers, *Florence Purington*, William J. Davidson, Elbert Harvey, *Harry P. Kendall*, Henry K. Hyde, *Howell Cheney, Edgar Furniss, Alva Morrison*, Paul Davis, *Mrs. Frank G. Wilkins, Mrs. Mary Hume Maguire*, Amy Rowland, *Susan Doane Arnold*, Lottie G. Bishop. The names in italics are the Trustees who in that year constituted the Committee on the Succession to the Presidency.

CHAPTER 13

[1] The Rt. Hon. Arthur Henderson, President of the Disarmament Conference: "It is literally true to say that the will of hundreds of millions of men and women has been expressed in favour of disarmament, as the essential condition of an abiding peace."

CHAPTER 15

[1] The committee women were Mrs. Caroline O'Day (then in Congress); Mary

E. Woolley, Chairman of the Peoples Mandate Committee; Mrs. Hannah Clothier Hull, Chairman of the Executive Committee for the Mandate and President of the Women's International League for Peace and Freedom; Mrs. Gerard Swope, Treasurer of the Mandate Mrs. W. A. Newell, Member of the Mandate Committee and a prominent officer of the Methodist Missionary Council; Charl O. Williams, a past president of the National Education Association; Elizabeth Christman, Secretary-Treasurer of the National Women's Trade Union League; and Mabel Vernon, Campaign Director of the Mandate Committee.

[2] Published by Macmillan in the Kappa Delta Pi Lecture Series.

[3] 1934 Committee on Succession to the Presidency: Alva Morrison, Howell Cheney, Henry Kendall, Rowena Keyes and Mary Maguire.

[4] In April of 1935, an official alumnae group, *not* unconnected with the members of the Trustee group of men and women, placed themselves on record as follows with regard to an incoming President:

1. The President must make Mount Holyoke her major interest.

2. *The President should in collaboration with the faculty guide the educational policies of Mount Holyoke College.*

3. *The President should consult with the faculty. . . .*

4. *The President inspires, understands and sympathizes with the undergraduates.*

5. *The President must be able to apportion funds wisely to departments,* appreciate the financial problems involved in so large a physical plant, increase endowment, and be able to administer the business affairs of the college wisely. . . .

6. *The President must be able to impress the public with her own and Mount Holyoke's significance.*

February 17, 1936.

[5] Mrs. Ralph White, 177 Mullins Street, Watertown, New York.

My dear Mrs. White:

The following are names of possible successors in the Presidency, all of them strong "candidates":

1. Mrs. Anna Brinton, Ph.D., a Friend; Dean at Mills College, California; a classical scholar; leading member of the American Classical Society; successful administrator; world traveller; sister of the wife of Professor Miles of Yale University.

2. Mrs. Millicent Carey McIntosh, Ph.D., also a Friend; Head of the Brearley School, New York City; formerly acting Dean of Bryn Mawr; niece of former President M. Carey Thomas; able scholar; delightful personality.

3. Miss Meta Glass, Ph.D., a Virginian; President of Sweet Briar College; sister of Senator Glass; classical scholar; successful administrator; delightful personality; wide experience.

4. Miss Mary Yost, Ph.D., a Southerner; Dean of Women at Stanford University, California; formerly Professor at Vassar College; considered by Mrs. Rosenberry of Madison, Wisconsin, formerly Dean of Women at University of Wisconsin and a good judge, one of the strongest women in academic life in the country.

5. Mrs. Mary Ely Lyman, Ph.D., a graduate of Mount Holyoke; formerly Head of the Biblical Department at Vassar College; wife of Professor Eugene Lyman of Union Theological Seminary; distinguished scholar; very able speaker.

6. Miss Margaret Speer, A.M., graduate of Bryn Mawr College; daughter of Robert E. Speer, of New York City; Acting Dean of Women at Yenching Univer-

sity, Peiping, where she has had marked success as an administrator; the youngest of the group—somewhere in her thirties.

All of these women I know well; some of them I have known for years and can say honestly that I should be proud of any one of them as my successor; all have delightful personalities; are able women in the real sense of that word; have won distinction for themselves in scholarship and have had experience in administration. Miss Speer is the the youngest of the group, but no one of them is an "old lady!"

Three of the above are married; Mr. Brinton is also teaching at Mills College in the Department of Philosophy, and it is conceivable that a post could be arranged for him at Mount Holyoke. Dr. Lyman, an eminent member of the Union Theological Seminary in New York City, is much older than his wife and retires either this year or next. Dr. McIntosh is a physician and the possibilities in that case I do not know.

I am so convinced that the failure to appoint a woman to the Presidency of Mount Holyoke would be a mistake not only from the point of view of the College and its history of one hundred years, but also from that of the advancement of women in general, that I can say the possibility of not appointing a woman is the greatest anxiety upon my "horizon".

It was a pleasure to have the little visits with you this last week.

Cordially yours,
Mary E. Woolley

February 24, 1936

⁶ Dear Miss Woolley:

Thank you so much for your letter telling me the names of women you would like to see carrying on your work at Mount Holyoke. I am deeply interested.

I think I have come over to your point of view that your successor should be a woman. I enjoyed our talks and pondered on them. Personally, I want first what is best for Mount Holyoke, and then what is best for women in general. I hope we can be guided in our choice so that both causes may be served!

With deep appreciation of your confidence, I am

Most sincerely yours,
Maude Titus White
President of the Alumnae Assn.

CHAPTER 16

¹ Among Mary Woolley's files of notes, letters, papers and documents, in her own handwriting, there is this fragmentary memo for a letter: "Some of the difficulty & misrepresentation here—Increasing tendency of Boston group to run affairs of College—as an Exec. Com.—much guided by Mrs. Maguire. Conference Committee. 63 out of 96 faculty voting, emphatically favor a woman. Tell Wellesley procedure."

In the By-laws there is no number stated as a requirement for the election of a President of the College. In the ensuing closed meeting that afternoon, of the Trustees who asked for the delay there were nine and the vote was nine to fifteen. But it was at this time a clergyman on the Board decided to vote for a man, thus making the number who voted for a woman eight instead of nine. The number therefore became two-thirds of the vote taken, exactly the number required to elect a Trustee but supposedly not a President.

[1a] There were therefore: 18 men: 1 honorary; 8 women: 1 honorary, 6 alumnae.

November 4, 1936

[1b] My dear Mr. Morrison:

In answer to yours of November third, may I say that four of the members of the Board of Trustees—Miss Purington, Dr. Edwards, Dr. Day, and Mr. Pratt— told me that they had sent or left their vote in opposition to the acceptance of the report of the Committee on the Presidency.

You quote the By-laws "a two-thirds vote of the trustees present shall be necessary for the election of a trustee". I think it unfortunate that action should have been taken on so important a question in the absence of nearly one-third of the membership of the Board.

My statement that "the call for the meeting of the Board did not state that the election would take place at that meeting as the Secretary was not instructed to include it" referred as you say to the call for the meeting issued by the Secretary of the Board. It seems to me that a matter of business so significant as the election of a president of a college should have been included in the official call for the meeting through the regular secretarial channels. I have referred to the above matter only in the letter of October thirtieth sent in duplicate to each member of the Board.

As far as the alumnae are concerned, I have received and acknowledged many letters as well as heard many comments, but I have not taken the initiative in discussion or writing. It is inevitable that the trustees should meet with a want of sympathy and resultant protest in an appointment which set aside the wishes of the administration, a large majority of the faculty, as far as we can judge a majority of the alumnae and a multitude of friends outside the college.

Very sincerely yours,
Mary E. Woolley.

December 12, 1936

In view of the fact that the Trustees of Mount Holyoke College claim that the Alumnae as a whole do not favor a woman as president, this statement being based upon the fact that but few replied to their questionnaire which did not include this specific question, it would seem well to canvass the Alumnae to discover their feelings in the matter. Even though the appointment of the President Elect would seem to be a "closed issue" any false impressions as to the opinion of the Alumnae as a whole should be corrected. Please place a check in one of the squares on the enclosed slip to indicate your preference.

Enclosed slip:

I would prefer to have a man as president of Mount Holyoke College. ....
I would prefer to have a woman as president of Mount Holyoke College. ....

May 21, 1936

[2] To the Faculty:

The Faculty Conference Committee has been informed that the choice of a man as President of Mount Holyoke College is imminent. The Committee needs to know at once faculty opinion on the following questions:

1. Do you prefer to have a woman as President? Yes .... No ....
2. Check the names of any of the following women whom you would endorse:

    Jane Perry Clark   Mary Ely Lyman

    Meta Glass   Eunice M. Schenck

An immediate reply is *imperative*.

Return this blank to the secretary of the Conference Committee in the enclosed envelope.

Signature ....

May 26, 1936

To the Faculty:

The Conference Committee desires to make a further statement relative to the questionnaire issued May 21.

Apprised of the fact that early decision was likely, a decision departing from the precedent of the past (though the name of the nominee was unknown to it) the Committee ventured to ask for delay in the decision, and for time to present further consideration based on what it believed to be faculty opinion.

To test its judgment in the latter, it issued the questionnaire. The result of the first question was as follows: ("Do you prefer to have a woman as President?") 87 answered Yes. 11 answered No. 8 said in effect "the best person regardless of sex." 106 ballots returned.

These results have been transmitted to the President of the Board of Trustees.

The names listed were for the purpose of ascertaining, for the information of the Committee, whether there was any sharp crystallization of enthusiasm around any one of certain names previously under discussion in the Committee. The result was indecisive.

The Faculty Conference Committee

Emma P. Carr, Chairman   Amy Hewes   Abby Turner

Caroline M. Galt   Helen E. Patch   David E. Adams

From the Mary E. Woolley Papers, June 6, 1936. Votes in favor of a woman left by absent members: Dr. Edwards, Dr. Day, Miss Purington, Mr. Pratt. Votes by those present at the meeting: Miss Perkins, Mrs. Thompson, Mr. White, Mr. Speers and Dr. Potter. Votes opposed: Mr. Morrision, Mrs. Maguire, Miss Keyes, Mr. Cheney, Mr. Kendall, Mrs. Whitman, Miss Bishop, Dr. Furniss, Mr. Davis, Mr. Wiggin, Mr. Warren, Mr. Hazen, Mr. Harvey. (Mr. Davidson (?); Mr. Myers (?))

[3] Information received from Alumnae Secretary at Wellesley College, June 4, 1936.

Alumnae. A committee, known as Advisory Committee of Alumnae, was formed to canvass the Alumnae in regard to a new president The committee was composed entirely of Alumnae, selected geographically to some extent—that is, members were chosen from one general locality, so that they might be near enough for conference. The vote went in favor of a woman. The result was printed in the Alumnae magazine.

The statement from Wellesley. It is more explicit, and provocative of discussion. It embodies an appeal from Alumnae representatives, stresses importance of the action to be taken and the good will of the Trustees. Psychologically its tendency is to invite response . . . (For full information inquire at Wellesley for papers.) The results were made readily available through printing in the Alumnae magazine.

The statement from Mount Holyoke. The statement is vague, it makes no appeal, does not stress importance of action. It is sent from Trustees to Alumnae. Alumnae would not feel free to ask questions or initiate discussion. Response must inevitably be weaker and more indeterminate than in the case of Wellesley. No statement of results has apparently been made.

In answer to a letter in June, 1935, the Yale Secretary, a Mount Holyoke Alumna, and the Yale Dean of the Graduate School, placed themselves on record as in favor of a man and as "absolutely opposed" to a woman as President. In the spring of 1936 the Trustees added four more members, two women and two men, to the committee, thus creating a Committee of Nine. On this Committee of Nine one woman possibly (in the end she voted for a man) and one man possibly (though in the end he voted for a man) were opposed to the appointment of a man to succeed Mary Woolley. Thus there were seven set to appoint a man and two who might change their minds and did.

Mount Holyoke College comes under the definition of a corporation and as such is an "intangible being" which cannot be owned by anyone. Sir William Blackstone (1723-1780) has defined a corporation as "an artificial person created for preserving in perpetual succession rights which, being conferred on natural persons only, would fail in the process of time."

Study of the Charter and By-laws shows that the institution, under various names, was incorporated in 1836 and that the incorporators were five men. In January 1893, it was arranged that practically all moneys should be vested in the trustees of Mount Holyoke. In 1894, they were made eligible to hold all real and personal estate and again, in 1935, they were authorized to hold more real estate. Most of the amendments to the original incorporation seem to have been solely concerned with finances and always to the effect of granting more power to the trustees. There is very little reference to the scholastic interests of the college.

The trustees are exactly what their names would imply, having something more than power of attorney, but being in no sense of the word owners of the property. In the year 1936 under the By-laws, the trustees may consist of twenty-five elected members with the President of the College, ex officio. Twenty trustees are to be elected by the Board of Trustees as vacancies occur to serve for a period of ten years, the remaining five to be Alumnae Trustees, one to be elected each year by the Alumnae to serve for a period of five years.

Mount Holyoke is an endowed institution, and the Finance Committee of the Trustees cares for the investments. The By-laws, page 13, section 10, provide for a committee of four members, a vote of three being binding. At that time the Finance Committee was composed of Mr. Morrison, chairman, Mr. Harvey, treasurer, Mr. Warren, and Mr. Wiggin, a close circle of Boston business men.

[4] Those asked were: Miss Glass of Sweet Briar, Mrs. McIntosh, Miss Nicolson of Smith.

[5] In an open letter to the Trustees of Mount Holyoke College, Dr. A. Elizabeth Adams challenged as follows the "conclusions" of the Committee of Nine: "The expressed preference of the alumnae is for a woman. . . . Sixty per cent of the replies indicated that the president should be a woman or suggested only women

as candidates. . . . The number of replies to the questionnaire was small. This can be explained in part by the fact that direct questions, such as 'Do you wish to have a woman as the next president of Mount Holyoke?' and 'Do you wish to have a man as the next president of Mount Holyoke?' were not asked. Neither was adequate information on the subject given in an accompanying letter . . ."

A steady grinding down of the Faculty by the Board of Trustees had gone on for three years; cutting of salaries, cutting of appropriations, reduction of staffing, and usurpation of authority whether that authority was actual or traditional.

Some of the women Mary Woolley is known to have favored but for one reason or another were rejected by the committee, are: Dean Brinton (Mills College), Molly Ray Carroll, Jane Perry Clarke (Barnard), Meta Glass, Mary Ely Lyman, Mildred McAfee, Mrs. McIntosh, Frances Perkins, Josephine Roche, Dean Schenck (Bryn Mawr), Margaret Schlauch (New York University), Margaret E. Speer, Katharine Taylor (Shady Hill School), Dean Yost (Stanford).

CHAPTER 17

[1] In reply to an impressively sensitive and intelligent letter from Elise Belcher, Mary Woolley objected: "There is one part of your letter which I cannot follow— 'apparently the exceptional woman was not available'. My own conviction is that the exceptional woman was as available as the exceptional man!" But to the Mount Holyoke Alumnae on the Faculty at Wellesley, she said: "Now is the time for others throughout the country to rise up and express their opinion without circumlocution to the members of the Board of Trustees of Mount Holyoke. To a member of a different college Faculty she had written: "You know without my saying it, how hard this decision is for me to accept. Hard not for myself, I think I am right in saying, but for the College and the great cause. It seems to me a most terrible blunder, but − − !" And she went no further. In the second year of that struggle, she wrote an Alumna of whom she was personally fond: "As you know, the situation is far broader than personal, *affecting the cause of women, and that is what has made it so difficult for me.* However, we must go ahead with courage for the future."

To another Alumna, Mary Woolley closed her note with: "I am hoping that the stand for the right and just thing may be held without rancor." In acknowledgment of a letter received from an Alumna were these two sentences: "My emphasis refrained from personalities. I think you will agree with me that it is the principle which is the important thing."

[2] Dear Aunt May:

I want to tell you how perfectly amazed and shocked I was when I read of the appointment of a man as President of Mount Holyoke College. I cannot imagine that you feel otherwise, and hence you have my full sympathy. I do not doubt that a man can do the work very well, but Mount Holyoke was founded not only to educate women but to prepare them for places of leadership in thought and action. How absurd to have its own chief post of leadership occupied by a man!

I wish that he might have sense enough to resign, but perhaps that is overoptimism—even to express the wish.

Some day sensible colleges will have to adopt the provision which we have here at Westminster of having a certain number of faculty members elected by the faculty as advisory members of the Board of Trustees. Although they cannot vote, they attend trustees' meetings and have the right to speak on matters presented. Thus they can make faculty sentiment known to the trustees in a clear and direct manner before action is taken.

With much love,

Paul

January 22, 1937

Mrs. Ruth Wilson Tryon,
American Association of University Women,
1634 I Street, Northwest, Washington, D.C.

My dear Mrs. Tryon:

Thank you for your letter of the thirteenth. I have delayed answering until I could confer with two or three members of the Faculty who feel that there is need of education with regard to the situation as it affects women. For example, an English friend writes as follows: 'The color given by the suggestion that no other suitable woman exists in America will be damaging to the entire cause of women unless challenged. Thirty years ago . . . it might have been argued that there was not enough choice among qualified university women, but now that is an impossible argument and one which it is for American women to refute.'

I am including in this letter a brief "precis" for another friend of the college, which may be of interest to you or Dr. Kelly.

By this mail I am sending a special delivery to Dr. McHale, answering some definite questions which may be of use to you.

Cordially yours,

Mary E. Woolley.

³ With a show of fairness the Trustees took up a petition signed by 1172 which had been sent in by Dr. Amy Rowland and Carolyn Smiley. In the Trustee report on petitions from Alumnae no reference was made to either the Indianapolis or the Detroit petitions which Mary Woolley happened to know had been sent. Although the number of signatures on the petition being considered (!) was within 28 of a total of 1200, the number given by the Trustee reporting was 700. He called attention to the signatures of outside business men and women but the actual names of those who had signed it were not given.

CHAPTER 19

¹ Honorary degrees conferred, May 8, 1937. Doctor of Letters: Dorothy Canfield Fisher, Frances Lester Warner Hersey, Malvina Hoffman, Yau Tsit Law, Eva LeGallienne, Mary Redington Ely Lyman, Eileen Power, Alice Ravenel Huger Smith, Leonie Villard, Emily Susan Wilson, Roberta Teale Swartz Chalmers. Doctor of Science: Margaret Clay Ferguson, Margaret Tyler, Anna Pell Wheeler. Doctor of Laws: Katharine Blunt, Mildred Helen McAfee, Margaret Shove Morriss, Aurelia Henry Reinhardt, Virginia Crocheron Gildersleeve, and Margery Corbett-Ashby.

A brief list of honorary degrees and citations, and of honorary memberships, awards and medals which were received by Mary Emma Woolley appears on pages 290 and 291.

DEGREES AND DIPLOMAS

Date	Degree	College
June 25, 1884		Wheaton Seminary, Norton, Massachusetts
June 20, 1894	A.B.	Brown University, Providence, Rhode Island
June 13, 1895	A.M.	Brown University, Providence, Rhode Island
June 12, 1900	L.H.D.	Brown University, Providence, Rhode Island
1900	L.H.D.	Amherst College, Amherst, Massachusetts
October 15, 1910	LL.D.	Smith College, Northampton, Massachusetts
June 15, 1914	A.M.	Yale University, New Haven, Connecticut
June 20, 1923	LL.D.	Yale University, New Haven, Connecticut
October 16, 1931	LL.D.	Denison University, Granville, Ohio
February 20, 1933	LL.D.	Rollins College, Winter Park, Florida
June 20, 1933	LL.D.	Oberlin College, Oberlin, Ohio
June 13, 1934	LL.D.	Lake Erie College, Painesville, Ohio
June 14, 1934	L.H.D.	Wheaton College, Norton, Massachusetts
June 12, 1935	LL.D.	New York University, New York, New York
June 17, 1935	Ped.Dr.	New York State Teachers College, Albany, N. Y.
October 6, 1936	LL.D.	Western College, Oxford, Ohio
March 16, 1937	LL.D.	University of Chicago, Chicago, Illinois
June 1, 1937	Litt.D.	Columbia University, New York, New York
June 7, 1937	LL.D.	Bucknell University, Lewisburg, Pennsylvania
March 9, 1938	LL.D.	Mills College, Oakland, California
February 19, 1940	LL.D.	Rockford College, Rockford, Illinois
November 19, 1940	L.H.D.	College of Osteopathic Physicians and Surgeons, Los Angeles, California

1893 Daughters of the American Revolution (member)

1903 American Board of Foreign Missions (corporate member)

1914 Appointed United States Delegate to International Conference on Education to meet at the Hague

1914 Women's Council of Massachusetts Division of National Defense (member)

1921 Mary E. Woolley Foundation, established by Mount Holyoke College, Faculty

1927 College Entrance Examination Board (Life member. Chairman, 1924-1927)

1930 Tercentenary Commission of Massachusetts Bay Colony (member)

1931 Kossovo Medal—Royal Red Cross of Yugoslavia

1932 Appointed United States Delegate to Disarmament Conference in Geneva, by Mr. Hoover

1936 Federal Council of Churches of Christ in America, Congregational-Christian Council (Honorary member)

1937 National Board of the Young Women's Christian Association (Honorary member; served also as Chairman)

1937 National Commission, Columbus Memorial Lighthouse (member)

1937 Phi Beta Kappa (made Honorary Life Senator)

1937 Appointed Moderator of the Congregational Churches of America

1937 Awarded Susan Colver Rosenberger Medal of Honor—by Brown University

1937   Awarded Testimonial (hand illumined) by Faculty of Mount Holyoke College
1937   American Youth Hostel Association (hand-lettered Testimonial)
1939   Grand Official of Cristobal Colon—awarded medal and badge
1940   Associated Alumni of Osteopathic Physicians and Surgeons (member)
1941   Awarded "Scroll of Honor" by General Federation of Women's Clubs
1943   Delta Kappa Gamma Society (honorary member)
1946   Awarded King Christian X (Denmark) Medal of Liberation by Charge d'Affaires

Some organizations of which Mary E. Woolley served as President or Chairman—American Association of University Women: 1927-1933, President; 1933-1937, Chairman of Committee on International Relations; American Civil Liberties Union, Consumer's League of Rhode Island, League of Women Voters, National Child Labor Committee, National Woman's Party, United States Peoples Mandate for International Peace and Cooperation.

CHAPTER 21

February 6, 1942

[1] Dear Belle:

It is always a delight to hear from you, and it goes without saying that I wish I might see you. My last trip to Washington was from noon of December twelfth to morning of the fourteenth, two days full up with committee work. I hope for better fortune next time.

Since my retirement in 1937 I have been with the alumnae many times, and often said that I was seeing more of them than during my years at college. Large dinners or luncheons have been given in numerous places; twice in Baltimore, in Washington, Philadelphia, Rochester, Hartford, Cincinnati, Indianapolis, Chicago, Minneapolis, Pasadena and Los Angeles. There have been smaller and informal gatherings where there were fewer alumnae, as for instance, breakfast in Bloomington, Indiana, followed by a fifty-two mile motor trip with alumnae to Indianapolis. There have been other invitations, as for example, from St. Louis and from Cleveland, which I hope to accept when my wanderings take me in those directions. In these ways I have seen more than I could at class reunions where my evening was always divided among several groups.

The policy which I am following in not going back to Mount Holyoke is my protest against what was done. You know me well enough to realize that I never say a word against the present administration. The question is something bigger than the personal.

The summer after the new president was elected, Mrs. Lydia Sanderson Capen of Hartford, an alumna of Mount Holyoke, who was one of the instructors in my department at Wellesley, said to me: "A wicked thing has been done." I have often thought of that remark, and how directly Mrs. Capen saw to the heart of the question.

In the first place, the way it was done as I said to the Board of Trustees, "was more worthy of Hitler than of the United States of America." One of the Trustees of Wellesley College told me that when the Faculty and Administration of Wellesley expressed their wish that the policy of a woman as president be continued the Board dropped all thought of considering a man. A year before the election at Mount Holyoke I wrote to each member of the Board urging that only women be considered for the post; the spring before the election nearly ninety percent of the faculty of Mount Holyoke put themselves on record as wishing the election of a woman; the day of the election the Board of Trustees went into executive session lasting from the morning until the late afternoon, and when the report of the committee nominating a man was voted upon, it was accepted by one member less than the two-thirds vote required in the by-laws for the election of a new member of the Board of Trustees. I suppose that in framing the by-laws, the members of the Board never dreamed that anything less than an unanimous, or nearly unanimous vote, of the Board would be required for the election of the president of the college.

Among the number who voted for the acceptance of the report were several who a year before had written me that they were not in favor of a man as president. It is evident that they yielded rather than prolong the discussion. The alumnae were not given a chance to express their choice.

The above does not, however, go to the heart of the question. One hundred years before, Mary Lyon had given her life to the founding of an institution which should prepare women for service, especially in education. If, after a hundred years of that service, the college could not produce an alumna prepared to head the institution, why continue it?

There is more than that. We are living today in the most critical period of the world's history—a situation that is largely due to the failure of human beings to meet our human responsibilities. I have said many times that the "international hell of today is paved with neglected opportunities". I saw them time after time during my six months in Geneva, and I have realized that truth even more acutely since 1932. What does that mean! It means that women as human beings have a responsibility equal to that of men, and have a peculiarly natural fitness for this work of human relationships. As far back as 1929 at a dinner in New Orleans the British Consul General said to me: "There will never be a new international relationship except as it comes largely through women, but in order to bring that about you women must see to it that women are given posts of influence where they will have a chance to shape policy."

In the announcement of Henrietta Roelofs' death, a remark of hers was quoted something like this, in spite of the progress made by women they had failed to insist upon their admission to policy shaping posts.

I could say a great deal more along this line. Two or three days ago the *New York Times* listed eight new appointments at Mount Holyoke College, four men and four women. The posts given to the men were of professorial rank; the posts given to the women were of instructors rank.

This is a very long "screed". I could say much more; perhaps, however, it is sufficient to convince you that I cannot give up my protest. I am sure that you will realize that this is not an easy decision. I gave to Mount Holyoke thirty-seven years, exactly one half of my life.

My love for you all.

Affectionately your cousin,

Mary E. Woolley

October 13, 1943.

[2] Irving Fisher,
New Haven, Connecticut.
Dear Mr. Fisher:

Would you be willing to write a statement in favor of the Equal Rights Amendment? It would mean a great deal coming from you, and I hope that you will say "yes" to this earnest plea.

During the six years that I was National President of the American Association of University Women I was entirely in sympathy with the position of the Association regarding this Amendment, a point of view that I now find difficult to understand in myself. To ask that we "females" be rceognized in the Constitution on an equal footing with our brothers seems to me a mild request, and I am eager to do everything in my power to further the Amendment.

Yours,
Mary E. Woolley

CHAPTER 27

Westport-on-Lake Champlain,
New York
May 31-44

[1] Dearest Jeannette:

The Ferris-Woolley lot in the old "Joe's Hill" Cemetery—now called I think—by some other name—in Wilton, Connecticut, I should like to have as my resting place. Cremation should be or not be—as you think best.

I love you, Dear—as I have for almost fifty years.

Yours,
Emmy

(This sealed note was found by Mary Woolley's executor, Jeannette Marks, in the autumn of 1947.)

INDEX

(Compiled by Harriet Newhall)